VANSITTART

Study of a Diplomat

ALSO BY NORMAN ROSE

The Gentile Zionists: A Study in Anglo-Zionist Relations, 1929–39
'Baffy': The Diaries of Blanche Dugdale, 1936–47

VANSITTART

Study of a Diplomat

———————⊃•)ll(•⊂———————

Norman Rose

HOLMES & MEIER PUBLISHERS, INC.
IMPORT DIVISION
IUB Building
30 Irving Place, New York, N.Y. 10003

For Tslilla and Inbal

William Heinemann Ltd
15 Queen Street, Mayfair, London W1X 8BE

LONDON MELBOURNE TORONTO
JOHANNESBURG AUCKLAND

First published 1978
© Norman Rose 1978
434 64950 3

Printed and bound in Great Britain by
Butler & Tanner Ltd, Frome and London

CONTENTS

ILLUSTRATIONS

*Grateful thanks are due to the Vansittart family for permission
to reproduce family photographs*

Prologue

DURING THE WRITING of this book, I have been asked on numerous occasions: why a biography of Vansittart? Or, as a colleague of mine once humorously put it: why have I chosen to rescue him from the obscurity he so richly deserves? He was no Churchill or Hitler or Roosevelt. He was certainly not a decisive figure of world history whose stature and actions demanded, dare one say without question, an appraisal of his life. Yet, as will become apparent, he was not a figure entirely without consequence; and for a brief period he did exert a considerable influence upon British foreign policy decision-making. For all that, I have no wholly satisfactory answer to the question first asked, except to say that I found his personality and role sufficiently intriguing to warrant such an exercise, and that I hope others will too.

What then was the source of his appeal? I first encountered the name Vansittart as a student. He appeared to me then as the embodiment of everything pure and noble in British foreign policy tradition, a shining beacon of integrity in those dreadfully compromised years of the 1930's. There he was, so to speak, a knight on a white horse battling gallantly, and at times single-handedly, against the dark forces of appeasement. If ever one man personified the righteousness of the anti-appeasers, it was Vansittart. Not only that. By virtue of his opposition to the Chamberlain government, he also emerges as an anti-conformist figure *par excellence*. This combination was sufficient to inspire any but the most cynical and prejudiced of students.

No doubt, this was a *naif* view to hold. Certainly there are few scholars today who would defend the 'guilty men' of Munich theory. And the writing of this book has convinced me more than ever that such accusatory history is not only outdated but also positively harmful to a true understanding of those years. If this volume contributes anything to the debate on appeasement, it is simply to highlight, through Vansittart's own words and actions, the severely limited options open to those responsible for the formulation of British policy. It was far easier to present dramatic alternatives from the outside: from the safe confines of a newspaper column or an oppositionist political rally.

It is said that no man can remain a hero to his valet; or, one may confidently add, to his biographer. If some preconceived opinions have had to be amended, a few blemishes brought to light, the overall impression of the man remains substantially unaltered. Hopefully, a new, a more realistic, a more human dimension has been added to the previous conception of his personality. For me at least he remains one of the most appealing and compelling figures of those years, even if not the unflawed hero of my student days.

N.A.R.
The Hebrew University,
Jerusalem

Acknowledgements

MANY PEOPLE HAVE CONTRIBUTED to the preparation of this study. My chief debt is to Lady Vansittart for her encouragement of this project. Without her cooperation and unfailing courtesy and hospitality it is doubtful whether this volume would ever have been completed. I am grateful also for the reminiscences of the other members of Lord Vansittart's immediate family: his daughter, Mrs Cynthia Mackay, and her husband, Edward; his younger brother, Guy; and his two sisters, Miss Sibell and Miss Marjorie Vansittart.

My search for material led me to many private homes, offices and studies. For the time and patience expended upon me I wish to thank: Mr F. T. A. Ashton-Gwatkin; Flying Officer A. J. R. Banks; Sir Colville Barclay; Lord Butler; Lord Caccia; Mr Adam Ciolkocsz; Sir Laurence Collier; the late Mr I. Colvin; Mr and Mrs O. Corfield; Sir Michael Creswell; the late Rt. Hon. R. H. S. Crossman; Mr K. G. Dallas; Mrs M. Delderfield; Professor S. Friedlander; Mr J. Heffer; Mr P. K. Hiller; Sir Kenneth Hogg; Professor Rom Landau; Mr Valentine Lawford; Mr Peter Ludlow; Mr D. Marquand, M.P.; Professor W. N. Medlicott; Professor P. Mellini; Sir Clifford Norton; the late Sir Owen O' Malley; Count Raczynski; Sir George Rendel; Sir Frank Roberts; Mrs Zara Steiner; Sir Ralph Stevenson; Lord Strang; Mrs Kay Thomas; Mrs A. Turner; Mr P. Ustinov; Professor D. C. Watt; the late Sir John Wheeler-Bennett; the late Sir Arthur Willert.

I am grateful also for the gracious permission of Her Majesty Queen Elizabeth II to quote from material deposited in the Royal Archives, Windsor. My thanks are also extended to the archivists, librarians and staff of the numerous institutions in which I have worked: the library at Balliol College, Oxford; the Beaverbrook Library, London; the Bodleian Library, Oxford; the British Library of Political and Economic Science at The London School of Economics; the British Museum Library and its newspaper collection at Colindale; the Archives at Churchill College, Cambridge; the India Office Library, London; the Library at Eton College; the Institute of Historical Research, Senate House, London; the Kaplan Library of the Faculty for Social Sciences at the Hebrew University, Jerusalem; the Labour Party Library, London; the National Library at The Hebrew University; the Public Record Office, London; the Scottish Record Office, Edinburgh; the University Library, Cambridge; the Weizmann Archives, Rehovoth. Their patience and helpfulness greatly eased my task. Crown copyright material in the Public Record Office is reproduced by permission of the Controller of Her Majesty's Stationery Office. I would also like to thank the following individuals for granting me access to unpublished material in their private possession: Viscount Caldecote; Mr Martin Gilbert; Mr D. Marquand, M.P.; Sir Philip Magnus-Allcroft; Mr N. Nicolson; Dr D. Rotunda; Mrs K. Thomas.

I wish to thank the following authors and publishers for quotations I have used from works of which they hold the copyright: Earl of Avon, *Facing the Dictators* (Cassell & Co. Ltd.); G. Baer, *The Coming of the Ethiopian War* (Harvard University Press); B. Bond, ed., *Chief of Staff. The Diaries of Lt. Gen. Sir Henry Pownell* (Leo Cooper Ltd.); I. Colvin, *Vansittart in Office* and *The Chamberlain Cabinet* (Victor Gollancz Ltd.); H. Dalton, *Memoirs* (Frederick Muller Ltd.); D. Dilks, ed., *The Diaries of Sir Alexander Cadogan, 1938-1945* (Cassell & Co. Ltd.); F. R. Gannon, *The British Press and Germany, 1936-39* (Oxford University Press); Earl of Halifax, *Fulness of Days* (William Collins Sons & Co. Ltd.); J. Harvey, ed., *The Diplomatic Diaries of Oliver Harvey, 1937-1940* (William Collins & Sons Ltd.); M. Howard, *The Continental Commitment* (Maurice Temple Smith Ltd.); T. Jones, *A Diary with Letters, 1931-50* (Oxford University Press); R. R. James, *'Chips'. The Diaries of Sir Henry Channon* (Weidenfeld and Nicolson Ltd.); B. Lockhart, *Comes the Reckoning* (Putnam Ltd.); L. Lochner, *The Goebbels Diaries* (Fireside Press Inc., New York); N. Nicolson, *The Diaries and Letters of Harold Nicolson* (William Collins & Sons Ltd.); S. Roskill, *Hankey. Man of Secrets* (William Collins & Sons Ltd.); Z. Steiner, *The Foreign Office and Foreign Policy, 1898-1914* (Cambridge University Press); A. J. P. Taylor, *Off The Record. Political Interviews 1933-1943* (Hutchinson & Co.); Viscount Templewood, *Nine Troubled Years* (William Collins & Sons Ltd.); C. Thorne,

The Limits of Foreign Policy. The West, the League and the Far Eastern Crisis of 1931-1933 (Hamish Hamilton Ltd.)

I should like to register in advance my apologies for those cases which I have inadvertently overlooked.

I also owe a considerable debt to the officers of the Centre for International Studies at the L.S.E. – Professor G. Goodwin, Professor J. Joll, Professor E. Kedourie, Professor D. C. Watt – for kindly inviting me to spend a year at the centre as a visiting research fellow, thereby enabling me to collect much of the source material for this project.

In recent years the cost of historical research has grown enormously. I would like to place on record my appreciation to the following institutions for their generous and sustained support: the Central Research Fund of the University of London; the Deutscher Akademischer Austauschdienst; the Leonard Davis Institute for International Affairs at The Hebrew University; the Nuffield Foundation; the Research Fund of the Faculty for Social Sciences at The Hebrew University.

Professor S. Friedlander, Professor M. Verete, and Professor D. C. Watt read the book in typescript, either in whole or in part. For their informed comments and advice I remain greatly in their debt. A very special word of thanks is also due to Mrs Diana Reich. Over the past months she has generously given of her time, contributing to the research and making many invaluable suggestions concerning the contents of the book. I am grateful also to Mr Roger Smith and Miss Elizabeth Blair of Heinemann Ltd. for their constructive encouragement and good-natured understanding of the problems which accompanied this project. Needless to say, the sole burden of responsibility for any errors and for the opinions advanced here rest with the author alone.

Finally, I wish to record my deepest thanks and admiration to my wife and daughter. With commendable fortitude and enviable patience they endured my interminable journeys into the past when perhaps I should have been more receptive to the day-to-day problems of the present. This volume is dedicated, in gratitude, to them.

Abbreviations

―――――――――――――――――――

B.D.	Documents on British Foreign Policy
B.P.	Baldwin Papers
C.P.	Curzon Papers
F.R.U.S.	Papers relating to the Foreign Affairs of the United States
G.D.	Documents on German Foreign Policy
H.P.	Hankey Papers
Ll.G.P.	Lloyd George Papers
M.P.	The Mist Procession
P.D.	Hansard, Parliamentary Debates, 5th series, Commons and Lords
Ph.P.	Phipps Papers
P.R.O.	Public Record Office
R.A.	Royal Archives
Vnst.	Vansittart Papers

CHAPTER I

First Steps

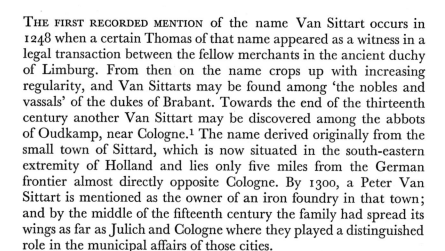

THE FIRST RECORDED MENTION of the name Van Sittart occurs in 1248 when a certain Thomas of that name appeared as a witness in a legal transaction between the fellow merchants in the ancient duchy of Limburg. From then on the name crops up with increasing regularity, and Van Sittarts may be found among 'the nobles and vassals' of the dukes of Brabant. Towards the end of the thirteenth century another Van Sittart may be discovered among the abbots of Oudkamp, near Cologne.[1] The name derived originally from the small town of Sittard, which is now situated in the south-eastern extremity of Holland and lies only five miles from the German frontier almost directly opposite Cologne. By 1300, a Peter Van Sittart is mentioned as the owner of an iron foundry in that town; and by the middle of the fifteenth century the family had spread its wings as far as Julich and Cologne where they played a distinguished role in the municipal affairs of those cities.

During the Reformation the family embraced the Protestant cause. Their conversion caused a sharp, though temporary, reversal in their fortunes. The protracted Spanish wars against the Netherlands during the sixteenth century brought in their wake much persecution of the dissenters. The area around Sittard and Cologne was a particularly vulnerable one, constituting as it did part of the main supply and approach routes of the Spanish armies into the Low Countries. In 1598 John Van Sittart, a counsellor of Aix-la-Chapelle, sought refuge from the persecutions of Archbishop Ernst of Cologne. He found it by escaping to the Hanse city of Danzig. It was here that Peter Van Sittart, the founder of the English branch of the family, was born in January 1651. The Cologne branch of the family seems to have died out towards the end of the seventeenth century. By comparison, the Danzig branch flourished, and by the end of the eighteenth century the Van Sittarts had succeeded in marrying into many of the patrician families of that burgher aristocracy.

Peter first arrived in England in 1670, though he did not settle finally in London until four years later. He was a merchant adventurer in the classic mould. A family history describes him as 'a man of daring and enterprise' who 'conducted divers trading expeditions in person to the East Indies, the South Seas, and the Baltic'. That he was a man of singular courage and daring can hardly be doubted. Those were fierce times and men travelled and traded in distant parts at immense risk. But although the risks were great so too were the opportunities. By the turn of the seventeenth century Peter had amassed a considerable fortune, had bought a vast mansion in St Mary Axe, where he resided until his death, and had swiftly established a reputation in the City of London both for astuteness and reliability. Peter reaped his reward. In 1700 he was elected a director of the East India Company. The Vansittarts' connections with the company lasted until its formal dissolution in 1857 and brought immeasurable material benefit and public distinction to the family.

In 1678 Peter married Susanna Sanderson, daughter of a country gentleman from County Durham. It was a stable and highly successful marriage. Their seven children struck deep roots and laid firm foundations for the future achievements of the English Vansittarts. There were two main branches of the family and they eventually based themselves upon two large estates in Berkshire: Shottesbrook and Bisham Abbey.

By the time of Peter's death in 1705, the family was secure in the knowledge that it had successfully penetrated the upper regions of London's *haute bourgeoisie*. With a sound economic base, and a family of rapidly expanding dimensions, the Vansittarts were all set to exploit the unlimited commercial opportunities offered by the eighteenth century and to stake their claim to high public office which would inevitably flow from the enrichment of the family fortunes. During the eighteenth century the family prospered. They produced Indian administrators, admirals, generals, academics, even a Chancellor of the Exchequer, and of course landed gentry in abundance. They never scaled the highest peaks; but they were always within sight of the top.

Probably the best known of the Vansittarts during this early period, or at least the one who achieved highest office, was Nicholas, fifth son of Henry Vansittart, later raised to the peerage as Baron Bexley. In 1812 he was appointed Chancellor of the Exchequer and remained in that office for the next twelve years. He was known for his activities in two areas: the employment of the house of Rothschild in order to provide sufficient specie for the needs of the army and the payment of foreign subsidies, in retrospect a life-saving innovation; and the universal unpopularity he acquired, in an already unpopular government, for imposing heavy rates of taxation in times of peace. A biographer wrote of him: 'A mild-mannered man, most ineffective in debate, he yet had many friends, and his mediocre abilities with accommodating and moderate views probably account for his holding office from 1801–1828 with the exception of only two years.'² It was Nicholas who acquired the great estates at Foots Cray in Kent.

After Nicholas's death in 1851 the family, at least in its contribution to public life, appears to have entered a definite decline. They played no prominent role in the expansion of British economic, political and imperial power which characterized the latter half of the Victorian age. Rather, they blended into the general, and by now well-established, pattern of upper-class English life: one of the best public schools, usually Eton, followed by a choice of careers in either the Army or Navy, the Indian or home civil services, the Church, or simply running the family estates. All this was in marked contrast to the rumbustious, swashbuckling pursuits of the earlier Vansittarts. Every age fashions its own leaders; and Nicholas, the unassuming, industrious, hard-headed, single-minded, public-spirited Chancellor, set the pace for the Victorian Vansittarts.

This period witnessed the first perceptible signs of decline in Great Britain's status as a great power. It was marked by two severe financial upheavals, in 1870 and 1886, each followed by an industrial and commercial crisis. In the late seventies the agricultural sector found itself overwhelmed by the sudden invasion of cheap American prairie wheat, an invasion which resulted in an almost endemic depression in rural areas until the turn of the century. These harsh economic facts should not, however, be judged in too unfavourable a light. Although in many respects Britain was slipping from her previous position of pre-eminence, in absolute terms her condition was thriving and prosperous. Great Britain mounted higher economic heights than ever before in her history. It is true that her affluence was marred by the emergence of a wave of militant social and industrial unrest which drew its strength from the evils of over-rapid and unplanned urbanization. Yet for those born into the privileged classes these problems were remote. The late Victorian age witnessed the zenith of Great Britain's economic power and political influence; and it was still firmly anchored on the traditional values of land, high birth, and great wealth.

It was in this comfortable setting that Robert Gilbert Vansittart was born at Wilton House, Farnham, on 25 June 1881. Van's* father, Captain Robert Arnold Vansittart, the only son in a family of nine, was an army career officer. In 1878 he married Alice Blane of Foliejon Park near Windsor, the third daughter of local, landed gentry. They had six children in all: three daughters, Sibell (born 1879), Honor (born 1883), and Marjorie (born 1888); and three sons, Van, Arnold (born 1889), and Guy (born 1893). They lived the routine life of a regular army officer's family, moving from one dreary garrison town to another. Then in 1886 fate intervened. On 14 April of that year their cousin, Coleraine Robert Vansittart, died suddenly, it was thought from diphtheria, at his residence at 15 rue Vernet, Paris. Coleraine was something of an eccentric. Owing to the peculiarities of the English inheritance system, the vast bulk of the Vansittart estates had fallen to him. Perhaps because of the responsibility of these unexpected windfalls he sought refuge in Paris. An intimate of the French nobility, Napoleon III trusted his judgement of horses and he was the first Englishman to be elected a member of the French Jockey Club. He helped make pigeon shooting a fashionable sport, and took an active part in 'Tir aux Pigeons' in Paris where a prize, 'Le Prix Vansittart', was annually shot for. These assorted activities came to an abrupt end in April 1886, and his cousin, Captain Robert Vansittart, read in the newspapers about the unexpected inheritence which had come his way: the estates of North and Foots Cray in Kent.

These were not the most auspicious times to inherit great landed wealth. But the estates at Foots Cray, situated as they were in Kent and based more on livestock, in particular dairy farming, and fruit-growing, were less affected by the general crisis in agriculture, though they could not have wholly escaped the consequences of the general decline in the agricultural sector.

The acquisition of Foots Cray necessitated a revolutionary change in the way of life of Captain Vansittart and his family. The estates have long since been swallowed up by the growth of suburban London, but they lay between Bexley and Sidcup, and could be found by following the old Folkestone road out of London. No

---

* I have adopted the familiar usage of his name throughout the narrative. Both his closest friends and his bitterest enemies called him Van, and it seemed natural and appropriate to follow their example in this volume of his life.

records remain describing the physical features of the estates. However, they must have been considerable in size, consisting of at least two thousand acres of rich, agricultural land devoted mainly to dairy farming, sheep raising and fruit growing – almost certainly apples, cherries and hops. The estate certainly realized enough rents and profits to sustain a more than comfortable existence for its owners. It supported a number of tenant farmers, and the new owner soon proved to be a considerate landlord, busily constructing model farm labourers' cottages and new village halls.[3] Captain Vansittart managed his own farm and took an intense, if paternalistic, interest in the welfare of his tenants and workers. Indeed, for a retired cavalry officer he seems to have plunged with a great deal of zest into the pleasures that awaited a Victorian squire.

It was a gratifying existence, well padded against the harsher exigencies of life. From now on the Vansittarts lived the life that befitted landed gentry at the end of the nineteenth century. The house in which they lived at Foots Cray was a large one, consisting of some thirty rooms; and its needs, as well as those of its owners, were amply administered by some fifteen servants.[4] The Vansittart children led uncomplicated lives. Their parents were neither unpredictable Victorian eccentrics nor restless *fin de siècle* intellectuals, desperately searching for cause and effect in every scientific-literary tract then in fashion. They were, in Van's own words, 'gentlefolk, who would not say boo to a gosling'.[5]

The outbreak of the Boer War brought this idyllic existence to a rude end. The Captain, to the applause of his children, volunteered his services. Too old for active duties, he served his country in the 'Re-mounts', transporting horses to South Africa and then on to the front line. In 1900 there was a brief panic at Foots Cray when he was reported missing in the Transvaal. But he came safely through, and immediately after his discharge from service he resumed his normal pre-war pattern of activities.

For her part, Alice Vansittart also played the role which fate had seemingly allotted her. A 'serene' and 'good-looking' woman to her children, she whiled away her time in traditional Victorian fashion on a diet of three-decker novels, croquet and archery. Nevertheless, she fulfilled her duties faithfully. The household was well organized; and the Sabbath strictly observed. Just across the lawn from the main house stood the church and, every Sunday, the young Vansittarts were shepherded off to pray not once but twice. Collective prayers were also practised daily before breakfast with Alice, or her eldest daughter Sibell, providing the musical accompaniment on a harmonium. Meals were taken at regular times and the children were expected to, and did, appear on time without undue fuss from their parents. The days slipped by pleasantly enough. Some pony riding or village cricket, some primitive lawn tennis, or even a little learning from French governesses, helped to relieve the monotony. Nostalgically, Van recalled that his

> Childhood, jolly and humdrum, comes back to me smiling in an odour of mignonette and blackcurrant tart, a vision of elms whence white owls flew noiseless in a noiseless countryside, of Dalmatian dogs who ran with coaches, an unrecognized survival of precaution against highwaymen.[6]

The Medway flowed placidly by, perfectly reflecting the life at Foots Cray.

At the age of seven Van was despatched to St Neot's, a preparatory school near Winchfield. The departure from home was not to his liking. He was predictably homesick, rebelling against the strict discipline imposed upon him in such an arbitrary fashion by total strangers. He was already regarded by his family as a mischievous child, forever in scrapes, frequently brawling with the local children. The pattern was repeated at St Neot's, though the odds now were more heavily weighted against him.[7]

The curriculum at St Neot's left little to the imagination and was the normal fare for most prep schools. Some French and Latin, a smattering of highly selective history, scarcely a look at geography, and, after a few terms, the doubtful pleasures of Greek grammar. There was one outstanding feature in this barren academic wasteland: the new-found joys of English literature. Van recalled in particular the enjoyment which the works of Sir Walter Scott and Macaulay gave him. It was a childhood passion which remained to comfort him throughout his life. Van was a minor poet and playwright though with literary ambitions of a grander nature, and he often sought refuge from the vicissitudes of public life by withdrawing into the romance of literature.

Van displayed a great enthusiasm for all forms of sport, another passion which he retained in later life: he was a dedicated, if indifferent, cricketer; a keen and moderately successful athlete; a boxer of promise; and an excellent tennis player. Tennis was his sporting forte. He improved his tennis in later life to become an accomplished player, competing in minor tournaments, and daily practising his game at Queen's Club before retiring to the Foreign Office. Eventually, towards the end of his life, he was appointed president of the All England Lawn Tennis Club at Wimbledon.

Of friends that he made at St Neot's, he tells us little or nothing. He merely recorded that 'most preparatory schools at the outset of the nineties were hard. The few friends whom I made – they were killed early in the first German war – came through the test with moderate pain and pleasure.'[8] But whatever the drawbacks of the system, Van adapted to it with the minimum of discomfort, and he was rewarded in his last year by being appointed head boy.

From St Neot's to Eton. The Eton at which Van arrived in the third-half* of 1893 was still recovering from the recommendations of a Royal Commission's report of February 1864. The Commission had suggested sweeping changes in the school's curriculum and management, in particular by placing the teaching of science, modern languages and mathematics on a proper footing. The headmaster during Van's years was Edmund Warre, a reforming head and an outstanding example of the scholar-athlete then so much in vogue. Academically the fare was similar to that offered at St Neot's, though now, owing to the new reforms, there was far more emphasis on modern languages – French and German – and science and mathematics. Van's house-master was a certain Arthur Cockshott, a mathematician of some repute; while his tutor was Hubert Brinton, a well-known classicist. Thus, the two sides were neatly balanced. One may assume that Van's house was run in the traditional fashion.

> We all had breakfast and tea in our rooms, and it was the duty of the fags to produce boiled or scrambled eggs and make toast and tea. The smoothness or otherwise of a fag's life depended very much on the temper of the fagmaster. An unreasonable and cantankerous fagmaster could goad the most long suffering fag to fury or despair, and from him there was no appeal. On the other hand nice fagmasters could make their fag's life very happy, with an occasional egg or the end of a pot of cream, or a sausage for Sunday breakfast . . . And every day in the dining-room at luncheon and supper, we were all given as much beer as we wanted, with the choice of a glass of port or sherry at luncheon on Sunday, solemnly handed round to all boys, large and small, by the fat old butler.[9]

And that he struggled up the hierarchical scale in the same manner as others.

* At Eton the terms are named halves. There are, therefore, three halves in every Eton year.

Van excelled as a scholar. One year after arriving at Eton he won the Assistant Master's prize in French. He sailed through the Trials (end of term examinations) with consummate ease, consistently gaining distinction grades. Only the mysteries of mathematics eluded him. Van's strength unquestionably lay in the field of modern languages. He had long shown exceptional linguistic talent. In 1899 he excelled himself by carrying off both the French and German Prince Consort prizes, a rare, if not unique, achievement.[10] On the playing field he was equally active, if somewhat less proficient in achieving spectacular results. His finest sporting feats were reserved for tennis, athletics and boxing; in team games he made less of an impression, and only just managed to scrape in as twelfth man for the Eton cricket eleven. It was a trait not easily shrugged off in later life and in more serious pursuits.

Van's finest hour occurred on the Fourth of June (founder's day) celebrations, when much thought and activity were given over to theatricals and speechifying. During his last years at school, Van expanded his repertoire of stirring, topical, not to say violently chauvinistic, recitations. Van's loaded perorations, which included a choice selection from Kipling, Tennyson, and an American poet, R. C. Rodgers,[11] were generally well-received, and his rendering of the 'White Man's Burden' was given an enthusiastic and positive notice in the *Eton College Chronicle*.[12]

> By that summer he had considerably polished his technique,

> and, as before, he varied his refrain so as to avoid monotony of cadence and to emphasise the changes of sentiment. He had completely got rid of the *tremolo* in his voice, but the unconsciously dilated nostrils showed how strongly he was feeling the splendid devotion to the mother country and the pride of race which thrills through the spirited verses [of R. C. Rodgers' poem, 'To The Race'].

But his farewell performance came at a singularly appropriate moment,

> on the day when we heard of the hoisting of the Union Jack at Pretoria, Vansittart should give us 'The English Flag' . . . the speaker held the audience spellbound by the vibrating earnestness of his voice . . .[13]

These quotations speak for themselves. This was not just playing to the gallery. They demonstrated in the most graphic and revealing manner the subject material Van found most attractive for public consumption. And they reveal equally that behind the facade of English *sang-froid* which Van preferred to display, lay a deeply emotional and histrionic personality. The heyday of imperialism had discovered a young and ardent advocate.

This latent patriotism burst into flame just as Van was about to embark upon the first of a long series of independent journeys to the Continent where, much to his bewilderment and shock, he encountered furious manifestations of anti-British sentiment. Towards the end of his Eton period it had become clear to him that his future career would lie in the diplomatic service. Family plans were set upon diplomacy and it seems as though Van voiced no serious objections to his parents' desires.

The primary requisite for a diplomat was proficiency in French and German. It was with this aim in mind that, in the summer of 1899, Van arrived at 174 rue de la Pompe, Paris, the residence of the redoubtable Jeanne de Hénault and the Mecca of many would-be candidates for the diplomatic or foreign service. Jeanne was already something of a legend in her own right. Esconced in her fifth-floor flat overlooking the Bois de Boulogne, surrounded by her cats and her aged mother, she imposed upon her young men an enigmatic discipline understood fully only by herself. Supremely confident in her own ability to translate the subtleties of the French language, she created great historic legends of her own invention. Another occupant at the rue de la Pompe recalled how she enshrined Van in a mythical aura: "There had been Robert Vansittart: he had written a French play at the age of sixteen and it had been performed at the Odéon: he had, after a bare six weeks of Jeanne, passed first into the diplomatic service.'[14]

It was not the most propitious moment to make acquaintance with the vagaries of French public life. The third republic was racked by a series of scandals involving the highest officials of state and kept on the boil by an eager and venal press. But even these improprieties paled into insignificance beside the deeper ramifications of the Dreyfus affair which had erupted with renewed fury into its second stage in 1899. Anti-semitism was by no means unknown in Great Britain. During these past two decades London alone had absorbed tens of thousands of destitute, *émigré* Jews fleeing persecution from Tsarist Russia. Problems were created; emotions set on edge. But the virus of anti-semitism never succeeded in poisoning the mainstream of British social and political life in the same deadly and insidious manner as it did on the Continent. Almost certainly the Kent countryside remained immune; at the most only the faintest echoes from London's Whitechapel must have penetrated as far as Foots Cray. Anti-Jewish prejudice among Britain's upper classes tended to be of a more genteel character. Anti-semitisim, in the obscene and virulent form given it by the wild men of *La Libre Parole* was, for Van, an unknown quantity. It surprised and shocked him beyond belief, not only because of the patent rubbish contained in the pseudo-scientific, racialist theories of Wilhelm Marr or Edouard Drumont, but also for the violent and uncontrollable passions it aroused. After a lifetime of experience he described anti-semitism as 'the prep school of violence'.[15] The impressions engraved by this lamentable episode remained with Van forever. He always retained a basic sympathy for the aims of Jewish nationalism, even if often critical of Zionist tactics. And it was the lunatic nature of Nazi racialism which did much to push him irretrievably along the path which led to the theory of original German sin.

These events were further complicated by the upsurge in French patriotism, and corresponding anti-British feeling, generated by the Fashoda incident. Compromise was finally reached, backed by the long arm of the British navy and the strength of the British position in Egypt. But France felt humiliated. The Paris press reacted in characteristic fashion, whipping up public feeling in an irresponsible manner, beating the drum, crying for war. 'I have gone through my life with those early impressions of senseless civil and foreign rancour.'[16] And so it was. This was one aspect of French life to which he never became reconciled: the frivolous irresponsibility of the press and the chronic instability of French public life under the Third Republic. In the future it would have disastrous effects upon his own policy, and he would return to this theme time and time again when in office.

Yet for all this, Van returned home an inveterate Francophile, and flaunted his new-found faith with all the ostentation of any recent convert. He was still very young. His infatuation with the French language and literature, the spontaneous gaiety of Parisian life at the turn of the century, the permanence of *La France*, all this must have more than compensated for the squalor of French public life, surely superficial and transient by comparison.

His Francophilia also resulted from his first experiences in Germany. Soon after winning the German prize Van felt the need to improve his knowledge of the language, and made arrangements to spend some time at a German crammer near Hamburg. The Boer War was then at its height and British popularity at its lowest. There was much talk of a 'Continental League' headed by Germany and aimed at curbing British arrogance. Van found the harsh, often brutal assault on Great Britain's integrity and reputation too repugnant to stomach. It was further exacerbated by the fact that Germany's animosity seemed directed against him personally.

> The Germans were positive; the young militarists at the crammer gloated at every British defeat, and the masters humiliated the alien by such tricks as opening the *Iliad* at false random, challenging him to continue the quotation, and putting up some primed accomplice to triumph. There was no escape from gibes in the house, press, theatre, street.[17]

The intensely personal nature of his reactions to the treatment he encountered in France and Germany can only confirm the impression that here was a young man in whom emotions ran deep, emotions which would burst into flame at the slightest provocation.

Many of his contemporaries at Eton – George Lloyd, Aubrey Herbert, Edward Wood, Percy Loraine, Arthur Willert* – were to serve with him in the Foreign Office. One of them remembered Van as an attractive and intelligent pupil who kept to himself and steered clear of any cliques or fashionable circles: 'A brilliant solitary who was not really accepted at Eton', as it was said. There were rumours circulating at the time that he had 'eastern blood', and Van's physical appearance must certainly have lent credence to this ludicrous assertion,† for he was handsome in the Latin manner with long,

---

* George Ambrose Lloyd (1879–1941): Hon. Attache at Constantinople embassy 1905; Conservative M.P., 1910–25; High Commissioner for Egypt and Sudan 1925–29. Cr. Baron, 1925

   Aubrey Nigel Henry Molyneux Herbert (1880–1923): Hon. Attache at Constantinople embassy 1900; Conservative M.P., 1911–23

   Edward Frederick Lindley Wood (1881–1959): Conservative M.P., 1910–34; Viceroy of India, 1926–31; Lord Privy Seal, 1935–37; Lord President of Council, 1937–38; Foreign Secretary, 1938–40; Ambassador to United States, 1941–46. Cr. Baron Irwin, 1925. Succeeded as Viscount Halifax, 1934

   Percy Lyham Loraine (1880–1961): entered diplomatic service, 1904; served at Constantinople, Peking, Warsaw, Teheran, Athens; High Commissioner for Egypt and Sudan, 1929–33; Ambassador to Turkey, 1933–39; to Italy, 1939–40. Succeeded as 12th baronet, 1917

   Arthur Willert (1882–1973): correspondent for *The Times* in Paris, Berlin, and Washington, 1910–20; Head of News Department of Foreign Office, 1921–35. Kn. 1919.

† This rumour stuck with Van throughout his career. The author once heard a high Foreign Office official, now retired, tell him in all seriousness that 'Van had black blood in him'. As was to be expected, the Germans often referred to his Jewish or Red Indian blood. See F.O. 371/22989, C. 8636/16/18

aquiline features. To make matters worse Van set himself unusual pursuits and was often discovered learning shorthand and typing in the common room.[18] No doubt these unmistakably bourgeois preoccupations were frowned upon in certain Etonian circles.

Despite these alleged quirks, Van terminated his Eton career as captain of the Oppidans. If nothing else his past record dictated it. By virtue of his new position, Van was also a member of Pop, the Eton debating society. He does not seem to have enjoyed the clash and thrust of open debate for he spoke only once in Pop and then 'ventured no more oratory for forty years'.[19] Even then he showed a marked preference for lecturing rather than persuading.

By the time he left Eton in the summer of 1900 he was nineteen years of age. He had spent a full seven years at the college, unusual at any time. He did not go on to university, which perhaps would have been the most natural thing to do. The precarious state of his father's finances was the deciding factor in this decision. In many ways Captain Vansittart was an unworldly, even gullible figure. He had no head for business; and almost from the outset of coming into his inheritance he had embarked on a protracted series of injudicious financial ventures, the net result of which was to lose him and his family the estates at Foots Cray. But although this unfortunate occurrence still lay far in the future, the first effects of Captain Vansittart's disastrous excursions into the world of business were already in evidence.

In any case, university education was not a prerequisite for a successful diplomatic career.[20] Rather, the emphasis was on travel and private education, a consequence of the important part which foreign languages play in diplomacy and the more rigorous linguistic tests imposed upon aspiring diplomats. Whatever the precise reason, Captain Vansittart could barely manage to scrape together an allowance of three hundred pounds per annum, roughly equivalent to the cost of keeping Van at Eton, and the minimum private income necessary for starting diplomats.[21] Van found no difficulty in surviving on this sum. Financial worries, however, were to pursue him well into the future until his first marriage solved the most immediate of them.

His father's monetary indiscretions also finally put paid to Van's ambitions, cherished since early youth, to follow a literary career. He accepted this blow with the minimum of fuss. After all, writing was a craft which could be pursued at any hour of the day. At any rate, this adverse decision did not dampen his enthusiasm or output, and he succeeded in producing a steady stream of literary works –

verse, plays and novels – until old age. Indeed, his literary style often crept into his official papers, sometimes to the amusement of his readers, but more often than not to their intense annoyance, and he would then be regarded as a *littérateur manqué* from whom nothing better could be expected.

In this way Van's immediate future was mapped out for him. He would spend the next years travelling in Europe and preparing himself for his future diplomatic career. By the turn of the century, recruitment into the foreign and diplomatic services was still based on a system which combined nomination and examination. Both services, though distinct and separate from each other, were regarded as outposts of an élitist, class system; and of the two, the diplomatic service had acquired the more class-ridden reputation.[22] Reform came slowly and grudgingly, and at least for the pre-war period with little visible effect. By the mid-eighteen-nineties candidates for both services sat for the same examination, though they were separately marked and appointed. Patronage still reigned. Entrance into either service could be obtained only by securing the nomination of the Foreign Secretary, and 'it was the weight carried by the position and interests of parents and sponsors, rather than the qualities of the candidates themselves, which decided the chance of a nomination'.[23] Certainly Van must have secured his nomination this way, for there was no other. Having secured it, he expected to compete for the examination sometime during the winter of 1902–3. Thus at least two years of travel and preparation awaited him before he submitted his candidature.

His journeys took him to familiar places; and although now undertaken with a more serious aim in view, he did not allow his academic pursuits to detract from the pleasures of foreign living. He spent the season at Bad Homburg, and succumbed to its oppressive charms. It was there that he fell in love for the first time. In later life he was extremely reticent about this affair. One does not know how it began, how it ended, or even with whom it was conducted.[24] In all probability his romance followed a pattern all too painfully familiar to young men of his class and education who have just been thrust out alone into the world. No doubt his first major encounter with the opposite sex left his ego bruised, his self-confidence in question, his pride shaken. But unless there was a basic flaw in his emotional make-up, he would certainly have looked back upon this episode with a mixture of smug satisfaction and nostalgic regret.

Great Britain was still at war in South Africa. During his first visit to Germany Van had experienced, in particularly odious form, the emotional, anti-British feeling generated by the Boer War. Now it was to involve him in a bizarre incident. During a tennis tournament a misunderstanding occurred on the courts. The honour of one of his opponents, a champion duellist named Captain Flesch, was slighted. He challenged Van to a duel. This was melodrama at its maddest. Future British diplomats were not expected to behave like German fencing masters. Van refused to be drawn. He argued:

> Look here, nothing would induce me to fight you with a pistol or a sword; but if you challenge me any more I shall hit you. And then as there will be no duel, won't you be dishonoured, and have to commit suicide? Let's go on with the game.[25]

Discretion triumphed. As it was obvious his welcome in Germany was wearing thin, he hurriedly packed his bags and left for the more congenial atmosphere of Vienna.

Vienna was more to his taste. He found the easy-going, often frivolous, Viennese infinitely easier to handle than the strait-laced Germans. Vienna possessed a unique charm of her own: the ancient churches; the great boulevard – the Ring – which encompasses old Vienna; the impressive Schonbrunn Palace and gardens; the baroque complex of the Hofburg. In particular he discovered the Viennese theatre and came away enchanted at what he had found. He struck up acquaintances with up and coming young Viennese *litterati* such as Hugo von Hofmannsthal and Jakob Wassermann, and departed suitably impressed with their nonconformist acts of creation. The weeks passed by in a round of sport, entertainment, high-flown discussion, and country visits. He became a close friend of George Franckenstein, later Austrian minister in London, and often visited the Villa Franckenstein in the Alt Aussee. They played lawn tennis together as doubles partners and toured the then limited European circuit. Van was an unpredictable partner: '[his] temper used to frighten, especially as I had a tendency to double fault'. But he obviously impressed his companions. 'We all prophesied a great future for Vansittart, for he was clever, witty, full of temperament, energetic and poetically gifted.'[26]

His Austrian experience stood out in marked contrast to the humiliations he had suffered in Germany. He recognized the feebleness of the tottering Habsburg monarchy, and the basic instability inherent in a multi-national Empire. Above all, he abhorred the increasing dependence of the 'worn Habsburgs' on 'the Hohenzollern upstart'.[27] He shrank from the thought of his elegant and cosmopolitan Vienna falling victim to a brash and parochial Germany. He soon became convinced of the fundamental incompatibility between these two German-speaking peoples; an incompatibility made more acute by the political rivalries of the period. As we shall see, the preservation of Austria as an independent national entity formed a cardinal principle in his European policy.

In the spring of 1902 he returned to Paris to prepare in earnest for the forthcoming examinations. During the summer months it had become apparent that the Foreign Office would open its doors to a limited number of applicants that winter, and Van, who had now reached the age of twenty-one, had no desire to prolong his apprenticeship longer than necessary. Most candidates proceeded, almost as a matter of natural course, from their residence abroad to a crammer in or around London, usually Scoone's on Garrick Street, where they were able to benefit from years of experience in learning the required texts in the required manner. Van did not avail himself of this luxury. Instead, true to his reputation as 'a brilliant solitary', he preferred to remain in Paris working at his own pace and according to his own method.

He could approach the forthcoming test with a considerable degree of confidence. Entrance into the service was heavily loaded in favour of those endowed with linguistic ability. On that score Van needed to have no fear.* He sat for the examination on 3 February 1903 together with thirteen other young hopefuls nominated to compete for three attachéships in the diplomatic service. A month later, on 4 March, the results were published. He had passed out top of his list.[28]

On the whole it was a result which invited self-satisfaction. He had overcome the last obstacle with comparative ease, and the final outcome must have pleased him and left him brimming with confidence at what the future held. The doors of the Foreign Office were now unlocked. The path to a diplomatic career lay open. 'Education was now over, and again the total sum seemed small; but with what was to hand a start must be made toward the range of *la haute politique*.'[29]

NOTES

1. Much of the information concerning the early history of the family derives from a privately printed history (1910) which was kindly made available to the author by Lady Vansittart.
2. *Dictionary of National Biography*, 144.

---

* He had to prepare papers in the following subjects: arithmetic, handwriting, orthography, English composition, *précis*, French, German, general intelligence, geography, and the history of Europe. In addition there would be two other language papers. Van chose Latin and Spanish.

3. Lord Vansittart, *The Mist Procession* (London, 1958), 19.
4. These remarks about the early history of the Vansittarts are based on interviews with Guy Vansittart, and Sibell and Marjorie Vansittart.
5. *M.P.*, 15.
6. *Ibid.*, 16.
7. *Ibid.*, 21.
8. *Ibid.*, 22.
9. Earl of Halifax, *Fullness of Days* (London, 1957), 48. Halifax was a direct contemporary of Van's. He was born in 1881 and joined Eton the same year as Van.
10. See *Eton Calenders* and *Eton College Chronicle* for this period.
11. The selection included Kipling's, *The Old Issue, The White Man's Burden*, and *The English Flag / The Flag of England*; Tennyson's, *Hands all Round*; and Rodgers' *To the Race*.
12. See *Eton College Chronicle*, 23 February 1899.
13. *Ibid.*, 9 June 1899, 23 February and 11 June 1900.
14. H. Nicolson, *Some People* (London, 1939), 119. This book contains a charming account of life under Jeanne de Hénault. However, the chronology in the above account is wrong, though the sentiments are laudable. The reference is obviously to Van's play *Les Parias*, first performed at the Théâtre Molière in Paris in 1905. Van was then twenty-four and a lowly third secretary at the Paris embassy. Even so, it was no mean achievement and rightly attained legendary status in Foreign Office folklore.
15. *P.D.*, Lords v. 140, 36–42, 12 March 1946.
16. *M.P.*, 25.
17. *Ibid.*, 29. See also *Black Record* (London, 1941), 35, 42.
18. These comments are based upon an interview with Sir Arthur Willert, 18 October 1972.
19. *M.P.*, 30.
20. See R. T. Nightingale, *The Personnel of the British Foreign Office and Diplomatic Service, 1851–1929* (Fabian Tract No. 232, London, 1930), 8; also Z. Steiner, *The Foreign Office and Foreign Policy, 1898–1914* (Cambridge University Press, 1969), 20.
21. It was assumed that applicants for the diplomatic service would have a private income of four hundred pounds. But this was no hard and fast rule, and by this time a certain degree of flexibility had crept in. See Steiner, *op. cit.*, 174.
22. Steiner, *op. cit.*, 20. For a detailed statistical analysis of the social structure and educational background of the foreign and diplomatic services, an analysis which clearly illustrates the class bias of these professions, see Nightingale, *op. cit.*
23. Quoted by Steiner, *op. cit.*, 17 from Cmd. 7748, *Report of Royal Commission on the Civil Service* (London, 1914).
24. This passage is based on a private communication.
25. Vansittart, *Black Record* (London, 1941) 43.
26. Sir G. Franckenstein, *Facts and Features of My Life* (London, 1939), 16.
27. *M.P.*, 34.
28. For the results, see P.R.O. Civil Service Commission, 10/2189.
29. *Ibid.*, 42.

CHAPTER II

The Young Diplomat

It has been noted that 'All the clichés about the Foreign Office staff were true; it was indeed the stronghold of the aristocracy and everything was done to preserve its class character and clannish structure.'[1] This image stemmed in large measure from the methods of recruitment into the service. Only the wealthy, the highly-placed, and the correctly educated were considered eligible for nomination. Those without the obvious social graces hesitated to apply for fear that, if accepted, they would find themselves out of their element.

Of the two services the diplomatic was the more socially exclusive. The glamour and romance ascribed to service abroad in an atmosphere still dominated by courtiers and an aristocratic society made this inevitable. But equally, and possibly of more importance, because an ample private income was necessary to sustain the glamour and the romance. Young attachés received no salary at all for the first two years of their service. Thereafter, the financial rewards were meagre until they had reached the summit of their profession. Even then ambassadors had a hard time making ends meet on their salary alone.[2]

Interchange between the two services was rare. Foreign Office officials were reluctant to take up posts abroad because of the extra heavy expenses involved. This was particularly true at the lower end of the scale. Only at the highest level was there some tradition of transfer. This sharp distinction between the diplomats and the officials came under increasing criticism, and there was a steady movement towards the idea of amalgamation. It met with entrenched opposition, almost entirely fuelled by the veterans of the Foreign Office who tended to regard the diplomatists as dilettantes and social butterflies. Quite naturally a degree of competition, if not latent hostility, developed between the two services which continued until 1919 when a formal amalgamation took place.[3]

Some improvements were achieved during the years immediately preceding the First World War. Lord Hardinge,* after becoming Permanent Under-Secretary in 1906 and possibly influenced by his own example, encouraged more interchange between the two services at the lower level. When they did take place, exchanges were almost always set in motion on the personal initiative of the clerk or diplomat concerned. Even then questions of rank and allowance intruded, and the number of exchanges permitted in any single year was severely restricted. Deciding which service to enter was, therefore, a matter of considerable importance. Once having made a decision it was extremely difficult, and often impossible, to reverse it.

Van opted for the diplomatic service. Paris or Vienna or St Petersburg, he reasoned, offered infinite variety when compared with the predictability of London. But first, all newly appointed attachés had to spend a few months in one of the Foreign Office departments 'to learn the technique of bottle-washing'.[4]

The old Foreign Office grandees developed an amiable eccentricity which must have helped to compensate for the tedium of office routine. It was all faintly reminiscent of public school pranks. One can picture Sir Francis Bertie,† an eminent diplomat, showing his juniors 'how high he could kick or how to cut candles in two with a sword'. Or the spectacle of otherwise staid Foreign Office clerks playing stump-cricket or football, whichever was in season, in the corridors of the Office. Or even the following terrifying exercise in one-upmanship:

> ... 'Lamps' Sanderson had remonstrated with him (Eyre Crowe) one day for wearing a bowler during the Season, when of course top hats were the rule or at any rate the fashion. 'You say I am not to wear a bowler', Crowe replied. 'Very well, your instructions shall be carried out'; and for the rest of the summer he came to the Office in a straw hat.[5]

When Van joined the Foreign Office the presiding Secretary of State was the fifth Marquess of Lansdowne. Lansdowne failed to

* Charles Hardinge (1858–1944): entered diplomatic service, 1880; Ambassador at St Petersburg, 1904–6; at Paris, 1920–22; Permanent Under Secretary at the Foreign Office 1906–10, 1916–20; Viceroy of India, 1910–16. Cr. Baron Hardinge of Penshurst, 1910.

† Francis Leveson Bertie (1844–1919): entered Foreign Office in 1863; Ambassador to Rome, 1903–4; to Paris, 1905–18. Kn. 1902. Cr. Viscount, 1918.

impress Van, at least when compared with the legendary Salisbury. But he took office at a critical time in his country's fortunes; and by the time he left the Foreign Office in 1906 there had been set in motion developments that were in many ways indispensable for an understanding of Van's career.[6]

In January 1902, the Anglo-Japanese alliance was signed; an alliance designed against Russian encroachment in the Far East and the possibility of a Russo-Japanese deal in the area at Great Britain's expense. It was a striking indication of Britain's need to safeguard her imperial commitments by arranging some sort of bargain with her potential rivals. The Anglo-French *entente* of April 1904 followed a similar pattern, as did the *entente* with Russia in August 1907. On the face of it these were mere colonial agreements; and in the eyes of many British statesmen and officials had little if any relevance to the European balance of power. But this was a misleading evaluation, for often the spirit of an agreement assumes a greater significance than its clauses. It generates a momentum of its own, pushing its partners into ever closer cooperation and mutual commitment. Certainly this was true of the Anglo-French *entente*, the act for which Lansdowne is best remembered. The preservation of the *entente* became an inviolable principle in Van's foreign policy schemes. It gained added strength by the growing feeling inside the Foreign Office, shared by Van among others, that in the face of permanent German enmity the preservation and strengthening of the *entente* had become vital to Great Britain's own security.

The new course was also a manifestation of internal developments. In the autumn of 1900 Lord Salisbury, declining rapidly and perceptibly in his physical and mental state, released the Foreign Office from the firm grip in which he had clasped it for so many years. Salisbury displayed a healthy scepticism about the advice of experts and the accumulated wisdom of bureaucrats. His officials were required to carry out his instructions swiftly and competently, but no more. Lansdowne, and his successor Grey, lacked the authority and prestige of Salisbury. Both were more susceptible to pressure from their private secretaries and other highly placed officials. In the Foreign Office a group of powerful functionaries holding vigorous convictions would henceforth voice their opinions with increasing regularity and with a marked degree of success. In particular, the anti-German element began to make its views felt,[7] and in the long run prevail.

Although these developments were already advanced, it would be wrong to assume that these men were somehow omnipotent, or that their views had conquered to the exclusion of all others. They represented well defined attitudes which were ultimately to be of tremendous importance. But quite obviously much of their impact in these early days was obscured by the weight of Foreign Office tradition. Nevertheless, this was the kind of transient Foreign Office world in which Van found himself in 1903. And the trends here enunciated: the basic anti-German bias; the changes in the structural and administrative running of the office; and the enhanced influence of the permanent officials, including that of the private secretary, were all to have an enormous bearing on Van's future career.

He entered the Foreign Office in March 1903. The pace of work was leisurely. Juniors began their day at noon:

> We docketed the newly arrived letters ... we ciphered and deciphered telegrams; ... we 'put by' in their proper files the papers which had been acted on; we made up, that is, packed and fastened up, the bags for our missions abroad. The only original work which I can remember to have done was a small contribution to the annual departmental memorandum.[8]

Van's initial impressions of his new tasks were slightly more picturesque, yet in essence were substantially the same.[9] Protesting against this lack of urgency, he attempted to introduce radical measures of reform. Finding a typewriter he began to finger it, only to be warned off by a senior clerk explaining, 'Don't you know we're in a hurry.'[10] It was all rather disillusioning and mundane. The chief consolation was that the mornings were free and left plenty of time for sporting activities.

The overall impression of life on the lower rungs of the Foreign Office is one of excruciating dullness and boredom. It is not surprising to learn therefore that Van expended more energy and thought, if not time, on social activities than on deciphering telegrams. Tennis took up much of his time, as did the added attractions to be found in the world of the theatre.

London suited him well. He lodged in the Temple in rooms overlooking the Thames, and seemed to have few cares to cloud his existence. But there was a certain nagging frustration in his day-to-day routine. It was too removed from the highways of diplomacy as he had envisaged them. He had not joined the diplomatic service simply to give himself social airs. He was more determined than ever to achieve a foreign posting.

Then good fortune intruded. A secretary at the Paris embassy was about to get married and sought a cheaper post at home. Sir

Sir Robert Vansittart's mother.

Sir Robert Vansittart's father.

Guy, Sir Robert Vansittart's brother.

Eric Barrington, Lansdowne's Private Secretary, without whose approval no such transfer could be effected, offered Van the vacancy. An exchange was arranged, and on 26 October 1903 he joined the staff of the Paris embassy. For the next eight years he served abroad and would not reside permanently in London again until ill-health prompted his return in 1911.

The Paris embassy lies between the fashionable rue du Faubourg Saint Honoré and the Avenue Gabriel. His first ambassador was Sir Edmund John Monson.* Although Van did not find Monson's shadowy personality attractive, the policy of a *rapprochement* with France was very much to his liking. He was already associated with that group within the Foreign Office which saw clearly the need to provide a counter balance to Germany's growing continental dominance. His own Francophilia had prevailed against deeply ingrained family prejudice. When he was about to go to Paris for the first time, a prim great-aunt of his threatened to cut him out of her will, and did so on the grounds that 'he would return home with no morals and a Latin mind'.[11] His aunt was concerned with his morals; others shied from contamination with a European political *malaise*. There is a sad continuity in Van's battles on this score. Many years of bitter experience did nothing to eradicate the hallucination of sophisticated Frenchmen dragging reluctant and innocent Englishmen into the European furnace.

The *entente* did not go far enough for Van who clearly would have preferred a more definite commitment.[12] Nevertheless he rejoiced in its signing. It was the great political event of his period in Paris. It polarized the European diplomatic scene. Anglo-French relations took a new course and were to be 'a *leitmotif* in Europe for the next thirty-six years',[13] despite much pressure to the contrary. Van could only have speculated on these negotiations from the outside. Otherwise he was concerned with the minutiae of embassy life which fell to the lot of an unpaid attaché. He was soon made to feel his place in the embassy hierarchy. A senior diplomat reviewed in public the individual merits of the staff:

> He began with some kindly words about the Ambassador and the counsellors, and a few more for himself; and so he descended the

* Sir Edmund John Monson (1834–1909); entered foreign service, 1856; Ambassador at Vienna, 1893; Paris, 1896–1904; tactfully settled disputes with French arising out of the *entente*. It is a curious fact that Monson was considered as a potential Foreign Secretary in the Liberal government of 1905. See J. Watson, *A Life of Sir Henry Campbell Bannerman* (London, 1973), 438.

B

ladder of eulogy, until at last the eyeglass rested on the least of God's creatures. He said, 'we do not know much about the new boy, but with that solitary exception, we can say there is not a fool among us'.[14]

The daily routine in an embassy was, if anything, even more soporific than in the Foreign Office. Work was still largely of a secretarial nature, and could be managed more than adequately without specialized training. Van soon found others more willing than himself to indulge in the pleasures of typing or filing telegrams. None of this appealed to him. The monotonous grind of his official duties must have profoundly disillusioned him and raised serious doubts as to whether he had chosen the correct profession. Advancement, if and when it came, would be the reward for many long and painful years of boring, routine drudgery. Many failed to stay the course. Was it worth the effort? Was there an alternative? Contemporaries of his in the theatrical world 'soon surged to the front in a quicker profession than mine'.[15] There remains the distinct impression that he felt stifled, both physically and mentally, by the inertia of the diplomatic machine. His literary dreams remained intact, even if he felt inhibited by present commitments from pursuing them to the exclusion of all else. Still, the period until the outbreak of the First World War would be the most creative one – from a literary point of view at least – in Van's career. He had much spare time on his hands.

Intellectual pursuits aside, he also developed a penchant for horse-racing, and, following the family tradition, was the first Englishman since Fashoda to be elected a member of the Jockey Club.[16] He became quite addicted to the pleasures of the turf. Financial embarrassment soon followed, and 'the problem of living twenty-four hours a day for the rest of the year became acute'.[17] Gambling in most of its forms took a firm hold upon him, and he neglected few opportunities of pursuing the excitement of the gaming table or the race-track. But one must not exaggerate.

He neither made nor lost vast sums of money. Lady Vansittart recalled that when Van gambled at Monte Carlo 'he would draw only twenty pounds of chips and then retire when he had lost them'; and moreover 'his hands would tremble as he placed his chips'.[18] But quite obviously the concept of a definite commitment coupled with inherent uncertainty, which is fundamental to most forms of gambling, pandered to a basic need in his character. Diplomacy often follows a similar course. Certainly in Van's case the element of positive commitment, often overcommitment, to a particular line was ever present. At times it blinded him to the more immediate realities of the moment. A gift for perceiving the correct line of action to be taken can already be detected; yet it was a gift flawed with a perverse inflexibility of approach which brought in its wake unforeseen and disastrous consequences for himself. All this however lay in the future.

Meanwhile, Sir Francis Bertie had arrived in Paris to assume his duties as the new Ambassador. Van was delighted with his new chief. Where Monson was cautious, Bertie sparkled. In Van's eyes, he was blessed with qualities which were indispensable for any diplomat: aristocratic, eccentric, fearlessly outspoken, intensely patriotic, passionately pro *entente*, violently anti-German. Bertie amassed considerable influence in Paris and never shrank from imposing his opinions upon his superiors in London or his colleagues in Paris.

> Once or twice a week he would tug up his white moustache, cock his high hat – immensely high with a narrow ribbon at the base – and strut into the Quai d'Orsay, where he would speak his mind to the transient Minister in a fashion no longer heard. He made one feel that the finest thing in the world was to be His Britannic Majesty's Ambassador in Paris. His influence there was soon established and he never lost his hold on London.

He was not an easy chief to work for:

> We called him the Bull because the only way to handle him was to wear him down early by junior *picador* and *banderillero* before the *matador*, or Counsellor, finished him with the day's signatures. We tamed him too by telephone ... We obeyed when he was visibly purple and his words heard far into the Faubourg.[19]

Despite Van's unconcealed admiration, Bertie possessed a puritanical streak which clashed with Van's continuous excursions into the bohemian *demi-monde* of Paris. Relations did not mellow as a result of Van's first incursion into the commercial theatre. He had decided to write a play in French in the hope that it would stave off an impending financial crisis. In order to avert Bertie's eyes from this venture, Van adopted a pseudonym, at once simple and obvious: Vancouver. *Les Parias* was a short one-act play. Originally intended as a satire on current trends in popular melodrama, it was eventually played straight by the theatre's management. *Les Parias* opened at the Théâtre Molière on 1 November 1905 and ran until

14 December, despite the critics, a not inconsiderable feat for a young Englishman aged twenty-four.*

Despite these theatricals, and Bertie's disapproval, *Les Parias* proved to be of some importance in Van's career. As he modestly put it: 'so reputation began'.[20] And so it was. Here was a young man, obviously endowed with great gifts, enviably independent, clearly destined for greater things. Legends once formed are difficult to disperse. Harold Nicolson† perpetuated it.[21] And it was generally agreed, at least at the junior level of the service, that Van was marked as a coming man.[22]

In March 1906 Van was appointed temporary Extra-Private Secretary to King Edward VII, and accompanied him to Biarritz to conduct his correspondence in French. It was his first introduction to royalty. His duties were light. His main occupation lay in completing the King's card parties. Stakes were high, or appeared so at the time; but Van quickly discovered that playing cards with the King 'was less hazardous than racing'.[23] His exertions did not go unnoticed. On 2 April he was appointed a member of the Fourth Class of the Royal Victorian Order, happy in the knowledge that his attainments were well above those required for members of the Fifth Class.

Immediately after his royal success the idea was mooted in the Foreign Office of his transfer from Paris to Buenos Aires. Bertie quashed the notion, claiming that the embassy could ill afford to lose him.[24] Van must have been considerably relieved. Latin America was a dull prospect when compared with Biarritz. He was still unsettled. He flitted between Paris and London and the pleasure spots of Western Europe. The theatre still beckoned, and he tried in vain to interest Herbert Tree‡ in the idea of producing a comedy in verse. Racing weekends at Moulton Paddocks, Sir Ernest Cassel's§ country

* See *Le Figaro*, 1 November 1905, and *Le Temps*, 2 November 1905. The reviews were on the whole luke-warm. A slight mystery remains concerning this episode. In the newspaper notices Van appears together with a certain M. Ch. Duflo as joint authors of the play. Who this gentleman was and what precise role he played in this episode remains a mystery. It might well have been a clever ruse by Van to throw the embassy bloodhounds off the scent.

† Harold George Nicolson (1886–1968): entered Foreign Office, 1909; served in Constantinople, Madrid, Teheran, Berlin; National Labour M.P., 1935–45; journalist, author, historian. Kn. 1953.

‡ Herbert Beerbohm Tree (1852–1917): actor–manager; appeared in over 80 productions; manager of Haymarket Theatre, 1887–97; opened Her Majesty's Theatre, 1897; half-brother to Max Beerbohm. Kn. 1912.

§ Ernest Joseph Cassel (1852–1921): financier and philanthropist with worldwide banking and railway interests. Kn. 1899.

place near Newmarket, tennis, cards, the theatre, all provided a steady diet which apparently satisfied his needs for excitement and relaxation. All this must have affected his health. Throughout 1906 his condition became the subject for some concern. 'Everyone says he looks so ill and ought to go away.'[25] Mallet* went on to recommend that Van should spend the winter in, of all places, St Moritz. Here, it was hoped, he would recover after having overdrawn so heavily 'on the banks of life'.[26]

By now it was abundantly clear that it was time for him to leave Paris. He had spent four years there. And although he showed great promise, his abilities had somehow become obscured by the glitter of his social life. None of this appealed to his conservative chief. Bertie was interested in the efficiency of his embassy, not in young diplomatic butterflies desperately pursuing 'happiness in every available form'.[27] His appreciation of Van's services was correct but hardly fulsome.[28] Bertie's message was clear. It was time for Van to become reconciled to a diplomatic career and to cease dissipating his energy and time in frivolous pursuits. Van had no option but to agree. But having decided he made one last flamboyant gesture. George Grahame,† then second secretary at the Paris embassy, enquired hopefully of his chief whether he had 'seen Vansittart who took a *short cut* from St Moritz by going round by Monte Carlo'.[29] His next posting, after Monte Carlo, was Teheran.

Van arrived in Teheran at the end of May 1907.[30] He was not altogether enamoured by the prospect of idling away his life in a hot and uncomfortable climate far removed from the benefits of Western civilization. Yet his first contact with the East had a profound effect upon him, as it did on so many of his contemporaries. The legendary romance of the Orient strongly influenced his literary work. One may look no further than his most celebrated literary achievement, *The Singing Caravan*, which reads as a kind of Persian Canterbury Tales.

His tour of duty in Persia also brought him face-to-face with the crude realities of the Russian question, yet another traumatic

---

* Louis Mallet (1864–1936): entered Foreign Office, 1888; private secretary to Grey, 1905; senior clerk, 1906; Assistant Under Secretary of State, 1907; Ambassador at Constantinople, 1913–14; participated in peace conference at Versailles, 1919; retired, 1920. Kn. 1912.
† George Dixon Grahame (1873–1940); entered diplomatic service, 1896; Ambassador to Belgium, 1920–28; minister plenipotentiary to Luxemburg, 1922–28; Ambassador to Spain, 1928–35. Kn. 1918.

experience. The Anglo-Russian *entente* was completed by the autumn of 1907 and Van was directly concerned with the closing stages of the negotiations. There was a strong vein of anti-Russian opinion within the Foreign Office. If not as vociferous as the anti-German faction, it was still deeply entrenched and it was buttressed by liberal opinion throughout the country. These were cogent reasons for approaching the forthcoming negotiations with the utmost caution and regarding their outcome with undisguised scepticism. Many high officials shared this view. Even for those officials who favoured the Russian connection, Nicolson* its architect, and Hardinge, the element of *faute de mieux* played a large part in their calculations. It was argued that a Russian agreement would give British policy greater flexibility of choice, would provide a solid continental check to Germany's ambitions, and possibly of greatest significance, would thwart a Russo-German combination.

If such was the feeling in London it was multiplied many times over by those officials who had to implement the *entente* on the ground. Agreements were relatively simple to sign in the chancelleries of Europe; they were infinitely more difficult to uphold outside of the conference hall. Sir Cecil Spring-Rice,† minister at Teheran, once remarked to Van that 'negotiating with the Russians is like boxing with a bad smell'.[31] These impressions were to remain. It is curious how these same considerations, almost identical in their reasoning, were to re-emerge during the latter years of the 1930's when once again Russia was needed as a check on German ambitions.

Van justified the agreement on these general grounds. The local aspect of the *entente*, that it in fact amounted to a partition of Persia, scarcely troubled him. This was diplomacy in the classic nineteenth-century mould. Colonial arrangements in Africa or Asia were fashioned to reduce tension among the great European powers, or to reinforce existing alliances between them. Van distinctly approved. Expediency and a correct order of priorities were decisive factors in international politics and could not always be balanced by absolute moral standards. Thus, in Van's own words, the *entente*

* Sir Arthur Nicolson (1849–1928): entered Foreign Office, 1870: Ambassador at Madrid, 1904–06; at St Petersburg, 1906–1910; Permanent Under Secretary at Foreign Office, 1910–16. Kn. 1888. Succeeded as 11th baronet, 1899. Cr. Baron Carnock, 1916.
† Sir Cecil Arthur Spring-Rice (1859–1918): entered Foreign Office, 1882; Minister to Persia, 1906–08; to Sweden, 1908–13; Ambassador to United States, 1912–18. Kn. 1906.

served its limited purpose by securing 'a covenant which kept us on terms with a gasping and grasping associate for ten years'.[32] When he was faced with the decisive crisis of his career, the Italo-Abyssinian conflict, he remained shackled to the same lessons he had first learned in Persia. The issues at stake were not dissimilar. But times had changed out of all proportion. Great powers were no longer able to juggle with territories in Africa or Asia with impunity. Public opinion was now a factor to be reckoned with, as Van discovered to his bitter cost. In this respect he remained very much a product of nineteenth century diplomatic practice.

A colleague of Van's recollected:

> Our own summer legation was at Gulhek under half an hour from Teheran but quite different in climate ... The grounds include a large area with houses and gardens for the staff but there are swimming pools and the whole property is well wooded and irrigated by running water ... Life at Gulhek was almost a dream of delight. In summer one could sleep on a balcony and I shall always remember the early mornings with the first sunlight striking the hills and soon afterwards the tree trunks, till the whole garden was bathed in light. A little work till about midday, a plunge into the very cold waters of the bathing pool, a glass of sherry, luncheon, an obligatory siesta in the burning heat of the summer afternoon, tea, tennis, dinner – what could be a more delightful programme ... picnics in the mountains and from time to time an expedition further afield ...[33]

The legation staff, from minister to physician, numbered seven in all. Van was the senior third secretary in the hierarchy; his immediate junior was Percy Loraine, a future ambassador to Italy and Turkey. Tying up the loose ends of the Russian *entente* involved an enormous amount of detailed, administrative work, particularly at the local level. Much of this burden fell on Van's shoulders as acting head of chancery. For the first time in his career he was obliged to accept responsibilities, not evade them. Curiously enough he became rather jealous of his new prerogatives. On the faintest suggestion that another diplomat be sent out from London to lighten the tasks of the legation, Van reacted swiftly:

> By the way I believe our cry for help has been delivered to you. I hardly suppose you'll be able to do anything for us. But may I take it on me to express my own hope that if anyone *was* sent out, he wouldn't be senior to me. It would be rather disappointing to

be superseded after 'having borne the best & burden of the day' during some mauvais quarts d'heure that have only been too frequent for me.[34]

He came through this test remarkably well. The result was plainly satisfying to his superiors, and not least of all to himself.

At the end of the summer of 1908 he succumbed to a serious bout of dysentery. Unable to recuperate fully in the primitive sanitary conditions of Teheran, he was obliged to return to London in the autumn to regain his health. He did so reluctantly for by now he had 'taken to the life, to my friends, even to work'.[35] Unlike Paris, the legation expressed high appreciation of Van's services. Work in the legation over the past few months had been exceptionally heavy,

> but in spite of occasional ill-health he has carried out his duties with unflagging zeal and cheerfulness while his marked ability and exceptional talent for mastering detail without losing sight of the main issue has been of the greatest value in the many complicated questions which as head of the Chancery he has been called on to deal.[36]

He received his just rewards. In the new year, on the eve of his posting to the British Agency in Cairo, he was appointed a second secretary in the diplomatic service at an annual starting salary of three hundred pounds.

Van arrived in Cairo on 12 January 1909,[37] almost two years after Sir Eldon Gorst* had replaced Lord Cromer as British Agent. Gorst, a lonely and sensitive figure who never quite realized his great potential, had attempted, without much success, to replace Cromer's paternalistic régime by one of a more liberal outlook. By doing so he aroused notably the hostility of the local nationalists who hankered after greater independence than Gorst was prepared to concede, but also the anger of the more reactionary British elements in Egypt who saw in Gorst's policies nothing less than total surrender to the extremists. By the time Van arrived, Gorst had succumbed to those pressures, and his policies while innovative were cautious rather than spectacular. Nevertheless, Van came to Egypt with a high regard for Gorst. Cairo's cosmopolitan attractions, while superficially enticing, left little lasting impression on him. Neither did the

---

* (John) Eldon Gorst (1861–1911): entered Foreign Office, 1883, and served in Egypt until 1904; Assistant Under Secretary of State at Foreign Office, 1904–1907; Consul-General in Egypt, 1907–11. Kn. 1902.

Egyptians. The Wafd (the Egyptian nationalist party) 'was a pyramid of corruption' while 'the Egyptians were spoiled by nobody but each other'. He also found little in common with the large British community resident in Egypt: 'the British in Egyptian service . . . the business community . . . and the Army of Occupation',[38] as he categorized them. Only the winter season brought relief when a rich variety of visitors from the Crown Prince of Germany to Theodore Roosevelt would brighten the local scene.[39]

Whatever was lacking in outside society, the British Agency and Consulate-General offered ample compensation. Harry Boyle, the Oriental Secretary, fascinated him and during his early months in Cairo acted as his mentor. Boyle, owing to his eccentric ways, soon fell into Gorst's disfavour and was transferred to Berlin. In his place Gorst appointed Ronald Storrs,* an accomplished and erudite official. Storrs proved to be an amiable companion; and together they concocted schemes, such as a carefully rehearsed brawl at an Agency garden party, in order to startle an otherwise unflappable community.[40]

The skill and experience of his colleagues† made it comparatively painless for him 'to settle down to the easy hours of the Chancery'.[41] Van expressed nothing but admiration for his new chief. Indeed, there is a definite touch of hero worship in the songs of praise he sings about Gorst.[42] It is clear that he closely identified himself with Gorst's liberal policies. Gorst reciprocated; not so much officially as socially. They played a great deal of tennis together, and Van frequently dined with the Gorsts and stayed on afterwards to make up a bridge four.[43] One of these occasions gave birth to another epic tale:

> Sir Ernest Cassel was on a visit to Egypt and, in due course, dined at the Agency. After dinner a bridge four was arranged, consisting of Gorst, Cassel, Vansittart and another. . . Vansittart, in early and even in later life, had, like other distinguished members of his Service, exhibited neither aversion nor lack of skill in games of hazard. He cut in with Sir Ernest and, the points having been

---

* Ronald Storrs (1881–1955): Egyptian government service, 1904–9; Oriental Secretary at British Agency, Cairo, 1909–14; military governor, Jerusalem, 1917–20; civil governor, 1920–26; Governor of Cyprus, 1926–33; of Northern Rhodesia, 1932–34. Kn. 1929

† In the two and a half years Van worked in Egypt his companions were: Ronald Graham, counsellor; Milne Cheetham, first secretary; Robert H. Clive, second secretary; and Raymond Parr, attaché. Van shared a room with Parr about whom he remained silent.

decided, presumed the addition of five pounds on the rubber. His opponents accepted; his millionaire partner, whether on principle or as a measure of deprecation, declined, when the Second Secretary, to the general stupefaction, announced that he would 'carry' him and, justifying his courteous insolence, duly won his double reward throughout the evening.[44]

His two-and-a-half years in Egypt passed quickly. Much of his time was spent in local travel and home leave.[45] Once at home, he was soon off socializing. He swiftly gained the reputation of a young man 'who could make a fourth at bridge, and knew the difference between claret and burgundy'.[46] Yet the same personal problems remained:

> I was still vainly trying to do something of everything, without itch to excel in anything, to touch life in all its rounded aspects, my profession, books, sport, travel, whatever came in a full day . . . It occurred to me that man might be like my tennis, good but not good enough to survive the competition on which he insists. Techniques were passing into another world; the age of the amateur was over, and now another age died too.[47]

After his successes in Teheran, he had halted in mid-stream. Even worse he appeared to have slipped back to his Parisian habits. Cairo, for him at least, constituted a slippery rung up the official ladder.

Whatever his good intentions to knuckle under to diplomatic routine it seemed as though life in embassies abroad offered little prospect for swift advancement in his profession. The temptations to climb aboard the social merry-go-round were too great to be resisted. But the obvious drawback was that Cairo, Teheran, or even Paris were too far removed from the centres of power. He was now thirty years of age. It was only right that ambition should begin to rear its head. He decided it was time for him to return to the Foreign Office.[48]

During the spring of 1911 he again fell victim to a serious attack of dysentery. This, together with his Persian experience, convinced his superiors that he needed a long spell at home to enable him to recover his strength. He left Egypt together with Gorst who was by then stricken fatally with cancer, and who died a few months later at his home in Castle Combe, Wiltshire. Van went straight into a London nursing home. After a few weeks of correct treatment in a more amenable climate, he was fit again for work. On 1 August 1911 he returned to the Foreign Office as a Clerk in the Eastern Department. He never left it again, except on short official missions, until his retirement from the service in June 1941 as Chief Diplomatic Adviser to the government.

NOTES

1. Steiner, *op. cit.*, 16.
2. For salary scales see Steiner, *op. cit.*, 175.
3. See C. Larner, 'The Amalgamation of the Diplomatic Service with the Foreign Office', *Historical Journal* (1972).
4. *M.P.*, 43.
5. These quotations are taken from: J. Tilley and S. Gasalee, *The Foreign Office* (London, 1933), 130–45; Sir R. H. B. Lockhart, *Memoirs of a British Agent* (London, 1932), 44–5; Sir O. O'Malley, *The Phantom Caravan* (London, 1954), 47, and quoted by Steiner, *op. cit.*, 12.
6. These developments can be followed in great detail in: Lilian M. Penson, 'The New Course in British Foreign Policy, 1898–1902', *Transactions of the Royal Historical Society*, 4th Series, XXV (1943); Penson, *Foreign Affairs under the Third Marquess of Salisbury* (London, 1962); J. A. S. Grenville, *Lord Salisbury and Foreign Policy* (London, 1964); G. W. Monger, *The End of Isolation* (London, 1963).
7. For a detailed discussion of these developments, see Steiner, *op. cit.*, 73–7.
8. J. Tilley and S. Gasalee, *op. cit.*, 127–8; quoted by Steiner, *op. cit.*, 14.
9. *M.P.*, 43.
10. *Ibid.*, 43.
11. Vansittart, *Lessons of my Life* (London, 1944), 21.
12. *M.P.*, 50.
13. *Ibid.*, 49.
14. *P.D.*, Lords, v. 191, c. 919–24, 10 March 1955.
15. *M.P.*, 47.
16. *Ibid.*, 49.
17. *Ibid.*, 55.
18. Interview with Lady Vansittart, 31 October 1972.
19. *M.P.*, 54.
20. *M.P.*, 55.
21. H. Nicolson, *Some People* (London, 1939), 119; R. Storrs, *Orientations* (London, 1939), 68, improved upon this story by insisting that Van wrote and produced two plays.
22. A private communication.
23. *M.P.*, 59.
24. F.O. 800/184. See Bertie to Mallet, 3 May 1906; Mallet to Bertie, 5 May 1906.
25. F.O. 800/164. Mallet to Bertie, 3 October 1906.
26. *M.P.*, 64.
27. *Ibid.*
28. F.O. 800/254. See Bertie to Grey, 26 April 1907.
29. F.O. 800/185. Grahame to Bertie, 1 March 1907.
30. F.O. 800/309. See Spring-Rice to Grey, 24 May 1907.
31. *P.D.* Lords v. 167, c. 31, 2 May 1950.

32. *M.P.*, 73.
33. H. Knatchbull-Hugesson, *Diplomat in Peace and War* (London, 1949), 75.
34. F.O. 800/70. Van to Tyrrell, 14 February 1908.
35. *M.P.*, 78.
36. F.O. 371/505. Charles Marling (counsellor at the legation) to Grey, 16 June 1908.
37. F.O. 371/659. Ronald Graham to Grey, 12 January 1909.
38. *M.P.*, 83, 87.
39. *Ibid.*, 83–84.
40. R. Storrs, *op. cit.*, 68–9, 90.
41. *M.P.*, 84.
42. *M.P.*, 85–6.
43. The Eldon Gorst Diaries for 1909–11. I am grateful to Mrs Kay Thomas of Upper Combe House, Castle Combe, for allowing me access to her father's diaries.
44. Storrs, *op. cit.*, 68.
45. See the Gorst Diaries; *M.P.*, 82–97; and F.O. 371/891, 1112.
46. See N. Nicolson, *Portrait of a Marriage* (London, 1973), 84.
47. *M.P.*, 93.
48. *M.P.*, 93.

CHAPTER III

Breaking New Ground

DURING THE INTERVAL between Van's departure in 1903 and his return in the autumn of 1911, the Foreign Office had altered considerably. A number of administrative and technical reforms, amounting in one commentator's view to a 'revolution',[1] had been pushed through which substantially enhanced the status of the junior members of the Office and their chances of more rapid promotion. The origins of this 'revolution' may be traced back to the return to Downing Street from St Petersburg of Charles 'Capability' Hardinge in January 1903 as the most junior of the four under-secretaries. Hardinge was a convinced reformer and he worked in close association with Bertie, another assertive personality, to ensure that his views were finally accepted. They were not only interested in effecting technical or administrative changes, important though these were. Bertie and Hardinge were also absorbed by the shifting balance of power in Europe and Asia, a balance which appeared to them to be moving against British interests. Monopolizing their fears was the growing German menace. As a result, they were concerned to actively promote changes, both in terms of policy, and Foreign Office and diplomatic appointments, in order to redress the balance in Britain's favour. Over the coming years their efforts were crowned with much success and their view became the prevailing orthodoxy under Sir Edward Grey.[2]

Hardinge's reforms, supported enthusiastically by Crowe,* were based on a new system of registering despatches. This may appear,

---

* Eyre Alexander Barby Wichart Crowe (1864–1925): entered Foreign Office, 1885; vigilant critic of German foreign policy; author of 'Memorandum on present state of British relations with France and Germany', 1907; Permanent Under Secretary at Foreign Office, 1920–25. Kn. 1911.

at first sight, to be a matter of little importance, or at best a technical question designed to beguile the experts. In fact, it profoundly changed the old Foreign Office and the functions of the first division clerks. Despatches were now first checked and noted by the juniors who could, if the occasion demanded, minute a possible course of action. The despatches were then examined by the responsible senior clerk. If the matter could be dealt with at this level, it was; if not, it was forwarded to the Assistant Under Secretary who dealt with it taking into account his juniors' recommendations. In this manner the process repeated itself until the issue under discussion reached either the Permanent Under Secretary's desk or that of the Foreign Secretary. Thus the minutes filtered upwards, enabling the senior officials to gauge both the aptitude and the diligence of their juniors.

Such a system was not without its pitfalls. Some argued that it could, under special circumstances, place excessive power in the hands of the officials. Combinations involving weak, inexperienced, or heavily-burdened ministers, with strong-willed, assertive and knowledgeable officials, held out dangers of a kind not experienced under the old regime. And as we shall see, such combinations were not as rare as might have been expected. For young, ambitious men like Van, anxious to ascend the official ladder as smoothly and as expeditiously as possible, the Hardinge–Crowe reforms were welcomed with enthusiasm.[3]

Van was assigned to work in the Eastern Department.* He still held the rank of a second secretary in the diplomatic service, and was not transferred fully to the Foreign Office establishment until 30 September 1913 when he was appointed a junior clerk. He was determined to make a success of his new post. Having spent eight years abroad he was anxious to remain in London. His younger brothers were growing up. Arnold, the elder of the two, had just come down from Oxford, while Guy, the youngest, was still at Eton. It was during this period that Captain Vansittart began to dabble in earnest on the Stock Exchange. The inevitable happened. He lost a great deal of money. The family never fully recovered from this setback. From then on, their financial position, though never desperate, was never healthy. For Van, his father's miscalculations had serious consequences. As his father's heir he saw his inheritance disappear overnight and with it any chance of financial independence in the future. His parental allowance had also vanished, and he was now forced to rely solely on his salary and what he could earn on the side

* The department was responsible for Greece, the Balkan States, Turkey, Russia, Persia, Afghanistan, Central Asia, Egypt.

through writing. He was by no means impoverished, however. As a second secretary in the diplomatic service Van's total salary would have amounted to about five hundred pounds. In Edwardian London this was more than enough to provide for a bachelor's needs provided he spent his money circumspectly.

Financial worries proved a weak barrier to his social activities. Continental holidays and tennis tournaments still occupied much of his time. These years were also his most prolific from a literary point of view. He published a great deal of poetry and two novels, *The Gates* (1910), a faintly autobiographical work, and *John Stuart* (1912), which is based loosely upon the history of his ancestor, Peter. In 1913 he staged two plays, *The Cap and Bells* and *People Like Ourselves*. Both were drawing-room comedies with political undertones, typical of their day, and both received mixed reviews from the critics.[4] His literary and theatrical work brought him into contact with many important political personalities, of whom Asquith, F. E. Smith and Churchill were to remain life-long friends.

Van's first interventions in foreign affairs concerned the Italian annexation of Tripoli in 1911, and further Russian designs in Persia. Van had no hand in formulating policy on these questions, but his occasional minutes convey to us some indication of the way his mind was working. On both scores, though hostile to Italian and Russian claims, Van was prepared to acquiesce in them.[5] In the general scheme of affairs both incidents appear as minor disturbances. His reaction points to the cardinal principle in his ideas on foreign affairs. Everything stemmed from German hostility. Given this absolute constant, other variables fell into place. Thus Italy could seize Tripoli and Russia manipulate the situation in Persia because both powers were essential to counter-balance German continental dominance. It was really a question of where to draw the line, or how far concessions in Africa and Asia would affect the European balance. For Van the answer to this question was clear. If agreements in these distant places weakened Germany, so much the better. In this context the fate of Tripoli or Persia, or perhaps at a later date Ethiopia, was only of marginal significance. They were to be sacrificial lambs for the European altar. Moral considerations were almost irrelevant. Only the European balance of power counted. Van was wedded to a purely continental outlook and he never wavered from this course.

'A chance for you, young man.'[6] These words greeted Van on his appointment as first British delegate to an international conference for the protection of the elephant and the rhinoceros which was to convene in London in May 1914. Wildlife conservation was not then the fashionable subject it has since become, and one can well sympathize with Van's frustration at having to concentrate on this inferior topic from which his 'attention soon wandered'.[7] However, by the close of the nineteenth century the need for international cooperation to protect wildlife had become increasingly urgent, not only because of the animals involved, but mainly because the subject gave rise to tension between the great powers. In Africa, for example, it was virtually impossible to check the illicit trade in valuable skins or ivory. Lack of uniformity of laws in the colonial territories, their vast areas and the enormous difficulty in patrolling them effectively, made smuggling a most profitable pastime. Poachers, in order to evade arrest and punishment, merely slipped across the most convenient frontier. In 1900 an international conference was signed 'for the preservation of vital animals, birds and fish in Africa'.* It was the forerunner for similar exercises in international cooperation.

Van's conference was designed to prevent the extermination of the elephant and the rhinoceros. But it was not simply a question of wildlife conservation. Both of these animals carried products of considerable value: ivory and rhinoceros horn. Some territories prohibited their export, others did not. It was not surprising, therefore, that a considerable amount of these valuables found their way through the ports of the 'free' territories to the outside world, to the enrichment of the customs' authorities of those countries. The British took the initiative. Their territories in East Africa were already subject to the proposals Van put before the conference which were intended to stop all trade in ivory and rhinoceros horn except under licence.†

The conference met at the Foreign Office from 19-22 May, 1914. Representatives of Belgium, Germany, Italy, Spain and Portugal attended. The business of the conference was carried out expeditiously. The British proposals, although finally modified in detail, were accepted in principle by all the delegates. Van's report singled

* The convention was signed by Britain, France, Germany, Italy, Spain, Portugal, and the Independent State of the Congo. It was never ratified.

† The precise terms were that a weight of 28-30 lb (13 kilos) should be agreed upon by all the powers as a legal weight, and that the killing of elephants whose tusks weigh less should be prohibited; and that it should be illegal to possess ivory or rhinoceros horn of whatever weight throughout Africa except under licence, or when confiscated and sold by a government. The principle objection came from the Belgians who insisted that 13 kilos was too high a standard and pressed to reduce it to 8. A compromise weight was reached on 10.

out the Germans for most criticism. He perceived in their attitude 'a far greater political importance than was represented by the conference'. Van was also highly suspicious of the chief German delegate, Richard von Kühlmann, counsellor at the German embassy. Kühlmann's rich wife often provided working luncheons or suppers for the delegates, but Van believed him to be hostile towards Britain, disloyal to his Ambassador, Prince Lichnowsky, and in short, 'equipped with strong appetites but no herculean principles'.[8] All in all he could claim that he had advanced his career. True, the conference was a very minor ripple upon the surface of international affairs. But the fact that he had negotiated it skilfully and with an obvious degree of success was a strong point in his favour.

On 14 February 1914, Van was promoted to Assistant Clerk. His new appointment brought with it a change in office and responsibilities. He moved to the Western Department; his new superintending Under Secretary was Sir Eyre Crowe. For the next twelve years, until Crowe's death in 1925, they were to work in close association with each other. The question must be asked whether or not Van saw himself as a latter-day Crowe, equally prescient but equally ignored. Van often made the comparison. 'The other premises of the faded masterpiece* were less ephemeral. . . reminding me of my memorandum thirty years later on the same topic.'[9] Others asked the same question, though not always in a tone flattering to Van. 'Vansittart is quite unbalanced about Germany; is he aping his predecessor of prewar days, Sir Eyre Crowe?'[10]

The two officials had much in common. Both were fluent linguists, knowledgeable and conversant in continental affairs. Both were painstakingly conscientious. Both flaunted a tendency to talk down to their ministerial chiefs whom they often considered as weak and ill-informed. Both detested, with a peculiar intensity, amateur diplomats, believing that diplomacy should be left strictly to the professionals. Above all, they were at one in their estimation of German intentions. Crowe's attitude never materially altered. He viewed

---

* 'The faded masterpiece' was Crowe's 'Memorandum on the present state of British relations with France and Germany', written in January 1907 and considered by many as a classic state paper. In it Crowe strongly defended the French entente and saw it as a buffer against Germany's aim to dominate Europe and eventually the world, and argued that unilateral concessions would only feed her appetite. The memo is published in Gooch and Temperley, iv, III, appendix A. It has been suggested (Steiner, *op. cit.*, n. 122) that 'Despite the historical importance of the memorandum, contemporaries did not view it as epoch-making.'

with growing apprehension the German obsession with *Weltpolitik* which, he was convinced, could never be attained except at the expense of British interests. Van's views on Germany were equally consistent and uncompromising.

Yet, to the contemporary observer, there were fundamental differences. Van acquired, and obviously relished, a social flamboyance which Crowe never attained or sought. His expensive tastes and his delight in playing the role of the grand seigneur left him open to accusations of dilettantism, and hence somewhat reduced his influence. Accusations of such a nature could never have been levelled against Crowe. His clinical professionalism and administrative ability were bywords in the office. The histrionic streak which pervaded much of Van's written work and which tainted him, unfairly, as a crude, anti-German racialist, was not evident in Crowe. These dissimilarities, in retrospect more of style than of substance, tended to obscure the common tenets of their outlook. Both men were in fact highly dedicated professionals, though almost diametrically opposite in their personal characteristics.

Although Van waxed enthusiastic over Crowe, the evidence suggests that his enthusiasm was not entirely reciprocated. Crowe, it may truly be said, rose to the top through the ranks. He curried no favours and received none, and was, on more than one occasion, passed over for promotion despite his obvious talents. He distrusted those whose careers prospered through a series of private secretaryships. Such men were, to Crowe, intriguers, bent on pushing 'private policies up backstairs'.[11] Van, unfortunately, was numbered amongst the 'backstairs' group, and when, in the early 1920's, he acted as Curzon's private secretary, he encountered an unexpectedly hostile Crowe.

Van had long suspected that the Balkan countries would, sooner or later, embroil the European powers in a great war. Even after the Balkan states had achieved their independence, the area remained dangerously unstable. 'Balkan statesmen are rarely able to see anything except the Balkans,'[12] he commented, expressing his fear that their short-sightedness and parochial ambitions would drag the European powers into war. The long expected crisis began on 28 June 1914 when Archduke Ferdinand, heir to the Austrian throne, and his wife, Sophie, were assassinated at Sarajevo. Although long determined to solve the Serbian question by force, Austria reacted tardily to this challenge. It was only on 23 July that she submitted an ultimatum to Serbia. This excessively long period of delay lulled the powers into a false sense of security. It also led some experienced officials – Nicolson and Crowe among them – to believe that Austria would act with restraint. Van held no such illusion. Almost alone among the permanent officials, he perceived the immediate danger. At the beginning of July he warned that Austria would follow 'a blindly anti-Serbian policy'.[13] After the Austrian attack on Belgrade on 28 July, Van, now at one with his superiors, believed war to be inevitable, and that Britain, in order to guarantee her status as a great power, had no option but to fight alongside her *entente* partners. Van's main fear, shared by Crowe and Nicolson, was that the anti-war faction in the cabinet would prevail. He despaired of the politicians; they hedged and wavered when they should have stood firm and resolute. Crowe warned Grey: 'The theory that Britain cannot engage in a big war means her abdication as an independent state.'[14] On 3 August Grey, claiming that the violation of Belgian sovereignty by Germany constituted a *casus belli*, carried the Commons in what Van described as 'a dreadfully apologetic effort'.[15] But it was enough. By 4 August Great Britain and Germany were at war.

The war was welcomed everywhere in an upsurge of national enthusiasm. Van's initial inclination was to join the British Expeditionary Force. As a civil servant engaged in work of national importance, his application was rejected. Both of his brothers enlisted, Arnold as a second lieutenant in the 11th Hussars, Guy in the Central Indian Horse. Early reports about the war filled him with horror. He had no doubt that the Germans were committing atrocities on a massive scale.[16] What could he do in the circumstances? Not a great deal. His war years were overshadowed by a growing sense of frustration. Young men of his generation and class were being butchered in a hideous war of attrition, while he was forcibly tied down to his desk in Whitehall composing endless memoranda. Van 'expected more useful employment'.[17] Instead he was appointed head of the Swedish section of the newly formed Contraband Department with Crowe as his chief.

The department was set up in the autumn of 1914 to deal with the complicated questions arising from blockade policy and trade with the neutral countries. Sweden held a special place in this scheme of affairs. Considered by Britain as 'the most intractable of the European neutrals',[18] her royalist government was avowedly pro-German and intensely anti-Russian. Sweden also exercised a dominant position over her Scandinavian neighbours. Norway, for example, though sympathetic towards Britain, feared the possibility of a Swedish reprisal for the secession of 1905, and hence was susceptible to pressure from her more powerful neighbour. Moreover, Sweden could, if she chose, choke off the flow of supplies in transit to Russia. This was a problem of crucial importance for the *entente* powers. Throughout the autumn and winter of 1914–15, the Russian armies had been savaged badly by the Germans. Their plight was desperate; a separate peace on the Eastern front appeared more than a remote possibility. It was clearly in the interests of the Western powers to ensure Russia's survival as a viable wartime partner.

The British had previously laid down the rule that contraband was liable to confiscation if there was evidence that its ultimate destination was an enemy consignee. This was the so-called doctrine of 'continuous voyage'. But in 1914, mainly in order to placate the Americans, the British set aside many of these restrictions. The result was an enormous increase in American trade with the Central powers by the simple method of using 'dummy' consignees based in neutral countries. By the early spring many important raw materials – tin, copper, lard, cotton, raw hides – were eluding, with official sanction, the Swedish export prohibitions, much to the material benefit of the Central powers and the intense annoyance of Britain.[19]

Was there any method of surmounting these difficulties? Van believed so. In a lengthy memorandum, he recommended that Swedish agents should be appointed to supervise the passage of goods considered by the British government as essential to the German war economy; that owners of goods in transit should be obliged to place deposits which would be forfeit should the goods be diverted from their original declared destination; and finally, that a checking system with the Russians should be set up to verify the authenticity of suspected 'dummy' consignees.[20] The situation was clearly in need of clarification. In June 1915 the government decided to send a mission to Stockholm to negotiate a new general agreement. Van was included as the Foreign Office representative.*

While preparing for his journey, a telegram arrived notifying him that Arnold had been seriously wounded at Ypres. Later that night his sister telephoned the Foreign Office to inform him that Arnold had died. The two brothers, though separated in age by eight years, were deeply attached to one another. Van acted the role of mentor and father confessor and perhaps saw in the younger Arnold a more carefree spirit which he himself envied. For Van this was a shattering blow, and he reacted with characteristic emotion.

* Other members of the delegation included: Mr Lancelot Hugh Smith, 'the ablest broker in London'; Mr Eric Hambro, a merchant banker; and Mr H. M. Cleminson, a lawyer.

I locked up my papers, lurched across Horse Guards Parade, plunged into the mutilated plane trees of the Mall, as far as possible from light or sound, and sobbed my heart out.[21]

He never fully recovered from the effects of Arnold's death. His sorrow, which was truly profound, provided a catalyst which polarized his previous anti-German convictions to an even greater extent. Personal bitterness was now inextricably interlocked with his political philosophy. This was an explosive mixture for any diplomat to contain. He later admitted that 'The personal element should not affect policy, but one cannot prevent experience from confirming conclusions already reached. Why ask for strength to reverse them?[22] For Arnold he wrote:

> I bow my head, O brother, brother, brother,
> But may not grudge you that were All to me.
> Should any *one* lament when this our Mother
> Mourns for so many sons on land and sea.
> God of the love that makes two lives as one
> Give strength to see that England's will be done.[23]

Meanwhile, Stockholm lay ahead. The primary concern of the mission, though not explicitly stated, was to ensure Swedish neutrality. The detailed negotiations proved abortive almost from the start. The Swedes were in a strong bargaining position. The continuous Russian defeats throughout 1915 gave them an immense leverage in the talks. From the outset, they took a high tone and would allow nothing to pass that appeared to question in the remotest degree their freedom of choice.* Eventually, both sides were prepared to admit failure. The stalemate was not as significant as might be imagined. It emerged that the Swedes were at least as dependent upon British exports, in particular coal, as the British were upon Swedish exports, or goodwill. Also, by the end of the year, the Eastern front had somewhat stabilized. Thus the British bargaining position improved. And with their main aim of continued Swedish neutrality achieved, Van and his mission returned to London with the thanks of Crowe and Grey ringing in their ears.[24]

As a reward for the lack of conspicuous failure of the Swedish mission, Van received promotion, of a sort. At the beginning of 1916 he was appointed secretary to the Prisoners-of-War Department under the

* The French ambassador defined the Swedish attitude as follows: 'Ils se grisent voluntiers d'odeur des bottes de Charles XII' (They like to intoxicate themselves with the smell of the jackboots of Charles XII). See Howard, *op. cit.*, 245.

direction of the Rt. Hon. Lord Newton,* 'a wordless wit who looked like a virginal satyr'.[25] The judgement was superficial, the inference unkind. Whatever his outward appearance, Newton deserved better of his junior. Almost certainly Van was more out of sympathy with his new job than with his new chief. Given the choice, he would have stayed in the Contraband Department which, in February 1916, evolved into the Ministry of Blockade offering greater chances of advancement. He felt as though the tumultuous affairs of the war were passing him by. 'Backwater Bob' was how he saw himself during this period.[26]

In fact his work was not as negligible as he imagined, as was reflected in the growth of his department which doubled in size in one year. His department was mainly concerned with improving the conditions under which prisoners-of-war and civilian internees were held, and arranging, if possible, mutual exchanges. On both these counts the department could claim considerable successes. In June 1917 a conference was held at the Hague to discuss these questions with the Germans. The agreement then reached substantially improved the lot of prisoners. Exchange schemes were to be speeded up and extended in scope; postal services were improved; breaches of camp discipline were to be more leniently treated; and the administration of camps made more efficient. As an immediate sign of goodwill, 16,000 prisoners were to be transferred to Holland for internment. The agreement was a popular one. The following December a similar accord was signed with the Turks at Berne.

Van's work in the department played upon his emotions and political judgement in a predictable manner. German methods of unrestricted submarine warfare had already earned his unconcealed disgust. Their treatment of Allied prisoners-of-war was, according to the reports reaching him, equally savage. Now, finally, he was face-to-face with even more conclusive proof of German barbarism. All doubt was banished from his mind; indeed, one might conclude that the spiritual torment raging in his mind was finally resolved.[27] Discussions were held in the department on how to react to German cruelties. Van's methods were not appreciated.

I advocated no reciprocal cruelty, but urged that German prisoners should receive no mitigation not enjoyed by the British. I

---

* Thomas Wodehouse Legh (1857–1942): Conservative M.P., 1886–99; Paymaster-General, 1915–16; Controller of Prisoners-of-War Department, 1916–19; wrote biographies of Lord Lyons and Lord Lansdowne; keen advocate of radical social reform. Succeeded his father as 2nd Baron Newton, 1899.

wished further to declare that we were listing the authors of all abuses in German camps, and would try them when we won.[28]

As the war progressed, and his experience deepened, his feelings grew even stronger.[29]

With the war drawing to its close, Van's attention began to be focused elswhere. His contribution to the war effort left him depressed and uncertain as to his future. It was quite understandable. He had been diverted to a Foreign Office backwater to write memoranda or to participate in meetings which, he felt, no one read or noticed, while his contemporaries, his friends, his family, had been decimated in the most ferocious war yet known to mankind. He returned to poetry. In 1918 he started work on *The Singing Caravan*, begun as a memorial to Arnold. There can be no doubt that he found more satisfaction in composing verse than in advising Lord Newton. He had again reached a crossroads.[30] Which way would he turn? There can be no categoric answer. Given the right opportunity, or inspiration, he might have realized his childhood dreams. Literature certainly held more appeal than politics. As it was, the inertia of habit triumphed over recurring youthful ambitions. He was thirty-seven years old, unfamiliar with any profession other than diplomacy. The Foreign Office, after fifteen years' service, was a tenacious taskmaster. Literature beckoned, but from afar.

> Then something happened: I was notified that I should attend the Peace Conference ... For a moment I felt a cockiness which I had not experienced since my small boyhood. . . I became briefly 'brilliant' . . . this conference was the finest and most promising thing in the world: It might be one of our last chances – they were frequent – but we would take it and right there would be a brave new world of sorts. So I ended *The Singing Caravan* on a cheerful note. . .
> Then I hurried the proofs back to Heinemann, and set out 'sworn to eclipse our sorry trades' and to remove the new mountains created by every upheaval.[31]

NOTES

1. Sir H. Nicolson, *Lord Carnock. A Study in the Old Diplomacy* (London, 1937), 325.
2. See Steiner, *op. cit.*, 70.
3. *M.P.*, 98–9.
4. See *The Times*, 18 April 1913 and 17 October 1913. The paper criticized Van's over-lengthy dialogue, comparing him in this respect with G. B. Shaw. There is indeed the barest comparison between his *The Cap and Bells* and Shaw's *Man*

and Superman if only one regards it as the story of a ruthless and resourceful upper-class girl out to get her brilliant, radical, working-class man.

5. See his memo on the Italian question, October 1911, F.O. 371/1110, no. 8896; for the Persian question, see Gooch and Temperley, *British Documents on the Origins of the War*, v. 10/1, 813.

6. *M.P.*, 115. See also F.O. 371/1908, no. 20458.

7. *M.P.*, 115.

8. See *M.P.*, 116. For a devastating attack on Kühlmann as a 'frustrated intriguer' with an 'innate disregard of the truth', see Sir L. B. Namier, *Avenues of History* (London, 1950).

9. *M.P.*, 63; also 45, 129.

10. B. Bond (ed.), *Chief of Staff, The Diaries of Lt. Gen. Sir Henry Pownell* (London, 1972), i. 38.

11. *M.P.*, 272.

12. Gooch and Temperley, v. 9/1, 573.

13. *Ibid.*, v. xi, 32-33.

14. Quoted by Nicolson in Carnock, *op. cit.*, 418.

15. *M.P.*, 128.

16. *M.P.*, 133.

17. *M.P.*, 137.

18. I am grateful to Dr A. Marsden of the University of Dundee for making available to me the relevant pages of his chapter on Grey's foreign policy for the forthcoming *Cambridge History of Foreign Policy*.

19. F.O. 382/265, 228. See Grey to Count Wrangel (Swedish Minister in London), 19 March 1915.

20. See F.O. 382/265, 34722, 36855. These suggestions originated from Sir Esmé Howard, British Ambassador to Stockholm, but they received Van's warm support. For the passage on the mission to Sweden, see also Lord Howard of Penrith, *Theatre of Life* (London, 1936), 243-7.

21. *M.P.*, 146.

22. *Ibid.*

23. From *Green and Grey: Collected Poems* (London, 1944).

24. On his return, Van wrote a long memorandum on the state of Anglo-Swedish commercial relations. (See F.O. 382/330, 238.) Little seemed to have changed. Despite the breakdown of negotiations, Van concluded that 'it would be most unfortunate if the impression gained ground that . . . we were closing down on Sweden'.

25. *M.P.*, 155.

26. *M.P.*, 198–9.

27. See *M.P.*, 157. Lady Vansittart also commented on his experience in the P.O.W. Department as convincing him of German brutality. (Interview, 18 August 1972).

28. *M.P.*, 157.

29. *Ibid.*, 186, 192.

30. See *M.P.*, 181, 187.

31. *M.P.*, 198–9.

CHAPTER IV

The Private Secretary

BY THE LATE SUMMER of 1918, with the German armies in retreat and the Allies in full pursuit, the Foreign Office began to prepare in earnest for the forthcoming peace conference. Expectations ran high. During the war, the Office had suffered in comparative silence as it felt its influence slipping slowly from its grasp.[1] Now that the peace-making was about to commence the officials expected to come into their own again. Complicated preparations had been in progress for the past six months. Scholarly handbooks, one hundred and sixty-four in number, were written to clarify every conceivable question that was likely to arise. At least the younger members of the delegation travelled to Paris certain in the knowledge that they were to be instrumental in reshaping the shattered world. Their hopes were to be quickly dispelled.[2] Lord Hardinge, who superintended the organization of the entire British delegation, expressed the mounting dissatisfaction, and often contempt, of the higher officials with the diplomatic techniques favoured by the politicians.

> Unfortunately, Mr Lloyd George, whose knowledge of many of the problems involved was non-existent, insisted on employing a staff of his own unofficial creation who had no knowledge of French and none of diplomacy, and the Foreign Office organization was consequently stillborn.[3]

Lloyd George's attitude towards his permanent officials was notoriously scornful, branding them to his intimates as 'narrow' and 'cranky'.[4] Yet, unlike many of his contemporaries, Van's particular standing was not seriously undermined by the Prime Minister's unorthodox diplomacy, even though Lloyd George's quarrels with the Foreign Office continued until 1922 and were a factor in his eventual downfall. Lloyd George was in constant attendance at Versailles from January until June 1919, when the German treaty was signed. Van remained on in Paris until the end of 1920, and was mainly occupied with two interlocking questions: the Turkish treaty, and the Palestine mandate. In this manner he escaped from the more immediate consequences of tripping over Lloyd George's feet, and was allowed to conduct his negotiations through the normal channels of communication between Paris and the Foreign Office. He exploited his opportunity to good effect.

His first months in Paris were difficult ones. The British delegation was housed at the Hotel Majestic. Staffed by British domestics, the catering standards were, apparently, beyond description: 'it has been a sad joke', Eyre Crowe, renowned throughout the service for his austere standards, wryly noted.[5] Nor was Van able to conform to the strict supervision imposed upon the delegates' private affairs by the Foreign Office establishment. When a friend offered him a vacant *garçonnière*, he fled to it with relief. His affairs were further complicated by the state of his finances. Throughout this period he found himself in dire financial straits, and was involved in a running, though unsuccessful, battle with the Treasury to increase the size of his salary,[6] a by-product of his own extravagances compounded by teething problems involved in the proposed amalgamation between the diplomatic service and the Foreign Office. Van discovered that the Treasury had decided not to pay bachelors serving on the Peace Delegation the war bonus of £220 on the grounds that they did not have an establishment to maintain at home and hence, apparently, did not need the money. The logic of this ruling escaped Van, and he appealed for justice to Crowe and Balfour:

> It is obvious that this is a very serious matter, especially in these times for people like me who are without private means and have to live on their pay.
> The Treasury know well enough that however unjust their treatment one would stay here to see the job through, but I really do not think they are entitled to take such an advantage of one's loyalty. I do not wish to make heavy weather about this, but feel most strongly that His Majesty's Government would not approve if they knew the spirit in which one was being treated as a reward for the hard work one has done.[7]

Balfour, himself a bachelor, was perplexed at this obvious discrimination which appeared to him 'altogether unjust',[8] and delegated the problem to Curzon's charge. Curzon showed no particular interest and it was left to Hardinge to battle in vain against the Treasury's decision. Van continued to survive on a very tight budget until a lucky run at cards relieved him of his more pressing cares.[9]

Matters were not made any easier by the death of his mother. The war finally put paid to any notions which the Vansittarts might have entertained about financial recovery. The estates at Foots Cray were sold off and the family moved to a smaller house.[10] Alice Vansittart, exhausted by her ill fortune, fell seriously ill towards the end of January 1919. She died on 13 February at the age of sixty-five, and was buried by the estates which had once belonged to the family. The precise relationship between Van and his mother remains unclear. His memoirs reveal little about her, except in the most general and non-committal terms. As Van left home at an early age and had lived an independent life, at least since his Eton days, it would be reasonable to assume that he experienced no more than the normal feeling of filial grief, and that his mother's death was not an occasion for a profound emotional upheaval, certainly not of the kind he endured when Arnold was killed.

The German treaty was signed on 28 June 1919. Although Van was not directly concerned with the treaty, his views about it must necessarily be the subject for some discussion as they form the essential basis for his attitude towards post-war Germany, perhaps the most important theme in Van's diplomatic career. His views on Versailles were never as clear-cut and uncompromising as in later life he would have had us believe. Although in public he championed the treaty in all its clauses,[11] in private he was much more critical.

It is important not to confuse Van the publicist with Van the diplomatist. Both played their well-defined roles. During his later life he was intent almost solely on justifying his public reputation as a consistent, unyielding, hard-line anti-German. He was certainly that. But his anti-Germanism, which flowered and attained its highest moral apogee during the Second World War, was flawed by doubts concerning the ethical propriety of some clauses of the treaty, particularly those relating to territorial and colonial arrangements. Throughout the 1930's he claimed that the treaty 'went too far, not individually perhaps, but cumulatively', and that it was 'a bad treaty'.[12] Even the contentious question of war-guilt did not appear so clear-cut in private as it did in public. In 1937 he even doubted whether Germany was wholly resposible for 'her unsuccessful war'.[13]

These observations were not spontaneous asides. They were measured statements intended only for the eyes of his colleagues and his political masters. We can be sure that they accurately represented his sentiments on the Versailles Treaty, sentiments which he had held consistently for many years. He blasted Keynes, and with some justification, for his classic presentation of the case for revisionism.[14] But the uncomfortable fact remains that 'the Britons who nibble the fruits of victory with the guilty conscience of Adam'[15] included him also. It was really only a question of the size of the nibble.

Soon after his arrival in Paris Van was appointed acting head of the Eastern Section, substituting for Louis Mallet who had returned to London owing to bad health. Much of his time was spent in transmitting to the Foreign Office the multitude of details concerning the Turkish negotiations. Liaison between Paris and London was far from perfect.[16] Van, however, performed his job with the utmost skill and tact, and was thus brought favourably to the attention of Curzon who had replaced Balfour as Foreign Secretary in October 1919. This proved to be of special significance for Van's career. Curzon considered himself an expert on the Eastern question, and Van's competent handling of this complicated issue greatly impressed him.

The complications arose from a series of so-called secret treaties and public declarations entered into by the powers during the course of the war* which provided for the partition of the Ottoman Empire. In December Van, who in Crowe's absence had been promoted to acting head of the political section of the British delegation, was ordered to return immediately to London to prepare for an Anglo-

* There were eight such obligations: (a) The Constantinople agreements, March–April 1915, by which Russia was to acquire Constantinople and the hinterland of the Straits on the condition that Britain and France achieved their aims in the Near East; (b) The treaty of London, April 1915, by which Italy agreed to enter the war on the allied side provided the eventual peace settlement assured her of *Italia Irredenta*, and territories at Turkey's expense; (c) the MacMahon–Hussein correspondence, June 1915–March 1916, interpreted by the Arabs as a pledge to erect an Arab state in Turkey-in-Asia; (d) The Sykes–Picot agreement, May 1916, which partitioned the Ottoman Empire into spheres of influence between Russia, Britain and France; (e) The treaty of St Jean de Mauriene, April 1917, which promised to Italy the Turkish provinces around Smyrna, also claimed by Greece; (f) The Balfour Declaration, November 1917, by which Britain promised to help facilitate the establishment of a national home for the Jews in Palestine; (g) the Declaration of the Seven, June 1918, which recognized the sovereign independence of the Arabs in those areas liberated by the Arabs themselves; (h) The Anglo-French declaration, November 1918, which promised the establishment of national governments and administrations deriving their authority from the choice of the indigenous population. For texts, see J. C. Hurewitz, *Diplomacy in the Near and Middle East*, i (N.Y., 1956).

French conference on the future of the Turkish Empire. Van and his colleague, Eric Forbes-Adam,* were required to work out a detailed plan of the projected Turkish settlement.[17] The French had already submitted a long memorandum, composed by Phillippe Berthelot, secretary-general at the Quai d'Orsay, setting out their views. Van's and Forbes-Adam's task was to see where it conflicted with British interests.[18]

Since the armistice the French had proved to be extremely awkward allies. Determined to exploit their victory to the utmost, they were raising maximalist demands everywhere, from the Rhineland to Syria to the Newfoundland fisheries. Van regarded most of these claims as ludicrous and advised applying the considerable British financial interests in France as a lever to persuade the French government to abandon its absurd pretensions.[19] By the end of the year the French position had softened. With the United States about to retire from world politics, the *entente* powers were forced back upon themselves. Compromise between them was essential if any progress was to be achieved over a whole range of outstanding problems, including the Turkish–Syrian question. The London conference of December 1919 was the first tentative move towards the re-establishment of the *entente*, a point made quite clear by Berthelot himself.

There was a general consensus over the four guiding principles of the Berthelot memorandum: the eradication of Turkish militarism; the establishment of an international authority to maintain the Straits; the liberation of Armenia from Turkish rule; and the emancipation of the Arab and Syrian populations from Turkish domination. Over the Turkish treaty itself there was little controversy, with one notable exception: the future of Smyrna. By an ill-judged decision of the Supreme Council in May 1919, Greece had been allowed to occupy the Turkish province. Van and Forbes-Adam saw in Greek ambitions a factor which threatened to sabotage the entire Turkish settlement. They proposed a reasonable compromise, European Turkey up to the Enos–Midea line[20] would be ceded to Greece; in return Smyrna would remain under nominal Turkish sovereignty. For the rest, the Van–Forbes-Adam proposals envisaged the establishment of an international régime for Constantinople and the Straits, and the maintenance of Turkish sovereignty, subject to Allied guidance, over Anatolia.[21]

* Eric Forbes-Adam (1888–1925): entered Foreign Office, 1913; third secretary at Paris Peace Conference; first secretary, 1922; participated in Lausanne Conference; served at Constantinople, 1923–25. Committed suicide as a result of mental depression in July 1925.

In the context of the period it was an enlightened scheme which, if acted upon, might have salvaged the Allied position in Turkey. But the cabinet rejected it.[22] For Van, however, its main significance lay in the fact that since January 1918 Curzon had been pressing upon the cabinet a plan similar in its broad outlines.[23] At least upon the fundamentals of the Eastern settlement their minds moved along the same track.

'The Secretary of State remarked to me the other day that you had covered yourself in glory at San Remo. Thought you'd like to know.'[24] 'Glory' was rather an imaginative word to use to describe Van's contribution to the conference. It is true that he was physically present at thirteen of the recorded twenty sessions.[25] But for the most part he remained in the background, a silent spectator. No doubt the major portion of his energy was expended in meeting, or possibly evading, the numerous lobbyists who invaded the hotels of San Remo throughout the conference.[26] At any rate, the main decisions were fairly easily settled. The Turkish treaty was drafted; the mandates for Syria and Lebanon were handed over to France, those for Palestine and Iraq to Britain; the resources of the Iraq oilfields were divided, France being apportioned twenty-five per cent of the net output. Only the details regarding the Palestine–Syria frontier remained outstanding.

Van felt instinctively that the right psychological moment to clinch the frontier question was immediately after the San Remo conference where he had found the French officials in an accommodating frame of mind.[27] Within a few weeks the French resolve to cooperate had exhausted itself, and they reverted back to their previous anti-British and anti-Zionist posture.[28]

It was the Syrian–Palestine question which gave rise to extreme concern. From the outset the French proved obdurate, not to say unreasonable. They clung to the provisions of the Sykes–Picot agreement until the very last moment, invoking every legalistic point to uphold its validity. The British now saw in the agreement an outdated and harmful document, arguing that it had been drawn up largely regardless of economic or geographical facts. They were spurred on by the Zionists as much as by their own interests. The British were under constant pressure from the Zionist organization to shift the Palestine frontier northwards, an aim incidentally which did not conflict with their own policy. Even so, Van often felt it necessary to resist the Zionists' maximum demands.[29]

Van suffered few illusions about the French. They were fundamentally anti-Zionist. For them the Palestine mandate was 'too judaised and too judaising',[30] and they made no secret of the fact that they regarded the British as 'foolish and asking for trouble'[31] by offering themselves as the mandatory power. Nor did the French attitude mellow with time. Quite the contrary, it hardened. Succumbing to the fantasies of the time, they saw in a Jewish Palestine 'a Bolshevik colony on their flank',[32] hence their determination to restrict that colony's frontiers to a minimum.

Van's difficulties were compounded by an additional factor. The instructions he received from home were often hopelessly out of touch with reality. He was convinced that this was mainly due to Zionist influence, pushing the government into making unattainable demands. Unable to negotiate calmly under this kind of pressure, he sent off a strong note of protest to London.

> We mustn't let the Zionists push us into attempting the temporarily unfeasible, or we shall be let in for trouble both with the French and the Arabs. We've fought their case for a year now, and there's really nothing more we can do for them (they do nothing for themselves here) short of a general deal with the French... *Territorially, as in the mandate, they will have to start slower.* Regrettable no doubt, but if they make good, these things can be added unto them in the future.[33]

The same pattern repeated itself over the debate on the Palestine mandate: the Zionists eager to race forward; the officials reluctant to move at the same pace. Again, some discussion arose over the expression 'self-governing Commonwealth', a phrase which had first been used in a draft version of the mandate in March 1920. Curzon thought this 'a euphemism for a Jewish State', and hence 'most dangerous'. The two chief British drafters, Van and Forbes-Adam, differed. Forbes-Adam admitted that the expression had been used in order to assuage the Zionists who argued that it would enthuse world Jewry. But, he added, it implied a self-governing Palestinian state or 'commonwealth', and not acceptance of the idea 'that the Palestine state set up by the mandate would ever become a Jewish state'. Van believed this argument simplistic and self-defeating. 'Why not be honest and say Jewish Commonwealth at once?' But like Curzon, he believed the concept to be 'contrary to every principle upon which we have hitherto stood'.[34]

Over another phrase – 'Recognizing the historical connection of the Jewish People with Palestine and the claim which this gives them to reconstitute it as their national home' – Van ran into hot water.

Curzon reacted hotly to the use of this expression, admonishing Van for having 'acted independently' by including it in a revised form of the mandate.[35] Van had restored the disputed phrase, originally drafted by Balfour, to 'make it easier for them (the Zionists) to swallow the other less palatable alterations' in the revised text.[36] Curzon remained highly sceptical.

Motivated by a desire to be entirely honest in his dealings with the Zionists, thereby leaving them no excuse for accusations of double-dealing, Van at the same time was compelled to tone down their more radical demands. Such logic required him to perform a delicate balancing act, successfully as it turned out, for on the whole the procedures he proposed were profitably adopted. Despite Van's impatience with Zionist lobbying, and Curzon's cordial distrust of the Palestine mandate, both fought hard to realize the Zionists' essential aims, seeing in them, no doubt, the furtherance of British interests in the area.*

Curzon was not alone in his high opinion of Van's abilities. Lord Derby, the British Ambassador in Paris, also came to rely heavily upon Van's professional skills. Derby had little experience of diplomacy. His was a political appointment, and as such it aroused much resentment in the service. Still, Van thought him likeable enough, though 'amiably inclined to agree with his last contact',[37] a characteristic which worked to Van's advantage.

Accompanying the Turkish treaty was a special tripartite agreement between Britain, France and Italy, whereby a self-denying ordinance in economic matters would apply equally to the mandated territories as well as to Turkey. Lloyd George held serious doubts as to the probity of such an agreement, hinting that the document would be represented as excluding other powers from commercial and economic gains.[38] But Derby had allowed himself to be pressured by the Italians into agreeing to sign. Van persuaded him not to do so, much to Derby's eventual relief: 'Vansittart . . . has been admirable in the advice he has given me.'[39] Curzon entirely

* It is interesting to note that Weizmann, the Zionist leader, when discussing this episode in his memoirs (*Trial and Error*, London, 1950, 348), singles out 'young Eric Forbes-Adam, highly intelligent, efficient and most sympathetic – who fought the battle of the mandate for many months', for special mention. Van is studiously ignored.

The frontier question dragged on for another two years. In December 1920 an Anglo-French convention (see Cmd. 1195) reached a provisional agreement concerning water supplies and established a special boundary commission which concluded its findings in February 1922; they were sanctioned by the League Council in July and ratified a year later.

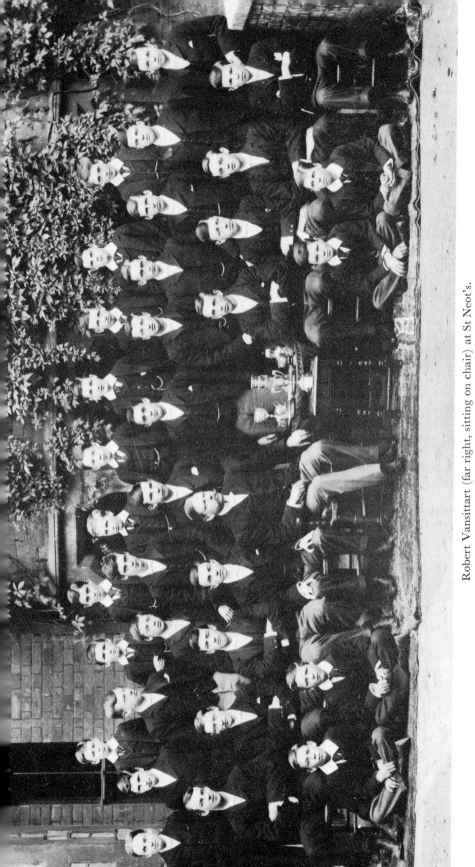

Robert Vansittart (far right, sitting on chair) at St Neot's.

Van (centre) with friends at Eton.

approved. The agreement, if published, would undoubtedly have proved an extreme embarrassment and most awkward to explain. Eventually it was swept away together with the Sèvres settlement. But Derby had found a reliable adviser and was careful not to lose him. He insisted that Van remain by his side in Paris, comforting Curzon with the knowledge that with Van 'to look after our interests nothing much can happen to them'.[40]

It would have been out of character had Van concentrated only on work. Paris, he happily concluded, was no Keynsian nightmare. He continued with his sporting and theatrical pursuits. Limited by the dramatic talents of the British delegation, he organized two productions – Cecil Clay's *A Pantomime Rehearsal*, and Tristan Barnard's *L'Anglais tel qu'on le parle* – in the basement of the Hotel Majestic. One wonders what the other delegations thought of these spectacles.[41] In 1919 *The Singing Caravan* was published. It sold five thousand copies in two editions. Heinemann, his publisher, consoled him with the thought that only 'Five thousand Britains at most are regular readers of poetry'.[42] His distant cousin, T. E. Lawrence, proved an ardent admirer: 'Did I ever put you on to the Vansittart? . . . it is that rarest English thing, light poetry.' The story went that Lawrence carried it about with him, as he had carried *Arabia Deserta*, and that when he came down in a plane crash he was found to be wearing 'khaki (without any insignia or rank) and "sneakers" and to have as sole kit Vansittart's book'.[43] Later Lawrence was instrumental in securing the publication of *The Singing Caravan* in a special de luxe edition by the Gregynog Press.[44]

During the autumn of 1920 Van's immediate future became the subject for debate. A counsellorship was about to become vacant in the Paris embassy. Van was the natural choice to fill it. The two alternatives open to him were limited: either to remain in the Foreign Office, or to take a foreign posting with the certainty of promotion and extra financial benefits. The issue was further complicated by the fact that in 1919 the main recommendations of the MacDonnell Commission were put into effect. Diplomatists and clerks were now included in a joint seniority list up to and including the rank of counsellor, and promotions, either at home or abroad, were to be drawn from this list. The amalgamation provoked much internal discussion.[45] Powerful critics – including Hardinge, Crowe and Tyrrell* – ranged themselves against the scheme, on the grounds that the

* William George Tyrrell (1866–1947): entered Foreign Office, 1889; precis writer to Grey, 1905–7; private secretary to Grey, 1907–15; Assistant Under

c

amalgamation glossed over the disparate tasks which diplomatists and clerks had to fulfil.[46] Sir John Tillet, the chief reformer, put Van's case:

> Vansittart is a very able person who wants to get promotion and we are going to try and stop him by telling him the door is shut. Very likely the Foreign Office needs strengthening, but no service was ever strengthened by forcing able men to remain in subordinate positions against their will.[47]

Van would have been amused had he known about the controversy he was inadvertently stirring up. In fact he was keen to remain in Paris. It was the Paris embassy which exhibited little enthusiasm to acquire his services. Derby, previously a great fan of Van's, now saw nothing ahead but difficulties:

> I like Vansittart and I would not like to do anything against him but at the same time I am not very favourably impressed with his capabilities as head of Chancery. I do not refer to his capabilities as a Diplomat but to his powers of exercising control and discipline.[48]

This seems a rather ingenious argument, for while it would be accurate to say that Van was not an organization man, his record during the peace conference had been beyond reproach and had been acknowledged by all as such.

Derby's true motive lay elsewhere. It was about this time that Van first met and became engaged to Gladys Heppenheimer, later to become his first wife. His fiancée was the daughter of an American banker. She was 'smart, attractive, pleasant and a good conversationalist', 'cosmopolitan, spoke French admirably, [and] had a sense of the ridiculous'.[49] But more to the point she was married, had two children, and was in the process of being divorced. Derby hinted that such a match would be most unsuitable:

> Quite between ourselves there is I believe another reason which might make his appointment somewhat undesirable but I have only heard it by a roundabout way and I would not say anything to you officially on the subject.[50]

To Hardinge he was more specific:

> . . . had Vansittart obtained that appointment his marriage to the lady of whom we spoke the other day was to come off; the marriage

Secretary of State, 1919–25; Permanent Under Secretary, 1925–28; Ambassador in Paris, 1928–34. Kn. 1913; Cr. Baron, 1929.

was dependent upon that. Under the circumstances Lindsay's appointment* appears to have been a useful obstacle.[51]

In the event the obstacle proved a frail one, for Van and his fiancée were married a year later.

Van ultimately benefited from Derby's intervention. Some weeks after this incident, while on holiday in Biarritz, he received a letter from Curzon inviting him to become his political secretary.[52] Curzon wanted him to act as liaison between the Foreign Office and 10 Downing Street, and to assist him 'with ideas'. He would begin his new duties, at the rank of Assistant Secretary, in the New Year.

Van's private and professional quandaries were resolved by one letter. Curzon showed great understanding and allowed him to travel frequently between Paris and London while the divorce proceedings were in progress.[53] Inevitably, there were rumbles of discontent at Van's appointment. This was understandable. His rise in rank over the past two years had been spectacular: from first secretary at the beginning of 1919 to counsellor at the end of 1920. Moreover, he was an able man; and although he tended to belie his ambition he had come into a powerful inheritance. How would he choose to use it? Certainly for his own benefit, but hopefully not to the detriment of others.

He had no doubt as to where his future lay. Duty, inclination and ambition all pointed in Curzon's direction, but knowing Curzon he regarded his unexpected advancement with a mixture of apprehension and excitement. Curzon was a severe taskmaster. His idiosyncracies were notorious; and his appointment as Foreign Secretary was viewed with considerable alarm by most of the officials.[54] The years Van spent by his side, though of crucial importance for his career, were often trying and irritating ones, and on more than one occasion Van debated seriously whether or not to abandon his imperious chief to his own devices.[55]

On the whole, however, Van's relations with Curzon were extremely cordial. For there was another side to his mercurial character. To those who served him loyally he reciprocated in kind. Van profited greatly from the benevolent despotism of his new chief. His first marriage was blighted by the continuous ill-health of his wife. Often this involved absenting himself from important conferences.

---

* Ronald (Charles) Lindsay (1877–1945): entered Foreign Office 1898; Ambassador to Constantinople, 1925–26, to Berlin, 1926–28; Permanent Under Secretary, 1928–30; Ambassador to Washington, 1930–39. He was moved from Washington to Paris as Counsellor in 1920.

Curzon understood. Van was deeply grateful. His correspondence to Curzon clearly reveals his deep sense of obligation.[56] On the eve of his marriage, he made a solemn promise to Curzon:

> No, being married won't make any difference to my ardour as Private Secretary, for, you see, my future wife and I have had to wait so long for each other that it won't seem much matter to wait for dinner . . . With gratitude – and, if I may say so respectfully, with affection.[57]

He married in the late autumn of 1921. At the last moment there was an unexpected hitch. Gladys, a Roman Catholic divorcée, was barred from a church wedding. The ceremony, after hurried family consultations, finally took place in a registry office. After spending their honeymoon in Venice, they returned to London where they found suitable accommodation at the Corner House, Catherine Street, just off Buckingham Gate. Later they moved to a far more expansive mansion at 103 Park Street. In the summer of 1922 they acquired a weekend cottage, Church Farm, at Herstmonceux, Sussex.[58]

His marital responsibilities – he had also acquired two step-sons – introduced an element of stability into his life. Regular hours and less gallivanting around town made him a more conventional figure. His relationship with Curzon deepened. They exchanged confidences regarding their respective illnesses – Van at the time was suffering from acute pyorrhoea and some form of stomach disorder.[59] And when Curzon himself was bed-ridden with phlebitis Van continued to prop up his spirits, enquiring assiduously after his health, keeping him *au courant* with the latest political developments, and amusing him with some spicy political gossip.[60]

Van's influence with Curzon must have appeared considerable. Crowe at least was convinced that this was indeed the case, and seized upon an internal scandal at the Paris embassy* to try to separate Van from his position of power. He wrote to Curzon:

> I do not know what your present views about Vansittart are. But if you still think of selecting some other Private Secretary, here would be a suitable opportunity . . . I believe Vansittart would do

---

* It was a particularly complicated affair. The counsellor at the Paris embassy was Sir Milne Cheetham (Van's old colleague from his Cairo days). Cheetham's wife, Anastasia, daughter of a veteran Russian diplomat, M. Mouravieff, had been involved in an affair with a junior member of the staff, Mr Nigel Walter Law. Nor, according to rumour, was this the first example of Lady Cheetham's behaviour. Cheetham had filed divorce proceedings and the case was due to appear before the courts in October. In the eyes of some officials, it was essential to remove Cheetham from Paris before then as the public scandal would

well at Paris. His wife would there be more of a help than in his present post. Failing his going abroad he would have to take on one of the departments in the office, the most naturally the Eastern one – I do not know how that would suit you. My own idea remains that he would be better abroad. And I imagine that he would jump at Paris. I know that at one time it was his ambition.[61]

But it was no longer. He was married; had set up two homes; and his wife was pregnant. Curzon eventually decided to keep him.[62]

Van shared Curzon's intense dislike of Lloyd George's high-handed methods of conducting foreign affairs. Like his chief, he deplored the manner in which the Foreign Office had been eclipsed, and firmly believed that the Prime Minister's foreign policy initiatives, particularly in the Near East and in the field of Anglo-Russian relations, were leading the country to catastrophe. In March 1921, with the resignation of Bonar Law from the leadership of the Conservative Party, Van felt the moment was propitious to break Lloyd George's grip on the Foreign Office. In a truly extraordinary letter, he urged upon Curzon a plan of campaign designed to exploit the new political scene:

> I said in my letter [not found] that I thought this was the psychological moment for action to strengthen your position and that of the FO . . . When you first spoke to me of his [Bonar Law's] retirement, you said it would weaken the government. That is true, but it is that which makes the opportunity, and, if turned to account, will strengthen the government; for he was steadily weakening the Unionist party, which is the strongest element in the coalition – perhaps in the country. Mr Bonar Law could blow the horn and crack the whip, and keep them together – for the benefit of Downing Street. All that is changed with the succession of Mr [Austen] Chamberlain to the mastership. He cannot, and would not, keep them together for a twisting turn.

Van went on to criticize Lloyd George's foreign policy in the strongest possible terms:

> . . . I will take two instances . . . The Russian Trade Agreement [of July 1920] and the Eastern policy. The two are incompatible.

make his position untenable. Hence the decision to rid the embassy of his presence. All ended well, however. Milne Cheetham was sent off to Berne; the Cheethams were divorced in 1923; and Lady Cheetham married Mr Law in 1929.

By a bias, which is a lack of balance, Downing Street has backed Greece in such a manner that she must turn back Turkey upon Russia, and so create a *casus* that must destroy the agreement . . . For Turkey cum Russia will react upon us throughout the East, upon us as the Greek backer. This is tortuousness run into a circle – a vicious one. But, in foreign policy, if one lives from hand to mouth, one is apt to see no further than one's nose.

Our position in the East has been imperilled . . . and a weak European powerlet has been straddled into Asia, where even Great Britain finds the foothold increasingly difficult. Greece must get between our legs and trip us at every turn. I don't want to criticize Mr Bonar Law, though many Unionists like myself hold strong opinions on the methods and results of him; but I do feel that the change of Mr Chamberlain offers a great chance of putting things on a sound basis again . . . The first essential is that Foreign Policy should return whole to the Foreign Office, and not to be run spasmodically behind its back (Greece) and over its head (Russia).

If the insistence is rightly taken it will strengthen the government. If the chance be not taken the government will take a toss anyhow, for it will not now be possible to keep the Unionist party in a pack, and it will run riot in covert or in the open . . .

I venture to think this may be worth considering, and, if I am not quite wrong, the corollary would be an early conference with Mr Chamberlain on your return.[63]

Van's hopes of Chamberlain taking a new initiative, typical of so many Unionists, were unfounded. Lloyd George applied all his charm to capture the new Conservative leadership. The coalition continued, until, eighteen months later, as a result of Chamberlain's exaggerated loyalty, the Unionists finally ran 'riot'. There is no evidence to indicate how Curzon reacted to his private secretary's presumptious advice. There can be few precedents for any official, let alone one of Van's rank and position, attempting to inveigle his superior in political intrigues of this kind. But Van was rarely reticent, particularly on paper. In any case, he felt on safe ground. His comments struck a ready chord on Curzon's wounded pride.

All of Van's predictions about the iniquity of the government's Greek policy eventually came true, though at the time he was not nearly as far-sighted as he later pretended to be. In the early stages of the crisis he had argued strongly in favour of the government's policy of neutrality.[64] To do otherwise would only 'alienate and destroy Greece without winning the already swollen Angorites'. It was for this reason that he resolutely opposed a reckless suggestion by Churchill that Britain impose her mediation by force upon the two conflicting powers, particularly in order to bring the Greeks into line.[65]

Churchill's proposal was rejected. But by the end of 1921 it had become clear that the British were playing a lone and dangerous game in the Near East. Their allies, France and Italy, had come to terms with the nationalist government at Angora, while the Soviet Union had signed an agreement with Mustapha Kemal thereby stiffening Turkish resistance to Greek ambitions. By the autumn of 1922 British policy had been overtaken by events. The Greek armies had broken and were in full flight before the Turkish advance. On 9 September Turkish troops entered Smyrna. At Chanak, on the eastern coast of the Dardanelles, a small British force faced the victorious Turks alone. A crisis of major proportions confronted the British government.

Through the summer, while the crisis was building up, Curzon was ill. Balfour, his substitute, by now an elder statesman, was unable to give decisive leadership and unwilling to stand up against Lloyd George. He exerted little influence upon affairs. When the crisis broke the Foreign Office realized that the game was up, and that no amount of mediation would rescue the Greeks from their own folly. Lloyd George was carried along by his own enthusiasm. He did not survive this crisis. Criticism had been mounting against his government for some time and on many counts. The Conservative Party, at a meeting at the Carlton Club, decided to free itself from his tutelage. The coalition dissolved. Lloyd George left office, never again to return.

The Foreign Office rejoiced at this belated and somewhat shady triumph. At the General Election of November, Lloyd George's faction – the National Liberals – returned only sixty-two seats. His downfall was absolute. Curzon was free at last of his *bête noire*. Van gloated together with his chief.

> The best comment I have yet heard on the Election comes from an old servant of my father's: 'I always said the country would sooner be governed by gentry than a Jumped-Up-Saturday-Night like Mr Lloyd George'. We've all been wondering exactly what the expression means, but it *sounds* very graphic.[66]

Although Van remained with Curzon for another year, they were to share no further triumphs. During these past years Van had succeeded in consolidating his personal position. Having the ear of the

Foreign Secretary at all hours of the day gave him considerable influence in Foreign Office and diplomatic appointments. A potential power-house of this kind, particularly when operated by a capable and ambitious man, was viewed by the Foreign Office hierarchy with intense misgivings. As we have seen, Crowe, by now Permanent Under Secretary, fell into this category. In January 1924, a minority Labour government took office under Ramsay MacDonald, who also acted as his own Foreign Secretary. Van wished to continue as private secretary to MacDonald, but Crowe, convinced that Van was amassing too much power, would not have it. Instead, he appointed Walford Selby,* a less controversial figure 'whom he considered unlikely to exercise influence'.[67]

Van, though disappointed, had little cause for complaint. Since 1919 he had experienced only success. His reputation was firmly established. True, he was regarded by some as a private secretary on the make. Suspicions were rife, perhaps inevitable. Those who had risen through the ranks found it difficult to accept those who had entered the inner sanctum through the side door. Perhaps it was fortunate that Van departed together with Curzon. He needed a spell of departmental work to set the balance straight again. His last meeting with Curzon was painful. 'Curzon', Van concluded, 'had a great presence, great ability, great application, but not quite the greatness which he greatly desired'. He was 'an A-1 Class 2 man'.[68]

NOTES

1. See R. H. Warman, 'The Erosion of Foreign Office Influence in the Making of Foreign Policy, 1916–18', *The Historical Journal*, 1 (1972); also G. A. Craig and F. Gilbert, *The Diplomats, 1919–39* (New York, 1965), i, 17–22.
2. See H. Nicolson, *Peacemaking* (London, 1964), 30–42; Hugh Knatchbull-Hugesson, *Diplomat in Peace and War* (London, 1949), 24–5; and *M.P.*, 198–9.
3. Harding of Penshurst, *Old Diplomacy* (London, 1947), 229.
4. See Lord Riddell, *Intimate Diary of the Peace Conference and After* (London, 1933), 126; also on this topic, Craig and Gilbert, *op. cit.*, 27–8, and Warman, *op. cit.*, *passim*.
5. See Eyre Crowe to Ronald Graham, 18 July 1919, F.O. 371/3747; also a minute by Van, 12 July 1919, and Hubert Montgomery (chief clerk) to Van, 9 July 1918, *ibid*.
6. This was not only a problem which concerned Van, but was general to a wide range of officials of Van's rank. See his minute, 12 July 1919, Hubert Mont-

---

* Sir Walford Harmwood Montague Selby (1881–1965): entered Foreign Office, 1904; private secretary to Gray, MacDonald, Austen Chamberlain, Arthur Henderson; minister plenipotentiary in Vienna, 1933–37; Ambassador in Lisbon, 1937–40. Kn. 1931.

gomery to Van, 9 July 1919, and Eyre Crowe to Ronald Graham, 18 July 1919, F.O. 371/3747. Also C. Larner, *op. cit.*

7. See Van's minute, 12 July 1919, Hubert Montgomery to Vansittart, 9 July 1919, F.O. 371/3747.

8. Crowe to Graham, *ibid.*

9. *M.P.*, 230.

10. See *M.P.*, 208.

11. See his speech in the Lords, in May 1942, *P.D.*, L., v. 122, c. 1066–1976; and *P.D.*, Lords v. 133, c. 409–34, 10 October 1944; and *P.D.*, Lords v. 143, c. 873–82, 30 October 1946. This theme is scattered throughout Van's later written work. See *Lessons of My Life* (1943); *Bones of Contention* (1945); *Events and Shadows* (n.d.); *Even Now* (n.d.). See also *M.P.*, 220–27.

12. See 'An Aspect of International Relations, 1931'. F.O. 371/15205 or C.P. 4 (32), CAB. 24/227.

13. See Vansittart Papers (hereafter Vnst.), 1937, 2/31.

14. See *M.P.*, 224–5.

15. *Ibid.*, 220.

16. See H. Nicolson, *Peace Making*, 291, 314.

17. See *B.D.*, 1, iv. 930–31.

18. See their instructions from Crowe, *B.D.*, 1, iv, 930–31. The French memorandum, with Van's and Forbes-Adam's comments, appears in *B.D.* 1, iv, 942–56, 577–87. The latter pages are devoted to Syria, Palestine, Mesopotamia and Arabia. The comments on this section were not communicated to the French, unlike the first which dealt with the less controversial Turkish question.

19. Minute by Van, 11 March 1919, Lloyd George Papers (hereafter Ll.G.P.), F/3/4/18. Hardinge approved of this suggestion; Lloyd George rejected it on the grounds that 'it would be undesirable to mix up these two questions'. One can perhaps detect in Van's current demand the forerunner to his 'keep Germany lean' policy in the 1930's. See also minute by Van, 20 December 1921, F.O. 800/329.

20. See *B.D.*, 1, iv. 750, for map giving exact position of the line.

21. For the minutes of the conference, where this scheme was raised, see *B.D.*, 1, iv. 938–42, 956–64.

22. Edwin Montague, Secretary of State for India, argued that, if put into effect, it would have a disastrous influence upon Moslem opinion in India. The cabinet allowed itself to be persuaded by this dismal prophecy. See Nicolson, *Curzon, The Last Phase* (London, 1934), 112–15.

23. See Nicolson, *Curzon*, 76–7.

24. Ronald Campbell to Van, 11 May 1920, F.O. 800/329.

25. See *B.D.*, 1, viii, nos. 4, 5, 6, 9, 10, 11, 12, 13, 15, 16, 17, 19, 20.

26. See J. Nevakivi, *Britain, France and the Arab Middle East* (London, 1969), 242.

27. See Van to Curzon, 6 May 1920, F.O. 371/5244, E. 4438/4164/44; also Van to Major Young, 29 June 1920, *B.D.*, 1, xiii, 298–301.

28. *B.D.*, 1, xiii, 291.

29. See *B.D.*, 1, iv, 580, 598. No early agreement was possible on the frontier issue, and a final decision was left in abeyance until after the San Remo conference.

30. See Van to Major H. Young, 21 June 1920. *B.D.*, 1, xiii, 292.

31. Van to Major Young, 29 June 1920, *ibid.*, 299.

32. Van to Curzon, 16 November 1920. *ibid.*, 391.

33. Van to Curzon, 7 October 1920. Curzon Papers, India Official Library (hereafter C.P.), F/3/3(O–W), 1920. Van was as bitterly critical, if not more so, of the American Zionists. See Van to Curzon, 4 November 1920, F.O. 371/5247. E. 13762/4162/44.
34. See F.O. 371/5199.
35. See *B.D.*, 1, xiii, 328.
36. *Ibid.*, 329.
37. *M.P.*, 183.
38. For discussion and text of agreement, see *B.D.*, 1, viii, 132–43; also, Nevakivi, *op. cit.*, 248.
39. Derby to Curzon, 11 May 1920, C.P. F/6/3, F/7/1; also Van to Curzon, 11 May 1920, *ibid.*
40. Derby to Curzon, 13 May and 27 July 1920, C.P., F/6/3, F/7/1.
41. See *M.P.*, 216; also Nicolson, *Peacemaking*, 329.
42. *M.P.*, 214.
43. T. E. Lawrence to Edward Garnett, 5 December 1930. Quoted by Edward Thompson in his introduction to *The Augustan Poets* (London, 1943); also *M.P.*, 214.
44. See T. Jones, *A Diary with Letters, 1931–1950* (O.U.P. 1969), 1, 67.
45. This entire question can be followed in C. Larner, *op. cit.*
46. Hardinge to Curzon, 6 August 1920. F.O. 366/789, X1495. I am grateful to Mrs Zara Steiner for bringing this document to my attention.
47. *Ibid.*
48. Derby to Curzon, 15 August 1920, C.P. F/6/3, F/7/1.
49. Private communications; and *M.P.*, 251.
50. Derby to Curzon, 15 August 1920, *op. cit.*
51. Hardinge to Curzon, 31 August 1920, C.P. F/7/2.
52. *M.P.*, 252–3.
53. See, for example, Van to Curzon, 3 September 1921, C.P. F/4/3.
54. See, for example, the Dalton Diaries, 9 May 1930; Hankey to Curzon, 22 April 1921, C.P., F/4/3; and *M.P.*, 272–3. Also J. D. Gregory, *On the Edge of Diplomacy* (London, 1928), 245.
55. See *M.P.*, 272–3, 274–5. In this connection, see also Lord D'Abernon, *An Ambassador of Peace* (London, 1929), 1, 156.
56. See his letters to Curzon, 1921–22, C.P.
57. Van to Curzon, 3 September 1921, C.P. F/4/3.
58. See 'Church Farm' in *Tribute* (London, 1926).
59. Van to Curzon, 15 and 31 May 1922, C.P.
60. See his correspondence with Curzon, May–July 1922, C.P.
61. This passage is based on Hardinge to Crowe, 16 August 1922, and Crowe to Curzon, 19 August 1922, C.P. F/5.
62. See Tyrrell to Curzon, 5 September 1922, C.P. F/5.
63. Van to Curzon, 30 March 1921, C.P. F/4/3.
64. Van to Curzon, 19 April 1921, F.O. 800/154.
65. For the Churchill proposals and Van's minutes of 27 June 1921, see C.P. F/4/3.
66. Van to Curzon, 23 November 1922, C.P.
67. *M.P.* 307; also a private communication.
68. See *M.P.*, 307–8; and S. Roskill, *Hankey, Man of Secrets* (London, 1972), ii, 400.

CHAPTER V

The Permanent Under Secretary

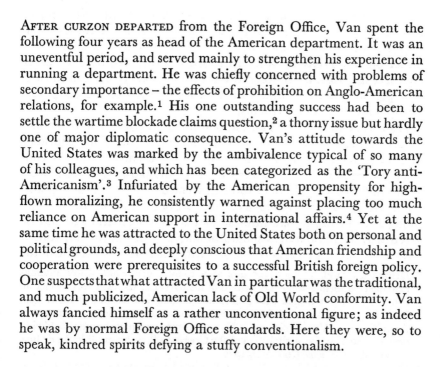

AFTER CURZON DEPARTED from the Foreign Office, Van spent the following four years as head of the American department. It was an uneventful period, and served mainly to strengthen his experience in running a department. He was chiefly concerned with problems of secondary importance – the effects of prohibition on Anglo-American relations, for example.[1] His one outstanding success had been to settle the wartime blockade claims question,[2] a thorny issue but hardly one of major diplomatic consequence. Van's attitude towards the United States was marked by the ambivalence typical of so many of his colleagues, and which has been categorized as the 'Tory anti-Americanism'.[3] Infuriated by the American propensity for high-flown moralizing, he consistently warned against placing too much reliance on American support in international affairs.[4] Yet at the same time he was attracted to the United States both on personal and political grounds, and deeply conscious that American friendship and cooperation were prerequisites to a successful British foreign policy. One suspects that what attracted Van in particular was the traditional, and much publicized, American lack of Old World conformity. Van always fancied himself as a rather unconventional figure; as indeed he was by normal Foreign Office standards. Here they were, so to speak, kindred spirits defying a stuffy conventionalism.

Van's steady run of success since his appointment as Curzon's private secretary brought him to the favourable attention of the leaders of both major political parties, Stanley Baldwin and Ramsay MacDonald. In February 1928 Baldwin, searching for a new private secretary, offered Van the job. Van did not hesitate. On 2 February he crossed

over to 10 Downing Street to begin his new duties, newly promoted
to the rank of assistant under secretary.

What prompted Baldwin to choose Van? We have no precise
knowledge of Baldwin's motives. Van's past record, his American
triumph, even his literary accomplishments, must have furnished a
positive image in Baldwin's eyes.* But in all probability Baldwin's
decision was chiefly a consequence of his determination to reorganize
his private office.[5] Baldwin had long formed clear-cut ideas on this
matter, though it remains a subject for speculation as to why he
waited so long to put them fully into effect. Shocked by the Byzantine character of Lloyd George's personal court and guided by
Warren Fisher's† inspiration, he resolved that his office should be put
on a permanent, regular-service basis, manned by officials seconded
by selection from the civil service lists. His principal private secretary
would hold the rank of assistant under secretary of state (the equivalent to a major-general, according to Fisher's scale of values), and
would draw an additional allowance of five hundred pounds borne
direct on the Treasury vote. In short, Baldwin required a career
civil servant, able, loyal, tolerably ambitious, experienced in the arts
of a private secretary, and with a proven record of success.‡ Van
satisfied all these requirements.

However one explains Van's appointment, there was no precedent
for seconding a senior Foreign Office official as the Prime Minister's
private secretary, and the strangeness of the choice aroused considerable comment. *The Times* called it 'unusual'.[6] Questions were
raised in Parliament. Labour radicals seemed to detect in the appointment a devious political move on the part of the Prime Minister and
thought it 'in the public interest that some information should be
given why all these moves should be made at this particular time'.[7]

One reason was clearly connected with the ambitions of one of the

* Despite his carefully contrived airs as a country gentleman whose interests
  extended no further than the welfare of his livestock, Baldwin was in fact an
  extremely cultivated man with a deep and abiding interest in literature. Tom
  Jones (T.J.), Baldwin's confidant, chief speech writer, and deputy secretary to
  the cabinet, was Van's colleague at No. 10. He may well have brought Baldwin's
  attention to Van, for as chairman of the Gregynog Press he published a de luxe
  edition of *The Singing Caravan* in 1932.
† (Norman Fenwick) Warren Fisher (1879–1948): permanent secretary to the
  Treasury and head of civil service, 1919–39. Kn. 1919.
‡ The situation was particularly acute because Baldwin had inherited Sir Ronald
  Waterhouse (Van's predecessor) from Bonar Law and Ramsay MacDonald.
  Waterhouse has since acquired, justifiably so, a notorious reputation as an
  intriguer, and there can be little doubt that at this phase Baldwin thought him
  incompetent and dangerously ambitious and wished to get rid of him.

most powerful and influential figures in Whitehall, Sir Warren Fisher. Throughout Van's career Fisher hovered somewhere in the background. There were those who insinuated that he manipulated Van in much the same manner as he wished to manipulate the entire civil service. During their years in office they were to work closely together, particularly on questions of defence and rearmament on which they shared a similar outlook, though Van's final judgement about him – 'He was the best friend that I ever had in adversity, less good in better days'[8] – was far from complimentary and reflects a parting of the ways in the twilight of both their careers. To what extent he was responsible for Van's appointment is not apparent. Clearly he was consulted; and equally clearly his advice was positive. Fisher believed firmly in the creation of a unified civil service, to include the staff of the Foreign Office, the members of which would be promotable, according to merit, between departments.[9] The appointment of a top Foreign Office official to Number 10, borne on the civil service vote, would constitute a convincing precedent for breaking down the inter-departmental barriers which frustrated Fisher's long-term aims. Obviously Van was not party to Fisher's ambitions, but he was forever conscious that it was politic to keep on the right side of Fisher; and experience proved him correct. 'Make friends with Fisher', he warned one of his juniors. 'It's no good to quarrel with the Treasury.'[10]

No sooner had he settled in at 10 Downing Street than personal tragedy struck. On budget day 1928, Van was hard at work at the House of Commons. Suddenly he received an urgent message to return home without delay. On arrival, he found that his eldest stepson, Robert, had met with a fatal accident: the safety lift had caught and crushed him. Van's relationship with him, at first restrained, had later developed into one of genuine affection. Towards the end, Van saw in him a younger version of his brother. 'Another Arnold gone', he mourned. 'He had only goodness and courage.'[11]

But this calamity was only the prelude to an even greater tragedy. His wife, of an acutely nervous disposition, long sick despite all efforts to cure her, was unable to withstand the shock of losing her eldest son. Exhausted physically and mentally, she suffered a severe relapse. Three months later, at the age of thirty-six, she died in her sleep. She was buried at the family church at North Cray on 5 July 1928. Van, whatever his innermost feelings, preserved an outward reticence about the circumstances of his wife's death. He merely recorded: 'I have cried a lot in my time. We will not "go on about it".'[12] Shortly afterwards the father of Van's younger stepson, Jay Robinson-Duff, returned to London to claim his surviving son. Van resisted. He fought and lost an expensive lawsuit. It was an agonizing footnote to the most shattering personal episode in his life. At one fell swoop his family was reduced from five to two.

Van sustained himself in work. In Baldwin he discovered a sympathetic support to guide him through his personal crisis. 'Make Downing Street your home',[13] he wrote to Van. Accepting the invitation, Van found in the older man's wider experience and outward calm refuge from his personal distress. On the occasion of Baldwin's death, Van recollected that 'it was just not possible for one man to have been kinder to another'.[14] His final portrait of Baldwin is both sympathetic and perceptive.[15] Inevitably they disagreed about foreign affairs, and Van's persistent harping on the dangers that lay ahead earned him, for the first but not last time, the epithet of 'Cassandra'.[16] But Van was careful to tone down his criticism. He went out of his way to dispel the legends surrounding Baldwin on this score and reduce them to more human proportions. Even when Baldwin's reputation had sunk to its lowest level, he reminded his forgetful audience that although he dissented from much of Baldwin's foreign policy, the scurrilous criticism levelled against him 'was uttered with insufficient knowledge of the inner man and the inner facts, and was therefore unjust'.[17]

With the formation of Ramsay MacDonald's second minority government in June 1929, Van's future appeared uncertain. Having just joined Baldwin's staff, there was no reason to expect a Labour administration to retain him. Quite the contrary, there was every reason to expect a purge among the staff at 10 Downing Street. But MacDonald's mind did not move in so straight a line. Immediately after the elections, Van was approached by an intermediary of his, Wing Commander Sir Louis Grieg, and asked whether he would be willing to continue to serve at Number 10. In a letter to Lord Stamfordham, the king's private secretary, Grieg explained that MacDonald had long been 'impressed by Vansittart and how sorry he was not to have had him when P.M. He further declared that if ever he was back in power, his intention was to get him as private secretary.'[18]

Something of his affection for Baldwin flowed over into his relations with MacDonald. MacDonald's first period in office, though short in time, had been fruitful in foreign policy-making initiatives; and Van, like many of the Foreign Office staff, had been agreeably surprised by MacDonald's energy and ability. These were telling reasons for remaining on at Downing Street; but there were others. For eighteen months he had sat in the very centre of the country's power structure, dealing with a multifarious collection of problems, and participating in their solution when necessary. He enjoyed his position of authority and the scope it offered him. Van was clearly reluctant to return to the more drab routine of Foreign Office work.

There were last-minute hitches, however. Insinuations had already been voiced regarding the propriety of Van's first appointment. Now the situation was infinitely more involved. Elements among Labour's rank and file publicly questioned the political neutrality of the civil service. By way of answering his critics, MacDonald decided upon a clear division of labour between his private secretaries. One would act as the liaison between himself and the Labour Party; the other would be responsible for contact with the Palace and government departments. Van was offered the second of these posts. Unsure of what lay ahead, and perhaps already sensitive to public criticism, he explained to MacDonald the difficulties he envisaged in accepting such a job. MacDonald was adamant: 'I haven't changed my mind. My need is for somebody who will say No to me, and I think you will.'[19] Obviously flattered by MacDonald's response, he accepted. Whatever Van's relations were like with MacDonald, he was clearly out of step with Labour's ideologues and their minions. And Van reciprocated in kind. It was not the most conductive atmosphere in which to work.

Van remained with MacDonald until the end of the year. His main task was to help MacDonald improve Anglo-American relations, and he worked closely in cooperation with the Prime Minister to attain this aim, accompanying him on his successful trip to the United States and Canada in the autumn of 1929.[20] Soon after their return, on 13 November 1929, a communiqué was issued to the press stating that Van would replace Sir Ronald Lindsay as Permanent Under Secretary at the Foreign Office.[21] Lindsay, a rather pedestrian figure, had been head of the Office for two years. From the outset his relations with Arthur Henderson, the Foreign Secretary,* had been strained.[22] It was clear that, given the right pretext, Lindsay's days as PUS were numbered. Accordingly, when Esmé Howard

---

* Arthur Henderson (1863–1935): Labour M.P., 1903–31, 1933–35; Secretary of Labour Party, 1911–34; member of war cabinet, 1916–17; Home Secretary 1924; Foreign Secretary, 1929–31; President of World Disarmament Conference, 1932–34; awarded Nobel peace price, 1934.

retired from the Washington embassy, Henderson replaced him with Lindsay.

The Times had noted that 'There is no other candidate in Downing Street with his [Van's] experience, distinction of mind and versatility.'[23] Judicious though this verdict might sound, Van's appointment did not pass without some envious eyes being cast in his direction. Van later recollected that he had no ambition to become PUS. 'Why hurry back to a trade on which politicians steadily encroached?. . . What if my views were too simple for the intellectuals who discover *pro and con* where I could only find *pro or con*.'[24] Yet it is inconceivable that a career diplomat like Van, whatever his inner doubts and uncertainties, would not have leapt at the opportunity of heading his profession. Perhaps he feigned indifference because it was the gentlemanly way of saying Yes. Nevertheless, his appointment caught the Foreign Office by surprise, at least at the junior level. Having left for Downing Street only two years previously, it was not expected that he would return so swiftly and in such a spectacular manner. Some of the senior officials scarcely concealed their resentment.[25] There was also the question of his age. Van was only forty-eight years old when he took office, together with Capability Hardinge the youngest PUS of this century.* Usually the post was offered when the candidate had reached his mid-fifties; and the appointment was generally considered as the last lap before retirement, or as the penultimate stage to one of the great embassies. In some circles it was felt that Van had been elevated too quickly; 'a shade too early', in one official's words.

Were there any rival candidates? The most talked-of alternative was Sir Eric Drummond.† Five years older than Van, a product of Eton where he too had been Captain of the Oppidans and had carried off the Prince Consort Prize in French, Drummond had worked his way up the ladder by a series of private secretaryships. After ten years at Geneva he could reasonably claim to be amongst the most experienced of British diplomats. However Drummond, for all his administrative skill, was a somewhat remote and unpopular

---

* Their ages on the assumption of office as PUS were: 'Lamps' Sanderson, 53; Hardinge, 48; Arthur Nicolson, 61; Eyre Crowe, 56; Tyrrell, 59; Lindsay, 51; Vansittart, 48; Cadogan, 54; Orme Sargent, 62; William Strang, 56; Ivone Kirkpatrick, 56. Average age, 54.9

† James Eric Drummond (1876–1951): entered Foreign Office, 1900; private secretary to Asquith, Grey, and Balfour; Secretary-General to League of Nations, 1919–33; British Ambassador in Rome, 1933–39. Kn. 1916. Succeeded as 16th Earl of Perth, 1937.

figure, and it was suspected that behind the façade of success lurked an indolent and indecisive character. At least one source states categorically that Drummond was offered the post but that he rejected it on the grounds that 'he honestly did not feel it right to leave the League until the international situation improves'.[26] Some other indirect evidence points in the same direction. Van himself admitted to having been 'foisted'[27] upon Henderson, though he may have been referring to his alleged reluctance to accept the post.

Sir Walford Selby, a fierce opponent of Van's who had served as Arthur Henderson's private secretary, wrote that it was Sir Warren Fisher, in his capacity as head of the civil service, who 'defeated Mr Henderson's intentions as regards the filling of the vacancy in the post of Permanent Under Secretary'.[28] Selby was quite a prickly individual and not at all popular with his colleagues, two of whom described him as 'a lightweight'.[29] Selby mentions no names, but the inference is clear that Henderson did not want Van. Rumours to this effect were current at the time. One official described the appointment as 'scandalous', and was convinced that it came to pass only because of Van's friendship with Fisher and because of the latter's uncontrollable appetite to swallow the entire civil service.[30] Another implied that it was the result of 'string-pulling', of an 'intrigue' concocted by Van and Fisher while they were at Number 10.[31] While discarding the exaggerated nature of these claims, one cannot entirely discount this hearsay. But there is no tangible evidence to back it up. Fisher's alleged influence over Foreign Office appointments has been adequately discussed elsewhere,[32] and a reassessment of the evidence, on the whole circumstantial in nature and lacking in any solid documentary backing, only confirms the conclusion that the main charges against Fisher are considerably inflated.

The main reason, however, for Drummond's exclusion lay in his lack of departmental experience, and, perhaps of more importance, in his relationship with MacDonald.[33] MacDonald disliked him intensely. In the Prime Minister's nonconformist eyes his fellow Scot had committed an unforgivable sin by converting to Roman Catholicism. MacDonald's enmity was decisive. Henderson may well have put forward Drummond's candidature. But if so, MacDonald must have vetoed it. When Drummond retired from the League, MacDonald refused him the Paris and Washington embassies. Instead he was exiled, ironically enough, to Rome.

MacDonald regarded Van as a much happier choice, as did most of the Foreign Office staff.[34] They had been on close terms since

1924. There were no 'ideological' differences separating them such as ruined the relations between Drummond and MacDonald. Rather their extrovert characters tended to harmonize, or at least not clash overtly. No doubt MacDonald saw in Van his own man. Perhaps he believed that Van would direct Henderson in accordance with his own plans; that he would become MacDonald's eye and hand in the Foreign Office. If so, this proved to be a fallacious assumption. Van was of too independent and forceful a character to accept such a humble role. He was nobody's tool, neither Fisher's nor MacDonald's, and he did not hesitate to stand up to any of his chiefs when the occasion demanded it.

When Van took up his appointment as Permanent Under Secretary, he was forty-eight years of age. Tall, he stood six feet and one inch, and lean in appearance, with a darkish complexion and high oriental-like cheekbones, he generated an impression of vitality and warmth. There was something theatrical and mysterious about his appearance, and he seemed to foster the image of the dynamic actor-manager type that he had been all too familiar with in his youth. This was partly a result of his physical characteristics, and partly due to his mode of dress. He was a fashionable, though not ostentatious dresser, and was usually to be found with a fresh, white carnation in his button-hole.[35] Sartorially, the most telling accusations levelled against him were that 'he wore co-respondent's shoes in August' and dressed 'with such unspiritual smartness'. It all added to the impression of the debonair man-about-town, socializing, dabbling in the theatre, and not averse to a flutter on the horses or to the turn of a card. It was an image, needless to say, which contained an element of the truth but which was far removed from representing his total personality.

If one had to employ one word to describe the essence of Van it would have to be that indefinable yet highly expressive noun 'charm'. Every acquaintance of his encountered by the author emphasized this aspect of his character. Most succumbed to it. Once, after two hours of talk with a highly-placed Foreign Office official, the lady of the house burst into the room to insist upon 'the utter charm of Van', and then, her duty done, she lapsed into silence for the remainder of the morning. It was difficult to resist the pervasive influence of his charm. He also made the most of his ability to radiate his magnetism though never in any contrived manner. Although entrenched at the pinnacle of his profession, he was not an unapproachable figure, and certainly not like one of those 'God-like under secretaries who didn't talk to anyone'. Of course, the degree of contact depended upon where you stood in the pecking-order of the Foreign Office hierarchy. Those closer to the top had easier access. But many of the juniors remember being invited to breakfast or lunch at Van's Park Street mansion where he would put his diffident guests at ease and invariably amuse them with his unconventional small talk. Sessions of tennis or squash or swimming would also occasion an opportunity to break down Office barriers. The more favoured juniors were blessed with a visit to his country estate at Denham. Here, in his rural setting, they were pleasantly surprised by his lack of social convention; and at times amazed by his patience. One unfortunate individual recollected how he put his foot accidentally through a concealed ceiling and, expecting the worst, was astonished at 'how well Van took it'.

Yet for all his efforts to break the ice, Van remained, inevitably, a somewhat remote figure to his staff. No doubt this was partly due to his style of living, but also, and perhaps mainly, because of the rigid hierarchical structure of the Office which did not permit too close a contact. Some of his juniors felt as though he was patronizing them, though in the most inoffensive way. As one official wryly put it, 'it was like being asked to tea by the headmaster'.

Van took an almost paternalistic interest in the welfare of his staff. Shortly after his second marriage, as a wedding gift to the service, the Vansittarts launched a kind of civil service benefit fund for those members who were not well off and who needed financial assistance in moments of personal crisis.[36] At times, his generosity exceeded the limits of his fund. It was known, for example, that he personally contributed towards the hospital bills of Allen Leeper,* one of his closest aides, shortly before Leeper's untimely death in 1935.[37] They did not sustain their interest after the first initial period of enthusiasm. Lady Vansittart believed that the scheme had petered out by the time war came. By then Van certainly had other things on his mind, but his encouragement of the sports ground at Hillingdon remained until his retirement.

The main duties of a PUS are to ensure the smooth administrative functioning of the Office; to recommend promotions and dismissals; to act as the chief contact with ambassadors abroad, and to receive foreign ambassadors in London; and, of course, to tender advice to

---

* Alexander Wigram Allen Leeper (1887–1935): seconded to Foreign Office from British Museum, 1915–18; member of British delegation to Versailles conference; first secretary, 1924; counsellor, 1934.

the Secretary of State on matters appertaining to foreign affairs. Van's working day was planned in accordance with this new routine. He arrived at the Foreign Office at ten and remained until five in the afternoon, with just enough flexibility at both ends of the scale. His staff accustomed themselves to his habits. One could not understand why he insisted upon a two-hour lunch break, gently hinting that they could get through more work if they would cut down their eating habits. Van retorted: 'I want the young men of the Office to be free to go into the City or Clubs, and they must have two hours for that.' About one quarter of his working time was spent in interviews and meetings; the remainder on paper work. During the evenings and over the weekends he had his boxes to cope with.

Even the kindest of Van's critics would be forced to admit that administration was not his chief forte, and on this score he clashed with both Fisher and Hankey* as will become evident later. Nevertheless, the enormous quantity of work involved in his new duties left him no option but to plead for greater efficiency and swiftness when dealing with the ever-mounting piles of despatches. Often Van saw a paper ten or eleven days after it had been registered. 'This is much too slow going', he wrote, pleading for a greater sense of urgency among his staff.

Van also took criticism well; or at least he showed no outward sign of anger when confronted with a contradictory viewpoint. Although his opinions were held with a passionate conviction – Eden, in this respect, called him 'ruthless', and Hoare underlined his 'singleness of purpose'[38] – he had an abundant capacity to listen to the other person's point of view. One official noted that after a strong exchange of opinion over a question of great importance he felt that 'their relationship grew even stronger'. In a sense this was simply a general manifestation of the attentiveness – perhaps politeness – which he invariably displayed towards those who worked under him, revealing perhaps a slight feeling of unease at the unexpected position of power which he had acquired. 'The very modesty with which he would receive some minor, routine service – the quick, wide, startled grimace of a smile, the machine-gun fire of grateful phrases – suggested that he still couldn't bring himself to take even his own subordinates' good-will for granted.'[39]

Humour too was a quality not lacking in his character. Sir David

---

* Maurice Pascal Alers Hankey (1877–1963): Secretary to Committee of Imperial Defence, 1912–38; to Cabinet, 1919–38; Minister without Portfolio, 1939–40; Chancellor of Duchy of Lancaster, 1940–41; Paymaster-General, 1941–42. Kn. 1916. Cr. Baron, 1939.

Kelly* has written that 'his witty comments always imparted a cheer-ful and soothing note into our frenzied conveyor-belt of files and boxes'. On one occasion Kelly, then working in the American De-partment, sent up a report explaining a programme of festivities to commemorate the second centenary of the birth of George Washing-ton. They were planned to extend some nine months. Van rejoiced: 'It is evidently intended to celebrate the conception as well as the birth of George Washington.'[40]

The passing of years only mellowed his sense of fun. At the out-break of the Second World War, a certain baronet had the habit of sitting under the stairs at St James's Club and chattering endlessly to the despair of all around him. One day a soldier, exasperated beyond reason by this infuriating phenomenon, referred in a loud voice to that 'f . . . ing old bore'. The baronet took offence and demanded that the soldier resign immediately. Van was requested to intervene. He asked the baronet what in this description he objected to. *Every-thing!* . . . Van: 'I can quite understand your feeling insulted if he had merely called you an old bore, but I should have thought that men of our age would think it quite a compliment to be called what he called you.' Apparently this interpretation had escaped the notice of the baronet. He abandoned his claim mollified and with a new lease on life.[41]

Not in all matters did Van evince such a liberal and understanding attitude. His daughter thought that 'he set high moral and ethical standards for himself and expected others to live to the same stan-dards'. An admirable proposition no doubt; but only on the assump-tion that all people are alike and hence subject to the 'same standards' in their personal life. Such a rigid conception of human behaviour leads one inevitably into the morass of intolerant generalizations and often bigotry. Take, for example, Van's attitude towards sexual mores. 'People thought the better of you if you had a mistress, and better still if she was well-known', he once joyfully reminisced to one of his officials. This was man's traditional role, that of hunter, and he heartily endorsed it, provided it was accomplished circumspectly and with the correct degree of grace. Any deviation earned his displeasure. He developed an almost pathological hatred of homo-sexuality, condemning out of hand the 'new laxity towards *ces messieurs* of perversion'.[42] In May 1954 he rose in the House of Lords to warn

* David Victor Kelly (1891–1959); entered diplomatic service, 1919; served at Buenos Aires, Lisbon, Mexico, Brussels, Stockholm, Cairo, and Foreign Office; counsellor, 1938; minister at Berne, 1940–42; Ambassador at Buenos Aires, 1942; to Turkey, 1946–49; to U.S.S.R., 1949–51. Kn. 1942.

'that this vice cannot be checked without a revival of the reprobation with which it was once regarded'. He argued against any liberalization of the laws governing homosexuality. 'If we smooth the path of the adult evil-doer, we automatically increase the prospect of the perversion of the young.'[43] It was a prejudiced, insensitive speech. It seemed sad that Van, who was normally flexible and rational, and who was in so many areas of his own life unorthodox and nonconformist, should have adopted such a regressive and puritanical attitude. 'You have a rigid mind,' Churchill once told him. Van admitted it in respect to his 'attitude towards communism, Deutschism, and homosexuality'.[44]

St James's Club was Van's favourite refuge. Although he was elected to membership of the Athenaeum in February 1947, he rarely used its facilities. St James's – 'where the grandest diplomats go' – remained his first choice for more than fifty years. The Club's physical presence appeared less imposing than that of other fashionable London clubs. The rooms were smaller, the members less in evidence, the servants more unobtrusive. (They too remembered Van well: 'a charming man, so quiet'.) The decor was restful, 'distinguished' to use one member's proud definition. The green motif seemed to dominate.

On the first floor one enters the bridge room. This is a small, overwhelmingly green room, which exudes an aura of seclusion and decorum. It was in this sanctuary that Van spent many of his free hours. From his early youth he had been attracted by most forms of gambling. Horse racing, cards, the roulette wheel, had all competed, on occasions successfully, with his official duties. Bridge became a more mature substitute for his youthful endeavours. Almost every day, duty permitting, Van would spend the hours before dinner at the Club playing bridge at his favourite corner table with some of his cronies in an atmosphere 'thick with smoke'. He was a competent enough player. His card bill always balanced, or very nearly so.* But he did not play for gain. For Van the card-playing sessions, the camaraderie of his clique, the cocoon-like atmosphere, were a necessary distraction from the buffetings of his official life. And as the 1930's wore on to their grim finale, so Van's need to escape to more sympathetic surroundings increased. At the Foreign Office he found himself more and more an isolated figure. Around the

---

* One official insisted that he 'was known to lose £50 or £100 in one evening'; but this is certainly an exaggeration and does not tally with any other evidence which the author heard.

bridge table his cares dissolved in an atmosphere of social congeniality and comradely partnership. In many ways his card sessions were psychologically necessary for him to break loose from the nervous tension and personal frustration which suffocated so much of his official life.

For Van, despite, or perhaps because of, his outward show of social affability and confidence, was in fact a sensitive, emotional and highly strung individual. On some he left 'the impression that he was always on the verge of bubbling over'. These were characteristics which conditioned much of his behaviour and, at times, his health. Of course, this was not so apparent to those who came into contact with him only fleetingly, or even to his colleagues at Whitehall. But those who knew him intimately, away from the bustle and role-acting, were aware of his inner misgivings and his inability to relax. This expressed itself in day-to-day mannerisms. Although by no means a *gourmet*, he was moderately fond of good food and wine, and enjoyed eating at his favourite restaurant, the *Coq d'Or*. Yet he ate and drank as though 'unaware' of the delicacies placed before him, racing through each course and eating 'far too fast to appreciate the cooking'. He was apprehensive of great heights, possibly of high speeds. He never flew, preferring the leisurely, nineteenth-century mode of travel by ship and train. He never learned to drive, though this may well have been an indication of his inability to grasp the mysteries of twentieth-century technology. At any rate, when being driven he would immerse himself in his official papers, blithely ignoring the passing countryside, refusing to be disturbed by the twists and turns of the speeding car, and displaying 'a wonderful sense of balance'. During the Second World War he developed into an accomplished orator, and became a familiar figure on the public platform or on the benches of the House of Lords. Yet he was racked by nerves before each performance: 'his hand would tremble when preparing the outline of the speech'.

His nervous disposition also impressed itself upon his young daughter, Cynthia. 'Don't say anything to upset Daddy today', she would be warned constantly. Cynthia also remembers Van's persistent premonition about having his house burgled. Although he had many servants, he would personally check all the doors and windows to make sure they were locked before retiring. He would never relinquish a key of the house to anyone, not even Cynthia, who would therefore have to return home at the unlikely hour of 11 pm or else find herself locked out.

During periods of acute political tension he was subject to bouts of melancholy. On one occasion, just before the outbreak of war, he abandoned in despair an official engagement at Buckingham Palace, totally dejected by the opulent display of luxury and amusement at a time when the country was on the brink of war. After the war, with the horrifying disclosures of German atrocities, he sank into a deep depression. He said to Lady Vansittart: 'The world has turned so ugly that but for you I wouldn't mind going.' He began to ruminate on the mysteries of death, wondering if it was not like 'a long night'.

Often his health was affected. At the height of the Munich crisis he confided to Hugh Dalton* that he was sleeping only four hours a night, and that 'he did not want to become dependent upon drugs for his sleep'.[45] With the approach of war his anxieties increased. He developed a duodenal ulcer. During the winter of 1940–41, when he was preparing the controversial *Black Record* broadcasts, he decided 'to starve over Christmas' on a milk diet, a decision easier reached than kept, for he soon began to eat and drink normally. Dalton noted that 'His judgement is now very uncertain.'[46] At the same time he contracted a skin disease which first attacked his arms. He wore gloves as a protection but it later spread to other parts of his body. His doctor was convinced that this was a psychosomatic ailment brought on by his generally nervous frame of mind.

Altogether the first months of the war were a distressing time. He was obsessed with the notion of falling captive to the Nazis should they overrun the country.† Eventually, Lady Vansittart secured from their doctor a potent sedative. It helped him to relax. On one occasion he was asked what he would do if invasion came. 'Then he paused, slowly moving his right hand to softly pat his left waistcoat pocket, remarking almost casually: "I always carry here my ultimate protection should the very worst happen".'[47] It was during these months that Van destroyed many of his private papers, fearful of compromising his friends and political contacts, particularly those in Germany.

But the most poignant expression of Van's state of mind was his decision to send Cynthia to the United States. He was not an unaffectionate father. Indeed to his immediate family he was quite

---

* Hugh John Neale Dalton (1887–1962): lecturer at London School of Economics, 1919–36; Labour M.P., 1924–31, 1935–59; Under Secretary of State for Foreign Affairs, 1929–31; Minister of Economic Warfare, 1940–42; President of Board of Trade, 1942–45; Chancellor of Exchequer, 1945–47. Cr. Life Peer, 1960.

† Van occupied a prominent place on the Nazis' blacklist. Hitler himself placed Van third among England's 'guilty men', after Churchill and Hore-Belisha. See H. Trevor Roper, *Hitler's Table Talk* (London, 1953), 276.

demonstrative. Cynthia was studying at Heathfield, a boarding school near Ascot. 'Van was an attentive father', taking an interest in his daughter's education and visiting the school regularly on sports' day and such like occasions.* In the general panic of 1940 he judged that his daughter would be safer with her American relatives. Of course, his was not an isolated decision. Almost seventeen thousand children were sent overseas, five thousand of whom found homes in the United States.[48] Yet this was not 'a family decision', but Van's alone. Cynthia resented being sent away. Van insisted. She left England in September 1940, at the age of seventeen, as it happened for ever. They did not meet again until 1947. Cynthia became a resident of the United States, married there in 1955, and visited Van five times in all until his death in 1957.

In July 1931 Van remarried. His bride, Sarita, was the widow of Sir Colville Barclay, a diplomatist and an old acquaintance of Van's who had died two years earlier. Sarita was the elder daughter of Herbert Ward, the artist, who had at one time accompanied Livingstone on his journeys in Central Africa. Ward later retired to Paris, a very wealthy man. On his death he left to both his daughters (the younger, Frances, married Sir Eric Phipps, British Ambassador to Germany and France during the 1930's) trust funds to be operated from the United States by the Guaranty Trust.† Within the closed circle of Foreign Office social life, Van had known the Barclays well for many years. After Sir Colville's death they drew closer together, perhaps bound by the common tragedy in their lives. They were seen much in public together. Sarita would often watch Van play tennis. Reporters began to link their names. When Sarita spent her Easter holidays at her villa in the South of France, Van pursued her. Together they read a notice in the *Evening Standard* that they had become engaged. Sarita registered her amazement, for she had been widowed for only two years 'and was not thinking of getting married again'. Van argued: 'Wouldn't it be silly to change it?' They did not do so. They were married on 29 July, at St Mary's Church, Denham. It was a small and unpretentious wedding, with only the immediate family circle present.

Sarita introduced into his life a stability and balance which had

---

* Among the other pupils at the school was Joachim Ribbentrop's daughter, Bettina. Cynthia remembered that 'they were awful' to her. It does not appear as though Van and Ribbentrop met on the sports field at Heathfield.

† The exact size of the trust fund was a matter for inspired speculation, but it was certainly considerable and rumoured to be in the region of £40,000 p.a.

been lacking since 1928. His home, instead of being a place to escape from, became an additional source of strength. At least in his personal life he had found a secure anchor. Although Van was certainly an attractive man and seemed to enjoy the company of pretty women there was never the whisper of a scandal attached to his name. All were agreed that his marriage was a love match. Those who came into contact with them recall, almost without exception, the 'quite exceptional charm and beauty and kindness of Lady Vansittart'. She was deeply in love with Van. So much that in later years she developed an almost embarrassingly uncritical attitude towards his career and achievements. The overwhelming impression is one of conjugal bliss.

When in London, the Vansittarts lived at 44 Park Street. It was an enormous house, long since destroyed to make way for a smart office block. Overnight Van had acquired a large family. Cynthia, his own daughter, and the three Barclay boys, Colville, Cecil, and Robert, all came to live at Number 44. He managed very well with his step-sons, who soon felt that 'they could talk to him man-to-man', while Cynthia and Lady Vansittart developed a close friendship which has remained to this day. Cynthia remembered 'a lot of social activity' at Park Street. Many foreign dignitaries were entertained there. Churchill was a regular visitor, as were Edward VIII and Mrs Simpson. Van often lunched at home, so-called business lunches, and when there were not too many visitors, or it was not too late, the whole family would dine together.

The village of Denham lies some twenty miles west of London along the Oxford road. To the visitor it contains all the necessary ingredients of the 'typical' English village: a twisting, narrow central road, flanked by a number of pubs, picturesque cottages, slightly more substantial residences, and some quaint shops. At the farthest end of the village one encounters the village green. Bordering one side of it is a high, brown-brick wall. Beyond the wall one discovers 'The Beautiful and Well Known William and Mary Residence, Denham Place.'[49] The origins of this stately and dignified home are ancient and can be traced back to the mid-sixteenth century. By the end of the century it came into the possession of the Bowyer family, well-known as 'staunch loyalists'; it was rumoured that after the Battle of Worcester, the Royal Princes were harboured at Denham. In 1688, the year of the 'Glorious Revolution', Sir Roger Hill purchased the estate. An active supporter of the House of Orange, he decided to build himself a residence more suitable to his rank and status than the old, fairly modest establishment. It took him thirteen years and cost him £5,591.9d before he was finally satisfied with the result. The house that stands today is the product of Sir Roger's industry. Succeeding generations of the Hill family occupied it until eventually, through marriage, it came into the hands of the Way family who retained it until Lady Vansittart first saw it in early 1930.

Ever since the death of her first husband, Lady Vansittart had been searching for a country house which would enable her to be close to her two boys at Eton. In April 1930, the Duke of Leeds told her about 'a fine house just outside London'. She quickly made arrangements to see it. When she arrived 'It was a foggy day, but after inspecting only two rooms, I decided to take it. I felt from the beginning a strange feeling of familiarity with the house.' Lady Vansittart remained there until 1969 when the high cost of its upkeep forced her to move to smaller premises in London.

It would be difficult to overestimate the importance Denham Place fulfilled in Van's life. In a sense it rekindled memories of his childhood days. His family too had been the owner of vast – even vaster – estates. His father too had succeeded to the position of country squire late in life, and had revelled in his new responsibilities. So too with Van. He loved to play the role of the country gentleman; or later, after his retirement, the role of monarch-in-exile. And Denham Place provided him with a magnificent tableau to act out his part. Despite the vagaries of fortune, Van had finally come into his own. Sir John Wheeler-Bennett* related how Van would meet him at the station and 'take him off to Denham via the fields of the estate, with a servant to carry the bags and assorted acknowledgements from the peasants on all sides'. Richard Crossman,† in a characteristic aside, stressed the theatricality of Denham: 'A castle with a moat‡ and inside the French duc with his Lady embroidering tapestry.'

---

* John Wheeler-Bennett (1902–76): official of League of Nations Union and Chatham House; employed in British propaganda programme in the United States, 1941–44; in Political Intelligence Department of Foreign Office, 1944–45; attached to British prosecuting team at Nürnberg trials; historian and author of many works on contemporary international relations. Kn. 1959.

† Richard (Howard Stafford) Crossman (1907–74): fellow and tutor at New College, Oxford, 1930–37; assistant editor of *New Statesman and Nation*, 1938–55, editor, 1970–72; Labour M.P., 1945–74; Minister of Housing and Local Government, 1964–66; leader of House of Commons and Lord President of Council, 1966–68; Secretary of State for Social Services, 1968–70; journalist and author of works on political thought and government.

‡ Needless to say there is no moat at Denham Place. But a river does run through the grounds.

Although Denham was only listed as a manor house, it was a very grand manor house indeed. Along the staircase-hall and round the dining-room hung portraits of Vansittart notables. The pictures are not worth a great deal in themselves, though the frames are very finely ornamented. Van made little effort to acquire them, relying on Lady Vansittart's sense of judgement. But the prominent position they held throughout the house suggests that they contributed to his sense of history, and that he, Sir Robert Vansittart, was continuing the family tradition of service to the state.

Some of the other attractions of Denham included a private chapel, with a sixteenth-century screen; five entertaining rooms, including a tapestry room and a dining room with a white Adam fireplace; six bedroom suites – the Vansittarts had an unusual addition, 'a wig room'; the usual domestic quarters; vaulted cellars; stables; and garaging for up to ten cars, though the Vansittarts had only three, including a Rolls-Royce and Vauxhall 14. On the immediate grounds were six cottages; a kitchen garden; a rose garden; and a formal garden – modelled on the gardens at Hampton Court. Through it all flowed the River Misbourne to form an ornamental lake fringed by willow trees. The total area of the estate ran to ninety-six acres. To run this large establishment the Vansittarts were helped by twelve servants* and five gardeners. Even today, though the house is closed (the gardens, happily, are still cared for) the overall impression is one of superb magnificence, albeit of a bygone age.

Van became deeply attached to Denham and towards the end of his life rarely spent a night away from it.[50] Every weekend, and often during the week, he would travel to his domain. Once there he would immerse himself in country life. Pottering around the gardens, weeding, keeping an eye on his vegetables, tending his Chinese geese and pigs, listening to the troubles of his tenants. Visitors were frequent. Some added their own eccentricities. Sir George Clerk,† by reputation the best dressed man in the service, would come to Denham and insist on spending his time sawing logs.

Ensuring that Denham remained 'One of the Show Houses of England' was no easy matter. Burglars pestered them, but their designs were usually frustrated by the alertness of Van's two alsatian

---

* The breakdown was as follows: a butler; two footmen; an odd job man; three housemaids; a companion to Lady Vansittart; three kitchen staff; and a chauffeur.

† George Russell Clerk (1874–1951): entered foreign service, 1899; Ambassador to Turkey, 1926–33; to Belgium, 1933–34; to France, 1934–37. Kn. 1917.

guard dogs, Peter and Paul.[51] Fire was a much more dangerous hazard. At the end of December 1952, a large quantity of burning soot fell into the oak-panelled library. The Vansittarts immediately began to roll back the carpets and rugs and started carrying out the furniture. It was only owing to their prompt reaction that very little damage was caused.[52]

The upkeep of the house and grounds must have been an enormous commitment. It is a striking indication of the Vansittarts' income that they maintained Denham Place together with their Park Street mansion without undue scrimping. However, the ownership of such splendid properties raised problems not necessarily connected with material considerations. It was once pointed out that Van had no need to indulge in social climbing 'as he had already arrived'. His material well-being, indeed luxury, was probably without precedent among the Permanent Under Secretaries of this century, or even of the nineteenth century. He could, and did, entertain on the royal scale. At the height of war-time austerity, Harold Nicolson went down to Denham to stay overnight. 'He gave me a marvellous dinner: trout, lamb, fruit and a bottle of Pomerdy '98. I slept in an enormous four-poster bed in an enormous room, and my feet, when I crossed the carpet, made a long trail of footsteps in the pile.'[53]

It was at Denham Place or at Park Street that Van received foreign representatives and conducted much of his diplomacy. His ability to entertain on so lavish a scale and in such glorious eighteenth century surroundings set him apart not only from his colleagues at the Office but also from the ministers he served. It would not be extravagant to conclude that some resentment was nursed in high places, particularly by those ministers who were unable to compete with their Permanent Under Secretary. By the same token it may well be that Van himself began to believe in the omnipotence which derived from his own setting. Ivan Maiskey,* a frequent visitor of those years, told him bluntly: 'You should not have been a public servant.'[54] Another experienced commentator noted that Van had a tendency to patronize his ministers. 'He was supremely confident in his own ability and judgement, and considered his ministers as inferior in experience and as amateurs.' In this respect, Eden, who had cause to know Van in his many roles, made, perhaps unwittingly and in a different context, the most pertinent comment: 'The truth is that Vansittart was seldom an official giving cool and disinterested advice based on study and experience. He was himself a sincere,

* Ivan Maiskey (1884–1975): counsellor at Soviet embassy in London, 1925–27; Ambassador to Great Britain, 1932–43.

almost fanatical crusader, and much more a Secretary of State in mentality than a permanent official.'[55] Van himself later admitted: 'I conceded no superiority to politicians except that in a clash they must win.'[56]

As has been observed, Van's literary and theatrical occupations formed an integral part of his life. During the early years of his career he often toyed with the idea of abandoning his profession in favour of writing. Despite his predilection he lacked the necessary self-confidence in his own abilities to take the risk. Perhaps he was right not to have done so. For the truth of the matter was that he never rose above gifted amateur status in his literary achievements. One critic, with a touch of typical exaggeration, put it most cruelly: 'In everything he did he was brilliant as an amateur, but second-rate when judged by the highest standards to which he aspired.'[57] A sweeping, in fact meaningless, generalization concerning his diplomatic work, but regarding his literary *œuvres* it contains a large element of truth. Conceivably, he attempted the impossible. His greatest ambition was to be recognized as an artist of the front rank as well as an outstanding man of public affairs. Such a romantic conception of human versatility was, by the twentieth century, severely outdated. Renaissance man had long since disappeared; and none of Van's efforts proved equal to the task of reviving him. Sadly for Van, he belonged to the era of the specialist.

But there was no easy escape from the twin goals he had set himself. Hankey said of him that he was 'very cultured for a civil servant'.[58] The Office regarded his literary activities as 'amusing'. Yet their consequences were far from amusing, particularly for Van himself, for his literary style flowed over into his official prose with dire results. His prepared memoranda were saturated with epigrams, sparkling metaphors, and tortuous allegorical comparisons. There was no easily discernible meaning to his compositions. They contained a strange and multi-dimensional character that was quite unique. The overall effect was so bewildering as to flummox the average reader. Many of his sentences have to be read at least twice before they can be fully understood. Someone once said of Van: 'I have just been translating one of Van's papers for my master.' Sir Alexander Cadogan, his successor as PUS, complained: 'If he has any ideas or impressions, why can't he put them down straight on paper instead of dancing literary hornpipes.'[59] His style has been variously described as 'boring . . . though we agreed with his views'; 'untactful'; 'Proustian'; 'unbalanced'; 'over-elaborate'; 'like advertising copy'; 'ornate, affected, ghastly'. A minister wrote of his 'keen, active mind, sometimes obscured by tortured language'.[60] It was common knowledge that Van's memoranda made little impact upon his ministers. Arthur Henderson told his private secretary that he 'couldn't understand them'. 'Oh, some more from Van', sighed Halifax when faced with the prospect of tackling more of Van's papers. They were altogether too intense, too allusive, and too repetitious, faults which were commonly attributed to his artistic temperament.[61] All this was in direct contrast with his conversation, or with the minutes he wrote spontaneously on a day-to-day basis. Here he was neither complex nor longwinded. His minutes were pungent, witty, often brief, and had a refreshing vibrant quality about them that stood out from the drab, formal contributions of some of his colleagues.

Of course, his writings were highly polemical. He made no pretence otherwise. And this was perhaps the most compelling reason why his memoranda went unheeded. He was preaching a message which most of his political masters did not wish to hear. He was convinced that there could be no lasting, permanent settlement with Hitler's Germany. This belief separated him from those of his ministers who reasoned that Nazi Germany could be returned to the European fold by rational discussion and sensible compromise. Politicians do not like being told incessantly that their calculations have no basis in reality. Their natural reaction would be to seek advisers who would buttress, not sabotage, their own convictions, however misguided. And this is precisely what they did.

Van's attitude towards religion was correct and proper, certainly less than enthusiastic.[62] His upbringing had been typically Victorian, with church-going and collective family prayers forming a regular part of his daily routine. He accepted it as a natural, even inevitable, burden. Probably all this religion had an adverse, counter-productive effect, for he quickly detected a widening gap between true spirituality and the bureaucratic, entrenched character of organized religion which fed off its own vested interests. For Van religion was not conditioned by association with a particular denominational establishment; it was a wholly personal, private affair. He never cast aside those Christian ethics upon which he had been nurtured. But he did not wait upon the Church to interpret them for him. He railed against the dogma and ritual to which the Church had succumbed, and which, in his estimation, was deflecting it from its original path.

What particularly riled Van was the Church's dithering attitude towards the horrors of Nazi Germany. Here the issue was crystal-clear. Nazi Germany was anti-Christian, anti-civilization. Should not the Church have risen up in defence of Christian ethics, unequivocally and without compromise, against this pagan phenomenon? Instead the Church shilly-shallied, it prevaricated, or worse it played the pacifist game. When a vicious monster attacks you, knife in hand, you do not turn the other cheek. You seek to eliminate it, for that is the only way to ensure that the ethics you wish to preserve will not be submerged beneath a sea of barbarism. The clergy, on the whole, did not live up to Van's expectations.

For the German church he expressed nothing but the greatest contempt. It had betrayed every Christian value without so much as a murmur.

> For generations the German Churches have been infected by militarism, like everything else in Germany. They have aided and abetted every aggressive war, have never lifted a finger to restrain, but have often raised a finger to bless, the excesses of German Authority, civil and military, not only in the heat of battle but in the cold-blooded persecution of the Poles ever since the iniquitous partitions.

When he was at Denham he would read the lesson at church service. And this became a matter of habit during his retirement. He had a preference for the Book of Ecclesiastes, and would often read this instead of from the appointed lesson.[63] This did not signify a return to the Church. He was still playing his own game, choosing his own readings, appearing by request. In a sense it was a game expected of him as the local squire. He enjoyed it. And no doubt he used the pulpit to give free rein to his theatrical talents long since extinguished on the legitimate stage.

Maisky wrote of Van that he was 'flesh of the flesh of the ruling class of Great Britain'.[64] There could be no denying his conventional English upper-class background. The pedigree was impeccable: from a Kentish squirearchy to Eton to the Foreign Office. Few would deny his brilliant gifts, yet for all that he remained something of an outsider. A contemporary of his at Eton remembered that Van was 'a brilliant solitary', 'a loner who did not belong to any clique or circle'. So he remained throughout his life. For some he was 'the undiplomatic diplomat', 'an unusual kind of official', 'a many-sided man' whose wide variety of interests and talents set him apart from the

Van and his first wife, Gladys (née Heppenheimer) on their honeymoon in Venice.

adys, Van's first wife, with her two sons,
Robert (left) and Jay (right).

Van and his two stepsons, Jay (left) and
Robert (right). 'Nanny' is on the right.

Sir Robert Vansittart (far right) at a rehearsal of his play 'Dead Heat' in 1939.
(*Radio Times Hulton Picture Library*)

general conformity of the Foreign Office representatives. Others envisaged him as a kind of guru, above and beyond those he sought to teach and lead. One should beware of succumbing to stereotype definitions. Yet the conclusion cannot easily be avoided that for all Van's Englishness he did not quite belong to the club.

Of course his physical appearance lent great credence to the discredited myth that his origins were from more exotic climes, and this somehow explained his lack of English under-statement, his tendency to exaggerate, his volatile, Latin character. His appearance may have added to his sense of not belonging, but it was not the reason for it. In fact it is almost impossible to explain this phenomenon in either social or professional terms; its roots were more in his temperamental make-up – an imprecise and unsatisfactory conclusion. He did not, for example, shrink from making enemies when in pursuit of his aims. In fact, in a perverse way he seemed to glory in it. His directness and tenacity, almost to the point of professional suicide, were a case in point. He revelled in being too provocative, in shouting his views from the roof-tops. And through his ornate literary style, refined and polished, he flaunted his contempt for those who obstinately refused to comprehend.

Let a foreign diplomat give his impression.

> He had a pleasant, deep, and warm voice. He had an expressive face, though wrinkled. He was 'artistic' and could therefore establish contact much more easily than the typically English, public school type which inhabits the F.O. He was different from that type: far more direct, and did not give the impression that he was trying to be too smart or too stand-offish. In that sense he was more continental than English.[65]

A much closer observer believed that 'Van was the quintessential "outsider"; an outsider to those "inside", but equally an outsider to the conventional "outsider".'[66] A realistic assessment.

NOTES

1. See F.O. 371/10637, A. 52/52/45, and 12048, A. 364/364/45. Also, *F.R.U.S.*, 1926, ii, 350–55.
2. See F.O. 371/11163, A. 4579/6/45, A. 4692/2/45, and 11165, A. 6553/6/45. Also *B.D.*, 1A, ii, 865, 867, 900–01, 913; and *F.R.U.S.*, 1926, ii, 294–308.
3. R. C. Allen, *Great Britain and the United States* (London, 1954), 747.
4. See, for example, his minutes of 4 February 1934, F.O. 371/17593, A. 785/785/45.
5. See Sir Warren Fisher to Baldwin, 3 March 1928, B.P., v, 163.
6. *The Times*, 2 February 1928.

D

7. See *The Times*, 14 March 1928.
8. *M.P.*, 350.
9. See D. C. Watt, *Personalities and Policies* (London, 1965), 104.
10. Private communication.
11. *M.P.*, 356.
12. *M.P.*, 357.
13. *Ibid.*, 358.
14. *P.D.*, Lords, v. 153, c. 324, 17 December 1947.
15. See *M.P.*, 352–6.
16. *Ibid.*, 366.
17. See *P.D.*, Lords, v. 153, c. 324, 17 December 1947.
18. Grieg to Stamfordham, 4 June 1929. Royal Archives (hereafter R.A.), GV K2223/39. The following passage is based, except where stated otherwise, upon this letter.
19. *M.P.*, 371.
20. See *B.D.*, 2, i, 67–8, 106–16, K. Middlemass, ed., *Whitehall Diaries* (London, 1969), ii, 213–14, 217; and *M.P.*, 389–91.
21. *The Times*, 13 November 1929.
22. See H. Dalton, *Memoirs*, i (London, 1953), 219; also *Dalton Diaries*, 9 May 1931.
23. *The Times*, 29 November 1929.
24. *M.P.*, 394.
25. Private communication. See also H. Dalton, *op. cit.*, 247.
26. See D. T. Rotunda, *The Rome Embassy of Sir Eric Drummond* (unpublished Ph.D. thesis, University of London, 1972), 93. No authority is quoted for this statement.
27. *M.P.*, 398.
28. See Selby, *Diplomatic Twilight, 1930–40* (London, 1953), 4. This story is repeated in D. Carlton, *MacDonald versus Henderson* (London, 1970), 23, relying on Selby as the source.
29. From private communications.
30. *Ibid.*
31. *Ibid.*
32. See D. C. Watt, *op. cit.*, 100–102; also G. K. Fry, *Statesmen in Disguise* (London, 1969) 52, n.3. It must be remembered that Fisher, as head of the civil service, was, one assumes, entitled to voice an opinion regarding Foreign Office appointments. Perhaps on occasion his enthusiasm got the better of him. In August 1936, Rex Leeper, an avowed opponent of his, revealed to a friend that Fisher 'hates the Foreign Office, wants to reform it, and was proposing to put Leith-Ross [the government's chief economic adviser] into Van's place if Van went to Paris'. See K. Young (ed.), *The Diaries of Sir Robert Bruce Lockhart, 1915–1938* (London, 1974), 351. Eden provides the weightiest evidence against Fisher. He cites two occasions when Fisher attempted to exert his influence: the first, at the beginning of 1936, when he wanted to put a number of ambassadorial appointments to the Prime Minister; the second, when he proposed Sir Findlater Stewart, PUS at the India Office, to replace Van as head of the Foreign Office in 1938. Eden successfully withstood these attacks. See Avon, *Facing the Dictators* (London, 1961), 319–20, 521.
33. I am grateful to Professor James Barros for information on the following points. See also his book, *Betrayed From Within* (Yale University Press, 1969), 3.

34. Private communications.
35. As much of the material for this section is based on interviews, it would be tiresome to cite references for every quotation or opinion mentioned. I have done so only when absolutely necessary. The interested reader may consult the author for more detailed references. In connection with Van's sartorial habits, see V. Lawford, *Bound for Diplomacy* (London, 1963), 270.
36. Private communication. Also Ramsay MacDonald to Vansittart, 28 May 1932, MacDonald Papers, 2/6.
37. K. Young, *op. cit.*, 352.
38. Avon, *op. cit.*; Templewood, *Nine Troubled Years* (London, 1954), 137–8.
39. Lawford, *op. cit.*, 27.
40. Sir David Kelly, *The Ruling Few* (London, 1952), 210–11.
41. *Dalton Diaries*, 17 June 1941.
42. *M.P.*, 204.
43. *P.D.*, Lords, v, 187, c. 755–7.
44. *M.P.*, 413.
45. *Dalton Diaries*, 5 September 1938.
46. *Dalton Diaries*, 18 December 1940.
47. A. P. Young, *The 'X' Documents*, S. Aster (ed.) (London 1974), 201–2.
48. See A. Calder, *The People's War* (Panther Books, 1971), 149.
49. Much of the information about the early history of Denham Place is derived from a brochure put out by Druce and Company, estate agents, when the estate was being sold in 1969.
50. *M.P.*, 422.
51. See, for example, *The Times*, 19 August 1939.
52. See *The Times*, 29 December 1952.
53. N. Nicolson (ed.), *The Diaries and Letters of Harold Nicolson* (Fontana Books, 1970), ii, 293.
54. *M.P.*, 399.
55. Avon, *op. cit.*, 242.
56. *M.P.*, 399.
57. See R. H. Crossman's notes, *New Statesman*, 10 May 1958.
58. *Dalton Diaries*, 29 April 1931.
59. D. Dilks (ed.), *The Diaries of Alexander Cadogan, 1938–45* (London, 1971), 13.
60. Avon, *op. cit.*, 241.
61. See *M.P.*, 427.
62. Much of the material for this passage is based on *Lessons of my Life*, pp. 148–168. Unless stated otherwise, all quotations are taken from these pages.
63. A private communication.
64. Maisky, *Who Helped Hitler?* (London, 1964), 45.
65. A private communication.
66. A private communication.

CHAPTER VI

The 'Old Adam'

————————⟨⟩————————

IN MAY 1930 THE enigmatic, discredited and half-forgotten figure of 'old Adam', the symbol of pre-1914 diplomatic practice, began to stalk the corridors of the Foreign Office. There he strode, 'jovially overt and unconscious of incompatibility of temperament' with the new era of the League of Nations and international cooperation.[1] Much has been made of this memorandum, the first of Van's 'old Adam' series, perhaps too much. It has been interpreted as a ferocious attack against German ambitions, prophetically warning Europe of the dark future which awaited her as a consequence of Germany's insatiable appetite. True, Van envisaged 'Germany's natural object' as being two-fold: to re-enter the family of European nations on a footing of equality; and to 'modify the penal provisions of the peace settlement which has galled her pride and hampered her national development'. Within this general framework he sketched Germany's foreign policy aims: the re-establishment of Germany as a world power, which would entail the acquisition of colonies and mandates; *Anschluss* with Austria; rearmament, so as to obtain at least parity with Poland; and the drastic modification of Germany's eastern frontier. He also noted the recent rise in popularity of the National Socialists, though he declined to exaggerate its importance, only pointing out that 'under the leadership of the half-mad and ridiculously dangerous demagogue Hitler' the Nazis advocated a policy of uncompromising hostility to the Versailles peace settlement and the policy of fulfilment. Germany, he went on, had already achieved a great deal: the termination of the Allied military commissions; the evacuation of the Rhineland; the Hague reparations settlement. But impressive as these achievements were, the totality of the Allied victory and the humiliation of Vesrailles still lay heavily upon Germany, and her bruised national pride would inevitably push her towards demanding further concessions.

It was an accurate enough summary of the German position; but there was nothing startlingly novel about it. Quite the contrary, these basic objectives of German diplomacy had stubbornly dogged the heels of every post-war German politician from Rathenau to Stresemann to Hitler. They were typical, commonplace slogans fed to almost every German political audience since the débâcle of 1918–19. Small wonder that they should be reflected in a Foreign Office memorandum discussing German foreign policy.

The really curious point about the first of the 'old Adam' series is how little space Van devoted to the German question and how much he bestowed upon 'the Latin sisters', Italy and France. He castigated Mussolini's policy of prestige. About France he was even more critical. Her system of alliances, her obsession with the balance of power, her virtual hegemony over Europe, all created a state of affairs unparalleled since the days of Napoleon. The French, he concluded, were conducting a policy incompatible with the new post-war concepts of 'moral disarmament and cooperation'. Van was pleading for greater morality in international politics and arguing against the selfish *Realpolitik* blindly pursued by France and Italy. To all this he added one fundamental rider. It was of absolute importance to accord to British policy sufficient strength to command respect, if not fear, in 'old Adam's' eyes. He struck an early note in his campaign for increased British rearmament.

There were, however, some glaring omissions in his paper. It was in fact almost wholly European oriented. The only non-European country to receive any attention at all was the United States – barely one page; while the Soviet Union was rewarded with twenty-three lines. The Middle East was completely ignored, as was the Far East where a major international crisis was brewing. His preoccupation with European affairs was perfectly understandable, even if it did reveal a certain lack of perspective. Most British politicians and diplomatists accepted the axiom that the European balance was central to Britain's security. Nevertheless, the relegation of the rest of the world to a comparatively insignificant position tended to blur the connection between African or Far Eastern questions and the more crucial ones facing the government in Europe. Rarely was it possible to deal with them in isolation and most attempts to do so only tilted the European balance even further against the government.

*   *   *

By the end of 1932 the international situation had deteriorated considerably, mainly as a result of the economic crisis. In the Far East
the Japanese seized control of Manchuria while the League of
Nations stood by helplessly. In Europe the attempt to effect an
Austro-German Customs Union collapsed, chiefly due to French
pressure, leaving in its wake even greater economic and political
havoc. It was the position in Central Europe that troubled Van most.
Van's initial reaction to the Union was one of reserve, though he
contemplated that at some future date it might be necessary to act
against it.[2] But he took strong exception to the secretive manner in
which the scheme had been foisted upon Europe: 'this sudden and
clumsy move by Germany'.[3] Two months after the announcement he
clarified his views:

> Morally, we do quite clearly think that the proposed union is
> wrong, because it would lead to the loss of Austria's economic inde-
> pendence (economic liberty of action), and that it is undesirable
> because it would inevitably lead to a political *Anschluss*, for which
> the present European situation is not opportune, if indeed it ever
> is.[4]

But on reflection he warmed to the idea in principle, seeing in it
the first tentative step towards a European federal union possibly
on the lines initially proposed by Briand in September 1929. He now
disputed the French argument that the Union was 'purely, simply
and entirely a political move, the first step to the *Anschluss* and must
be fought as such'. He feared that the French would over-react,
blockade Germany, and thereby aggravate European tension.

> Thus, [he concluded] the whole of Europe, against maybe its better
> judgement, in any case by a bitter paradox, is being forced to treat
> what can be represented as the first step towards European federa-
> tion as an objectionable political manœuvre destined to wreck the
> peace of Europe . . . Nor do I personally believe that this *coup* was
> conceived, or is intended as any preface or approach to a political
> '*Anschluss*'.[5]

The project also had an adverse effect on Van's relations with his
political chiefs, MacDonald, Henderson and Dalton. The French, as
a counter move in their campaign against the Customs Union, had
proposed a general European tariff programme known as the Reuff
scheme. The Foreign Office, after telephone consultations with other
relevant government departments, had drawn up a memorandum
which concluded that the scheme 'is an improvement from our point

of view of previous French schemes and, if we secure the necessary safeguards, there is no inherent reason why we should object to it', though of course there could be 'no question of our entering the arrangement ourselves'.[6] Only the Dominions Office objected to the main conclusions of the memorandum. They raised the question at a meeting of ministers called to consider the Agricultural Reserve Fund on 18 May. Dalton, in the absence of Henderson, represented the Foreign Office. To his amazement he had to defend a memorandum which he had neither seen nor heard of. It was a most embarrassing situation. Van swiftly penned a lengthy note of explanation accepting 'full responsibility' for the mishap.[7] The Foreign Office memorandum was withdrawn. The incident, small in itself, seemed to justify Dalton's intuitive comment that 'Van is a sound fellow, but not strong in action'.[8]

Although Van had opposed the purely bilateral nature of the customs project, anticipating that the sheer weight of German economic might would result in the political demise of Austria, he was not averse to controlling and extending it to include other European countries – though not Britain – thereby contributing to the stability and pacification of Europe. Instead of his sensible compromise, French intransigence had sharpened the economic slump and heightened political tension. Nowhere was this more evident than in Germany where the Nazis would shortly emerge as the largest single party in the *Reichstag*. He predicted the radicalization of German foreign policy. 'The Nazis are coming', he warned. 'The old German spirit is abroad in plenty and predominance, contained only at present by a tight belt.'[9]

He was by now quite disillusioned with French policy. The whole tenor of his argument turned fiercely, at times unreasonably, anti-French:

No one, of course, contemplates any avoidable friction with France. We are, in any case, in no position for high words or dudgeon with our nearest and most powerful neighbour, who has of late virtually attained the very thing that we have traditionally sought to avoid in Europe, hegemony, if not dictatorship, political and financial. The advocates of 'cooperation' with France must, however, show us on what specific points it is practicable otherwise than by concession on our part . . . The historian of the future will not be indulgent to French and American post war policy. Both have been blind and selfish, and the former has been unduly vindictive as well.[10]

Living in the shadow of the depression, Van felt that it was impossible to divorce politics from economics, or in his words, that it was no longer feasible to continue applying 'political cataplasms to economic complaints'. Fully conscious of the dangers ahead, he advocated embarking upon a full-scale policy of treaty revision which would encompass his new-found insight into economic affairs. He threw the whole weight of his authority behind a memorandum recently composed by Orme Sargent* and Frank Ashton-Gwatkin,† which itself relied heavily upon Van's previous papers, and which supported the case for the revision of Versailles.[11]

He began with an astonishing defence of German policy, displaying a deep understanding of the German case over the Customs Union, and arguing that Germany was 'entirely within her rights' in building the pocket battleship, *Deutschland*, an act which she had been 'positively driven into . . . by the Treaty of Versailles'. He had no doubt that the German case 'is on every ground of morality and equity exceedingly strong', and asserted unhesitatingly that no British government would side with the French against the Germans.

But Van knew that in order to make any scheme acceptable he had to allay French fears about a resurgent Germany. To this purpose, he devised a comprehensive agreement which included treaty revision but which also broadened the British commitment to European, in particular French, security. It included the strengthening of the Locarno agreements to encompass the French northern ports, the establishment of a Mediterranean Locarno, and a European protocol to satisfy the French system of alliances in Eastern Europe. But equally he was intent on removing the most pressing German grievances. Thus he proposed the abrogation of the disarmament clauses of the Versailles treaty, admittedly in a controlled manner, but which in effect envisaged the enlargement of the German armed forces.

Here was a programme, at once imaginative and far-reaching in scope, which, if accepted, might have immeasurably reduced European tension. But what if it were rejected? Van was convinced that in those circumstances Britain would have no option but to move

* Orme Garton Sargent (1884–1962): entered Foreign Office, 1906; first secretary, 1919; counsellor, 1926; head of Central Department, 1928–33; Assistant Under Secretary of State, 1933–39; Deputy Under Secretary of State, 1939–46; Permanent Under Secretary of State, 1946–49. Kn. 1937.

† Frank Trelawny Arthur Ashton-Gwatkin (1889–1976): entered consular service, 1913; first secretary at Foreign Office, 1920; counsellor, 1934; attached to Lord Runciman's mission, 1938; advisor to minister of economic warfare, 1939; Assistant Under Secretary of State, 1947.

into a period of isolation and allow Europe to stew in its own juice; or at best to wait until wiser counsels prevailed:

> For us European politics are mostly other people's feuds and grievances. We have espoused some foreign causes, but a point has come where we can go no further . . . Beyond a certain point, the quarrels of Europe are not our quarrels, and the point may now be reached when, failing agreement on our contribution, we must say so . . .

Unlike the continental powers, Britain did have an alternative, and, if provoked beyond endurance by the egoistic, short-sighted policies of the European powers, she would adopt it.

But it was not only on the Continent that Van encountered opposition. His own government displayed the utmost reservation towards his policy of wooing the Germans by stiffening British commitments to France. His papers came before the cabinet on 15 December. The whole tone of the discussion rejected entering into further obligations over and above those already contained in the original Locarno agreements and the Covenant of the League.[12] The cabinet, apprehensive about extra European entanglements, declined to follow Van's lead.

Despite the government's lukewarm reaction, Van did not abandon all hope of progress. He believed the World Disarmament Conference, due to convene in February 1932, might occasion the breakthrough he was seeking. If the conference could make more headway, it could pave the way for some substantial political agreements. Van's optimistic expectations rapidly vanished. The conference soon lost its way in a maze of plans and counter-plans, mutual recriminations and suspicions, and a general lack of unity of purpose among the participating powers. The main stumbling block was how to square French demands for security with the German claim for *Gleichberechtigung* (equality of status), a claim that was finally granted on 11 December through the meaningless formula of 'equality of rights in a system which would provide security for all nations'. By the end of the year Van had almost abandoned any hope of success. He wrote to Hankey:

> My general feeling is that it is 'now or never' with disarmament – that is to say, that if the next few months are allowed to pass, the Disarmament Conference will be dead by the summer. We shall then be faced with a most serious situation. Germany on the strength of the 11 December agreement will maintain that the Disarmament

Conference having irretrievably failed, the *Gleichberechtigung* to which she is entitled may be brought about unilaterally . . . If so, we are in for a new race in armaments which this country could only join in at great expense or abstain from at great hazard.[13]

Although Van had graphically identified the pre-1914 spirit, he hesitated to allot to it a permanent address. From 1930–32 he tended to see Paris or Rome as providing the most fruitful atmosphere for 'old Adam's' regressive behaviour. His constant harping about the 'Latin sisters' and their interminable squabbles bears ample witness to his anger at their selfish policies. By the beginning of 1933 he no longer had any doubts as to where 'old Adam' resided. Hitler's rise to power on 30 January 1933 settled that particular argument. His accession to office placed European politics on a completely new, and far more dangerous, footing. Less than one month after Hitler's appointment as chancellor he forecast that 'These wild men and killers' would not be easily displaced.[14]

By May 1933 Van was convinced that:

The present regime in Germany will, on past and present form, loose off another European war just so soon as it feels strong enough. Their only fear is that they may be attacked before they are ready. Meanwhile it will endeavour to cog and lull so as better to eat the artichoke leaf by leaf. This is crude; but we are considering very crude people, who have few ideas in their noddles but brute force and militarism . . . This crude barbarism which denies all liberty may of course change its idea. I don't believe that it will.[15]

How did Van propose to meet the German challenge? His answer was unequivocal: by large scale rearmament and the closest cooperation with France. Van admitted that he was offering 'almost a counsel of despair', but he added that it was better 'than no counsel at all'.[16]

Gone were the days when he contemplated a balanced policy towards Germany and France. All his suspicions about the incurably evil nature of Germany and German politics rose to the surface again. His 'gut reaction' to all things German once more dominated his thinking. Everything was grist to his mill. One morning he strode into his private secretary's office and flung a book of German martial songs onto the desk: 'Read those if you don't believe me,' he cried.[17] Nor did his first meeting with a top Nazi personality, Alfred Rosenberg, the erstwhile 'philosopher' of the Nazi movement who had come to London on a goodwill mission to justify Nazi racialist theory, allay his fears. Rosenberg cut no ice with Van: 'A Balt who looked like cold cod.'[18] The mission could only be termed a disaster.[19]

In common with many other observers, Van also had difficulty in relating the Nazi movement to the sweep of German history. For a brief period he held the view that the Nazis were mere stooges of the old ruling cliques, the Junkers and the militarists. The Rohm purge* seemed to verify this assumption. The horrible events of that night were of course decisive proof of the barbaric nature of the new régime and its leader whom he now defined as a 'dangerous paranoic'. But the ultimate beneficiaries of this blood-letting would be the traditional ruling classes.

> We shall have back in full control the class and system that made the war of 1914. *Plus ça change*. The danger to Europe is going to be greatly increased by the increasing power of the more competent section of these savages.[20]

These general sentiments were widely held in the Office. Sargent and Wigram† both expressed themselves strongly in the same vein, as did Eden, though in somewhat more restrained language.[21] It was some time before Van realized that Hitler was not clay in the hands of the old ruling circles, and that the distinction between 'moderates' and 'extremists' within the top Nazi leadership was one totally without meaning. Many of his colleagues and political chiefs were slower off the mark.

The establishment of Hitler's régime did not exclude the possibility of reaching a negotiated settlement with Germany. On the contrary, Van was clear in his mind that discussions should proceed. Diplomatists had to deal in facts, however unsavoury. It was not within the province of the Foreign Office or the British government to impose upon Germany a system of government more compatible with liberal standards in Western Europe. Germany could not be ignored. Whatever civilized Europeans felt about the inherent brutality of Nazi Germany, Germany would remain the most powerful continental power, restless, energetic, seeking to overthrow the

---

* On the night of 30 June 1934, the 'Night of the Long Knives', Hitler purged his party of its so-called radical elements, at the same time exploiting the opportunity to settle many old scores with his political opponents. About 400 people met their death at the hands of Hitler's gunmen, including the top leadership of the S.A., the ex-chancellor, General von Schleicher, and his one-time colleague, Gregor Strasser.

† Ralph Follett Wigram (1890–1936): entered foreign service, 1916; first secretary at Paris embassy, 1924–33; counsellor and head of Central Department at Foreign Office, 1934–36.

status quo. Better to draw the sting from German demands through negotiation than fatalistically slip down the path that led to open confrontation and war. Diplomacy, Van argued, could not be conducted by saying 'No' to everything.[22]

Van quickly shed the argument he himself had used to such good effect regarding the iniquities of Versailles. It was no longer a question of righting ancient wrongs but of tying Germany down to rigidly defined agreements which would bind her in an overall European settlement. Van was not conducting a moral crusade on behalf of Germany. What concerned him was to rectify the balance-of-power which he now saw as swinging heavily against Britain, and which if allowed to deteriorate or even drift would result in war. How to achieve this? In his own mind he was quite certain that the new Germany was bent on aggression and that the chances of persuading her by rational discussion to adopt a more conciliatory policy were infinitesimal. 'It is conceivable that the Germans may change their minds. If they do, it will not come from any change of heart but from isolation and external pressure.'[23] Thus Germany would be compelled, in her own interests, to adopt a more pacific attitude.

The guiding principles of his policy were clear. Cooperation with France was fundamental. Whatever criticism he had levelled against France in the past would have to be subordinated to the greater aim. He travelled much farther in this direction than any of his contemporaries. He spoke of 'an alliance with France or something mighty like it'.[24] The French persevered in exasperating him. Their unreliability, their political instability, their selfishness, the poor quality of their leadership, led Van to despair of their ever being moulded into an effective weapon against Germany. But was there an alternative? Only by reconciling France to her 'Latin sister'. Van's overtures to Italy were not conducted out of any sympathy with the Fascist régime but simply because Italy was yet another pawn in his power game. He acknowledged the differences between Fascist Italy and Nazi Germany and endeavoured to exploit them to British advantage. Admittedly, he held an exaggeratedly high opinion of Mussolini. Thus he dismissed the German leadership as 'incompetent' with not 'a tittle of Mussolini's ability'.[25] Later he claimed that 'Mussolini is really a very sensible man, who sometimes thinks somewhat like us on foreign affairs'.[26] Perhaps it was a case of the wish being father to the thought, for Mussolini's 'ability' turned to dust at the first decisive test.

In this way a Western combination would emerge, backed by the formidable power of the United States, which would act as a brake on extreme German demands and enable the West to negotiate from a position of relative strength. In the course of approximately one year he had substituted one Grand Design for another. But he was well aware that practically every link in his new chain was a weak one. The United States were reluctant to be involved; France was unreliable; Italy, whatever Mussolini's qualities, was notoriously capricious with longstanding revisionist ambitions in the Adriatic and East Africa. Of vastly greater importance, Great Britain herself was unable to set a strong example. Since the end of the First World War her defence system had been systematically run down and she stood, like the proverbial Emperor, naked before the German challenge. It would be a long and arduous and uphill struggle to weld these flawed components into a greater whole, with no guarantee of success at the end. How to contain Germany in the meantime? Almost by chance Van hit upon a method which appeared to him highly relevant in the existing circumstances, and which confirmed a level of approach he had long contemplated. It emerged from the so-called Metro-Vickers affair in March 1933.

In the early morning of 12 March 1933, GPU agents entered the Metro-Vickers compound at Perlovka, just outside Moscow, and arrested two British employees of the firm, Allan Monkhouse and Leslie Thornton.[27] Within twenty-four hours four other engineers were placed under arrest. All were accused of 'economic espionage' and of deliberately attempting 'to wreck' Soviet industrial projects which they themselves had set up. The prisoners were subjected to the usual humiliations and eventually put on public trial. Five out of the six accused were found guilty. Thornton, judged the leading saboteur, and Monkhouse were sentenced to short prison terms, the rest were banished from the Soviet Union.

These events were recorded against a background of renewed Anglo-Soviet trade negotiations. The government had long been dissatisfied with the previous agreement of 1930 which the Soviet Union had exploited by 'dumping' up to one-third of her total exports onto the British market with no appreciable rise in British exports to the Soviet Union. The government's decision to renegotiate the agreement was in effect an attempt to force Anglo-Soviet trade into balance. From the outset of the talks Van determined on a tough line, thinking in terms of a complete trade embargo should the Russians fail to comply with British demands. Van was convinced that the government held all the trump cards. Access to British markets was vital to the Soviet Union: 'they will meet our wishes' rather than lose it.[28] The trade embargo was the one effective weapon at the disposal of the government. But if used, it must be absolute: 'It must be a threat of complete exclusion,' Van ruled.

He was in a particularly favourable position during the crisis to guide the government's policy. MacDonald and Simon were in Europe on a diplomatic mission and did not return to London until the end of March. This enabled Van to seize the initiative in order to ginger up the cabinet. Knowing MacDonald's predilection for the Soviet Union it was essential to set out the main lines of his policy as quickly as possible. He met Maisky, the Soviet ambassador, on 16 March. Although the two men were on good terms the interview was a stormy one. Van lashed out: the allegations against the accused were 'grotesque and hysterical', the arrests merely

> a stage performance, and a very bad one at that, mounted simply to disguise, by serving up scapegoats, the ill success of certain industrial undertakings in Russia. If the Soviet government did not regain its senses, and quickly, the commercial negotiations would be discontinued. It was essential that the Soviets went into this affair with their eyes open.

Of course, the strategy was not his alone. Ashton-Gwatkin planned the details and it was vigorously upheld by Laurence Collier.*[29] But it was Van who set the tone. On more than one occasion he had to stiffen the resolve of his hesitant chief, Sir John Simon.[30]† He had no doubt that pressure should be exerted only on the economic front, and opposed the suggestion of the Moscow embassy to break off diplomatic relations and recall ambassadors.

With the conviction and imprisonment of Thornton and Monkhouse, the cabinet decided to enforce a trade embargo. About £25 million of Russian exports were involved. A mini trade war ensued with measures and counter-measures being taken by both sides, but with the Russians getting decidedly the worst of the confrontation. The British estimated that the Russians would not last a month. They held out for six weeks. On 1 July the two engineers were

---

* Laurence Collier (1890–   ): entered Foreign Office, 1913; First secretary at Foreign Office, 1923; counsellor, 1932; Head of Northern Department, 1932–41; minister to Norway, 1941; Ambassador to Norwegian government, 1942–50. Kn. 1944.

† John Allesbrook Simon (1873–1954): barrister; Liberal M.P., 1906–18, 1922–40; Attorney-General with seat in cabinet, 1913–15; Home Secretary, 1915–16; 1935–37; Foreign Secretary, 1931–35; Chancellor of the Exchequer, 1937–40; Lord Chancellor, 1940–45. Kn. 1910. Cr. Viscount, 1940.

released. Trade negotiations were resumed two days later and ultimately brought to a successful conclusion in February 1934. Van's policy had paid handsome dividends. 'Here was success for resolve.'[31]

Van regarded Nazism and Communism as two variations of the same disease. His Metro-Vickers triumph strengthened his resolution to play the economic card against Germany for all it was worth. This was the origin of his 'keep Germany lean' policy. After only eight months experience of the Nazi régime, he concluded: 'The only thing that might bring Hitler down is economic adversity . . . I would suggest, therefore, that in the general interest Germany should be kept underweight.[32]

Van remained constantly on the alert to ensure that Germany remained lean. He reacted forcibly the moment he sensed any kind of deal between the City and financial circles in Germany. To Warren Fisher he wrote:

> I have always thought that financial stringency in Germany was going to be our principal safeguard against wholesale German re-armament; and that we should do all we can here to keep Germany lean, even, at a cost to certain people here . . . politically anything that keeps the Germans lean at the present time naturally appeals to me.[33]

And the Treasury responded sympathetically to his warnings.[34]

As part of his economic strategy, Van also actively encouraged the establishment of an independent Economic Department within the Foreign Office, a long overdue innovation. Hitherto there had been no distinct department which dealt with economic affairs. Until the early 1930s, economics had been largely ignored by the Foreign Office. Instructions had gone out in 1906 that additional economic information was to be included in the annual report of diplomatic missions; but this was a fairly haphazard procedure. Commercial attachés were regarded with some contempt by the career diplomats, and were often ostracized socially. Little weight was attached either to their views or to their activities. Until 1931 economics was not even a required subject for Foreign Office entry examinations. Aspiring diplomats had not the slightest motivation to familiarize themselves with questions of trade or commerce. Obviously this was a most unsatisfactory state of affairs.[35]

These problems had by no means been resolved by the time Van took office. He was perfectly aware that he could not afford to antagonize the Treasury. Cooperation and consultation were imperative.

Apart from questions of high policy, problems of extra manpower, finances, even more office space were involved. These might appear mundane considerations when compared with the intricacies of foreign policy decision making, but they can be decisive when setting up in practice a new department or section. These bureaucratic obstacles had first to be overcome, and the Treasury, through some typical Whitehall in-fighting, fought a stubborn rearguard action to preserve its prerogatives.

But first the Office had to define for itself the precise functions of the new department. Quite simply, it had to prove its case, to its own satisfaction and to everyone else's. This it did at the end of 1930. Sir Victor Wellesley* set out the main lines of development of a political economic section which would investigate the effect of economic development on foreign policy and not, as had previously been emphasized, its effect on British trade.[36] (It was this impertinence which prompted Fisher's celebrated reaction: 'Sock him [Wellesley] on the jaw.'[37]) Ashton-Gwatkin then submitted a series of evaluations dealing with various aspects of the new section's work. They were approved in February 1932. At the same time an economic section was brought into being with Ashton-Gwatkin as its chief, though it was still in the experimental stage with no official recognition.

From its inception, Van gave the new section his warmest support, and any accusations that he was indifferent, or even antagonistic, to the consolidation of the Office's economic side may be confidently disregarded. 'Mr Gwatkin's work has been most useful during the past year ... There is of course no doubt that it is going on. Its utility is going to increase. His department must therefore be increased.'[38] A year later he had 'no doubt as to its future: indeed it will have to be, and will be, expanded'.[39] His enthusiasm for the section's future did not dampen, and he nicknamed it 'the Cuckoo's department', claiming that it would soon oust all the other departments from the nest.[40] But his enthusiasm was linked to his wider strategy, for only by the continuous gathering and sifting of economic intelligence would his 'keep Germany lean' policy make any sense at all. 'Old Adam', as personified by the spirit and actions of the new Germany, would be brought to heel by a combination of economic pressure and Western diplomatic unity.

---

* Victor (Alexander Augustus Henry) Wellesley (1876–1954): entered Foreign Office, 1899; controller of commerce and consular affairs, 1916–19; counsellor, 1920–24; Deputy Under Secretary of State, 1925–36. Kn. 1926.

NOTES

1. See F.O. 371/14350, C. 3358/3358/62, 'An Aspect of International Relations in 1930'. It is almost impossible to estimate the precise number of 'old Adam' memoranda Van wrote, as practically every memorandum penned by him as PUS could, with very little imagination, be included in this classification. However, the following ten, composed by him over the period 1930–40, can clearly be identified as belonging to this category.

   F.O. 371/14350. C. 3358/3358/62, 'An Aspect of International Relations in 1930', 1 May 1930.

   F.O. 371/15205, C. 3277/321/62, 'An Aspect of International Relations in 1931', 1 May 1931.

   'The United Kingdom and Europe', 1 January 1932, C.P. 4 (32), CAB. 24/227.

   F.O. 371/17380, W.2322/117/98, 'The Crisis in Europe', 2 March 1933 or C.P. 52(33), CAB 24/239.

   'A Memorandum on the Present and Future Position in Europe', 28 August 1933, C.P. 212(33), CAB. 24/243.

   'The Future of Germany', 7 April 1934, C.P. 104(34), CAB. 24/243.

   F.O. 371/19949, C. 8998/8998/18, 'The World Situation and British Rearmament', 31 December 1936.

   'Germany', 3 February 1936, C.P. 42(36), CAB 24/260.

   F.O. 371/22986, C. 19495/15/18, 'The Origins of Germany's Fifth War', 28 November 1939.

   F.O. 371/24389, C. 4229/6/18, 'The Nature of the Beast', 14 March 1940.

   Copies of these papers may also be found in other departmental files in the Public Record Office, and in the Vansittart collection at Churchill College, Cambridge.

2. See his minute of 21 March 1931, *B.D.*, 2, iii, no. 2.

3. See 'An Aspect of International Relations in 1931', F.O. 371/15205, C. 3217/321/18.

4. F.O. 371/15162, C. 3542/673/18. His minute of 25 May 1931.

5. See 'An Aspect. . . . .', *op. cit.*

6. For general minutes on the Reuff scheme, 7 May 1931, see F.O. 371/15162, C. 3490/673/3.

7. Van to MacDonald, 20 May 1931, *ibid.*

8. See *Dalton Diaries*, 30 March 1930.

9. See 'The United Kingdom and Europe', 1 January 1932, C.P. 4(32), CAB. 24/227.

10. *Ibid.*

11. For the Sargent–Ashton-Gwatkin proposals, see C.P. 301(31), CAB. 24/225. For Van's support, 'The United Kingdom and Europe', *op. cit.*

12. For cabinet discussion on 15 December, see CAB. 23/69. See in particular C.P. 17(32) and C.P. 27(32), CAB. 24/227, for a cabinet committee's negative conclusions in regard to his advocacy of a Mediterranean Locarno.

13. Van to Hankey, 18 January 1933, CAB. 63/46. In this connection, see also Van to Simon, 24 November 1932, F.O. 371/16467, W. 12577/1466/98.

14. See Van's minutes of 6 and 22 February, 1933, Vnst. 2/1, 2/5.

15. Minutes of 6 May, 1933, Vnst. 2/3.

16. See his paper, 'The Crisis in Europe', 2 March 1933, C.P. 52(33), CAB. 24/239; original draft in F.O. 371/17380, W. 2322/117/98.
17. A private communication.
18. *M.P.*, 475
19. See *B.D.*, 2, v, no. 138, and *G.D.*, C, i, no. 237, for accounts of the visit. See also R. Cecil, *The Myth of the Master Race: Alfred Rosenberg and Nazi Ideology* (London 1972), 174–76.
20. See his minutes of 2 July 1934, Vnst. 2/15.
21. *Ibid*; also minutes of 10, 25 and 31 July and 1 August, 1934, Vnst. 2/19.
22. See his minutes of 1 December 1935, F.O. 371/18852, C. 8852/55/14 and Vnst. 2/24.
23. See minutes of 11 July 1933, Vnst. 2/14.
24. Minutes of 26 February 1933, Vnst. 2/3.
25. Minutes of 22 February 1933, Vnst. 2/8.
26. Minutes of 4 December 1933, Vnst. 2/12.
27. This passage, unless stated otherwise, is based on: A memorandum compiled in April 1933, F.O. 800/288 (Simon Papers): *B.D.* 2, vii, chaps. iv, v, vi; and D. N. Lammers, 'The Engineers Trial (Moscow 1933) and Anglo-Soviet Relations', *The South Atlantic Quarterly* (Spring, 1963).
28. From a memo. by Van, 22 November 1932, B.P., v, 118.
29. See minutes in F.O. 371/17266, N. 2104/1610/38.
30. See Lammers, *op. cit.*
31. See *M.P.*, 459–61 for Van's later recollections about the incident.
32. See his paper of 28 August 1933, C.P. 212(33), CAB. 24/243. Printed in *B.D.*, 2, v, no. 371.
33. See Van to Fisher, 8 January and 15 August 1934, T. 175/86, X. 1/7034 (P.R.O.): also his note to Simon, 28 September 1935, F.O. 800/295.
34. *Ibid.*
35. These comments are based on a Foreign Office 'Statement of Existing Instructions with regard to Economic Reporting and an Outline of their General Requirements', 3 March 1934, F.O. 371/18487, W. 3928/293/50.
36. See his memo. of 1 December 1930, F.O. 371/14939, W. 12855/12855/50.
37. A private communication.
38. His minutes of 22 January 1933, F.O. 371/17318, W. 278/278/50.
39. His minutes of 30 January 1934, F.O. 371/18487, W. 293/293/50.
40. A private communication.

CHAPTER VII

Foreign Affairs

VAN ASSUMED HIS responsibilities as Permanent Under Secretary on 7 January 1930. Most of his senior officials were men whom he had known and worked with for close on thirty years. Many were older and more experienced in office routine. The impression remains inescapable that his relationship with his senior officials, with the notable exception of Orme Sargent, was strained, or at best rigidly correct.* He fostered his own circle of younger men: Ralph Wigram, Rex Leeper,† and his private secretary, Clifford Norton,‡ who were known as 'Van's boys' in Whitehall.[1] To the informed observer it was apparent that to get on in the Foreign Office you had to be 'one of Van's men'.[2]

Towards his first political chief, Arthur Henderson, Van showed a distinct reserve. The social and psychological gap between them was too wide and too deep for them ever to be on really close terms. Paradoxically, perhaps this was the reason why he never quite established the same kind of ascendency over Henderson as he did over succeeding foreign secretaries. With Henderson's deputy, Hugh Dalton, a product of Eton and King's College, Cambridge, he was on firmer ground. 'I found him easy to work with and open to argument,'[3] a remark more revealing about its author than about

---

* Neither of his deputy under secretaries, Victor Wellesley and Hubert Montgomery, or his Assistant Under Secretary, George Mounsey, are mentioned in his memoirs. Only Lancelot Oliphant is singled out for special praise (see *M.P.*, 399).

† Reginald Wilding Allen Leeper (1888–1968): entered Foreign Office, 1918; first secretary, 1924; counsellor, 1933; Assistant Under Secretary of State, 1940–42; ambassador to Greece, 1943–46; to the Argentine, 1946–48. Kn. 1945.

‡ Clifford John Norton (1891–): entered Foreign Office, 1921; private secretary to Vansittart, 1930–37; counsellor at Warsaw embassy, 1937–39; minister to Switzerland, 1942–46; Ambassador to Greece, 1946–51. Kn. 1946.

its subject. Dalton shared many of Van's views on foreign affairs, particularly over the German issue and rearmament. They were to work in close harmony over the coming years.

With the breakup of the second Labour government in August 1931, Lord Reading replaced Henderson at the Foreign Office. It was a transient appointment. After only ten weeks in office, he in turn was succeeded by Sir John Simon. During the interim period, MacDonald's newly formed National government had gone to the country and had received a convincing mandate from the electorate.* Owing to the severe economic and financial crisis which had brought the Labour government down, Neville Chamberlain, the new Chancellor of the Exchequer, emerged as a key figure in the cabinet. By virtue of the authority of his office, and helped along by his principal adviser, Sir Warren Fisher, he exerted a considerable influence on most aspects of defence and foreign policy. Compared with the energetic, efficient, and interfering Chamberlain, Simon cut a poor figure.

Simon went reluctantly to the Foreign Office, the Treasury being his first preference, even though he remained in office until June 1935, the longest reigning Foreign Secretary of the 1930's. Much criticism has been levelled against him; and little has been offered in his defence.† Seemingly unable to form any close relationship, Simon, despite his acknowledged intellectual virtuosity, appeared as a remote and distrusted figure, clinging to office, any office, come what may.[4] No doubt his fifteen years in the political wilderness explains his consuming desire for office.[5] Van's relationship with Simon is difficult to fathom. There is a carefully restrained, though perceptive, portrait of him in *The Mist Procession*.[6] Later, in an unguarded moment, he was more explicit. Simon, he claimed, had never 'liked him' and was the 'snakiest of them all'.[7]

Simon's chief defect as Foreign Secretary lay buried in his own temperament. Meticulous and often incisive analyses of inter-

* The National government captured 554 seats in all; 473 Conservatives, 13 National Labour, 35 National Liberal (Simonites), and 33 Liberals (Samuelites). Against this formidable combination were ranged 52 Labour members, 4 Independent Liberals (Lloyd Georgites), and 5 Independents. After the cabinet reshuffle in November 1931, MacDonald continued as prime minister, Baldwin as Lord President of the Council, and Samuel as Home Secretary; Chamberlain replaced Snowden as Chancellor; and Simon moved into the Foreign Office in place of Reading.

† Least of all by Simon himself. His memoirs, *Retrospect* (London, 1952), must be classified among the least revealing ever written. As Professor Medlicott has pointed out: 'He mentions Vansittart once, misspells Wigram's name, and omits Sargent altogether.' W. N. Medlicott, *Britain and Germany: The Search for Agreement 1930-37* (London, 1969), 9.

national questions, setting out the pros and cons, weighing up the various alternatives, pointing out the different options, were his special talent. In all fairness to Simon it should be remembered that many of his papers were first rate analytical surveys, admitted as such in the Foreign Office, and hardly bettered by any of his successors.[8] But invaluable as his symposiums were, they were hardly likely to set the Foreign Office alight. Lacking in enthusiasm himself, he failed to inspire it in others. Van confessed to Eden that he was melancholy at Simon's continuous indecision.[9] An advocate by training, he provided neither the cabinet nor the Foreign Office with the right kind of leadership or initiative. 'Vansittart drives him his way,' Eden complained, 'but J.S. is reluctant to travel. Yet he clings to the F.O. It is an unhappy situation for us all.'[10] He experienced infinite difficulties in carrying through a policy to the end. Forever seeking to forestall criticism, he earned a reputation as a trimmer and a hedger. An aura of confusion enveloped his policies.[11]

Nor was Simon's deputy, Eden, or 'young Eden' to quote Van, well suited to fill the gap. 'Desirous and deserving of praise, he avoided suspicions of brilliance or originality and pruned protusions with sense. He said the right things so often that he seemed incapable of saying anything else.'[12] Eden came to the Office at the age of thirty-four. He was not entirely without experience, having acted as Austen Chamberlain's Parliamentary Private Secretary for three years. But his years told against him. Lacking in self confidence, his minutes for this period were for the most part quite undistinguished and unoriginal. Only after some years in office did Eden cast aside his inhibitions and express some ideas of his own. But his was a popular appointment. Elegant and stylish, he endowed the Foreign Office with the glamour of public relations in an age when public relations were not yet the vogue.

The lack of firm guidance at the ministerial level enhanced Van's own position and, of course, that of his senior officials. The situation was not to alter radically until the beginning of 1936 when Eden, now Foreign Secretary, began to display an independence of mind, if not authority, which he had not previously shown. It was about this time that his relations with Van began to sour. One might conclude, in a most general fashion, that for five to six years it was the senior officials at the Foreign Office who called the tune, carrying their ministers along with them.

The first major international crisis to confront Van resulted from the Japanese attack against Manchuria in September 1931. The

Japanese aggression coincided with the political-economic upheaval in Britain. Preoccupied with fresh elections and urgent economic problems, the cabinet had little time to devote to the Far East. After initially noting the Japanese action, it did not discuss it again until mid-November.[13] It was during this decisive period, when all the actors in the crisis were intent on defining their roles, that the Foreign Office, almost by default, fashioned the main principles of British policy.

Among the officials there was general condemnation at the manner of the Japanese action, but equally there was general agreement that they had acted only after severe provocation. 'The Chinese', wrote Van, 'had been asking for trouble, and they got it.'[14] Japan, it was reasoned, had considerable economic interests in Manchuria which could not be ignored or put in jeopardy by Chinese incompetence.* Everything pointed in the direction of a compromise solution, with the Japanese appearing as the aggrieved party. But if China proved intransigent, she would have to 'take the consequences'.[15]

Within the Foreign Office differences of emphasis did emerge, however, regarding the role the League should play in the crisis. One camp, inspired by Wellesley, aimed at minimizing the activities of the League on the grounds that its overt anti-Japanese disposition would only inflame the conflict and provoke Japan into even more extreme measures. Others, including Van and Simon, contended that it was necessary to keep the League in play lest it slide into 'helpless abdication'.[16] But Van held no false illusions as to its capacity to restrain Japan. Nor was he bound, either on ideological or practical grounds, to automatic League intervention: the League, he reminded Wigram, is neither 'a principle' nor 'a quasi-religion'.[17]

Hamstrung by their incapacity to act alone, and influenced by genuine feelings of sympathy towards Japan, the government decided that 'it was not worth the heavy cost of using coercion to impose one's will upon Japan'.[18] Sanctions, Simon minuted three days after the cabinet's decision, were out of the question. Instead he counselled seeking any course which would preserve the moral authority of the League.[19] Confrontation having been rejected, the Foreign Office fell back on reconciliation as the one feasible method of resolving the dispute. In practice, given the mood of Japan, this was an admission of failure; or rather an uneasy acceptance of the Japanese *fait accompli*.

After the Japanese landings at Shanghai in February 1932, a new

* It should be noted that the British had already acted on this principle when, in 1927, they had protected their interests in Shanghai by force of arms.

sense of urgency crept into the official papers. Major British interests were now at stake. Van's main proposition was brutally frank:

> *We* are incapable of checking Japan in any way if she really means business and has sized us up, as she certainly has done. Therefore we must eventually be done for in the Far East unless The United States are eventually prepared to use force.[20]

Van was not entirely convinced that the United States would not ultimately be compelled to intervene; though not, of course, as a result of her own initiative. The Japanese may end 'by kicking in the US too'. This was the crucial point: to clarify the attitude of the United States, for without her active intervention the British position was doomed and the government must eventually swallow 'any and every humiliation'.

In the event the American response was cool: and it is now clear that the United States had no intention whatsoever of intervening in the crisis.[21] This fact explains Van's restrained reaction, even after the Shanghai landings, when he opposed the suggestion of economic or diplomatic sanctions against Japan.[22] He thus reluctantly reconciled hinself to the position of dominance which Japan had carved out for herself in the area.

Yet he was fully conscious of the grave danger to British interests, not only in the Far East but also closer to home, of a Japan bent upon aggression and apparently impossible to stop. He had volunteered no foolproof scheme to counter this threat. It was simply a case of choosing the best out of a series of bad alternatives. But whatever happened, he had no intention of allowing Britain to act as policeman for the League.

> Presumably Japan will huff out of the League ... What then? Why should anybody's withers be wrung – if we are prudent ... I would of course prefer that Japan should be reasonable and stay in the League, but if – or as – she won't, why worry too much, unless we have been fools enough to take the lead in provoking her.[23]

It might be argued that it was a thoroughly evasive, even dishonourable, role which he envisaged; but it was an entirely realistic one.

The Manchurian episode provided the first unambiguous indication that there were definite limits beyond which British foreign policy could not venture without provoking the very gravest risks. Van had no hesitation in rejecting the latter alternative. And it would be difficult to deny the essential responsibility of his choice.

Apart from the grave deficiencies in British defence, a myriad of social, economic and political factors at home acted as crippling restraints upon the foreign policy decision-makers. The conditions which fashioned the British response over Manchuria did not disappear overnight. Neither did the conclusions drawn from this affair, namely that Britain could not act alone or pursue a sanctions policy – either economic or political – which might involve her in a war for which she was totally unprepared. Collective security could not become the sole responsibility of the British government. When the next crisis broke between the League and a recalcitrant power, this time Italy in pursuit of gains in Abyssinia, these lessons had to be relearned.

As the sounds of the Far Eastern crisis died away, Van became increasingly preoccupied with the problems posed by the emergence of Nazi Germany. In truth the Manchurian episode was never more than a sideshow for him, more important for the shock-waves it engendered than for the actual expansion of Japanese power into Manchuria. He soon became absorbed in an infinitely more crucial question: German designs on Austria.

German agitation against Austria began in earnest almost immediately after Hitler became Chancellor. It took three main forms: economic pressure; a continuous barrage of seditious propaganda; and the subversion of the Austrian state from within. The purpose of this activity was clear: to effect the *Anschluss*. There was hardly any other issue about which Van held such definite views. Convinced that 'Austria can quite well exist independently, and it is most important to the safety of Europe that she do so',[24] Van's chief concern was to organize a European front to warn Germany off.[25]

From 15 July until 29 August Van was in charge of the Office while Simon took his summer holidays. He was clearly working under a tremendous strain. The news from Austria led him to believe that a European explosion was imminent. His imagination fired, he penned a fiercely-worded memorandum giving full vent to his darkest suspicions. On 23 August he sent it off for approval to Ramsay MacDonald.[26] Two days later MacDonald replied:

> In some places you 'let yourself go', and I am not sure that that is wise in a state document like this. I have therefore underlined some words and expressions which I think you ought to put in a more reserved form . . . One or two sentences are also constructed in a way that the Foreign Secretary might object to, because they seem to bear the meaning that you are dictating the policy of the

Office. I know that you do not mean this but be careful that the wording does not bear out such an interpretation.

Van replied:

I quite appreciate all you say. The paper was written at great speed, because I was afraid of the possibility of the cabinet being confronted with a crisis . . . In this I am referring particularly to a *putsch* (in early September. The Italians believe this too) . . . Therefore the need for speedy action and hence insufficiently pruned drafting to which you rightly allude. I have now rewritten in the light of your comments. I have also been careful in trying to eliminate any phrase to which the Foreign Secretary might possibly take exception. I know you realize that 'I know my place' very well, and should of course never wish to give any possible impression of exceeding it.

He declined MacDonald's invitation to take a holiday.

Two days after this counsel of caution MacDonald wrote to Simon in slightly more unguarded terms. He was not

very happy about Van's work and worry. I have reason to believe that he is a bit overstrained, and complete rest away from papers is much required for him. It may be difficult to let him cut himself off altogether whilst this Austrian problem is being handled, but he ought not to be left in sole charge of the Office, lest he should break down under the strain or show nerves in dealing with the matter.

MacDonald was close to Van and relied heavily upon his advice. In April he had taken Van on a short trip to the United States. Now MacDonald, whose own powers were in a state of evident decline, had touched upon a raw spot. Van's gifts were undoubted; but equally his ability to cope with a major crisis was suspect. In the future he would be unable to escape fully from the widely-held suspicion that in a moment of crisis he would crack under the strain. His own temperament, his inner nervous tension, carefully controlled though it was, his rich imagination, all lent a certain credence to this belief. Above all, it was the histrionic character of his language which caught his superiors off balance, and made them fearful lest he attempt to translate his vivid phraseology into concrete action.

Despite MacDonald's caveat he expressed his views with clarity and decision.[27] 'We are all backing the losing horse in Austria', he wrote. Hitler's ultimate aim was to destroy Austria and incorporate her in a greater Germany. The future of Europe turned on the Austrian question. Hitler's challenge could only be withstood by bringing together Italy, France and Britain into a common diplomatic front, while at the same time propping up Austria economically. 'If that demonstration can be made sufficient for the coming winter, Germany may yet lose the game.' There was little wrong with this advice provided the Italians could be brought into line. Unfortunately, the Italians showed extreme reluctance to play Van's game, preferring to go their own way.[28] Only frustration, and ultimately failure, awaited Van's efforts to unite the Western powers against the German menace.

Van's assessment of the Austrian situation was also coloured by the reports he received from the British minister at Vienna, Sir Walford Selby. He had little confidence in Selby's judgement; and Selby reciprocated in kind. Selby was one of Van's most scathing critics. The title of his memoirs, *Diplomatic Twilight, 1930-40,* speaks for itself, and it is riddled with damaging remarks about Van's term of office as PUS. Much of his criticism was grossly exaggerated. But as a result of it relations between the two were highly charged. Some of Van's most bitter complaints were reserved for Selby's dispatches, many of which were, upon examination, quite unrealistic. On one occasion Selby had written: 'No one can quarrel with Germany desiring to tear up the whole peace settlement.'[29] This was too much for Van. He minuted:

> The despatch concludes with an observation that is really stupefying . . . The *whole* peace settlement, Sir Walford Selby? Really? All you venture to protest about is that Germany should take our time and not hers about it! I have never read a more astounding composition by one of His Majesty's Representatives abroad . . . And of course I repudiate it entirely.

Selby beat a hasty retreat before this onslaught and amended his despatch in accordance with Van's wishes. As far as Van was concerned the quality of British diplomacy in Vienna left much to be desired.

The situation in Berlin was far better. Sir Horace Rumbold, Britain's first ambassador to the Nazi régime, suffered few illusions as to the essential brutality of Hitler's government and its *revanchist* aims. During his last seven months in Berlin he left the Foreign Office in no doubt as to his views; and they confirmed much of

what Van already suspected.[30] He was replaced by Sir Eric Phipps,*
Van's brother-in-law. On the surface their relationship was perfectly
amicable, and Van often went out of his way to praise Phipps for his
prescient and amusing reports; indeed, on the whole, he continued
the Rumbold tradition to Van's satisfaction. Misunderstandings did
occur, but were usually brushed aside.[31] Beneath the surface however there lurked a controlled tension, based perhaps more on an
ambivalent family relationship than on differences in policy. By
1938–39, their relationship had cooled to such a degree that Phipps,
now ambassador in Paris, was briefing his confidants in London
about Van's subterranean activities designed, no doubt, to undermine his own position.[32] Years later, reflecting on the effect of
Phipps's despatches, Van found himself in agreement with Baldwin's
well known quip that 'they had too much wit and not enough
warnings'.[33] His day-to-day minutes contain no hint of his later
judgement.

Phipps arrived in Berlin at the beginning of October 1933. Prior to
his appointment, Owen O'Malley† had suggested to Van the idea
of issuing instructions to Phipps, later to be published, which would
clarify the attitude of the government to the new German régime.
A revealing discussion ensued. O'Malley's brief was simple.[34] He
advocated 'a friendly and intimate attitude' towards Germany,
based on the recognition of legitimate German grievances dating
back from Versailles. Taking the broader view, his paper anticipated a loosening of the French connection, thereby enabling
Britain to restrain French policies contrary to her interests and
allowing her to act as an impartial mediator in the Franco-German
dispute.

These principles were quite foreign to Van's overall conception of
the direction British policy should take; and his minutes indicate
clearly his fundamental belief that any understanding with Germany would be enormously difficult, if not impossible, to achieve.
In any case, Van had thought of

> something much simpler & briefer. . . he [Phipps] should do all he
> could to cultivate good personal relations with the powers that

---

* Eric Clare Edmund Phipps (1875–1945): entered diplomatic service, 1899;
served at Constantinople, Rome, Paris, Madrid, Brussels; First Secretary, 1912;
counsellor, 1920; minister at Vienna, 1928–33; ambassador at Berlin, 1933–37;
Paris, 1937–39. Kn. 1927. In 1911 he married Frances Ward, Sarita's younger
sister.
† Owen St Clair O'Malley (1887–1974): entered Foreign Office, 1911; counsellor and head of Southern Department, 1933–1937; minister to Mexico, 1937–

> be in Germany . . . but that, in adopting this attitude, his friend-
> liness should be tempered by firmness and frankness . . . and he
> shd leave the German Govt under no illusion of the effects caused
> in this country by their methods . . . I feel that it is premature to go
> beyond this, and that we shall get onto dangerous ground if we do.

Van waved the rest of O'Malley's suggestions aside on the not unreasonable ground that they 'would start a controversy with every
paragraph'.

No published instructions were issued to Phipps. Of course, this
did not mean that the discussion was terminated. The search for an
agreement with Germany continued.[35] Despite the grave misgivings
of many of the officials, Van included,[36] the debate focused upon
how an agreement could be attained and on what terms, and not
whether it was worthwhile to achieve one at all. In principle at
least there was little to divide the officials.

Van therefore agreed that exploratory talks in Berlin should continue. 'Herr Hitler is bound to be opening his mouth wide at this
stage: it need not be filled, though something has got to go into the
maw.'[37] A tolerable agreement could be squeezed out of Germany
only by a combination of three factors: a drastic increase in the
British rearmament programme; the limitation of German rearmament to an acceptable level; and widening the basis of Anglo-
French cooperation. All these factors were connected, for France
would only accept a measure of German rearmament if Britain
proved herself a capable and reliable ally. Van was aware that time
was running out. Disarmament euphoria was widespread and acted
as a brake upon the government. By February 1934 Van noted that
'There is no prospect of a strong policy anywhere to arrest Hitlerism
now. The French would have adopted it if they had thought we
were willing and able. They well know we were emphatically neither
– above all not able.'[38]

The deficiencies in British strength led Van to believe that Germany could best be contained within an overall European settlement, to include Germany, and not by a bilateral Anglo-German
agreement. This was the theme he attempted to pursue in the coming
years. It differed little from the overall concept of Louis Barthou, the
French Foreign Minister, and when the two met in July 1934 Van
submitted a plan of his own which was similar in content to Barthou's

---

38; to Hungary, 1939–41; ambassador to Poland 1942–45; to Portugal, 1945–
47. Kn. 1943.

schemes.* For both statesmen such an agreement made no sense at
all without the inclusion of the Soviet Union. Owing to his anti-
Soviet prejudices, Van reached this conclusion reluctantly. But the
prospect of Soviet cooperation held an added attraction as it would
minimize the danger of a Russo-German deal, a not inconsiderable
bonus. In June, apparently on the initiative of Lady Vansittart,
Van first invited Ivan Maisky, the Soviet ambassador, to his house in
Park Street, and they continued to meet thereafter on a regular
basis.[39]

These feelers for a preliminary agreement broke down on the
barrier of German intractability. In September 1934 Germany
rejected the West's overtures, pleading that she could not be a
party to the pact while her own claim for equality in armaments
remained unsatisfied. Van rejected this excuse as entirely 'inadequate'.[40] Feeling that Britain had done her utmost, he advised
waiting upon a new French initiative. This failed to materialize.
After the assassination of Barthou in October, French policy fell
under the sway of Pierre Laval,† a highly intelligent though unscrupulous politician who was deeply suspicious of the Soviet Union and
more than anxious to build a bridge to Rome. It was almost impossible to pin Laval down to a straight answer. 'You are not a statesman,' he was once told, 'you are a tendency.'[41] Cooperation with
France, Van's basic postulate for restraining Germany, became that
much more difficult to attain.

Yet by the beginning of 1935 fresh ideas for a new approach to
Germany were under discussion. Plainly there existed a widespread
feeling that every effort, however forlorn it appeared at the outset,
should be made to break the deadlock. But also, as Professor Medlicott has pointed out, because 'Hitler in his moody, incalculable
way, was still ready to do business of some sort with England.'[42]
And his vague, ill-defined statements of conciliation and hints of
better things to come fell upon receptive ears in Whitehall.

The Anglo-French communiqué of 3 February 1935 laid out in

---

* There were three main components to Van's proposals: (a) a treaty of mutual
  assistance between Germany, Poland, Czechoslovakia, the Soviet Union, and
  the Baltic states; (b) a Franco-German convention to which the Soviet Union
  might later be associated; (c) a convention linking the assistance pacts with the
  Locarno agreements and the League Covenant. See also Van to Sir Clive Wigram, 10 July 1934, R.A., GV, M.2417/2.
† Pierre Laval (1883–1945): French Prime Minister, 1931–32, 1935–36; Foreign
  Minister, 1931–32, 1934–35; served as vice premier to Pétain in the wartime
  Vichy administration; chief of govt., 1942–44; executed for collaboration with
  the Nazis, 1945.

general terms the outline for an overall European settlement.* The scheme, though outwardly attractive, had little to commend it to the other powers. In particular, the Germans remained indifferent to the entire programme, with the exception of the air pact. With the programme disintegrating before it had got off the ground, the Foreign Office made a concerted effort to answer the innumerable arguments against it. Inter-departmental discussions were held with the aim of ironing out the objections and fashioning a programme acceptable to all.

On Van's instructions a memorandum was prepared which incorporated the opinions of Laurence Collier, Ralph Wigram, and Charles William Orde, heads of the Northern, Central and Far Eastern Departments, on the international position of the Soviet Union with special reference to the proposed Eastern pact. It was completed on 12 February.[43] Van marked it as 'a wise and excellent' contribution. But however much Van was impressed by this joint effort, its conclusions did not go unchallenged. Orme Sargent thought the memorandum faulty because it ignored 'the disadvantages and dangerous repercussions of a Franco-Russian alliance'. One of its authors, Collier,† vehemently rejected this argument on the grounds that British public opinion did not care

two hoots about the so-called encirclement of Germany; nor could I say that a Russo-French understanding would bring a German-Japanese or German-Italian alliance appreciably nearer than they are already.

* The declaration promoted the idea of an air Locarno; German agreement to an overall political-security system to include an eastern Locarno; a Danubian pact; revision of the disarmament clauses of Versailles; and the return of Germany to the League.

† If anyone in the Foreign Office at this period deserves the accolade of 'arch anti-appeaser', it is surely Laurence Collier. His minutes brooked no compromise, neither with Germany nor Italy. Of course, it can be argued, as indeed it was, that you cannot conduct diplomacy by saying 'No' to everything. Collier did; at least as far as the European dictators were concerned. And there is a shining honesty and consistency in his comments which bears favourable comparison with most of his contemporaries.

Collier made the interesting point that the policy of 'agreed memoranda' was practised only in the Central Department, 'but not, I think, elsewhere in the Office – certainly not in the Northern Department'. His reasoning was persuasive: 'It seems to me that Vansittart – and, when necessary, the Secretary of State himself – ought to be in possession of the real, individual views of his subordinates, in order that he may then choose between them by use of his own

Van minuted his agreement. He strived hard to achieve a consensus of opinion, preferring not to put conflicting memoranda before the cabinet. But the differences of outlook were too great to bridge.

From this internal debate, Van pasted together his own contribution.[44] Basing his argument on the assumption that the Soviet Union had two enemies 'of real political importance, Japan and Germany', he included the Soviet government among the 'wholehearted supporters of the present territorial status quo in Europe and Asia'. How to prevent her from joining the revisionist bloc? Only by finding an alternative to the Eastern pact in its present form of a general guarantee of mutual assistance. And here Van proposed 'to build up something on the basis of the non-aggression arrangements already in force in the East of Europe'. Soundings to this effect were already being taken in Paris. But even at this very early stage in the proceedings Van was beset by a nagging doubt as to the prospects of success. Here were the two sides to his policy, one possibly eroding the other. On the one hand an intuitive feeling that it was necessary to keep the momentum of negotiations moving, hoping perhaps that by the very act of talking something positive would emerge; while on the other, a growing realization that the Germans were playing their own game according to their own terms of reference.

Van had laid out yet another grand design, and the cabinet approved it. But having defined the final goal, the government, in the most perverse manner, proceeded to block its own path by a series of clumsy diplomatic manœuvres which left Britain dangerously isolated from her potential continental allies. Van cannot escape his share of the responsibility for the eclipse of British credibility during these critical months.

It was the preparations relating to the Simon–Eden trip to Berlin which set the pattern. They were marked by indecision and hesitancy. Simon's ability to carry the negotiations to a successful conclusion did not infuse confidence in his officials,[45] particularly after they received information from Belgium that Hitler's position had hardened on practically every issue.[46] Van minuted this depressing report that 'No settlement on these lines is possible.' In these circumstances was there any point in going ahead with the visit? Van obviously had his doubts. Unquestionably, the officials instinc-

---

judgement; otherwise each individual view has to be distorted in order to appearance of unanimity.'

tively distrusted this playing at summitry, and would much have preferred, both on professional and practical grounds, a well-trained, seasoned diplomat assuming responsibility for the talks, pinning down the Germans at every twist in the negotiations. In the event it was Hitler who made the first move. As a result of the publication of the British defence white paper in early March he contracted a diplomatic chill and the visit was postponed. Within a few days the Germans had overturned the disarmament clauses of Versailles. Hitler had taken what he knew was about to be offered. The British bargaining position had been destroyed even before the negotiations had begun.

Despite the obvious provocation of the German move, it was decided that the visit should take place. Simon, Eden, and particularly Phipps, favoured this course, and the cabinet acceded to their views.[47] Van was not so certain. Convinced that German demands were 'going up and up' he felt that the cabinet had gone too far and too fast: 'Unless we are extremely careful, indeed *more* careful in future, we may find that the German jack o' lantern has led us into a deep and irretrievable bog.'[48] Three days before his ministers were scheduled to arrive in Berlin, Van warned Phipps in the strongest possible language of the necessity to take a 'very firm line' with the Germans. He went on:

> In this I feel that the reputations of you all from the Secretary of State downwards are at stake, and not only the reputation of the Mission itself, but yours which stands very high. I hope therefore that I may count on you, Eric, to put all your weight into the maintenance of the only line which can be of any avail . . . and that this firm line will be maintained unflinchingly by you *all*.[49]

But Van was equally disturbed by the fact that the decision to go to Berlin had been taken without first consulting either France or Italy. If a European front were to be maintained, it was vital that all three powers should act in concert, and should be seen to do so. If not, the suspicion would inevitably arise that Britain was planning a separate deal with Germany. Van reflected that by ignoring her allies Britain was treading on dangerous ground, and indeed threatening the success of the mission, as Hitler would be bound to exploit this breach in allied solidarity.[50] However, when the meeting eventually took place on 25–26 March, Hitler, contrary to his expectations, proved much less refractory than he had imagined, and did not reject outright any of the proposals put to him.[51] Although Simon was disappointed at not having achieved a greater measure

Anthony Eden (far left) and Sir Samuel Hoare (second left) attending a memorial
service for Arthur Henderson in 1935. Van walks next to Sir Samuel Hoare.
(*Radio Times Hulton Picture Library*)

Robert Vansittart leaving his home in Park Street, Mayfair, 1934.
(*Radio Times Hulton Picture Library*)

PHEW!—By POY

Phew! This cartoon shows the way in which Van was caught between the policies of Sir Samuel Hoare and Sir Anthony Eden.

Life has not become less strenuous for Sir Robert Vansittart, the Permanent Under-Secretary for Foreign

(By courtesy of the Evening

of agreement, the impression remained strong that Hitler was open to persuasion: the talks could continue. But to a certain degree the damage had already been done. In Paris and Rome suspicions deepened as to Britain's ultimate intentions.

This pattern was repeated by the Anglo-German naval agreement of 18 June 1935 which allowed Germany to build up to thirty-five per cent of Commonwealth naval strength. As a result, the already tenuous ties between the Western powers were impaired even further. The Stresa front, signed the previous April, proved to be an extremely fragile affair.*

Even after much reflection the naval agreement remains one of the most puzzling events of 1935, particularly in view of the disastrous diplomatic repercussions which followed in its wake.[52] Why then did Van aquiesce in it? He was certainly aware, as his minutes indicate, of Germany's record of 'mendacity' in naval affairs.[53] Thus, though he did not 'welcome' the agreement, he did not 'object' to it, and mainly, it seems, because he held the general view that it was just a technical, limiting accord desired in particular by the Admiralty to ward off the Japanese challenge in the Far East.[54] He was also swayed by Robert Craigie's† analysis of the way the negotiations were expected to develop. Craigie, the Foreign Office expert on naval matters, believed that the Germans had raised the thirty-five per cent ratio as a bargaining device, and that once the negotiations got under way it would be possible to cut the German demands down to more modest and acceptable proportions.[55] Ribbentrop,‡ the chief German negotiator, sadly disappointed him, for he presented the thirty-five per cent figure as an ultimatum and refused to budge from it. 'Tactless rather than faithless', was Van's final verdict on the agreement.

After the agreement was signed he congratulated Ribbentrop and told von Hoesch§ that he would defend it 'with complete conviction'.[56] Were these diplomatic platitudes? Not entirely. Van's acceptance

---

* The Stresa front was constructed by Britain, France and Italy to protect the German denunciation of Versailles and reaffirm the powers' adherence to Austrian independence. See also, pp. 159–63.

† Robert L. Craigie (1883–1959): entered Foreign Office, 1907; first secretary, 1919; counsellor, 1928; Assistant Under Secretary of State, 1934–37; ambassador to Japan, 1937–41. Kn. 1936.

‡ Joachim Ribbentrop (1893–1946): German ambassador to Britain, 1936–38; Foreign Minister, 1938–45; sentenced to death at Nüremberg, 1946.

§ Leopold von Hoesch (1881–1936): German ambassador to Great Britain, 1932–36. His sudden death in April 1936, ostensibly as a result of his exertions during the Rhineland crisis, became the subject of much speculation.

E

of the agreement must be seen in relation to the wider concepts of British policy as laid down in the Anglo-French communiqué of February and his own memorandum of the same month. Hitler had already beaten the Foreign Office to the post by his March initiative; it was essential not to allow him a repeat performance. Once the Germans were tied down over a relatively minor issue, at least when compared with an air Locarno or an Eastern pact, it would be possible to go on to more meaningful agreements. It was a question of priorities; and for the Foreign Office, Van included, the naval question apparently came down low on the list. In this way, it can be argued that the British were really doing the French a great favour in coming to a naval agreement with Germany. And this perhaps explains why the Foreign Office took for granted French approval.* If so, it was a grievous miscalculation, for a wiser Van later confided to von Hoesch that by signing the treaty the British had lost favour in Paris.

Van had manifestly failed in his duty to assess the diplomatic consequences of the agreement before it was concluded. However, once the agreement had been reached, and he had begun to absorb some of its shock-waves, he had second thoughts. With the Abyssinian question coming to the fore, he was desperately in need of French support and could not afford to generate further mistrust in Paris. Van now accepted without qualification the French line that a future settlement with Germany must only be a comprehensive one, a package deal.[57] As far as he was concerned, the day of bilateral agreements of any description was over.[58]

But even his comprehensive settlement was as far off as ever. He was convinced that the desire to placate Germany, if pushed to unreasonable lengths, would lead to the alienation of France and Italy, as had already happened to some extent over the naval agreement, and therefore the increased isolation of Britain.[59] The negotiations lost their momentum. In any case, Van was deeply pessimistic as to their outcome.[60] The government continued to voice public approval of the Eastern pact, but the voices carried neither conviction nor enthusiasm. In the event, it was Germany who finally withdrew. Von Hoesch informed the Foreign Office that, owing to the Franco-Soviet alignment,† his government had lost

---

* This kind of reasoning can easily be detected in the interviews quoted above, and also in a report of a conversation between Eden and Laval on 22 June 1935 (CAB. 24/255).

† On 2 May 1935, a Franco-Russian alliance was concluded, due to be renewed after five years. Each side promised to aid the other in case of unprovoked

interest in the Eastern pact.[61] The lapse in German interest came at a convenient moment. By this time Van was wholly absorbed in the Abyssinian crisis; it was to be the most decisive issue in his career.

NOTES

1. A private communication.
2. K. Young, *op. cit.*, 327.
3. *M.P.*, 398.
4. For a critical note on Simon see M. Cowling, *The Impact of Hitler: British Politics and British Policy* (Cambridge University Press, 1975), 33, 55–7; and A. L. Rowse, *All Souls and Appeasement* (London, 1961), 15–17.
5. He admitted that his resignation in 1916 was a mistake, 'paid for at a heavy pace'. *Retrospect*, 108.
6. *M.P.*, 427–8.
7. *Dalton Diaries*, 3 May 1939. 'Them all' referred to the Big Four: Chamberlain, Hoare, Halifax and Simon.
8. See, for example, some of Van's remarks regarding Simon's views on the disarmament question. Correspondence in Simon Papers, F.O. 800/291, 9242.
9. Avon, 125.
10. *Ibid.*, 187.
11. *Ibid.*, 26, 28, 30, 219–20, for criticism of Simon's methods.
12. *M.P.*, 429.
13. See C. Thorne, *The Limits of Foreign Policy. The West, the League and the Far Eastern Crisis of 1931–33* (London, 1972), 149.
14. See 'The United Kingdom and Europe', C.P. 4(32), CAB. 24/227.
15. Quoted by Thorne, *op. cit.*, 156.
16. *Ibid*, 188.
17. Van's comments in Wigram to Phipps, 2 October 1935, *Ph.P.* 2/25.
18. Thorne, *op. cit.*, 189, quoting from cabinet records of 11 November 1931.
19. Simon's minutes of 14 November 1931, *B.D.*, 2, viii, no. 720.
20. See Van's minutes on a memorandum by Sir J. Pratt, 1 February 1932, *B.D.*, 2, ix, no. 238.
21. See Van to Simon, 8 February 1932, *B.D.*, 2, ix, no. 378. Also Thorne, *op. cit.* 225–72; and W. R. Louis, *British Strategy in the Far East, 1919–39* (O.U.P., 1971).
22. See notes of a conversation between Lord Cecil and Van, 9 May 1933, *B.D.*, 2, ix, no. 553.
23. Quoted in Thorne, 362; see also Van's comments in *B.D.*, 2, ix, no. 419.
24. Minutes of 30 September 1933 on draft instructions to Sir E. Phipps, drawn up by the late Sir O. O'Malley (hereafter 'Draft Instructions'). I am grateful to Sir Owen for allowing me to see his copy of the correspondence. I have been unable to trace it in the files of P.R.O.
25. These themes may be followed in *B.D.*, 2, v, nos. 254–370.
26. The following correspondence is in the MacDonald Papers 2/7 at the time of writing in the possession of Mr D. Marquand, M.P.

---

aggression. This agreement was not buttressed by any military convention. Though it was unpopular in conservative circles in France, it was ratified on 27 February 1936.

27. Unfortunately, his original draft remains untraced, probably destroyed. His revised version may be seen in C.P. 212(33), CAB. 24/243 (printed in *B.D.*, 2, v, no. 371).
28. See interview between Van and Grandi, 23 August 1933, F.O. 371/16654. C. 7618/2092/3; also Vnst. 1/8.
29. See F.O. 371/18358. R. 7108/37/3. For Selby's version of the incident see *Diplomatic Twilight*, 40–41.
30. See, for example, *B.D.*, 2, v. no. 229; and *M.P.* 476–78. See also M. Gilbert, *Sir Horace Rumbold: Portrait of a Diplomat, 1869–1941* (London, 1973).
31. See, for example, Van to Phipps, 26 April 1935, *Ph.P.* 2/17. This file contains correspondence which illustrates perfectly Van's method of mollifying Phipps.
32. See Phipps to Sir Horace Wilson, 13 December 1938, *Ph.P.* 3/5, also 'Eclipse', pp. 212–13.
33. *M.P.*, 445.
34. See 'Draft Instructions', *op. cit.*
35. This is the subject of Professor Medlicott's illuminating essay, *Britain and Germany: The Search for Agreement, 1930–37* (University of London: London, Athlone Press, 1969).
36. See his minutes of 11 July and 1 December 1933, Vnst. 2/7, 2/10.
37. Minutes of 12 December 1933, Vnst. 2/13; also 2/35.
38. Minutes of 10 February 1934, Vnst. 2/14.
39. See Van's minutes of 28 July 1934, Vnst. 2/16; *B.D.*, 2, vi, nos. 537, 544; notes of an interview with Maisky, 9 August 1934, F.O. 371/18299, N. 4718/1/38. Also Maisky, *op. cit.*, 43–5; and an interview with Lady Vansittart, 31 October 1972.
40. His minutes of 16 September 1934, Vnst. 2/19.
41. See Templewood (Sir Samuel Hoare), *op. cit.*, 158. Nicholas Titulesco, the Rumanian Foreign Minister, was the perceptive observer.
42. Medlicott, *op. cit.*, 12.
43. See F.O. 371/19460, N. 927/135/38.
44. See 'International Position of the Soviet Union in Relation to France, Germany and Japan', 21 February 1935, F.O. 371/19460, N. 880/135/38.
45. See Avon, 125; and Medlicott, 15.
46. See F.O. 371/18828, C. 1818/55/18.
47. Eden minuted to this effect on 15 March (F.O. 371/18828, C. 1818/55/18) i.e. a day before the German government adopted compulsory military service and announced the formation of an army of 36 divisions, but six days after they had verified the existence of the *Luftwaffe*. His memoirs are much vaguer on this point, where he claims 'we ought to have returned the diplomatic cold' (p. 129).
48. Quoted by Medlicott, 16.
49. Van to Phipps, 22 March 1935, *Ph.P.* 2/17; also Medlicott, *op. cit.*, 16.
50. See Avon, *op. cit.*, 129–30.
51. For a summary of the talks, see *G.D.*, C, iii, nos. 555, 564, and F.O. 371/18831, C. 2580/55/18. Also C.P. 69(35), CAB. 24/254.
52. For discussions of the agreement and its background, see D. C. Watt, 'The Anglo-German Naval Agreement of 1935: An Interim Judgement', *Journal of Modern History*, v. xxviii, no. 2 (1956), and Hines H. Hall III, 'The Foreign-Policy Process in Britain, 1934–35, and 'The Origins of the Anglo-German Naval Agreement', *The Historical Journal*, 19, 2 (1976).

53. See his minutes of 3 June 1935, F.O. 371/18860, C. 4372/206/18.
54. See *M.P.*, 525–8. This version received indirect confirmation by Ribbentrop, who negotiated the agreement on behalf of Germany. 'Although he [Vansittart] welcomed the agreement in general terms, he seemed to be extraordinarily nervous, and I had the impression that he did not like the course which events had taken.' *The Ribbentrop Memoirs* (London, 1954), 42.
55. See Hines, *op. cit.*
56. See notes of their interview, 19 June 1935, F.O. 371/18847, C. 4952/55/18; and *G.D.*, C, iv, no. 201.
57. See the Eden–Laval interview (CAB. 24/255) where Laval argues this point strongly.
58. Minutes of 30 July 1935, Vnst. 2/18.
59. Minutes of 5 July 1935, Vnst. 2/22.
60. See minutes of 3 June 1935, F.O. 371/18860, C. 4372/206/18.
61. See *G.D.*, C, iii, 234, 249, 252, 253, 281.

CHAPTER VIII

'Bricks Without Straw'
The Problems of Defence

———————————————⊰✧⊱———————————————

VAN ABIDED BY GREY'S DICTUM that 'You must not rely on your foreign policy to protect the United Kingdom'.[1] Complementing his keep Germany lean policy, he laboured to boost Britain's defence capacity which he saw as a prerequisite for a successful foreign policy. In June 1931 he attacked the basic assumptions underlying the ten year rule.[2]* Successive governments had imposed upon the Foreign Office an impossible undertaking. 'This perpetual making of bricks without straw is a heartbreaking task',[3] he complained on more than one occasion. Under no illusion as to the difficulties, particularly on the home front, he wrote:

> Germany will attract friends to her camp if she is allowed to grow while we remain weak. Were that to happen, there would eventually be a landslide in Europe and the democratic principle would vanish. It is a pity that this sleepy and complacent democracy of ours is still so very far from realising how much its existence is menaced, unless it is prepared to make some sacrifice to defend it. It has a respite before it, but not a very long one. Will it utilise the interval properly? . . The possibility of averting the danger at an early stage has passed. We must now begin looking clearly into the future. I wonder if this country is capable of realism.[4]

Above all, were the politicians capable of realism? Van told Baldwin: ' "You have a *caisse de jeu* to make any gambler's mouth water. You

* The ten year rule was devised by Lloyd George in 1919 who informed his military staff that they need not anticipate a major war within the coming ten years. This ruling was renewed periodically until, in 1928, on Churchill's initiative, it was agreed that this assumption should be reviewed annually.

could lose a packet and still have a majority of 250." He rightly reminded me that he knew much more than I about this sort of thing. Whereas I merely guessed that by pressing on with rearmament he might drop 50 seats, 100 on a division, he feared a landslide.'[5]

By the autumn of 1933 it was patently obvious that the disarmament conference had entered its terminal stage. The government was faced with the unhappy prospect of having to initiate a measure of rearmament in the face of widespread internal opposition to any increase in arms expenditure. Van's aim of steady progress towards disarmament augmented by international commitments faded away. Britain would now have to attend first and foremost to her own defences. If this could be combined with an overall political settlement, so much the better. But it was now of cardinal importance to guarantee that Britain's defence capability matched the challenge confronting her security.

Nevertheless, Van clung to the hope of salvaging something out of the Geneva wreckage even after Germany left the disarmament conference and the League on 14 October. Hitler had astutely covered up his move by throwing to the Western powers a variety of substitutes for their consideration: non-aggression pacts; the renunciation of Alsace-Lorraine; even a convention on the limitation of armaments. Thus throughout the winter of 1933–34 negotiations of a sort were in progress with Germany. Ultimately they came to nothing. But differences did emerge as to how seriously to treat Hitler's overtures. Hankey, for example, inclined to believe that Hitler 'means business' and that his proposals deserved 'to be taken very seriously'. Hence he argued that direct negotiations with Germany should take first priority, avoiding 'a political Manifesto' as 'the method of Geneva' which 'Hitler has publicly claimed that he detests'. Van was not 'so hopeful' about the outcome of the dialogue; but he too did not contemplate any public announcement 'so long as the German conversations . . . offered any prospects'.[6] Clearly sceptical about Hitler's motives and pessimistic as to the outcome of the conversations, he hoped, in any eventuality, to use Geneva as a platform to discredit Hitler even further, and as a buttress to, not substitute for, Britain's own rearmament programme.

Baldwin was not unaware of the consequences of a breakdown of the disarmament conference. At his request Van, Fisher and Hankey were invited to prepare a paper for the cabinet on just such an eventuality. The three officials submitted their conclusions on 4 October. They bore all the hallmarks of Van's ideas. Certain that Germany intended to abrogate unilaterally the disarmament restrictions of the Versailles treaty, they postulated that

> This step is essential to further stages of the [German government's] programme, since the recovery of the Polish corridor and the alteration of the Eastern frontier of Germany (and perhaps, incidentally, the *Anschluss* with Austria) cannot be accomplished without force, since it is only to force that Poland could yield. Once Germany was free from any menace on her Eastern frontier the next objects in her programme are the recovery of her lost possessions in the West and of her colonies. These final stages become of vital concern to the British Empire.[7]

Throughout, the German menace was hammered home: its warlike spirit, its massive military potential. They enquired of the cabinet whether Britain could afford to disinterest herself in a European war. If not, and the authors of the memorandum left no doubt as to their opinion on the matter, the only alternative lay in giving a clear, unambiguous warning to Germany that Britain would never abandon her international obligations. In any eventuality, the cabinet could not ignore 'the necessary corollary, namely, an increase in expenditure on Imperial Defence'.

Van, not content with this explicit advice, submitted a supplementary question of his own. Outraged by German behaviour at the disarmament conference, he warned the cabinet that if the Germans were allowed to get away with such wild demands*

> the future of Europe will indeed be black; for the Germans will be in a position to make (and will therefore make) war at such a relatively early date that their present regime will not have had time to settle down. The present exorbitant demands of Germany . . . are another clear indication of her eventual aggressive intentions, of which, as I have often ventured to point out, there can be no permanent doubt.[8]

These warnings were immediately followed by the annual report of the Chiefs of Staff.[9] Their review emphasized the deteriorating international situation and in particular the dangers inherent in Germany's rearmament programme. It also pointed to the possibility of military intervention on the Continent should Germany embark

---

* The Germans had demanded an unspecified quantity – 'elastic' as Van defined it – of weapons forbidden under the Versailles treaty, together with the retention of $1\frac{1}{2}$ million trained men composed of the para-military units of the Nazi party.

on a policy of aggression. The upshot of this analysis was that additional increases in defence expenditure were inevitable. The government's chief advisers, both military and political, appeared to be of one mind.

On the strength of the above evidence the government appointed a special sub-committee of the Committee of Imperial Defence 'to consider the influence the international situation would have on the priority of provision of Service requirements'.[10] It became known as the Defence Requirements Committee (DRC). Hankey was appointed its chairman; Van and Fisher were the other civilian members; and the Chiefs of Staff* completed the forum. The civilians dominated the committee. There was no secret here. With the exception of Chatfield, the service chiefs found themselves overshadowed by the civilians, lightweights floundering in the heavyweight division. Ellington was quite unable to grasp the strategic needs of his service and relate them to the changing international situation; he had to be constantly coaxed forward, and even then he was reluctant to advance. Montgomery-Massingberd was scarcely better. One of his political chiefs thought him 'very inadequate and out of date'.[11] Fisher is reputed to have despised the Chiefs of Staff, and, with the exception of his Whitehall associates, 'felt himself to be a titan among minnows'.[12] On the other hand, Hankey, Fisher and Van made up a very powerful combination indeed, not that they were always in full agreement. Hankey, for example, went on record as strongly distrusting Fisher's judgement, particularly on naval questions and the defence of the Pacific.[13] On one occasion, he even offered the opinion that Fisher 'is rather mad' due to 'some mysterious nerve disorder' which affected his judgement.[14] All this, however, did not prevent Van and Fisher from working closely together; they were in general agreement on most of the major issues that confronted the committee.

The DRC first considered a recent conclusion of the Chiefs-of-Staff that for the moment the main danger lay in the Far East. Hankey and Chatfield were the chief advocates of the 'Imperial' school. This report had already been the subject of a detailed

---

* (Alfred) Ernle (Montacute) Chatfield (1873–1967): Admiral, 1930; C.-in-C., Mediterranean fleet, 1930–33; First Sea Lord and Chief of Naval Staff, 1933–38; Admiral of Fleet, 1935; Minister for Co-ordination of Defence, 1939–40 and member of war cabinet under Neville Chamberlain. Kn. 1919.

Sir Edward Leonard Ellington (1877–1967): Air Chief Marshal and Chief of Air Staff, 1933–37; Inspector-General, RAF, 1937–40. Kn. 1920.

Sir Archibald (Armar) Montgomery-Massingberd (1871–1947): Chief of Imperial General Staff, 1933–36. Kn. 1919.

Foreign Office inquiry. The overwhelming majority of departmental opinion had endorsed its conclusion. There were two exceptions: Sir Victor Wellesley and Van. Van put his case before the Committee:

> The order of priorities which put Japan first pre-supposed that Japan would attack us after we had got into difficulties elsewhere. 'Elsewhere' therefore came first, not second; and elsewhere could only mean Europe, and Europe could only mean Germany . . . Our resources were not sufficient to meet a menace from both Japan and Germany, and . . . of the two Germany was the greater menace.[15]

The committee was assured that if the Foreign Office were allowed a reasonably free hand, diplomatic relations with Japan could be prevented 'from deteriorating into a rupture'. The meaning of his statement was clear: squaring up to Germany; accommodation with Japan. Fisher supported him entirely. The final report reflected their views. Germany was designated as 'the ultimate potential enemy against whom our "long range" defence policy has to be directed', while towards Japan they envisaged an 'ultimatum policy of accommodation . . . and an immediate and provisional policy of "showing a tooth".'[16]

There were two main aspects to the discussions of the DRC. First, he political implications of elevating the German menace to first priority. Since it was obvious that Great Britain did not have sufficient resources to fight simultaneously two major wars on two widely distant fronts, it followed that Anglo-Japanese relations would have to be improved even at the expense of the American connection. The entire concept of British Far Eastern policy since the Washington treaties would have to be reversed, or at best radically amended.

Van accepted this verdict with equanimity, seeing in it a logical conclusion to the unhappy story of Anglo-American relations since the end of the war. Of course, he was quite aware of the complications which would result as a consequence of the proposed new course. Britain's relations with both China and the United States would be adversely affected. He did not view this prospect with overt enthusiasm, and would much have preferred keeping both the Japanese and the Americans in play, if possible.[17] Fisher, on the other hand, jumped at the idea with positive glee. Both harped upon this point at the end of January.[18] Some days later Van recorded:

> I will only repeat my strengthened conviction that we have been too tender, not to say subservient, with the US for a long time

past. It is we who have made all the advances, and received nothing in return. It is still necessary, and I still desire as much as ever, that we should get on well with this untrustworthy race ... We shall never get very far; they will always let us down.[19]

This was followed by a fierce letter from Fisher on the same theme. The United States were 'a serious obstacle to our getting on terms with Japan; and I believe we have got to "disentangle" ourselves from the USA. They are no use to us, but make use of us – to our detriment – vis à vis Japan.'[20] Fisher made it clear that Britain could not afford to dissipate her resources in any way which would expose her 'to be overwhelmed by an eventually rearmed and bellicose Germany – which country is in my opinion our ultimate danger'. Fisher never lost an opportunity of repeating his views. Indeed he did so with such ferocity that he appears almost pathological in his dislike of the Americans. It was Baldwin who made the apposite remark that Van 'hates the Germans as much as Fisher hates the Americans'.[21]

During 1934 an attempt was made to attain an Anglo-Japanese *rapprochement*. Fisher took a leading role in these affairs, with Van's firm backing. Eventually they terminated in failure, and Britain was forced back upon the 'self-seeking and unreliable' Americans, to the intense disapprobation of Fisher and the annoyance of Van. Whatever may be said of the moral issues involved in coming to terms with a bellicose Japan bent on expansion, there can be no doubt that the foreclosure on the Japanese alternative severely restricted Britain's diplomatic options, particularly in view of the United States' barely disguised reluctance to cooperate in Far Eastern affairs. Certainly the danger of a major war on two widely distant fronts remained.

Having agreed upon the political order of priorities, the DRC now set out to translate it into a series of practical proposals designed to remedy 'the worst deficiencies' of service requirements. Van's main concern was Britain's lack of ability to repel an air attack. Perfectly aware that Germany was constructing a powerful air fleet, he was haunted by the vision of a 'knock-out blow' which would eliminate Britain at the outset of a war. Fisher shared his apprehension. And they in turn merely reflected a wide measure of informed opinion throughout the country and in the government.[22]

Long before the DRC was convened Van had expressed himself forcibly on this subject:

I feel myself that the real crux is air disarmament and I know you [Hankey] share this. If no serious progress can be made with this, I think it does not matter much what happens to the rest of the disarmament programme since this is the arm in which we are likely to be faced in the future with the most bitter armament race . . . The speed and ease with which new types are being developed makes it a far more formidable danger than anything in the way of naval or military armaments.[23]

A month later he wrote that Germany will rely in the future on

the mechanized weapons such as tanks, big guns, and above all military aircraft . . . Aviation in particular offers to Germany the quickest and easiest way of making her own power effective. With her vast industrial system and her already flourishing civil aviation, she will have no difficulty and no insurmountable expense in proceeding promptly to the creation of one of the leading air forces of Europe . . . Aviation is the field above all others in which Germany could attempt with some hope of success to catch up France without undue delay. Against military aircraft the extensive fortifications of the French frontier cannot avail.[24]

Nor did German behaviour diminish his fears. During the first months of 1933 there had been unmistakable signs that the Germans were secretly rearming. In May, Brigadier A. C. Temperley, the British military representative to the League, composed a strongly worded 'mad-dog' memorandum on the state of German rearmament, recommending that there should be no relaxation of the treaty of Versailles 'unless a complete revision of present military preparations and tendencies takes place in Germany'. Van warmly supported these views, and instructed that the paper, together with other evidence which he had collected, be circulated as a cabinet document.[25]

The following month the Germans ostentatiously announced that unidentified aircraft had dropped subversive literature over Berlin. There was of course no foundation for this claim; but a high-ranking official in the German air ministry immediately proclaimed that 'in no circumstances can we admit further postponement of the question of equality of rights in the air and on land'.[26] Further disclosures by responsible German officials made it abundantly clear that Germany was engaged upon the construction of a powerful military air fleet. On 15 July Göring, seemingly throwing all caution to the wind, requested from the British government twenty-five to fifty aircraft 'for policing purposes in Germany'.[27] This astonishing request was turned down politely but firmly.

Van began his work on the DRC fully conscious of the German air threat, and convinced that the indiscriminate, irresponsible nature of aerial warfare was particularly well suited to the Nazi mentality.[28] In many ways British rearmament plans in general were a function of her air build-up in particular. Air expansion dominated British rearmament strategy throughout this period. And although the Royal Air Force was the junior service, Van, apparently, was intent on securing its future: ' "Charlie", he informed Lord Londonderry,* "I'm going to make yours a great department".'[29]

Thus the DRC's recommendation that the 'fifty-two squadron scheme', originally adopted in June 1923, should be speedily completed, was of crucial importance. This meant, if put into effect, an additional forty squadrons to cover home defence and to provide air support for an army expeditionary force. Van considered even these figures quite inadequate. Two days before the report was due to be signed he insisted on absolute clarity in its formulation which should state 'what is really necessary, thus leaving to the Cabinet to decide how far the necessary provisions proposed should be undertaken'.[30] He had in mind improvements in anti-aircraft defences which, even after the committee's recommendations, would leave Britain virtually defenceless north of the Wash. But of greater importance, he argued for an extra twenty-five squadrons as the barest minimum to meet the country's needs. Again Fisher backed him. But Hankey, not entirely convinced of Van's case, and anxious to terminate the committee's work at an early date, hastily composed a harmless formula:

> Owing to the accumulating evidence that Germany has increased her Air Force and intends to expand them rapidly, some of us accept this limitation with no small misgiving, and only on the understanding that the question is kept under close observation.

Van agreed to this weak compromise with some reluctance, but mainly because the committee also recommended that 'it remain in being in order to review the scheme, as finally approved by the Cabinet, at appropriate intervals'. In other words there would be further opportunities for Van to make his case. The report was signed on 28 February 1934.

There then occurred an incident which can only be explained by the total inability of the Chief of Air Staff, Ellington, to grasp the most elementary needs of his own service. He wrote to Hankey on

---

* Charles Stewart Henry Vane-Tempest-Stewart (1878–1949): Under Secretary of State for Air, 1920–21; Minister of Education, Northern Ireland, 1921–26; First Commissioner of Works, 1928–29, 1931; Secretary of State for Air, 1931–35. Succeeded as 7th Marquess of Londonderry, 1915.

the 28th that the fifty-two squadron scheme would not be sufficient to include an air contingent for an expeditionary force. This point had been under continuous discussion for almost three months, and Ellington himself had claimed that 'for a war on the Continent no extra units would be needed'.[31] When Van heard of Ellington's second thoughts he exploded. He told Hankey that Ellington's letter threw everything 'into the melting pot again'. He asked for another meeting of the committee, and requested that the report be pigeon-holed until further clarification. Moreover, Ellington had had the temerity to intrude upon Van's special province, questioning the reliability of France. 'Whether we can rely on France', Van retorted, 'depends entirely on circumstances, and in particular (a) whether we are worth counting on, and (b) how we handle them in these crucial coming years.' He castigated the large and stupid school of thought in this country always ready to vent its spleen on France. 'Why then should we assume that the French will step into every breach with or for us?' Van felt unable to accept such a 'hazardous doctrine where our national safety is concerned'. What particularly galled Van was the Air Marshal's lack of support for his own pro-posal for an extra twenty-five squadrons at their last meeting. This 'puzzled' Van, as well it might. Montgomery-Massingberd also came in for harsh criticism, along more or less the same lines, for Ellington's silence directly affected the strength of the territorial army, also, in Van's opinion, in dire need of reinforcement.*

At the time of the incident Van was bed-ridden with 'flu. Hankey succeeded in lowering his temperature. He himself was by no measure persuaded by Van's arguments. Though concerned with the German air menace, he doubted the ability of the Germans to build as rapidly as Van forecast. 'They have also to build up a navy and that is not going to be done very quickly.'[32] Again he questioned Van's figures

* The emphasis here placed on air expansion should not be interpreted as neglect for the needs of the Army. During the sessions of the DRC Van argued for the reinforcement of the territorials and the strengthening of an expeditionary force whose rightful place would be alongside the French army. He explained his reasons in a letter to General Dill, then Director of Military Operations and Intelligence at the War Office, in March 1934: 'those who question the neces-sity of an Expeditionary Force are in danger of following the will o' the wisp that led straight to 1914. We should again be written off – continentally.' (Quoted by P. Dennis, *Decision by Default* (London, 1972), 39.) French support could not be taken for granted under all circumstances. Indeed, only by raising a credible land force to be used in the event of war against Germany would it be possible to convince France that it was in her interest to support Britain. The inability, or lack of resolve, to intervene militarily in a continental war would lead to political

about the growth of the German air force, contending that they were larger than any he had yet seen. But the differences ultimately, he stressed, were of 'degrees, or, rather imminence'. To create a fuss now, after the report had been signed and sent off to the printers, would be embarrassing for all. Van resigned himself to a tactical retreat: 'Keep my letter in pickle by all means if you prefer. I shall perhaps ask for it to be taken out later in the year.' Hankey noted: 'with infinite difficulty I have achieved a unanimous report.'[33]

Despite the unanimity of the report the differences remained, and were to grow steadily with the passing of years. Some experts at the Air Ministry seriously questioned the Foreign Office's estimation of the German air threat. They forecast 1942 as the critical year when Germany would be ready for all out war, and in consequence advised gradual, certainly not too rapid, expansion of Britain's first line air power.[34] Nor did the Air Staff accept with equanimity the implication of the report's assertion that the fifty-two squadron scheme would be used for home defence. Under the tutelage of Trenchard,* the Air Staff had come to accept an offensive doctrine as the conventional wisdom. They wished to expand the RAF's striking force, and to curtail all attempts, particularly from unenlightened civilians, to impose upon them a defensive role which in their estimation would be wholly illusory. Arguments over the pace of German air expansion and the strategic role of the British and German air fleets in the event of war continued to divide Van from many of his colleagues.

Van was most disturbed by this turn of events. The lack of expertise, of professionalism on the part of the service chiefs was beyond

---

and diplomatic isolation. These arguments did not change fundamentally over the years. 'It is obviously impossible to limit our military effort in advance without receding into impotent isolation' (minutes of 8 Jan. 1937, F.O. 371/20701, C. 205/205/62). Or, 'This is a fantastic and impossible situation. It may not be impossible to accelerate the date at which our infinitesimal army will be properly armed because, owing to lack of foresight, capacity has not been created in time, but what we can do is to see to it here and now that our larger military contributions, which would have to be in the nature of let us say at least 20 divisions, should not be put in the same position, and that the capacity for equipment, including guns and tanks, should be authorised and initiated at the beginning of February 1939.' (Minutes of 24 January 1939, F.O. 371/22922, C. 940/281/17, also of 21 and 30 January, *ibid.*) In this connection, see also M. Howard, *op. cit.*, 105–6.

* Hugh Montague Trenchard (1873–1956): General Officer Commanding Royal Flying Corps, 1915–17; Chief of Air Staff, 1919–29; Marshal of RAF, 1927. Kn. 1920. Cr. Baron, 1930.

his comprehension.* Ellington's behaviour, by any estimation, was unbelievably inept. When asked the number of army cooperation squadrons required, he replied that the Air Staff had taken no account of this at all and therefore he could not answer the question.[35] His utterances before the committee were 'most confused', and he proved to be 'extremely weak in discussion'. The Chiefs of Staff had continuously to be prodded and pushed into taking up arms on their own behalf. Pownell,† who acted as one of the secretaries to the committee, and whose sympathies were usually with his military chiefs, observed:

> It is curious how, all through, the Chiefs of Staff have been the moderating influence in the Committee. The civilians, whose presumable line was to keep down impossible service demands, have continually been the alarmist party, demanding quicker and heavier rearmament, whatever the price.[36]

Van signed the report with extreme misgivings. In April the Germans published details of their rearmament budget, promising massive increases in Germany's military potential, particularly in the air.[37] This latest revelation from Germany confirmed all of Van's worst fears. The DRC's report had already become outdated, overtaken by events. Even his plea for an extra twenty-five squadrons was no longer sufficient. For the record he wrote to Simon:

> I only concurred in the report in regard to the air – i.e. leaving the question of the 25 squadrons to higher authority – because I thought the higher authority might take a different view of this, and would reconsider it from a point of view other than the technical one. I believe that if the Government only work to these 65 squadrons, as here proposed, in *ten* years they will be considerably behind what the country expects or is ready for. I think that whatever it *was*, it has become an inadequate proposal.

* Prof. Howard (*op. cit.*, 106) gives the following explanation for the lacklustre performance of the Chiefs of Staff. 'Starved of resources for years, uncertain of their ability to recruit the necessary manpower and conscious of the lack of any armaments-base to make major expansion possible, the timidity of the service chiefs, pathetic as it now appears, is understandable.' These are all perfectly valid points. But however one juggles the reports of the DRC, the service chiefs emerge from them in a very bad light: unimaginative, lacking in initiative and originality of thought, and totally ill-equipped to withstand the intellectual challenge imposed on them by their civilian counterparts.

† Henry Royds Pownell (1887–1961): assistant secretary of Committee of Imperial Defence, 1933–35; Deputy Secretary, 1936; Director of Military Operations and Intelligence, War Office, 1938–39; Chief of General Staff, BEF,

I wish to put on record therefore that not only did I agree to the report in its present form with known reluctance (known to my colleagues, I mean), but that I would not have agreed to it *at all* had not the report been written *before* the publication of the German rearmament budget and before the knowledge that we have recently acquired in regard to the building of German bombers. To talk of a ten year programme in these circumstances and in view of the rate at which the situation is developing, is not, to my mind, realism . . . and I therefore hold the more to my original view that an extension to ten years would be practically and politically inadequate.[38]

Immediately after the report had been signed Van wrote a lengthy memorandum justifying the basic assumptions of the DRC.[39] In it he proved his case by quoting extensively from the past reports of British ambassadors to Germany, from D'Abernon to Phipps, backed by the more candid statements of the Nazi leaders. All this demonstrated that 'the German spirit', warlike, militaristic, and *revanchist*, had never reformed. So overwhelming was the evidence that no other conclusion was feasible. He emphasized that the Committee took 'no immediately alarmist view'. 'There is probably no immediate danger. As the Defence Requirement Committee put it, "We have time, though not too much time, to make defensive preparations".' He did not rule out the possibility of a 'long-range policy' which aimed 'at the reconciliation of revisionist ideas with anti-revisionist fears and obstinacy'.

But Nazi Germany had rudely disturbed the atmosphere in which alone such a consummation can be achieved, and her citizens are daily being inoculated *en masse* with the fanatical doctrine that force is not only the sole but the intrinsically noble and desirable means of realising her ambitions . . . Even if she returns [to Geneva] under prayer and pressure, these ambitions and these consequences will not be changed unless she changes her heart and her teaching of the rising generation. There lies the only acceptable test.

Two weeks later he forwarded to the cabinet, as further proof of German intentions, details about the construction of air bombers 'on a considerable scale'.[40]

In June he warned the government, then considering the report, against producing a 'mountain's mouse'.[41] After fifteen years of work

---

1939–40; C.-in-C. Far East, 1941–42; C.-in-C. Persia and Iraq, 1943; Chief of Staff to South East Asian Command, 1943–44. Kn. 1940.

it must be admitted that our 'policy has failed'. Unless a measure of strength, 'a little more weight', was injected into British policy it will become increasingly difficult to secure

> the adoption of our pacific views and counsels. And here I venture to put the point very briefly. The execution by 1940 of an air programme approved in 1923 is no deterrent . . . Events in Germany are already leaving it behind, for the situation has changed since the report of the Defence Requirements Committee was signed; and it will change still more rapidly.

Conciliation through strength was the slogan he was now advocating.

These warnings were intended to stir up a ministerial committee which had been reviewing the report since early May.* Neville Chamberlain proved to be its guiding spirit; and it soon became apparent that he was bent on drastically cutting back the total expenditure recommended by the DRC.† By July the government had decided to stand by Chamberlain's cuts. Expenditure was reduced to £50·3 million. The army, its portion cut by half, was the chief casualty. Air expansion remained the dominant theme; and the DRC scheme was even enhanced, though in a curiously negative fashion. The balanced allocation of resources between the services, favoured by Hankey and the Chiefs of Staff, and to some extent reflected in the Committee's original report, had been shelved. Instead, clear priority was given to counter the air threat. Other defence problems were assigned a secondary role. The fifty-two squadron scheme was abandoned. It was replaced by Scheme A which, when fully implemented by the end of 1938 or early 1939, would provide the RAF with a total strength of 1252 aircraft – 111 squadrons.[42] Chamberlain was party to this decision, indeed he was mainly re-

---

* Although the report had been signed at the end of February, the cabinet did not begin to discuss it in earnest until May. During the intervening months the British were still angling after a convention within the framework of the disarmament conference. But on 2 May the French rejected a British proposal for a convention which would have included recognition of a measure of German rearmament. Thus the mirage of an agreement finally faded away, and the cabinet turned its full attention to the DRC report.

† The entire cost of the DRC recommendations would amount to £82·3 million. Apart from the 52 squadron scheme, the army would acquire an expeditionary force of 4 infantry divisions, 1 tank brigade, and 1 cavalry division; while the navy, owing to existing treaty regulations, would not be enlarged by any new capital ships though the older ones would be modernized and auxiliary services improved upon. The major part of these proposals was to be implemented within 5 years; the entire programme within 8–9 years. See C.P. 64(34), CAB. 24/247.

sponsible for it. He had long been concerned by Britain's obvious lack of readiness to repel an air attack, and, clearly under the influence of his Permanent Under Secretary, Warren Fisher, had argued consistently for 'a large increase in the Air Force concentrated at home'.[43] In effect Chamberlain had resolved Van's dispute with Ellington. Van's struggle for extra squadrons had borne fruit; and from an unexpected source. Nevertheless Van remained uneasy. Despite all his efforts his 'mouse' had materialized, and its deterrent effect was, in his estimation, minimal.

For some time now Van had been privy to secret sources of information about Germany's rearmament schemes, particularly in the air. Nearly always they indicated massive increases in Germany's strength which compared most unfavourably with Britain's lackadaisical approach to her own defence problems. It was the contents of these reports which endowed Van's own arguments with extra force. Some confusion has existed as to the identity of Van's informants. The hazardous nature of their activities impressed upon all the need for absolute secrecy, and Van destroyed many of his papers in 1940 in order to protect their identity. There is nothing in what remains of the Vansittart papers to unravel the mystery. But fortunately it is now possible to compose a fairly comprehensive list of Van's contacts from other sources. Not all were concerned with feeding him with highly technical information about the state of Germany's air force. Indeed, the intelligence he received may be roughly categorized between the latter and more general surveys concerning Germany's internal situation, describing the conflicting forces at work within the German government, analysing the real aims of Hitler and his gang, and the struggle for power within the Nazi leadership.

Most of his information came, either directly or indirectly, from Group Captain Malcolm Grahame Christie.* Throughout the 1930's Christie hovered persistently in the background of Van's career. They had first met while Van was head of the American Department and Christie was air attaché in Washington. After his tour of service at Washington, Christie was transferred to Berlin where he remained until ill-health forced his early retirement in 1930. He then embarked upon a business career. His activities now took him frequently to

* Malcolm Grahame Christie (1881–1971): educated at Malvern College, and Aachen University – Doktor-Ingenieur; served with Royal Flying Corps, 1914–18, R.A.F., 1919–30; air attaché at Washington embassy, 1922–26; at Berlin embassy, 1927–30; general manager and director, Otto CokeOven Ltd., Leeds, and president of Otto CokeOven, New York.

Europe, where he renewed and developed contacts he had made while in government service. Apart from his wide range of musical and artistic interests, he was a man of extraordinary physical courage. On one occasion he chose to crash his damaged aircraft into a hangar sooner than expose the ground staff to unnecessary risk.[44] He was also extremely wealthy, and possessed a house on the German–Dutch border where he was able to conduct his cloak and dagger transactions in comparative secrecy.[45] On the closest terms with Göring and General Milch,* he had easy access to official circles in Berlin, especially those connected with air affairs. In the main his contacts were traditional, nationalist, right-wing Germans, though of course vehemently anti-Nazi. Many were Catholics. As we shall see, Van's attitude towards them was somewhat ambivalent, but for the present they served him a useful purpose.

One of Christie's informants, indeed it appears as though he was the most important of them, was a gentleman named Hans Ritter. Ritter was a retired officer of the German General Staff and an ex-First World War pilot. From 1934–38 he served at the Paris embassy in an honorary capacity as assistant to the military and air attachés, and also as adviser to the Junkers aircraft company. Ritter and Christie worked uninterruptedly to procure and pass on all possible information

> regarding developments in Germany, both political and military. During the years that Ritter was employed at the German embassy in Paris he was in the closest touch with me and supplied me with extraordinarily correct and valuable information, which I passed on to you almost weekly. He paid regular visits to Berlin, and of course had access to almost all Departments there.[46]

In the Christie papers the informants are invariably disguised as 'X', 'Dr Y', 'Z', or 'an important industrialist', and so on. A certain 'Fish' is mentioned, whose information came from 'only the highest proven sources', as is 'Johnnie', an ex-German staff officer and diplomat.[47] 'X' has since been identified as Carl Goerdeler,† and from the same source it is evident that the leading industrialist was Robert Bosch.[48]‡ Van first met Goerdeler in 1935 and he seemed to him

---

* Air General Erhardt Milch, later Field Marshal (1892–1972): Inspector-General of Luftwaffe, 1939–45; adjutant to Göring, 1938. Sentenced at Nürnberg to life imprisonment; released in 1954.

† Carl Friedrich Goerdeler (1884–1945): recognized leader of the German resistance; chief burgermeister of Leipzig, 1930–37; resigned in protest at removal of statue of Mendelssohn from the public square by the Nazis.

‡ Robert August Bosch (1861–1942): German engineer and industrialist, founder

then the 'only genuine German conspirator'.[49] But he ultimately detected in Goerdeler the all too familiar symptoms of the German nationalist, longing to restore Germany to her pre-1914 frontiers. Goerdeler and his circle became more important with the approach of war.

Van himself was infuriatingly discreet about his contacts. His papers reveal nothing; and his memoirs name only Goerdeler – even Christie is excluded. But it is known that he also maintained the closest contact with Desmond Morton* and Sir Stuart Menzies, head of the secret intelligence service. Van was in fact connected with foreign intelligence in an official capacity, for the Secret Service fund was administered jointly by the heads of the Foreign Office and the Treasury, the details of which were, reportedly, kept personally by Fisher and made up in his own hand.[50] Hence Van was also privy to official sources of intelligence. Regarding his air ministry contact, all that can be gauged is that 'One of my sources was in the German Air Ministry'.[51] Who was he? It is impossible to say with absolute certainty. Lady Vansittart remembered him as 'a functionary in the German air ministry . . . very quiet and nervous and sensitive'.[52] He was unquestionably one of Christie's men, and in all probability Ritter.

On the political-diplomatic side his sources are relatively easier to identify. Certainly members of the German resistance: Goerdeler, Bosch, the Kordt brothers,† Ewald von Kleist-Schwenzin,‡ and others in the same circles. Peter Ustinov's father, one time press attaché at the German embassy, was another.[53] His work made him a particularly valuable contact. Ustinov was well acquainted with Sir Vernon Kell, head of the counter-intelligence service, and Van. His deep disillusionment with Nazi Germany, and the increasingly

---

of Bosch precision machines and electrical equipment company; invented Bosch spark plug; developed Bosch magneto and lamp. He was numbered among the industrialists who had helped Hitler to power, but then became disillusioned with him.

* Desmond Morton (1891–1971): soldier; head of CID's Industrial Intelligence Centre, 1929–39; personal assistant to Churchill, 1940–45. Kn. 1945. Morton was at one with Van about Germany's air potential and intentions, and together with Van leaked a great deal of highly confidential information to Churchill on these matters. A private communication; *M.P.*, 496; see also M. Gilbert, *Churchill* (London, 1976), v, 554 *passim*.

† Theo Kordt, counsellor at the German embassy in London; Erich Kordt, senior counsellor at the German Foreign Ministry.

‡ A conservative politician and landowner. Retired to his estates in Pomerania in protest at the Nazi régime.

precarious nature of his undercover activities, led him to apply eventually for British nationality. Mr G. Mooney, president of General Motors Overseas Corporation, was yet another contact. He knew Van through Guy Vansittart, at the time European Manager of General Motors. Mooney's position afforded him great influence and easy contact with the highest circles in the German industrial establishment. He became particularly important after the outbreak of war in September 1939, when he continued to supply Van with top-secret information.[54]

One other source must be mentioned: Wolfgang Gans Edler zu Putlitz, scion of a Prussian Junker family, and related to the Koenigsmarck and Bismarck families.[55] Putlitz was a junior secretary at the German embassy in London and was the principal contact with the Foreign Office, at least at that level. He held genuine anti-Nazi views and made no secret of them to his Foreign Office friends, some of whom were quite embarrassed by his outspokenness. It is clear that he supplied Van with general information about the German government's intentions, and possibly about the effectiveness and strength of the German opposition. Van obviously felt in his debt, for in 1940 he helped Putlitz to escape from Holland and for some time during the war even sheltered him at Denham Place. Van later recalled that:

> A few brave men knew that I realized a war to be nearing. They thought that, if they fed me with sufficient evidence, I might have influence enough to arouse our Government and so to stop it. Of course they were wrong, but we tried. These men deserved well, though one of them went sadly astray after the war.[56]

The one who went astray was Putlitz who, after the war, turned up in East Berlin as an official of the German Democratic Republic's foreign service.

Thus Van relied upon a formidable private intelligence system, apart from the traditional sources of the secret intelligence services. Such a mass of information often posed more questions than it answered. How to sift the chaff from the wheat? Which were the reliable sources? How genuine were the anti-Nazi sentiments of the source? Nearly always there remained a lingering suspicion that the eager recipients of the information were being taken for a ride. There was no foolproof method of surmounting this obstacle. Van was accused of believing what he wished to believe. And undoubtedly the contents of his intelligence reports confirmed and strengthened the dogmatic opinions he already held about Germany's military-political intentions. This is not to suggest that the reports were invariably inaccurate. Naturally there were always elements of exaggeration and speculation, but on many occasions, as will become apparent, they came very close to the truth.* But the suspect nature of the information, combined with the burning intensity of Van's presentation of it, very often produced the reverse effect from that intended. His reputation as a scaremonger grew.

There was one aspect in particular about Germany's air rearmament which deeply disturbed him, and which pushed him more and more into the solitary role of the Cassandra of the Foreign Office. Understanding the mentality of the Germans as he did, he was quite certain that they would exploit the use of air power to extract political concessions. As early as January 1934 he had told the DRC:

> It was impossible to expect to find reasons in their methods. It was notorious that the Germans were not actuated by reason in their foreign relations ... the younger spirits among the Nazis regard air power as the means by which, through threat of action or by action itself, they would demand their Colonial Empire back.[57]

His remarks were listened to with unconcealed scepticism, but this notion continued to haunt his thoughts.

In November 1934 intelligence sources indicated that Germany was about to embark upon a massive air expansion programme. The figures showed that by 1 October 1936, with the completion of their second stage, they would have attained a first line air fleet of 1296 aircraft with one hundred per cent reserves. Equally disturbing was the fact that German industrial potential to expand was far in advance of anything previously anticipated, and that their output was now estimated at about one hundred and forty aircraft per month. Sharp increases in the German air budget lent added weight to government fears. On 28 November there occurred the celebrated Churchill–Baldwin confrontation in the Commons over the German air threat. Churchill warned that the German air force was rapidly approaching equality with the British, and that given the comparative rates of expansion the Germans would have doubled their strength relative to the RAF by 1937. There was less force in his first assertion than in his second. Certainly the figures now available indicate that Churchill's predictions of Germany's future performance – unques-

* At the height of the Second World War Hankey said: 'When the pre-war records are opened on the origins of the war it will be found that the intelligence given was accurate and ample, the opinions sound, and the warnings, though given, were by no means always followed.' See *P.D.*, Lords, v. 126, c. 961, 25 March 1943.

tionably prompted by Morton, Van and Wigram – were uncomfort-
ably close to the truth. Obviously much depended upon how the
information received was interpreted. How, for example, were first
line strength and reserves calculated? Equally the implications of
any interpretation depended greatly upon how the evaluator estimated the German air threat.* These were questions which gave rise
to much dispute in the future. But Baldwin's fumbling reply, a performance he repeated in another parliamentary debate in May 1936,
gave extra credence to the view that the government was not tackling this problem with sufficient vigour and foresight.

On 1 January 1935 Christie passed on further alarming details
about the rapid growth of German air power.[58] Profoundly disturbed
at the impotence of the Western powers to arrest Germany's illegal
air rearmament, Van searched for another way to neutralize her
continual infringements of her obligations which at the same time
would guarantee a measure of security against air attack. He believed he had found it in the concept of an overall air pact. Concluding that it was no longer feasible to halt German air expansion,
Van reasoned that the most hopeful alternative was to control it, to

* In the November debate Churchill relied heavily on Desmond Morton's figures.
Morton, who put the existing German first line strength at between 800–900,
based his calculations on military aircraft equipped with bomb racks and
machine guns, and civil aircraft 'capable of conversion to military use as above
in a few hours'. (I am grateful to Mr Martin Gilbert for allowing me to read an
advance copy of his fifth volume of the Churchill biography from which the
above quotation was taken.) Regarding civil aircraft, this was a fairly elastic
definition and did not meet the operational standards of the RAF. But this was
not in fact the cardinal issue. Dramatic though the revelations – and denials –
of German first line strength were, the most decisive point was Germany's
industrial capacity to expand her air power. On this question there was little to
differentiate between the estimates of the Air Staff and the Foreign Office. The
government's failure to act upon the persistent and prescient warnings of its professional advisers, to say nothing of Churchill's public campaign, was the most
disturbing feature of this unhappy story. Even so, it should be noted that there
was often a wide discrepancy between German plans and performance, and that
even the most experienced observers of the German air scene were capable of
making mistakes. By 1939, for example, production was actually 33% less than
that originally planned; while after the Munich settlement, planning and production contracted in relative terms until the outbreak of war. Nevertheless, the
warnings of Van, Wigram and Churchill ultimately proved true. By the latter
1930's the Germans had constructed the largest military air fleet in the world,
and were producing more aircraft per month than any other country. In this
connection see: R. J. Overy, 'The German Pre-War Aircraft Production Plans:
November 1936–April 1939', *English Historical Review* (Oct. 1975); Collier, *op.
cit.*, 25–48; Bialer, *op. cit.*; Roskill, *Hankey*, iii, appendix B; M. Gilbert, *op. cit.*;
and *G.D.*, C, iii, app. 1.

cut it down to more manageable proportions. He was in fact advocating the legitimization of a German military air force, though one which would be strictly supervised and hence would present a minimum danger to the West.

Van's intention was to refine previous Foreign Office proposals for an air convention which had been promoted as early as November 1933.[59] Towards the end of January 1935, this complex issue was given a fresh impetus.[60] The French now took the initiative, hoping thereby to involve the British in their security in return for French agreement to waive the disarmament clauses of the Versailles treaty. Van latched on to this idea. Time, he sensed, was not working in favour of the Western democracies. On 10 January 1935 he told William Crozier, editor of the *Manchester Guardian*: 'The sands were running out fast . . . if we do not get a convention within the next six months I doubt whether we shall get one at all.'[61] By the beginning of February a Foreign Office memorandum had been prepared incorporating the suggestion of an Anglo-French air pact. Van pressed Simon whose job it was to sell this idea to the cabinet: 'We are unanimous in hoping that you and your colleagues will approve its findings.' Simon concurred. But the cabinet refused to be swayed by his arguments, and rejected it on the grounds that Germany would interpret it as a further move in her encirclement. Instead, a broader formula was advanced to include all the Locarno powers. Although this was not what the Foreign Office had planned, it was a considerable step forward in the right direction, and one taken largely in consequence of continual Foreign Office pressure.[62] As a result, a joint Anglo-French communiqué was issued which, within the framework of 'a general settlement freshly negotiated between Germany and the other powers', envisaged revision of the restrictive disarmament clauses of Versailles and an agreement of mutual assistance against air attack.

These negotiations hung fire for another month. Opposition to the Foreign Office plan was widespread and very influential. In Hankey's view it presaged 'an unlimited military commitment . . . the most serious . . . that we have entered into for centuries, if at all'; and his opinion was upheld by the Chiefs of Staff who anticipated being 'plunged into a war with all our forces'. Hankey and the service chiefs mounted a powerful counter attack against the air convention.[63] But it was not only on military grounds that Hankey fought the Foreign Office initiative. He was particularly incensed at the way the Office, and especially Van, had ridden roughshod over accepted civil service procedure to ensure that their views were accepted at ministerial level. For the Foreign Office, or so it appeared, had taken the offensive before the French had actually raised the topic as one for official deliberation. Was this simply negligence or bad management? Or a combination of both? Such possibilities cannot be entirely ruled out. But there might have been more in this than met the eye at first glance. It was more than conceivable that here was a deliberate ploy on Van's part to force his colleagues to accept his views, or at least to strike his blow first. If so, it was an effective scheme, for his efforts were crowned with more than partial success. At any rate, Hankey felt aggrieved, smarting under the impression that he had been outmanœuvred: Foreign Office behaviour had been 'outrageous' and 'an act of bad faith'. Fisher, though inclined to favour the pact, 'was very wroth with the Foreign Office on procedure', and complained of the same lack of consultation on economic and financial questions, hinting at a possible inquiry into the organization of the Office.[64]

Unlike his colleagues, Van was not so much concerned with procedural details as with working with France in restricting Germany's freedom of action. 'There will be no question', the Foreign Office cautioned, 'of joining Germany against France and Belgium.' In this way the pact could never be operated on Germany's behalf, only against her. Van was offering restrictions on German air rearmament but without any compensation. Even if the objections of Hankey and his supporters could be met, there was nothing in this programme to appeal to the Germans. The air pact was abortive almost from the moment it was first mooted.

Nevertheless, at the beginning of March the government decided to press forward with the comprehensive settlement it had devised. Simon and Eden were to go to Berlin, while Eden planned to visit the capitals of Eastern Europe to seek general approval of the plan. Van too had received an indirect invitation from Hitler to go to Berlin for an exchange of views.[65] He rejected the offer. He wrote to Phipps that it would be impossible for both the Secretary of State and himself to leave England at the same time,[66] a feeble excuse for during the course of 1935 he accompanied Simon to Stresa and Hoare to Paris. But apart from this technical pretext Van expanded on deeper reasons:

It has come to me, not only from you but from many sources as well, that the Germans have a deep antipathy for me personally, and attribute to me any lack of success which may attend their efforts vis-à-vis this country. They say freely and violently that I am anti-German . . . It is of course completely untrue. I am not anti-German in the least. I have always thought that Germany got far too rough usage at Versailles and have always wished to see minimised the imprudences then committed . . . the whole of my attitude towards *recent* Germany – I emphasize that word recent – can be put in a nutshell. I consider that the military preparations, both material and moral, being made by Germany (and I need hardly tell you that I keep as close an account of them as is possible for any one man) far exceed in dimensions anything which could possibly be necessary for internal consumption . . . If these warlike preparations of body and spirit and steel were changed, I should be the first to change also with a great sigh of relief. I should revert instantly to my old and very friendly feelings. But until those facts, and they are *facts*, are changed I am not going to have my attitude changed by words alone . . . and so long as those in authority in Germany are not spiritually disposed to such a change, any conversation would be really a waste of time and would, I think, do little good. . . . these are not only my own feelings: they are the frame of mind and attitude which I expect from those who work with me in the Foreign Office. In a word I expect them to be as realistic as I am, and there is no-one on whom I count more in this direction than yourself as you already know.*

An unmistakable evangelical fervour emanates from the closing sentences of this revealing letter; a divine conviction that he was right and that any deviation from his chosen path would lead to certain disaster. A degree of rigidity had crept into his thinking which somehow contradicted his own efforts to obtain a political settlement. His ceaseless preaching on this theme and in this vein displeased those who sought more pliant advisers and more flexible policies.

On 4 March the government published its defence white paper.[67] Both Fisher and Van had a hand in drafting it, though Hankey was its chief author. Some discussion arose over the formulation of the paper, with Hankey anxious to cut out 'a lot of [Van's] fiery stuff', particularly paragraph five.[68] After ministerial intervention, Van's draft was restored.† Reviewing British disarmament policy, especially

* Van did not remain faithful to his own rulings for very long. The following summer he visited Berlin and saw all the Nazi leaders, despite the fact that there had occurred no appreciable change in German policy. (See above, pp. 196–99.)

† The offending paragraph read: 'The National Government intends to pursue without intermission the national policy of peace by every practicable means and to take advantage of every opportunity, and to make opportunities to make peace more secure. But it can no longer close its eyes to the fact that adequate

in the light of the failure of the conference, it noted the world trend towards rearmament with particular reference to Germany and her air preparations. These developments left the Government no alternative but to concentrate on her own defences: naval requirements were to be met, and air defences improved upon. Extra expenditure on armaments could no longer be delayed. If the language of the paper was restrained, its meaning was clear.

With the publication of the paper Hitler caught an unexpected diplomatic chill and postponed the Simon–Eden visit. Van interpreted this stratagem as blatant interference in British internal politics, an attempt to 'feed the opposition and weaken the present Government'.[69] But Hitler continued to unsettle the Western powers. On 9 March it was officially announced that Germany had established a military air force. A week later Hitler restored conscription and set up a peacetime army based on thirty-six divisions – five hundred and fifty thousand soldiers. In Van's estimation this was a blatant and typical example of German double-dealing. He began to have second thoughts about an agreement: 'We have only been complaisant to her [Germany's] proceedings, I assume, so long as there was a faint chance of agreement. If that spark fails, Germany should no longer profit by our connivance'.[70]

But the government, wishing to explore all possible avenues, decided to go ahead with the ministerial visit which was now rescheduled for 25–26 March. On the second day of the discussions the question of Germany's air requirements was raised. Hitler demanded parity with France, by which he included the French forces stationed in North Africa. Simon reserved for last the vital question of the current strength of the German air force. Hesitating for a moment, Hitler replied that Germany had already attained parity with Britain which, according to Hitler's calculations, gave him 2100 aircraft including reserves.[71]

Hitler's claim, though unfounded in fact, seemed to justify the panic of the previous winter. Moreover, the Foreign Office was now informed of the Air Ministry's latest estimate of Germany's air strength, which, apparently, confirmed Hitler's boast and even improved upon it. Van elucidated the meaning of these new figures for Simon:

[they] should be known to every member of His Majesty's Government. The Foreign Office have given long and ample warning to

---

defences are still required for security and to enable the British Empire to play its full part in maintaining the peace of the world.' It is difficult to see what Hankey found objectionable in this rather tame formulation.

His Majesty's Government. I wish the Air Ministry had seen and spoken as plainly as we have done during these last years. The number of service aircraft in Germany is already *greater* than (not equal to) the number in the United Kingdom. What then are we to think of the Air Ministry?[72]

Four days later Simon, relying on Van's sources, wrote to Mac-Donald claiming that German first-line superiority 'now seems to be some 30 per cent', amounting to a grand total of three thousand machines of every type. Even more alarming was the German capacity to expand, now estimated at two hundred per month 'and very probably more'. Ultimately Germany was aiming 'at a factory output sufficient to double her first-line strength in two months'. These first-line strength figures were disputed by Londonderry in a memorandum circulated to the cabinet the same day that Simon sent off his letter. Basing his appraisal on Ellington's calculations, he called only for an increase in home defence. But his paper lacked a complete sense of urgency, particularly when compared with the dramatic presentation of the Foreign Office case:

> There is no ground for alarm at the existing situation, whatever first-line strength Germany may claim, we remain today substantially stronger *if all relevant factors are taken into account.*

On the most crucial issue, however, not over current figures of first-line strength but over the organization of the air industry for war production, Londonderry admitted that the future 'must cause grave concern', though he was quick to point out that 'Germany will not be ready for, and is not intending to go to, war before 1942'.[73] Van reacted sharply to this complacent optimism which he noted 'was shared by no one in Europe'.[74] A short while later, after he had become still more disillusioned at the chances of an air agreement, he wrote: 'things will move more quickly than either the CIGS or the Air Staff believe. In any case we cannot delay our own preparations beyond the end of 1938 at latest, or 1 January 1939.'[75]

By now the question had entered the public domain. The parliamentary debates, the defence white paper and Churchill's public campaign had highlighted the essential issues. At the end of March reports of Hitler's parity claim had been leaked to the press and the BBC on Van's initiative to gain support for 'our own estimates'.[76] At the end of April, the *Daily Telegraph* published a thoroughly authoritative article on the state of German air rearmament. There is every reason to suspect that the information was leaked to the paper's diplomatic correspondent, Gordon-Lennox, by Wigram on Van's authority. Van later recalled that: 'The revelation caused a stir, and from that moment the prospects of rearmament brightened'.[77] During these months Van laboured endlessly to ensure that this case was heard. On the train journey to the Stresa conference, Van, together with his aides Ralph Wigram and Rex Leeper, buttonholed Wing Commander Charles Medhurst, deputy director of air intelligence, and insisted that he clarify to MacDonald the grave weaknesses inherent in Britain's air capability. This was to put Medhurst, a comparatively junior officer, in a totally false position. But Van was adamant and the meeting eventually took place over breakfast at Stresa.[78] Whether MacDonald was impressed with what he heard, or even whether he was capable of taking any decisive measures at this stage of his career, must remain open to doubt. But he was an obvious target for Van's lobbying. The choice of Medhurst as a Foreign Office lever was no accident. During 1934–35 the Foreign Office, in particular its air experts, Michael Cresswell,* Wigram and Van, had, for obvious reasons, deliberately fostered close relations with him, and the Stresa confrontation was a natural continuation of these contacts.†

Soon after this incident Van weighed in with another 'fearsome memorandum' urging one hundred per cent increases in Britain's air expansion.[79] Towards the end of May he received further unnerving information from Phipps.[80] Göring had informed the British ambassador that Germany now aimed at 'parity with the French and 2000 first-line machines in the course of 1935'. Once again Van's own source, unquestionably Christie, elaborated the point: the Germans were already in a position 'to beat the French very easily'. Christie's pen-portrait of Göring – 'pathological . . . completely irresponsible . . . (and) much more dangerous' than Hitler – was most threatening; but Van accepted it without question. Given Göring's lunatic temperament, and the German government's knowledge of Britain's defence weaknesses, Van drew the most dramatic conclusions:

> They are convinced that no population could really stand more than a few days of intensive bombing, and that at the end of that

* Michael Justin Cresswell (1909–   ): entered Foreign Office, 1933; served in Berlin, Madrid, Athens; counsellor at Teheran, 1947–49; minister to Cairo, 1951–54; Ambassador to Finland, 1954–58; to Yugoslavia, 1960–64; to the Argentine, 1964–69. Kn. 1960.

† Medhurst's precise views are difficult to come by. On the one hand, he shared the Foreign Office's deep concern at Germany's rapid and uncontrolled air expansion. On the other, although he collaborated with the Foreign Office, he tended

time they would be able to impose any conditions they liked, even the handing over of the fleet or the colonies.[81]

A copy of this letter was also sent to Warren Fisher. It set off a triangular correspondence between these high officials about their respective attitude towards Germany and the chance of reaching a settlement with her.[82] On the whole Van and Fisher followed the same line, while Hankey revealed himself as a shade more optimistic than his colleagues and certainly more prepared to accept Germany's gestures in a conciliatory fashion. Van assured Hankey that the Foreign Office would not be backward in pursuing 'any genuine opening' with Germany. Strongly refuting the accusation (Hankey's?) that the Foreign Office had lacked zeal in the past in seizing opportunities to consolidate the peace, he claimed for himself the title of Hankey's and the Chiefs of Staff best friend at the Foreign Office. But he ended on his usual gloomy note, stressing the contrast between Germany's bellicose spirit and the impossibility of conducting a vigorous foreign policy without sufficient material strength.

Gradually Van's campaign began to bear fruit. Mounting public concern and parliamentary pressure, coupled with Hitler's blows against Versailles, pushed the government into taking more active measures. Lord Weir, an industrialist who had served as Secretary of State for Air at the close of the First World War, was appointed adviser to the government on questions of supply and production. At about the same time, an 'air-parity' committee was set up to ensure that Britain maintained her air credibility. Cunliffe-Lister,* who was soon to replace Londonderry at the Air Ministry, headed this committee with verve and imagination.[83] Finally the DRC was reconstituted, mainly as a result of the air panic, but also because by then it was generally admitted that the negotiations with Germany for an overall agreement had run into a blind alley. On this occasion

---

to make a more conservative, or professional, estimate of the situation. It would seem however that he fostered no illusions as to the comparative strength of the Luftwaffe and the RAF. What concerned him, rightly, was the rate of potential expansion. Interview with Sir Michael Cresswell, September 1975; Bialer, *op. cit.*, 116.

* Philip Lloyd-Greame, assumed name of Cunliffe-Lister, 1924 (1884–1972): Conservative politician; Secretary of State for Colonies, 1931–35; for Air, 1935–38. Kn. 1920. Cr. 1st Viscount Swinton, 1935. Cunliffe-Lister replaced the discredited Londonderry as Air Minister in 1935; three years later he too was eased out of that office, a scapegoat for the government's failings in air preparations.

the DRC was given a wide brief: to coordinate the service requirements in the light of the current international situation, and to make
suitable recommendations without regard to budgetry considerations.
The committee first met on 11 July.[84]

From the outset Van again found himself at loggerheads with the
Chiefs of Staff. They had calculated 1941–42 as probably the years
when Germany would be technically ready to launch an aggression.
Van challenged this assumption in the strongest terms. Not only
technical readiness had to be considered but also psychological factors. Germany might launch a pre-emptive attack if she thought her
enemies were not fully geared for war. It was therefore impossible
to guarantee the peace until 1942. Van regarded 1 January 1939 as
the more probable date, though it could not be assumed that Germany would remain quiescent until then.[85] His views were incorporated in the first recommendation of the interim report of the DRC
presented on 24 July.[86] The second recommendation stemmed inevitably from the first. As there were only three budget years remaining
until 1939, financial considerations would have to be of 'secondary
importance to the earliest possible security', an obvious dig at
Chamberlain and his cheese-paring tactics of just a year ago.

The final report of the DRC was issued on 21 November 1935 in
the shadow of the Italo-Ethiopian conflict. Politically the report reflected the deteriorating international situation. With Germany and
Japan out to dominate Europe and the Far East, Italy already on the
rampage in East Africa, France divided and unreliable, and the
United States more isolationist than ever, Britain could rely only on
her own strength. National and imperial security dictated as 'a cardinal principle' the avoidance of simultaneous hostilities with Japan
or with any power lying across the lines of communication between
the two. Again the DRC prescribed accommodation with Japan combined with every effort 'to promote and maintain friendly relations
with Germany'. But whatever political scenario emerged, one element remained constant. If peace was to be preserved, 'our armaments must be raised to a far more effective standard than has
hitherto been aimed at'.

Taking this concept as its basic premise, the DRC recommended
a new naval standard which would place a fleet in Far Eastern
waters to act as a deterrent against the Japanese while maintaining in
all circumstances a home fleet to ward off the German threat. The
army was now allocated five divisions, including one mechanized
division, three tank battalions, and a territorial force of twelve divisions to be mobilized at intervals of four, six, and eight months after

the outbreak of war. In the air the July 1934 Scheme A was to be accelerated, thereby raising the metropolitan first-line strength to one hundred and twenty-three squadrons or 1512 aircraft. Known as Scheme C, this system was to be completed by April 1937.* All this would be realized at the staggering cost of £417·5 million phased over a five-year period, half of which would be completed by 1938, Van's critical year.[87] Here was the kind of balanced expansion which had eluded the first DRC report.

Repeating their performance of 1934, the service chiefs again appeared conservative in their estimates, at least when compared with their more forthright civilian colleagues.[88] But Van also gave a repeat performance of 1934.

> A rare struggle today getting the DRC report signed. Went to Van first as I anticipated trouble there; sure enough it came. He signed up and then, producing a very serious despatch from Phipps on German rearmament,[89] said we weren't nearly strong enough on Germany and wrote out a para. for further inclusion. One which it was obvious the other members would not accept. Van said to me. 'It is quite certain there will be a European war in the next five years' – and he indicated two or three as being the limit ... Rang up Warren Fisher, who disliked Van's para. immensely. Finally caught Hankey and Van together and induced the latter to withdraw.[90]

These *prima donna* shock tactics could hardly have endeared him to his less temperamental colleagues.

One other aspect of the report troubled him: the perennial air question. The expansion programme accepted in July 1934 was in his judgment entirely inadequate. Just one year later he wrote: 'My view is a short and simple one. Anything that fails to provide security by 1938 is inadequate and blind. Even Scheme A (July 1934), therefore, is not what our situation and the situation of Europe requires.'[91] There is one passage in the report which appears to have been lifted from, or at least wholly inspired by, Van's letter to Hankey of 22 May. Van had then phrased his comments in strong and emotive terms, describing in graphic detail the devastating effects of aerial bombardment on civilian morale. His dismal forecast was accurately reflected in the report.[92] And no doubt partly as a result of his warnings the DRC improved upon Scheme A, both as regards first-line strength and the rate of expansion. Yet the current plan, Scheme

---

* This was obviously intended as a precise counter to the German rate of expansion, also calculated as 1512 machines by April 1937.

F

C, still dragged far behind Britain's actual requirements. Only three months after the DRC had reported, a new scheme, F, was approved which raised first-line strength to 1736 aircraft. An official historian has made this comparison: 'In general, Scheme F was a sound one, infinitely preferable to its successor, since it aimed at real strength in 1939 rather than a hollow pretence in 1937.'[93] Even so, it was not sufficient. Van had marked late 1938, or 1 January 1939, as the critical period. According to his sources the German rate of expansion was far superior to anything the British could match. By the autumn of 1936 – one-and-a-half years after Hitler's false claim – the Luftwaffe overtook the RAF. Parity had been lost.[94] It was not to be regained until after the outbreak of war. In this sense, Van, among others, had lost the battle.

But the debate continued unabated, with Van taking a prominent part. In February 1936 he resurrected the by now dog-eared theme of an air pact serving as a starting point for a more general agreement with Germany, a point which was duly accepted by the cabinet.[95] The same month he again clashed with Ellington and the Air Staff over comparative air figures between the Luftwaffe and the RAF. This particular round lasted until July when it was terminated somewhat abruptly by Ellington. Detecting little difference between the two sets of figures, which had been checked and re-checked by Van's old ally, Medhurst, he noted: 'but the methods of calculating first-line strength, output and wastage of aircraft, etc., differ, with the result that the deductions are different. This being the case I feel that little useful purpose can be served in prolonging what amounts to fruitless argument over relatively unimportant details.'[96] Nothing could be more designed to raise Van's hackles than this kind of apathetic, phlegmatic attitude. What Van wanted was an ample margin of safety for Britain's air defences. All his repeated attempts to inject a sense of urgency into the Air Staff's calculations were smothered by an indiscriminate blanket of complacency.

An attempt to clarify these 'unimportant details' occurred soon after this incident, with the Germans taking the initiative. General Milch hinted that, on condition of absolute secrecy, he would pass on official estimates of German air strength. He fulfilled his pledge in October 1936. The following January, in what reads like a carefully staged scene, Milch informed a high ranking Air Staff officer that by the autumn of 1938 Germany would reach a front-line strength of 1755 while Britain would not be far behind with 1736. Milch then conveniently proceeded to break down these figures into categories, and, as a last gesture, offered to keep Britain informed of any new

German programmes. These manœuvres were so obviously contrived that Van had no hesitation in denouncing them as a transparent exercise in sharp practice. He detected only one aim in Milch's play-acting: to lull the government into a false sense of security. And he was not at all certain that some innocents in government were not deceived by these theatricals:

> It was quite obvious to me that Milch was lying from the start, and I pointed that out at the time. (The *mise en scène* of the fraud was so childish that I could never understand how anybody could be taken in by it.)[97]

Milch had tried to show that the German and British air fleets were expanding at approximately the same rate. This estimation was contradicted in a report of the Chiefs of Staff circulated in February 1937.[98] It was a paper which told an appalling tale of neglect, and which made perfect copy for Van's caustic marginal comments. 'Who said parity in the air?' he queried, after reading that Germany and Italy would be 'considerably superior in first-line strength' over Britain and France. When he learned about the shocking state of Britain's air defences, he confessed that 'All this is frankly horrible'. 'A lamentable and incredible figure', he concluded, after discovering that Britain could match Germany's eight hundred long range bombers with only forty-eight of her own.

> I have little to say except of course that this is a dreadful record of all round imprudence, despite all the warnings put out by the FO for two years past. The WO has no redeeming feature in its tale of unreadiness ... I wonder what the public would say to this, if they knew even half as much about it as the Germans do. And there are no anti-aircraft defences to speak of, though I have been pointing out this also for years. If ever a country has gambled its existence, we have done so.*

* There is some evidence to indicate that in the late winter of 1937 Van was beginning to redefine his previous attitude towards air power as the ultimate weapon. When the Chiefs of Staff ascertained that it was open to doubt whether or not aircraft could halt armies, Van retorted 'No they cannot. *Vide* Spain. The Germans are now quite convinced that the air is overrated. The Germans and Italians have learned from the Spanish experience that infantry is still the dominant factor.' (Quoted by Dennis, *op. cit.*, 94.) Of course, Van was here referring to the use of air power against military targets, not its effect on the civilian population. The destruction of Guernica two months later seemed to reaffirm the horrifying results which could be attained by intensive aerial bombardment. In any case, this was a dubious point to make for a country which was still debating the extent of its continental commitment in the event of a war.

No programme devised by the Air Ministry whetted his appetite. He reminded Eden:

> I have pointed out on many occasions, from the beginning of 1934, that nothing can be guaranteed in Europe from the end of 1937; and that forecast – made at the outset of the first DRC – is proving accurate.
>
> The moral of all this is that the present scheme of the Air Ministry represents a rock-bottom minimum. Even so we shall be two years behind Germany, and even with a whole two years' time-lag we shall not be living up to Lord Baldwin's pledge.*
> After the adoption of this programme we shall be in a position of marked inferiority to Germany and our position vis-à-vis Italy will remain shocking.[99]

Van pressed his case on every conceivable opportunity. And he did so with little regard for the normal conventions of polite debates. Here perhaps lies the source of his reputation as the Cassandra of the Foreign Office whose prophecies could never be believed. His gift for over-statement, enhanced by his literary style and compounded by his blunt turn of phrase, flowed over into other aspects of his foreign policy. Once labelled an 'alarmist' he found it impossible to live down his reputation; and in a perverse manner he even strived to live up to it, perhaps deriving from it a psychological satisfaction in his running battle with his superiors. After all, he *knew* he was right. And so he was, if one takes the longer view.

Van's trial of strength with the air authorities was a consistent one. In it he revealed qualities of foresight and single-mindedness to a far greater degree than most of the politicians,† military chiefs, and Whitehall colleagues with whom he had to work. Dominated by the fear of a knock-out blow, he was obsessed by the vision of Britain

---

* In the November 1934 debate Baldwin had pledged that his government would not 'accept any position of inferiority with regard to what air force may be raised in Germany in the future'.

† That Londonderry quarrelled with Van should come as no surprise (see *Wings of Destiny* (London 1943), 131–32) though, characteristically, it by no means disturbed their social relationship. Far more surprising, and intriguing, is the fact that Cunliffe-Lister, Londonderry's successor, and a far more capable and energetic Secretary of State than he, should have found Van 'no help at all' over the air expansion programme (see Roskill, *op. cit.*, 196, n. 4). Perhaps the explanation lies in Van's methods of persuasion more than in the actual ideas he propounded. It is known, however, that by April 1938, Cunliffe-Lister was numbered among those who believed that Van 'must go' (see *Dalton Diaries*, 7 April 1938). But by then Van had almost gone.

spread defenceless before a relentless foe, open to physical destruction and political blackmail. Stubbornly he fought to impress his views upon the government and its bureaucratic machinery, only to find himself entangled in a maze of technical verbiage, sophisticated political calculation, and endless time-wasting discussions. At the height of the debate he bitterly complained:

> We have for years laboured under the burden of these endless committees and sub-committees which spend nothing but time. The results are nearly always astonishingly futile, particularly in this matter of Air Defence.[100]

Fortunately he was not deterred, even by the bureaucratic process, from voicing his views. In the final analysis he rendered an inestimable service to his country. His persistent warnings, despite the shock nature of his tactics, eventually had a cumulative effect. The pity is that they were not fully recognized, or acted upon, at the time.

NOTES

1. See his minutes of 15 November 1937, Vnst. 2/33.
2. See his paper, Vnst. 1/5.
3. For example, his minutes of 25 May 1936, F.O. 371/20279, F. 2872/89/23.
4. His minutes of 10 February 1934, Vnst. 2/4.
5. *M.P.*, 444.
6. Hankey to Van (two letters), and Van's note to Simon, 9 January 1934, F.O. 800/291, 9294. Parts of this correspondence have already been published in S. Roskill, *Hankey, Man of Secrets* (London, 1974), iii, 96–7. Captain Roskill infers that the difference between Van and Hankey over Geneva was clear-cut and one of principle. It certainly was over the estimation of Hitler's intentions; over Geneva there were merely procedural differences, as Hankey himself admitted.
7. See their joint memorandum of 4 October 1933, CAB. 63/64. 8204.
8. Van to Simon, 7 October 1933, CAB. 63/64. 9937.
9. C.O.S., no. 310, 12 October 1933, CAB. 16/109 or CAB. 53/23. See also M. Howard, *The Continental Commitment* (London, 1972), 103–04.
10. From the minutes of the 3rd session of the Committee, 4 December 1933, CAB. 16/109. The minutes of the DRC may be seen in CAB. 16/109–112.
11. Quoted by A. Marder, 'The Royal Navy and the Ethiopian Crisis of 1935–36', *American Historical Review* (June, 1970).
12. See D. C. Watt, *op. cit.*, 115.
13. See Hankey to Baldwin, 23 August 1934, Baldwin Papers, v. 1.
14. B. Bond, ed. *Chief of Staff. The Diaries of Lt. Gen. Sir Harry Pownell* (London, 1972), 36.
15. From minutes of 3rd session, 4 December 1933, CAB. 16/109.
16. From final report of DRC, 28 February 1934, C.P. 64 (34), CAB. 24/247.
17. Anglo-Japanese relations for this period are thoroughly discussed in Ann Trotter, *Britain and East Asia* (Cambridge University Press, 1975). See also

D. C. Watt, *Personalities, op. cit.*, 83–99 and a memorandum by Simon and Chamberlain, 'The Future of Anglo-Japanese relations', 16 October 1934, C.P. 233(34), CAB. 24/250.

18. See minutes of 9th session, 30 January 1934, CAB. 16/109.
19. Minutes of 5 February 1934, F.O. 371/17593. See also Van to Sir Ronald Lindsay, 24 September 1934, R.A., GV/M2433/3. Here Van complained that the American public and Congress were 'too stupid, and, above all, too self-righteous', concluding that 'In ageing I have lost my wind for running after the United States Government. It is a futile paper chase.'
20. Fisher to Hankey, 12 February 1934, CAB. 16/109.
21. Quoted by T. Jones, *op. cit.*, 129.
22. This topic is discussed thoroughly by U. Bialer, *Some Aspects of the Fear of Bombardment from the Air, and the Making of British Defence and Foreign Policy, 1932–39* (Unpublished Ph.D. thesis, London, 1974).
23. Van to Hankey, 18 January 1933, quoted by Bialer, 34.
24. Draft notes of 27 February 1933, F.O. 371/17380, W. 2322/117/98. Later revised and presented by Simon under his name as 'The Crisis in Europe', 2 March 1933, C.P. 52(33), CAB. 24/239.
25. Temperley's despatch is printed in *B.D.*, 2, v, no. 127. For Van's memorandum on German rearmament of 14 July 1933, see C.P. 183(33), CAB. 24/242; see also *M.P.*, 478.
26. See C.P. 183(33), CAB. 24/242.
27. See C.P. 198(33), CAB. 24/242.
28. See his minutes of 29 April 1935, F.O. 371/18840; also Bialer, 86–7.
29. A private communication.
30. This passage is based on minutes of 12th session, 26 February 1934, CAB. 16/109, and the final report of the DRC, C.P. 64(34), CAB. 24/247.
31. The correspondence for this incident is in CAB. 21/434.
32. This controversy may be followed in, Hankey to Van, 3, 5 and 6 March 1934, CAB. 21/434. 8204; and Van to Hankey, 2 and 6 March 1934, *ibid.*
33. A diary note, 4 March 1934. Hankey Papers, 1/7.
34. See Bialer, *op. cit.*, 118.
35. These observations are taken from the Pownell Diaries, *op. cit.*
36. *Ibid.*, 38.
37. See *G.D.*, C, ii, 707–08, 722–23; and iii, 1125–26.
38. Van to Simon, 14 May 1934, CAB. 21/388. 8204.
39. See 'The Future of Germany', 7 April 1934, C.P. 104(34), CAB. 24/248.
40. See C.P. 116(34), CAB. 24/249.
41. Minutes of 2 June 1934, Vnst. 1/11.
42. For details, see B. Collier, *The Defence of the United Kingdom* (London, 1957), 28.
43. Quoted by Roskill, *op. cit.*, 111. For Chamberlain's views, see also Bialer, *op, cit.*, 105–9.
44. *The Times*, 24 November 1971.
45. I am grateful to Mr Peter Ludlow for supplying me with some of the information about Christie and Ritter.
46. Christie to Van, 15 May 1941, Christie Papers, 1/18. When the author examined these papers, March–April 1973, they had not yet been catalogued in their final form, hence the references given here might not be up to date.

47. See Christie Papers, 180/1/29, 30.
48. See, *The 'X' Documents, op. cit.*
49. *M.P.*, 512–13.
50. Reported in John Bull, 1 May 1937.
51. *M.P.*, 498.
52. Interview with Lady Vansittart, 31 October 1972.
53. A private communication from Peter Ustinov, 27 July 1973.
54. See for example, F.O. 371/23099, C. 17419/3005/18.
55. I am grateful to Mr Valentine Lawford for much of this information, a private communication of 28 May 1973; also interview with Lady Vansittart, 9 March 1973.
56. *M.P.*, 497–98.
57. From minutes of 9th session of DRC, 30 January 1934, CAB. 16/109.
58. See T. Conwell-Evans, *None so Blind* (London, 1947), 27. This book was published in a limited edition of 100 copies. It contains an account of Christie's activities in the 1930's based upon his private papers.
59. See Bialer, *op. cit.*, 129–32. The cabinet had rejected the scheme in May 1934 on the ground that it might widen the country's military commitments while hindering air rearmament.
60. See Hankey's diary notes for February 1935, Hankey Papers, 1/7. These notes have been quoted *verbatim* in Roskill, *op. cit.*, 156–63.
61. See, A. J. P. Taylor, ed. *Off The Record, Political Interviews, 1933–43* (London, 1973), 30.
62. Bialer, *op. cit.*, 138–41, and Hankey's diary notes, *op. cit.* See also *B.D.*, 2, xii, p. ix.
63. See Hankey's diary notes, *op. cit.*
64. Hankey's diary notes, *op. cit.* To the author's best knowledge no such investigation was carried out.
65. Phipps to Van, tel. 23 February 1935, F.O. 371/18828, C. 1834/55/18.
66. Van to Phipps, 5 March 1935, *ibid.*
67. See Cmd. 4827.
68. Hankey to Phipps, 8 March 1935, Phipps Papers 3/3.
69. Minutes of 7 March 1935, F.O. 371/18828, C. 1780/55/18.
70. Minutes of 13 March 1935, Vnst. 2/20. See also W. N. Medlicott, *op. cit.*, 16.
71. See Avon, *op. cit.*, 132–141, 183.
72. Minutes of 6 April 1935, Vnst. 2/28; see also Van to Simon, 9 May 1935, F.O. 800/290. 3919; and M. Gilbert, *op. cit.*, 632–3.
73. Avon, *op. cit.*, 183–5.
74. *Ibid.*
75. Minutes of 29 July 1935, Vnst. 2/28, and of 5 July 1935, Vnst. 2/22.
76. See I. Colvin, *Vansittart in Office* (London, 1965), 45. This account is based on information related to Mr Colvin by Sir R. Leeper.
77. *M.P.*, 498–99; also M. Gilbert, *op. cit.*, 639–40.
78. Colvin, 129.
79. The Pownell Diaries, *op. cit.*, 70.
80. Van to Hankey, 22 May 1935, CAB. 21/540.
81. *Ibid.*
82. For the correspondence see CAB. 21/540.
83. See Pownell Diaries, *op. cit.*, 71–3.
84. The minutes of the DRC sessions are in CAB. 16/112.

85. From minutes of 14th session (the sessions were numbered consecutively from the first DRC meetings in November 1933), 19 July 1935, CAB. 16/112. See also his minutes of 17 and 29 July 1935 (Vnst. 2/28) on the same theme.
86. Report in CAB. 16/122. See in particular para. 14 where Van's opinions are quoted almost verbatim from the minutes of 19 July.
87. See DRC final report, 21 November 1935, pp. 39–42 (CAB. 16/112), for details of the military recommendations. Also Collier, *op. cit.*, 31, for a breakdown and comparison of Schemes A and C.
88. Pownell Diaries, *op. cit.*, 86.
89. Apparently his despatch of 13 November 1935, F.O. 371/18851, C. 7647/55/18.
90. Pownell Diaries, *op. cit.*, 88.
91. Minutes of 17 July 1935, Vnst. 2/28.
92. For a comparison, see final report, section X1, 6(e), CAB. 16/112, and Van to Hankey, 22 May 1935, CAB. 21/540.
93. See Collier, *op. cit.*, 31, 42, for a criticism of Scheme C, and a breakdown of Schemes C and F. Two other schemes followed: L – after the *Anschluss*; and M – after the Munich settlement.
94. *Ibid.*, 46–7.
95. See Van's memo., 'Britain, France and Germany', 3 February 1936, C.P. 42(36), CAB. 24/260.
96. Ellington to Hankey, 23 July 1936. The complete correspondence is in Vnst. 3/1. The figures of the German air build-up supplied by Christie were extraordinarily detailed; copies were sent to Hankey and Fisher.
97. Minutes of 30 June 1936, Vnst. 2/34; see also Avon, *op. cit.*, 484–5.
98. C.O.S. papers, no. 551, 9 February 1937, F.O. 371/20701, C. 1406/202, 205/62.
99. Minutes of 15 November 1937, Vnst. 2/33; also Avon, *op. cit.*, 492.
100. Minutes of 17 July 1935, Vnst. 2/28.

CHAPTER IX

'The Ethiopian Imbroglio'

———————————❦———————————

ULTIMATELY, IT WAS ITALY who held the key to the isolation of Germany. On any reckoning this was a flimsy foundation upon which to erect a grand strategy. Italy's long standing colonial grievances, her avowedly revisionist tendencies in Europe, the arbitrary nature of her régime, and above all, the capriciousness of her ruler, made an unstable partner in any coalition. Yet throughout 1934 there had been unmistakable signs that Italy considered herself part of the anti-German camp. Her main concern was for the future of the South Tyrol, a conspicuous target for German irredentism. In this connection it was of paramount importance for her to maintain Austria's independence. This issue, among others, divided Italy from Germany. Alone among the powers, Italy had reacted vigorously to the botched up attempt to overthrow Austria in July. One outstanding question threatened to shatter this improbable marriage between Italian fascism and Western liberal democracy: Mussolini's vision of a great Italian empire in East Africa.

Italian eyes had been devouring Ethiopia ever since the end of the nineteenth century.[1] In 1896 they had suffered a humiliating defeat at Adowa at the hands of the Ethiopian tribes, that 'shameful scar' as D'Annunzio, the Italian nationalist poet, put it. It cut deeply into the Italian national consciousness. By the end of 1934 Mussolini's plans for the conquest of Ethiopia were in their final stages of preparation. On 5–6 December there occurred an armed clash between Italian and Ethiopian forces, the so-called Wal Wal incident.* The

---

* Wal Wal was the most important watering spot in the north eastern part of the Ogaden desert. Control over its wells meant control over this arid region and its population. Although the Ethiopian– Italian–Somaliland border had never been properly demarcated, Wal Wal lay well inside Ethiopian territory, at least fifty miles. The Italians had been steadily encroaching upon the wells

reaction of both parties to what appeared on the surface to be a
puffed-up border skirmish ensured that it would evolve into a major
international dispute. The Italians, bent on exploiting their advantage to the utmost, demanded a full apology and reparations; the
Ethiopians, equally concerned to maintain their position, decided to
take the question before the Council of the League.

The rapid deterioration of the Ethiopian dispute was accompanied
by a marked improvement in Franco-Italian relations. Indeed it
is apparent that both processes were closely connected. On 7 January
1935 an accord was signed between the two countries. Its main
purpose was to consolidate Barthou's European front; and in this
it was eminently successful. Much confusion however has reigned as
to the precise nature of the agreement then reached over Ethiopia.[2]
Perhaps this question will never fully be answered. With two such
slippery customers as Laval and Mussolini the degree of uncertainty
in any conversation held *à deux* was bound to be high. Even the Quai
d'Orsay was unclear as to what precisely had taken place. Alexis
Léger, Van's French counterpart, 'had no idea of the extent of
Laval's private concessions to Mussolini – but he was sure they
existed'.[3] All the available evidence points to a definite indication by
Laval of French disinterest in Ethiopia, with all the political and
economic consequences which stemmed from such an assurance.

Certainly the Foreign Office interpreted the agreements as 'a
mortal blow' against Ethiopia.[4] Few officials regarded Ethiopia with
great enthusiasm. For Van, who was quite typical, it remained a
backward, semi-feudal kingdom, scarcely worthy of the independence

---

since the early 1930's; by 1932 they were in *de facto* control, a fact the British
authorities were well aware of. There were other complicating factors. Since
early 1934 Anglo-Ethiopian negotiations, unquestionably known to the Italians,
had been in progress which aimed at ceding the Wal Wal area, together with
minor frontier rectifications elsewhere, to Britain, in return for an Ethiopian
outlet to the sea at Zeila. These territories were important to Britain because
they included grazing lands used by the nomadic Somali tribes, nominally
under British protection; the uncontrolled wanderings of these tribes were a
constant source of irritation among the Powers. By the autumn of 1934, the
Ethiopians, spurred on no doubt by the prospects of a deal with Britain and in
the face of a general hardening of the Italian position, decided that the time
was opportune to reassert their waning authority. In November, a boundary
demarcation commission, consisting of British and Ethiopian representatives
with a strong military escort, appeared at Wal Wal. The British, whose role in
this affair appears to have been highly ambiguous, discreetly retired from the
scene, leaving the Italians and the Ethiopians in a state of uneasy confrontation.
Fighting broke out on 5 December.

it so awkwardly proclaimed. Van reluctantly resigned himself to
the prospect of the pruning of Ethiopian sovereignty:

> This is the best we can do. But I am afraid this is going to be the
> fable of the wolf and the lamb, a black and not blameless lamb,
> and that Ethiopia will undergo erosion at the least. We shall have
> to steer a course compatible with our position as a member of the
> League and our necessity, in the name of far greater issues than
> Ethiopia, of not breaking with Italy.[5]

Some days later he returned to the same theme. Now he set out in
great detail the foundations of his Ethiopian policy. In substance
they altered little until the crisis reached its climax at the end of
the year. Van hinted that the only acceptable solution might lie in
a territorial compromise; and he asked the cabinet to reflect on
such a possibility, unpalatable though it might be:

> I have sometimes thought it a pity we didn't let Italy have a
> German colony in 1919. We were really imprudently greedy.
> The impending episode is the inevitable sequel to our hogging
> policy then.[6]

Within the context of colonial concessions to Italy, he laid down one
basic proposition: the need to preserve Western unity against
Germany almost at any cost. On that principle rested 'the maintenance of peace' in Europe. Of course, everything should be done
to dissuade Italy from expanding at Ethiopia's expense. Failure to
do so would not only drive Italy 'into German embraces', it would
also deal a death-blow to the League. But Van warned, Britain must
not be manœuvred into playing 'an isolated and futile role of opposition'. Cooperation with France was still the first priority.

When the powers convened at Stresa, Van was determined that the
order of priorities he had arranged should be honoured. The conference was launched to settle European affairs: the Eastern and air
pacts, Austria, the German blows against Versailles. There was no
mention of Ethiopia, or any other non-European question, in the
British terms of reference for the conference.[7] It was only at the
eleventh hour, and then mainly as a result of Grandi's* lobbying,
that the Foreign Office specialist on Ethiopia, Geoffrey Thompson, was
invited to join the British delegation. Earlier he had pressed the same

---

* Dino Grandi (1895–   ): Italian foreign minister, 1929–32; Ambassador to
London, 1932–39; Minister of Justice, 1939–43; condemned to death *in
absentia* at Ciano's trial in 1944. Cr. Count, 1937.

course on Rome. Thus the experts materialized, prepared, no doubt, to debate their way round the problem. Where it mattered, at the top, no provision had been made for meaningful talks or decisions.

The conference opened on 11 April. Judging from contemporary reports it was a gay occasion. Set against the magnificent panorama of Lake Maggiore, the conference assumed a festive guise. The delegates were conveyed in two motor launches to the island of Isola Bella for the official opening of the conference in the Hall of Music in the Borromèo palace. Mussolini presided. The proceedings lasted until 14 April. On the surface the gathering was a huge success. A European front had been established. The well-rounded phrases rolled dutifully from the official communiqué.[8] What did all this amount to in fact? Not a great deal. If Austria is taken as a yardstick of British intent to act decisively in Europe, then her commitment was as vague as ever. MacDonald and Simon had both recently denied that Austria constituted a vital British interest, one for which she would fight.[9] Stresa did not alter that. No firm, unequivocal British commitment to maintain Austrian integrity emerged from Stresa. The much-vaunted Stresa front was little more than a paper combination ready to crumble at the first touch.

Van's strategy of first landing Mussolini in Europe and then controlling him in Ethiopia had not materialized.[10] He had been pressing for a definite undertaking to Austria since 1933. His advice had been rejected, his warnings dismissed as hysterical. Eventually he lost both Austria and Ethiopia, for, paradoxically, while his chiefs ignored his advice about Austria they heeded it about Ethiopia. Mussolini put it another way. Turning on his Ambassador Grandi, he remarked; 'You told me that on Austria the English answer would be "yes", and on Africa "no". As it happens their answer on Austria was "no", and on Africa "yes".'[11]

The French hoped that the British would follow their example and pursue friendlier relations with Italy, as no doubt did Mussolini. On his arrival at Stresa, Flandin* asked Van: ' Are you going to play this time or not, because if the answer is "no", it will be a practical Goodbye. We shall not quarrel, but we shall drift apart.'[12] Despite Van's urging, the British did not play; and their relations with both the French and the Italians deteriorated steadily throughout 1935. On the other hand Franco-Italian relations were on the upswing.

---

* Pierre Etienne Flandin (1889–1958): French conservative statesman; Prime Minister and Foreign Minister, November 1934–May 1935; Foreign Minister January–June 1936; from December 1940–February 1941 he served as Foreign Minister in the Vichy régime.

This was an asset the French would not easily relinquish particularly when there was nothing of substance to replace it. The British, whether consciously or not, were drifting into a policy of isolation.

A great deal has been made of the point that the British delegation at Stresa failed to warn Mussolini of the consequences of an expansionist policy in Ethiopia; and naturally Van has come in for his share of the responsibility.[13] Hugh Dalton, obviously overcome by the potency of his own rhetoric, proclaimed it as 'one of the most criminal blunders in the whole course of British diplomacy in these years'.[14] When Van came to explain why he had remained silent, one theme dominated all others: Austria.[15] It has been argued that 'There was a general acknowledgement in the foreign office that Austria was already lost even before Stresa began',[16] and in consequence Van's policy was doomed from the outset. This is clearly to overstate the case. At most, views in the Office were divided, even though the weight of informed opinion favoured making every effort to maintain Austrian independence. Van's commitment to Austria was absolute. He would do nothing to upset the chance of creating a European front against Germany, however slender and improbable, on the basis of a joint Austrian interest.

But there were other, equally valid reasons for not cautioning Mussolini. When Van's private secretary, Clifford Norton, asked him why he had not warned Mussolini, Van retorted: 'MacDonald is gaga; Simon is bad tempered at not being head of the delegation; and I am only an official.'[17] That MacDonald was physically and mentally incapable of firm leadership can hardly be questioned. Unable to administer to the simplest of his needs, he was not even fully aware of the scope of his officials' contacts or discussions.[18] In his memoirs, Simon skates peacefully over the Stresa conference, mentioning nothing of substance. But it is beyond dispute that he failed to raise the issue with Mussolini, despite his promise to Eden to do so, although it was discussed at a junior level.[19]

An opportunity had offered itself at the by now notorious session when Mussolini interpolated the words 'of Europe' in the final declaration, thereby announcing his intention of overthrowing the *status quo* in Africa:*

---

* Rotunda convincingly argues (*op. cit.*, 320–34) that this occurred at an *unofficial* meeting before the final session took place. In any case, undue importance should not be read into the words 'of Europe'. They first appeared in the original British draft presented to the conference, and were repeated, in different contexts, by both MacDonald and Flandin at various stages of the deliberations. This is a decisive point, for it implies that Mussolini did not surprise the delegates, and that they had ample time in which to reflect upon the hidden

As Mussolini read the statement . . . he paused and asked: was it not necessary to add the words 'of Europe' to the text? Twice he repeated the words 'of Europe', and he looked around the table at which he as the host presided. Africa had not been mentioned at the conference, although it was in everyone's thoughts . . . Mussolini waited for some protest. MacDonald and Vansittart looked at Simon. Simon sat absolutely still. Flandin and Laval watched them as carefully as Mussolini did. The French would not make a move unless the British led. The British leaders did not say a word. The French and Italians drew an identical and instantaneous conclusion: the silence was a tacit consent given by the British government to Italian ambitions in Ethiopia.[20]

Yet even this story, dramatic and full of atmosphere, can be amplified. Van later confided to Randolph Churchill that after Mussolini's staged intervention, he had turned to MacDonald and indicated the significance of the phrase. 'Don't be tiresome, Van,' MacDonald replied, 'we don't want any trouble. What we want is an agreement we can put before the House of Commons.'[21] If this story is accurate Van had fulfilled his duty. He had tendered his advice; it had been rejected by an ailing Prime Minister. Perhaps he should have turned to Simon; but then perhaps his first choice was intuitive, knowing full well that he could depend upon a negative reaction.

Alone among the senior officials, Eric Drummond pressed for a public airing of the problem.[22] This might have happened after the last session of the conference when the delegates were returning to the motor launches from the Palazzo Borromèo. Both Drummond and Van imply that Mussolini was approached, but that he 'speedily rode off on another track'. An approach was made, though no warning uttered. In any case, the timing was all wrong. A stroll down to the lakeside was not the most propitious moment to issue a stern warning to the Italian dictator. Obviously Van did not rate Drummond's advice highly. Apart from the personal antipathy between them, it was widely believed that Drummond took too soft

---

meaning of his, and their, words. In the official minutes of the session, since published (see *B.D.*, 2, XII, no. 722), there is no reference to Mussolini's interpolation. The relevant passage of the communiqué reads: 'The three Powers, the object of whose policy is the collective maintenance of peace within the framework of the League of Nations, find themselves in complete agreement in opposing, by all practicable means, any unilateral repudiation of treaties which may endanger the peace of Europe, and will act in close and cordial collaboration for this purpose.'

a line with the Italians. 'Lord Perth is very weak', complained Van in 1939.[23] Significantly, when Van's future became the subject for discussion at the end of 1935, it was Drummond who hinted that they should exchange posts.[24]

However one interprets the silence at Stresa, at least Van's behaviour was consistent. The Stresa front, fragile and delicate though it was, provided a tentative beginning; given time and goodwill it could have been consolidated. Both these ingredients were lacking. A coordinated policy with France was vital if Mussolini's plans were to be foiled. Having waited for so many years for the Latin sisters to get together, Van was reluctant to jeopardize their new friendship by an open confrontation at Stresa. Perhaps the shady nature of Laval's diplomacy inhibited any real intimacy between the Western powers. Both countries went fishing for Italian support, but in different ponds and using different bait. Where Van gravely miscalculated was in seriously underestimating Mussolini's impetuous nature; but in this too he was very much a creature of his age.

Having elaborated all these points, it remains to ask the most pertinent question of all: would a warning at Stresa have deterred Mussolini from his Ethiopian adventure? Only to pose the question suggests the answer. Forceful warnings were not lacking, neither before nor after Stresa. Despite them Mussolini went his own way.* And it would be fanciful to an extreme to imagine that yet another admonition would have tilted the balance towards peace. It may well have had the reverse effect. The Stresa conference, instead of terminating in a cloud of fine-sounding paper resolutions, could have ended in a humiliating fiasco, pushing Mussolini into even more extreme postures. Ultimately, that was the rationale guiding Van's policy.

On 7 June Baldwin succeeded to the premiership. At the Foreign Office, Sir Samuel Hoare† replaced Simon. Hoare, a shrewd and tough politician, had spent the last few years negotiating the highly controversial Government of India Act through the House of

* Whether the warnings reached Mussolini in their original form is another matter. Flattery and deceit were endemic to the Fascist régime, and there can be little doubt that the warnings were watered down during the act of transmission to Mussolini.

† Samuel John Gurney Hoare (1880–1959): Conservative M.P., 1910–44; Secretary of State for Air, 1924–29, 1940; for India, 1931–35; Foreign Secretary, 1935; First Lord of Admiralty, 1936–7; Home Secretary, 1937–39; Lord Privy Seal, 1939–40; Ambassador to Spain, 1940–44. Succeeded to Btcy, 1915. Cr. Viscount Templewood, 1944.

Commons. This massive effort had taken its toll. He was a sick man, given to severe attacks of arthritis and fainting-fits.[25] Apart from his health, he was disturbed by the internal controversies which seemed to rack the Foreign Office, at least when compared to the decorum and relative consensus of opinion he was used to at the India Office. 'Diametrically opposite views were pressed upon me, and sometimes with the intolerance of an *odium theologicum*.'[26] There is perhaps an element of exaggeration here, but Hoare must have been out of touch, perhaps out of his depth, in the livelier atmosphere of the Foreign Office.

He was also troubled by the anomalous position Eden, now Minister for League of Nations Affairs with a seat in the cabinet, held in the Office hierarchy. There appeared to exist the real danger of dualism in authority and advice. Eden's relations with Hoare were in any case strained. Disappointed at not being appointed Foreign Secretary himself, a note of pique crept into his relations with his chief. And as the League became inextricably involved in the Italo-Ethiopian dispute, Eden leapt into public prominence perhaps more than his position warranted and surely more than his senior colleague desired. But public prominence was one thing, foreign policy-making another. Hoare, prompted by Van, kept his hands tightly on the reins of office.

With a raw, and somewhat bewildered Foreign Secretary, Van was able to impose his authority in no uncertain manner. Hoare put it modestly, if accurately: 'Vansittart's fertile mind and unequalled knowledge of European politics and personalities were invaluable to me, whilst my more conventional methods may have been useful to him as a supplement to his sparkling *tours de force*.'[27] Van showed greater subtlety. 'At last', he claimed, 'I've got a Foreign Secretary I can work with.'[28]

He made no such claim with Eden. Tactical differences regarding the role of the League divided them. This was not a difference of principle but of degree. The distinction between *pro* and *anti* Leaguers is both simplistic and misleading. Basically the discussion turned on assessing the kind of role the League should play in the crisis. Eden revealed a greater predilection for League politics, perhaps even to the point of the expulsion of Italy from the League should she refuse to adhere to its principles. Outwardly Van paid every respect to the League Covenant. But he could never see 'the League's components tackling an aggressor of weight'.[29] Van's main complaint was that the 'Leaguers' had elevated their anti-Italianism to the status of an ideology, and over a minor issue in East Africa, when political reality dictated that they should give first priority to the German menace in Europe. He could not repeat his *idée fixe* often enough: Austria, not Ethiopia, was the cardinal question. The League was powerless to restrain Mussolini in Africa unless, ultimately, it was prepared for a military showdown. Everyone rejected this as a policy of desperation. Therefore why play at brinkmanship when the only tangible result would be to shatter the European front for Germany's benefit.

But the League would not be ignored. Quite the contrary, in every scheme concocted to resolve the crisis it was taken for granted that Britain was acting in the name of the League, not usurping its role. Any solution would have to gain the approval of the League as well as that of the interested parties. Van, in a surprising admission, considered the League 'even more vital in our national interests than France, as being the one umbrella under which most people in this country can be united'.[30] In this roundabout way Van and his supporters appeared as defenders of the League, anxious to boost its prestige with a striking success, not to hasten its demise with certain failure.

Throughout these weeks the Italian military build-up, now estimated at 100,000 troops, continued unabated, despite further British warnings. By June a new British initiative, originally mooted by Maurice Peterson* but almost wholly inspired by Van, was taking shape. Fearing an imminent explosion, he wrote:

> It is as plain as a pikestaff. Italy will have to be bought off – let us use and face ugly words – in some form or other, or Abyssinia will eventually perish. That might in itself matter less, if it did not mean that the League would also perish, (and that Italy would simultaneously perform another *volte face* into the arms of Germany, a continuation of *haute politique* and *haute cocotterie* that we can ill afford just now).[31]

The price Van had in mind was a land corridor through British Somaliland to include the port of Zeila in return for territorial concessions to Italy in the Ogaden region. This was the genesis of the so-called Zeila proposals of June 1935. The details were agreed

---

* Maurice Drummond Peterson (1889–1952): entered Foreign Office, 1913; served at Washington, Prague, Tokyo, Cairo, Madrid; private secretary to Balfour at Washington conference, 1921–22; Acting High Commissioner, Egypt, 1934; Minister to Bulgaria, 1936–38; Ambassador to Iraq, 1938–39; to Spain, 1939–40; to Ankara, 1944–46; to Moscow, 1946–49. Kn. 1938.

upon at a weekend meeting between Hoare, Eden and Van at Trent Park, Sir Philip Sassoon's* country house. On 16 June Van wrote eight pages of minutes to stiffen Hoare's and Eden's arguments at the forthcoming cabinet meeting.[32] In addition to the points he had already made, he added two basic conditions: that the proposals must 'be regarded as a minimum', and that the French should be consulted beforehand. The cabinet accepted his strategy.[33] On 28 June, after a final briefing by Van, Eden arrived in Rome to commence his mission.

Mussolini's reaction was wholly negative. The fact that the project had been leaked to the press did not ease Eden's task. But Mussolini's attitude was so uncompromising that, in the words of one official, it seemed 'unfortunately to kill the Zeila solution'.[34] Van disagreed: 'We must have a further shot at this', he countered, 'the issues are infinitely too great to take a first no, however uncompromising, for a final.' He had all along insisted that the proposals were 'a minimum'; and he refused to shut the door on a Zeila-like deal to solve the crisis.

Eden's mission failed in another, no less important, respect. The French became highly suspicious when they learned about the scheme from the political gossip columns, particularly when it followed so closely on the heels of the Anglo-German naval agreement. For some reason Eden failed to heed Van's advice to consult the French prior to the Italian talks, 'thinking it better to handle that first with Mussolini direct'.[35] It was a misguided decision. When Eden arrived in Paris on his way back from Rome he found an angry Laval awaiting him, accusing Britain of very nearly playing 'a trick' on France by reducing the profitability of the Djibouti railway through the cession of a rival port. Corbin, the French Ambassador in London, repeated the same complaint to Van.[36] The French were extremely sensitive on this point, hence Van's insistence that Eden sound out Paris before proceeding on to Rome. Van did his utmost to smooth things over. But at a time when Anglo-French collaboration was most needed, the British appeared to have spared no effort to needle their erstwhile partners. Within a few weeks Van would be complaining bitterly, and with every justification, about the anti-British venom of the French press. It was a fair complaint; but had the British revealed themselves as the most trustworthy and cooperative of allies?

Yet another sequel to the Zeila proposals which should have

* Sir Philip (Albert Gustave David) Sassoon (1888–1939): Conservative M.P. 1912–39; Under Secretary of State for Air, 1924–29, 1931–37. Succeeded to Btcy, 1912.

triggered off a red warning light in the Foreign Office was the reaction of public opinion to the project. Both wings of the political spectrum denounced the scheme: the right repudiating the cession of any British territory; the left up in arms at any concession to an acquisitive bully. Many years later Van reflected that only through 'quiet negotiations' had the plan any chance of success.[37] In any event, he had no intention of taking into his confidence politicians of the second rank. He told Eden: 'There is no reason why we should further impair our foreign relations [with France and Italy] to satisfy idle curiosity in the House of Commons.'[38] This was how he interpreted 'quiet negotiations'. He was advocating a return to the byways of secret diplomacy.

The outcry in the press naturally displeased Van for it severely limited his diplomacy. But he drew no conclusions from it save to have 'a further shot'. A wide gap divided the public image of British policy, with its strong adherence to League principles, from its private face, with its obsession for secret deals made at the expense of smaller countries. Although this was a crude oversimplification, this was how it appeared to the general public when confronted with dramatic headlines. Van may have sensed this discrepancy but he did nothing to remedy it. Clinging firmly to his nineteenth-century inheritance, he persisted in believing that it was possible to solve European problems by juggling territories around in Africa as if moving pawns on a chessboard. The Zeila incident was a dummy for the more sensational Hoare–Laval affair some six months later.

As the summer months passed Van's mood became increasingly pessimistic. Convinced that the Italians would attack Ethiopia come what may, he despaired of ever finding an effective combination to deter Mussolini. One factor in particular depressed him: the grave deficiencies in British sea power in the Mediterranean. Chatfield, the First Sea Lord, emphasized this point in a long conversation they held on 7 August.[39] From this discussion Van concluded that at the three power conference due to convene in Paris in mid-August, the French would have to furnish a definite assurance that in the event of war they would stand by Britain. But even if the French response was generous, there remained the need to tread warily for fear of provoking the Italians into 'a mad dog coup'.[40] Chatfield's remarks had deeply disturbed Van. The impression remains strong that they threw him into a minor panic. For the next day or two he bombarded his superiors with papers all designed to prove how right he was. Neither Hoare nor Eden dissented from the main tenet of his argument.[41]

The Paris talks terminated in failure. As expected, the Italians proved obdurate to an extreme, exploiting the occasion to parade extreme demands: the annexation of the non-Amharic territories and an Italian mandate for the remainder of Ethiopia. In public Laval stood up to these unacceptable claims. But in private the French attitude remained as problematical as ever. Laval told Eden that France was without an ally in Europe. 'The Russians were unreliable, the British unpredictable.'[42] On the 18th, the night the conference collapsed, a *post-mortem* was held in the British embassy:

> A tired and rather petulant Eden presided . . . the rest of us stood around as a worried and earnest Vansittart held the floor.
>
> 'Anthony, you are faced with a first-class international crisis. We've got to reinforce the Mediterranean fleet.'
>
> 'Well, Van', said Eden at last, 'you'd better draft a letter to the P.M.'[43]

Within three weeks naval reinforcements had been despatched to the Mediterranean; at the same time the main fleet withdrew from Malta, where it lay at anchor defenceless against air attack, to safer waters in Alexandria.

One unexpected result of the Paris talks was the suggestion that Van go to Rome to meet Mussolini to seek a way out of the impasse.[44] As Van was on his way south to the Antibes for a holiday, he was in a convenient position to pursue the matter further if it were so decided. His own inclination was that he would 'wreck the remains of a small rest by an unpleasant journey and a bad quarter of an hour'. The projected meeting did not materialize. As compensation he stopped off at Aix-les-Bains where he briefed Baldwin on the results of the conference.*

With the failure of the Paris talks the mood at the Foreign Office turned to strengthening the Geneva front and ensuring Anglo-French

---

* Lady Vansittart tells a slightly different version of this episode (interview 31 October 1972). She recollected that Grandi first put the idea to Van. He suggested that Lady Vansittart should travel to Italy, and then telegraph home that she had been suddenly taken ill. Van would then have a 'legitimate' excuse to go and join her without arousing suspicion, and could then meet Mussolini in secret. Van refused to be a party to this plot, claiming that it would be unfair and deceptive to his colleagues. No evidence has been found to substantiate this story in connection with the August talks; but Van wrote (*M.P.* 530) that, while the Zeila proposals were being hatched, the Italians had asked him to come out 'unobtrusively'.

cooperation. An atmosphere of impending crisis prevailed. Deeply conscious that events were gathering momentum, Van was uneasy at the lack of control over the crisis and pressed for an early cabinet meeting to decide on a clear-cut policy.[45] As usual, Van carried Hoare with him. He wrote to Chamberlain, sticking close to Van's text, forecasting 'a first-class crisis in the League at the beginning of September', and stressing the need 'for the Cabinet to consider what preparations should be made to meet a possible mad dog act by the Italians'.[46] Hoare reserved some harsh comments for his cabinet colleagues: 'Stanley would think about nothing but his holiday and the necessity of keeping out of the whole business almost at any cost. Ramsey has written me a curious and almost unintelligible letter warning me of the dangers that surround us.' Unwilling to act in a vacuum, Van and Hoare were clearly concerned at the extent the cabinet would back, or even grasp, their policy.*

The British were now faced with an acute dilemma. They could not stand by helplessly while the Italians destroyed Ethiopia. But neither could they act alone without incurring the gravest risk. This presumed solid Anglo-French collaboration. But the cracks in the *entente*, markedly visible since January, grew more pronounced as the crisis developed. The French harked back to a claim they had first made at Versailles: a definite British commitment in Europe against Germany. Only then would they move against Italy over Ethiopia. It was a harsh, logical policy, yet difficult to condemn and fully understood and recognized by Van. Without British acceptance of the French demand, there was little sense in acting upon the assumption of a united Anglo-French front. There was an element of self-deception, perhaps wishful thinking, in British policy during the latter stages of the crisis.

The element of self-deception was also painfully evident in Hoare's speech to the League Assembly in Geneva at the beginning of September. The speech was awaited with an eager sense of anticipation. Van was positive that it would have to be a tough one, both to boost the authority of the League and to gain the confidence of the French; and its first draft, to which he contributed,

---

* Baldwin's latest biographers vigorously, though not entirely convincingly, deny his basic indifference and lack of leadership throughout the crisis (see K. Middlemas and J. Barnes, *Baldwin* (London, 1969) 850–52). They suggest that Hoare 'was already imprisoned by mental stress behind a glass door of incomprehension'. The reference is a trifle obscure, but it may refer to the side-effects of Hoare's illness – he was bed-ridden with arthritis at the time. What is clear, however, is that no sooner had the government completed its consultations than Baldwin hopped back to France for another 'brief rest'.

reflected his views. Inevitably, there occurred the bureaucratic process of toning it down.* Van took strong exception to the redraft, fearing that it had lost the decisiveness he had insisted upon. His draft had included 'resistance to all unprovoked aggression in whatever quarter such a danger to the peace of the world may arise'.[47] He wished to avoid those well-meaning, though meaningless, phrases which had limited British diplomacy in the past. 'To say we stand for "the collective maintenance of the Covenant in its entirety" could not be used to reply to the French or to reassure Europe. It would not be taken as an answer and would therefore fail of its purpose.'[48]

The phrase remained; but the impact of the speech far exceeded Van's gloomy predictions. Hoare was 'amazed at the universal acclamation' it received.[49] Britain had at last taken the initiative in rallying the League. Italy was isolated; collective security had found a new champion. M. Paul Hymans, the Belgium representative, expressed everyone's thoughts: 'The British have decided to stop Mussolini, even if that means using force.'[50] Nothing could have been further from the truth.

Although widely acclaimed, the speech altered little. Military action against Italy had been ruled out beforehand by Laval and Hoare. The naval movements, menacing though they appeared, were solely precautionary measures. Economic sanctions, if applied, would be exercised modestly and in stages. Was the speech then a gigantic bluff? An exercise in self-deception? Hoare's revivalist appeal to the League was designed to browbeat Mussolini. He counted on deterring Italy by an upsurge in League fervour. To sugar the pill, Hoare offered Italy large-scale economic concessions, particularly free access to raw materials. The belief that the problem was economic rather than political was a wholly erroneous one, though it was widely accepted at the time. It was not shared by Van. Economic crumbs were no substitute for political and military glory. Having laboured in vain to harness France and Britain into an effective force to lead the League, he, at least, held few illusions that anything lay behind Hoare's stirring oratory other than bluster and lack of resolution.

Mussolini called the bluff. Perhaps encouraged by Laval's persistent references to the importance of Franco-Italian friendship, he

---

* Hoare wrote (p. 166) that 'Chamberlain had throughout helped me with the text'. He may well have had a hand in the watering-down, though he was most probably more concerned with the economic aspects of the speech to which Hoare attached the greatest importance.

rejected all last minute compromise proposals.* In the early morning of 3 October, Italian units crossed the Ethiopian frontier. Within hours news reached London that Adowa had been bombed. That same morning Grandi handed to Van an official communiqué to the effect that 'It had become necessary to Italy to undertake certain operations to ensure her military security.'[51]

Once hostilities had begun, the need for a settlement became more urgent. Laval put up a new proposal on 4 October. It originated in contacts between the Quai d'Orsay and the Vatican. In general terms it called for a revival of the Committee of Five scheme, with increased Italian participation and an Italian mandate over the non-Amharic regions. Van rejected this as an 'impossible suggestion'.[52] It went too far, and would moreover 'very deeply shock public opinion here'. He favoured a direct exchange of territories to Italy's advantage. Any settlement would have to reflect to a marked degree Italian interests. Van resurrected a scheme which included the cession of Bale and Ogaden and enhanced Italian influence throughout the remainder of Ethiopia.[53] Van thought this proposal 'a generous maximum'. Eden was initially more sceptical, doubting whether it could be sold to the League. But in fact it provided the basis for the involved and highly technical discussions which continued throughout the autumn and into early winter, and which of necessity also took into account the territorial gains Italy had made in the early stages of the war.

There was general agreement in the Office that this was the right approach. Hoare did not dissent. Neither did Eden who now preferred a 'frank exchange of territory' over an Italian protectorate, though he admitted 'the difficulties inherent in either course'.[54] It was the Office expert, Maurice Peterson, who voiced the first whisper of controversy, questioning the wisdom of rewarding an aggressive Italy with Ethiopian provinces, 'the price being paid by Great Britain'.[55] But Van made clear his preference for 'a clean cut on a smaller scale' over 'a thinly veiled protectorate over everything south of the 8th parallel'. Every solution, he predicted, would invite immediate and inevitable criticism, 'and yet no solution is

* The League had set up the Committee of Five to devise a compromise formula. It consisted of France (Laval); Britain (Eden); Poland (Colonel Beck); Turkey (M. Rushu Aras); and Spain (Señor de Madriaga, chairman). Italy was not represented on the Committee and did not recognize its legitimacy. The Committee's plan, which envisaged widescale Italian participation under the League's aegis, called for international economic and financial aid to Ethiopia, extensive internal reforms, and the possibility of an exchange of territory similar to that first proposed in June.

possible unless Italy gets a good deal'. Eden's position was hardly distinguishable from that of Van's, and it received additional support from Lancelot Oliphant. From then on the discussion turned on how many Ethiopian provinces to award to Italy, with the French generously raising Italian demands and the British trying to reduce them.[56]

The autumn of 1935 witnessed a new low in Anglo-French relations. The perversity of French policy exasperated the officials. They felt hemmed in by a growing sense of isolation. Charges and counter-charges flashed across the Channel in a manner reminiscent of the heady days of Fashoda. Anglo-French solidarity was rapidly crumbling, and it was particularly painful for an ardent francophile like Van to discover that in a moment of crisis the French proved themselves to be untrustworthy and double-dealing.

The French press circulated the most fantastic rumours. Was Britain about to launch a pre-emptive strike against Italy? Or to close the canal to Italian shipping? Or to blockade Italian ports? The Quai d'Orsay knew that the British government had no intention of initiating such spectacular moves. Yet the Paris press, either inspired or bought, did not shrink from fostering such dangerous illusions, and the Quai d'Orsay did nothing to prevent it.[57] Britain was presented as the real villain of the piece. Pilloried in the Italian press, taunted by the French press – itself heavily subsidized by Italian funds – the wholly false image emerged of a petulant Britain blocking the way to an amicable settlement. Commenting on this deplorable state of affairs, Van wrote:

> I do not believe that the French will ever play the game. Therefore only time and expense will induce the Italians to a settlement. If in time they become a danger we shall have to equip ourselves to meet it. I am worrying less about that now than about the danger of an Anglo-Italian war brought about not only by French lack of cooperation but disloyalty and treachery in its dirtiest and blackest form ... If that comes about, and we are left to it alone, it will be a disaster to our government, and I think we are entitled to avert that disaster, with all its consequences, without looking too far into the future or counting on two-pence worth of loyalty from our soi-disant collaborators.[58]

But short of threatening alarming consequences to 'Anglo-French relations in general and to Locarno in particular'[59] unless the French repaired their ways, there was little the British could do. Anglo-

French relations continued to deteriorate. The French, Van informed the Foreign Office, were 'impotent for aught but treachery and collapse'.[60]

Laval's conduct also deepened the suspicion between the two countries. Van had already marked him down as that 'treacherous creature'.[61] Of late, he had been acting more Italian than the Italians. Grandi made the most astonishing admission to Van: that he, Grandi, was out 'to obtain from this country, and to be able to represent himself in Rome as having obtained, more favourable terms for Italy than M. Laval was prepared to offer her.'[62] Laval and Grandi were now competing with each other for Rome's favour. Moreover, Laval was in direct contact with Mussolini and had evidently kept him fully informed on the progress of the Anglo-French talks. It is impossible to know what precisely materialized between these two characters. But Laval, apparently, was satisfied that he had extracted from Mussolini the basis for some kind of an agreement. He asked to come to London to put his case, but was put off by Hoare. Finally they agreed to meet in Paris at the beginning of December.

It is surely no accident that Laval's initiatives coincided with a 'peace offensive' launched by Mussolini at the end of November. Perhaps in order to lend greater credibility to his case he chose to ignore the Italian Ambassador to London, Grandi, and despatched a special emissary, General Garibaldi, grandson of the great Garibaldi and a wartime acquaintance of Hoare's. The gist of his message was that Italy would be prepared to cease hostilities and go before the League if sanctions, in force since mid-November, were brought to an end and if she were assured in advance of an honourable compromise settlement.[63*] Mussolini's honourable settlement signalled the demise of Ethiopia as an independent state. Van rejected

---

* Mussolini's terms were:
  (a) The territory in the Tigre province already conquered by Italy to remain under her direct suzerainty, or to be proclaimed independent.
  (b) The rectification of undemarcated frontiers, including gains for Italy in the Ogaden and Danakil regions.
  (c) A mandate for Italy over all non-Amharic territories.
  (d) A League of Nations mandate over the Amharic regions. In this eventuality the majority of the officials were to be Italian.
  (e) The disarmament of the Ethiopian army.
  (f) The creation of a port for Ethiopia at Zeila on condition that the above terms were agreed upon. If the British government wished to modify these terms, including clause five, Italy would be willing to give to Ethiopia the port of Assab, but only for commercial purposes.

it, as did Hoare. But the door appeared to have been pushed open, however hesitantly, for some kind of an agreement.

After Garibaldi it was Grandi's turn. He met Van three times at the beginning of December. Grandi's only reaction to Van's plea for moderation was to 'shake his head, to produce more maps, and to ask for more generous treatment'.* But the net effect of this feverish activity must have been to satisfy Van that a reasonable solution was just around the corner given a minimum degree of goodwill on both sides.

In Van's estimation time was running out. Sanctions had been in force since 18 November. Purely economic in character, they did not envisage military action against Italy.† The real crux would come with the debate on oil sanctions. The League was due to decide on this measure on 29 November. How would Italy react to what was widely regarded as the ultimate economic sanction? Evidence accumulated that she would not hesitate to go to war the moment sanctions began to bite and to affect her standard of living. When that occurred, Italy, in an act of desperation, would fling herself 'upon her principal enemy and do as much harm as possible even though defeat were inevitable'. War rumours poured in from Germany, Italy, France and Egypt.[64] Of course, there was no doubt

---

* Grandi's idea of more generous treatment consisted of:
  (a) The cession to Italy of Bale, Adowa-Adigrat, and a section of Danakil, together with part of the Harrar province to link up territorially Eritrea and Italian Somaliland to the east of Addis Ababa.
  (b) A special economic zone of influence for Italy in the south-east of Ethiopia. With the exception of the Harrar addition, there was little to distinguish this plan from Garibaldi's. (See minutes of the meetings, F.O. 371/19167, J. 8997/1/1.) These interviews may well have occasioned Grandi's oft-quoted, but quite inaccurate, remark that the Hoare–Laval plan was in fact the Van–Grandi plan. This was a typical piece of Grandi exaggeration. At the time Grandi was out of favour with Mussolini for having misled him as to the state of public opinion in Britain; he was also in Van's bad books for having inaccurately portrayed the British position in Rome. Grandi's intensive diplomacy was more an attempt to re-establish his personal standing than to reach a viable solution. Van took far more seriously the Garibaldi talks. However, the inflated nature of the reports Grandi sent back to Rome, known surely to Laval, may have compromised Van more than he realised.

† Article 16 of the Covenant provided for economic and military measures should any member of the League resort to war against another member in defiance of the Covenant. The economic measures enacted included the prohibition of Italian exports and of the export of certain categories of raw materials; the cutting off of financial credit; and an arms embargo. Even these rulings contained glaring loopholes. Austria, Hungary and Albania were within the Italian orbit; while the United States, Germany and Japan were not members of the League and were not bound by its decisions.

that the Italians were deliberately flaunting their bellicosity, hoping to reap as rich a military and political harvest as they could. Initially both Eden and Drummond tended to believe that Mussolini would not take the final step. But could they be absolutely certain that the Italians were bluffing? Van argued vehemently that it would be the height of folly to incur any foolish risk. 'The French and Europe', he noted, 'went on banking on Mussolini's bluffing until the eleventh hour. But Mussolini was not bluffing. He went to war. No instance can be cited of bluff on his part. He has always meant what he said – and done it, whether wisely or madly.'[65] He urged Hoare and Eden to adopt a more flexible line at the next cabinet meeting. Militancy should be avoided, he cautioned, until the deficiencies in British defence were rectified and the French swung into line. 'It must be clearly understood, and recognized in the political sphere, that we are neither the League's policeman nor its whipping boy.'[66]

Meanwhile, Peterson had been continuing his talks at the Quai d'Orsay. In answer to French extremist demands – the cession to Italy of the entire Tigre area – the British programme visualized a League plan of assistance for Ethiopia subject to the exchange of Adowa, Adigrat, Danakil, and most of the Ogaden region against a port and land corridor for Ethiopia, and the creation of a special sphere for economic development in the southern part of the country, again under League supervision.[67] These suggestions were agreed upon in principle in London.* As can be seen, they were fairly close in their territorial details to the Garibaldi–Grandi schemes, though the British placed great emphasis, indeed for them it became a matter of high principle, on the land corridor leading to a port to be conceded to Ethiopia as compensation for her concessions to Italy. The French gave no indication whether or not they accepted these ideas. The Comte de St Quentin, the chief French negotiator, maintained a discreet silence; while Laval conveniently disappeared from Paris for a few days.

At the General Election of 14 November, Baldwin's coalition coasted home to a comfortable victory. No longer inhibited by electoral considerations,† the government felt confident enough to pursue

---

* Eden's memoirs (op. cit., 292) are somewhat vague on this point, but he agreed to the new proposals on 26 November. See F.O. 371/19163, J. 8384/1/1.
† Not the least of which was the suspected enthusiasm in favour of collective security and what eventually became know as 'Leaguomania'. The results of the so-called Peace Ballot, published on 27 June, appeared to give decisive proof of the mood of the country. The most intriguing, and misleading, question asked was number five: 'Do you consider that, if a nation insists on attacking another,

the latest Laval–Mussolini peace initiative. At the crucial cabinet meeting of 2 December, Hoare spoke more or less in accordance with Van's ideas.[68] He proposed conditioning the implementation of oil sanctions with progress in the Anglo-French talks, and rejected outright unilateral British action. No one seriously dissented from these views, not even Eden who had previously demanded the immediate implementation of the oil sanction. A consensus was reached. It was agreed to wait upon the outcome of the forthcoming talks with the French. Should these prove unfruitful, the question of oil sanctions would be returned to the cabinet agenda. During the meeting Hoare announced that he intended taking a short holiday in Switzerland, but that he would stop over in Paris to see Laval and conduct the negotiations in person. Baldwin gave him a last piece of advice: 'Push Laval as far as you can, but on no account get this country into war.'[69]*

By the beginning of December the government had been manœuvred into an intolerable situation. Caught between a feeble League of Nations and an irresolute France, with a resurgent Germany on one side and a dangerously vulnerable Britain on the other, every policy alternative was fraught with risk. The Ethiopian crisis served only to screen the real issue, to focus attention away from the main field of battle in Europe to an essentially minor irritation in East Africa. Presented in such crude terms the conundrum resolved itself in a logical, though admittedly callous way. Certainly Van held this view. If a compromise formula could be attained, even at the Ethiopians' expense, he would have brought off a spectacular stroke: the Anglo-French alliance revitalized; the authority of the League restored; Italy saved from the clutches of Germany; and, most important of all, Germany confronted by a united Europe. With these ideas by now firmly entrenched in his mind, he prepared

---

the other nations should combine to compel it to stop by (a) economic and non-military measures? (b) if necessary, military measures? More than ten million people answered Yes to (a), 6·78 million to (b).

It is interesting to note that two independent polls taken by the *Morning Post* and *Daily Mail* in February and October 1935 produced directly opposite results to those achieved by the Peace Ballot. See D. Waley, *British Public Opinion and the Abyssinian War 1935–36* (London, 1975), 22–23.

* Once again Eden is vague on this point. He wrote that Hoare gave no indication that he intended 'to embark on a serious negotiation with Laval' (*op. cit.*, 298). This seems a strange remark to make considering all the preparations which had been made, and in view of the fact that Van was accompanying Hoare to Paris. Hoare himself later complained that he should have obtained cabinet agreement as to how far to go with Laval (*op. cit.*, 178). Still, all had agreed on the 'principles'. Perhaps it depended on the definition of 'serious'.

to accompany Hoare to Paris to continue the Peterson–St Quentin discussions on a higher level.

Van travelled to Paris on 6 December. The following afternoon Hoare arrived. He was met at the station by Van, Sir George Clerk, and Peterson. After first stopping at the British Embassy they drove to the Quai d'Orsay where the talks began at 5.30 pm. On the way Van asked Hoare whether the government intended to fight. The answer was negative. 'Then you will have to compromise,' Van retorted. 'That will be unpopular, but there is no third way.'[70] Before leaving London an apprehensive Eden had warned Hoare that in Paris 'Van can be more French than the French'. Hoare reassured him: 'I shall not commit you to anything. It wouldn't be fair on my way through to my holiday.'[71] Yet only a few days earlier he had written to Sir Clive Wigram, the King's private secretary, that 'we intend to go all out for bringing the conflict to an end . . . I hope M. Laval and I [can] agree upon a basis for negotiation.'[72] Either Hoare was not keeping Eden fully informed as to his intentions, a highly unlikely interpretation, or else Eden deliberately chose to ignore the potential significance of the Paris meeting. Whatever the explanation, it was an unhappy beginning to an unfortunate episode.*

The extraordinary scenes which preceded the discussions have been often described. The talks appear to have been conducted in a hothouse atmosphere of excitement and intrigue, with the British diplomats having to jostle their way through a crowd of journalists, photographers, and other hangers-on to reach the conference room.[73] Yet on the whole the British negotiators achieved their main aims.[74] First and foremost, Anglo-French cooperation. Despite Laval's evasiveness, Hoare and Van pinned him down until he finally agreed to extend the joint naval staff conversations already in progress to

---

* There is a widely held view that the Hoare–Laval meeting was a hasty, improvised affair which Hoare somehow managed to fit in on his way to his holiday. The leading players – Hoare and Van – both lent weight to this impression in their accounts of these events (see Templewood, 177–8; *Lessons of My Life*, 53; *M.P.*, 538), as did Eden (Avon, 298). Yet evidence does exist which indicates that Van at least believed that 'the second half of December' would be crucial for a solution of the crisis (see *G.D.*, C, iv, no. 404, a report by von Hoesch to German Foreign Ministry, 8 November 1935, on a discussion with Van). By the second half of November the diplomatic pace had considerably quickened: the elections were over; League sanctions were in force; Peterson was back in Paris; the Italians were fishing for a compromise; and Laval was ready to string along. By December it was obvious that fateful decisions could be avoided no longer. In this sense the Hoare–Laval meeting was no more fortuitous than any of the other diplomatic conversations which had preceded it.

cover the air force and the army. Van intervened in the first discussion to emphasize the need for carrying on all three processes simultaneously: the fixing of the date for the oil embargo; the peace negotiations; and the staff talks. (This had been a specific conclusion of the cabinet on 2 December.) Above all, there must be joint Anglo-French proposals; the French must cease acting as an intermediary between Italy and Britain. Laval succumbed, outwardly at least, to this pressure. At the conclusion of the talks Van and George Clerk congratulated Hoare on 'having re-established the Anglo-French front'.[75] This was the great achievement of the talks, one which Van had laboured incessantly to create over the past months. But it became obscured, in fact blotted out, by the details of the territorial settlement. These can be summarized briefly: an outlet to the sea for Ethiopia, either Zeila or Assab; the cessation of some of the conquered territory in Tigre to Italy, and frontier rectifications in the east and south-east; and a large zone in the south and south-west in which Italy, acting under the League, would have a monopoly for economic development.[76] By this deal roughly two-thirds of Ethiopia would fall under Italian control.

The cabinet approved these proposals on 9 December, not out of a sense of loyalty to Hoare, as Eden later implied,[77] but quite simply because the majority of ministers initially approved of the compact made in Paris.[78] Naturally, there were some misgivings. Eden in particular was dissatisfied. Even before the cabinet convened he had insisted on including certain procedural modifications which showed greater even-handedness towards Ethiopia. Van persuaded Laval as to their merit in a concentrated bout of midnight diplomacy. Laval, however, demanded his pound of flesh in return. He wanted a concrete assurance that, if Ethiopia rejected the proposals, the oil sanction would not be imposed. Laval reasoned, and Van concurred with him, that the Emperor would play this card with the intention of engineering a confrontation between Italy and the League. Once again, the answer from London was negative; Laval's request was a matter for the League to decide.[79] Intentionally or not, London had cut the ground from under their own feet. The Hoare–Laval scheme had been stretched to breaking point only hours after it was hatched.

Almost simultaneously with the conclusion of the talks the terms of the agreement were leaked to the press.* Newspapers hostile to

---

* It was widely thought at the time that Laval himself had leaked the information in an attempt to force the British government's hand – a singularly unsuccessful trick, if true. Van discarded this theory from the outset, believing that Laval's

Laval's government, particularly the *Œuvre* and the *Echo de Paris*, castigated the plan. The British press followed suit. *The Times* published a withering editorial, 'A Corridor for Camels'. General opinion in the House of Commons reacted angrily against the agreement. The politically minded – those who were moved at all by foreign affairs – insisted on raising their voices. Egged on by the League of Nations Union, their protests began to monopolize the correspondence columns of the press.* Bewildered by this unexpected onslaught the government began to backpedal. Eden's statement to the League, it 'sounded the death knell of the peace plan',[80] was ratified on 17 December. The following day half the cabinet rose in revolt against the plan. Apart from Chamberlain, Hoare found himself isolated.[81] That same evening his resignation was made public.† On 19 December Baldwin, making 'one of his take-you-into-my-confidence speeches'[82] officially buried the Hoare–Laval agreement.

Van remained in Paris until 12 December while the storm was breaking above his head. He had sensed that the plan would be misinterpreted in London. Before Peterson left Paris with details of the plan for the cabinet's consideration, Van urged him to emphasize 'the pressing need for closing the ranks against the coming onrush of Germany'.[83] When Van finally arrived in London he was met by Clifford Norton and Rex Leeper. They retired to Park Street for dinner. His aides explained to him how badly the situation had

---

numerous enemies at the Quai d'Orsay were seeking to dislodge him from office, a much more plausible explanation. Leakages were an inevitable and a day-to-day occurrence at the Quai d'Orsay where security precautions were practically non-existent.

* Mr Waley (*op. cit.*, 48–70) has convincingly demonstrated that the popular conception of a mysterious and spontaneous explosion in British public opinion which resulted in the famous 'deluge' of letters to members of parliament against the agreement has been considerably exaggerated. Baldwin was swayed by the hostile attitude of the House, not by 'public opinion' outside it. Public opinion, in any case a loose and often ambiguous term, has been defined by Mr Waley in this instance in a more precise and satisfactory manner.

† Hoare's personal story was one of high tragedy coupled with high farce. He left Paris immediately after the talks and arrived in Zuoz the following afternoon. Hoare was a skater of international quality, but on his first day on the ice he had a complete blackout. He fell and broke his nose in two places. While his colleagues were deciding his future he remained bed-ridden, at first in Switzerland, later in London. He arrived home on 16 December. His colleagues dutifully paid their respects and tendered their respective advice. But his duty was clear. On 19 December he rose from the backbenches of the House to deliver his farewell speech as Foreign Minister.

deteriorated. Van's first reaction was to play down the public outcry: 'A ten days' wonder, they'll soon forget all about it. We'll just have to ride it out.'[84] Norton was not so sanguine: the government was split, the House of Commons restless, the press highly critical. There was no room for complacency. He suggested going to see Baldwin that very evening. They arrived at the House at about 9 pm. Van pleaded with Baldwin to take the press into his confidence, to explain fully and frankly the motives for the agreement. Our case, he argued, was convincing enough to carry the House and the country. Baldwin seemed impressed. When they had concluded their talk, he threw a pile of telegrams he had received from the constituencies protesting against the agreement into the air: 'Tell the press we must have more aeroplanes', he ordered. Van emerged from the meeting smiling, confident that Baldwin would back the Foreign Office. 'He's all right,' he announced to Norton. Norton was again more sceptical. He had previously sounded out government officials about the need for Baldwin to brief the press. Thomas Dugdale, Baldwin's parliamentary private secretary, had retorted that 'He mustn't touch it.' Baldwin's instinct to preserve his government triumphed over Van's plea for frankness. As Van wrote: 'he scudded before the popular wind, so that our real case was never put'.[85]

Meanwhile Van found himself the object of mounting public criticism. He was dubbed 'The Man Behind It All'.[86] In a fierce article entitled 'The British Press Does Its Duty', the *News Chronicle* suggested that 'it would not be a bad thing if Sir Robert Vansittart . . . were transferred not too unobtrusively to some less perilous office'. Some days later the same newspaper again raised the delicate question of Van's future.[87] Even more disturbing, Van became the subject for cabinet censure. On two occasions, on 17 and 18 December, damaging criticism was voiced against him: first, for 'embarrassing' the cabinet by having doctored (?) the first report on the Paris talks which the cabinet received; and secondly, for having greatly 'misled' Hoare.[88] These allegations, imprecise and misleading, were without substance. But his position rapidly became untenable. He contemplated resignation. Forces antagonistic to him in the government and in the Office gathered momentum. 'Don't worry about Vansittart,' said the wife of a colleague to Flandin, 'he's done for.'[89] He told Austen Chamberlain of his difficulties and received a devastating reply: 'You had better go, you are getting rattled.'[90] He was offered an embassy, either Paris or Washington, but he turned the suggestion down, preferring to remain in London and 'stick it out'.[91]

Some friends remained. But the fire in their friendship had died

Brushing Up The Old Champion.

Brushing up the old Champion.

(Yorkshire Observer, 1938)

Monte Carlo Sensation. A Low cartoon of 1938.
(London Express Pictures)

Lord Halifax (left) and Sir John Simon leaving 10 Downing Street, 1939.
  (*Radio Times Hulton Picture Library*)

Sir Alexander Cadogan (right) and Sir Robert Vansittart leaving 10 Downing Street after a conference with Neville Chamberlain on the Czech crisis, 1938.
  (*Radio Times Hulton Picture Library*)

down. Despite their protestations of sympathy and goodwill, they saw clearly the writing on the wall. Phipps penned a note of support.[92] But a few days later he wrote to Hankey severely criticizing Van's Stresa policy: 'All the Ethiopian imbroglio springs from that hideous error.'[93] Hankey agreed, modestly acknowledging that if only he had gone to Stresa there would have been 'some plain speaking about Abyssinia'. He continued:

> I often think of your future. I fancy it is, as usual, connected with Van's. There has been a tendency to head-hunt over Sam Hoare's escapade in Paris and Van's name has been mentioned or hinted at . . . Warren Fisher and I and other friends will stand by him, but it may be that, after a decent interval, it may be thought that a change would be beneficial. . . I hope, however, that he will weather the storm, as he is (in spite of a certain impulsiveness) very good in his present job, and I owe him a lot.[94]

But Van's greatest source of comfort appeared from an entirely unexpected direction. Lord Beaverbrook sprang to the rescue where others hesitated or made no move at all. His powerful arguments were instrumental in persuading Van not to tender his resignation:

> It was indeed good of you to write, and in such terms. You have been the soul of kindness throughout this – when so many have failed – and I most truly appreciate it, and shall not forget it. You know what my aims have been, and I have followed them disregarding the cost to myself. I shall not desist from them myself; but there are many who want to stop me. But I shall remember what you say, and stick it out as long as it is made possible.[95]

On 16 December Van dined at Stornoway House, Beaverbrook's town residence, and used the occasion to defend his policy. 'This was a kind of dress rehearsal for a possible bigger show in two or three years' time. They had discovered no response in other countries. Even the French could not put oil sanctions over – not at least until they had proved to their people (i.e. by the plan) that the Italians were mad. Not a question of being afraid of the Italians. But a war would cost ships (which would take four years to be replaced) and lots of money. No one would be a whit better off – England would be definitely weaker – and in two years' time she might have to face a serious situation in Germany.'[96]

Although Van was on friendly social terms with Beaverbrook, he did not trust him politically, considering him irresponsible and wayward.[97] Why Beaverbrook should have intervened so decisively is

G

not clear. Magnanimity undoubtedly entered it, as did agreement on broad principles of policy. But perhaps it was yet another ploy in Beaverbrook's never-ending campaign against Baldwin.* Whatever his motive, his unstinting support was much appreciated.

Van's future, however, depended not on his friends' support but on his relations with the new Foreign Secretary, Anthony Eden. Eden entered into his inheritance with the unconcealed aim of easing Van out. Although he accepted the principle that Hoare, as the responsible minister, should be held accountable for the fiasco, he was also fearful of Van's special standing and the influence he wielded. In a revealing passage in his memoirs, he noted:

> In my long service at the Foreign Office as a junior Minister and as Secretary of State I have known many heads of the department and appointed some of them. I have never known one to compare with Sir Robert as a relentless, not to say ruthless, worker for the views he held strongly himself. The truth is that Vansittart was seldom an official giving cool and disinterested advice based on study and experience. He was himself a sincere, almost fanatical, crusader, and much more a Secretary of State in mentality than a permanent official.[98]

Eden would not tolerate divided leadership at the top, at least not when he was in the saddle. He wanted an official who would manage the Foreign Office efficiently and in accordance with his views. On neither count was Eden satisfied with Van. Sir Alexander Cadogan,† a more correct, manageable and less controversial figure than Van, was brought back from service in China with the intention of grooming him to replace a permanent official who acted more like a Secretary of State.[99]

Of course, it would be impolitic for Van to go immediately. Eden explained the reasons why in a carefully restrained letter to George V:

> On reflection Mr Eden is convinced that the best interests of the public service will be furthered by retaining Sir Robert Vansittart in his present post. The prime minister has been good enough to

---

* Mr Taylor suggests (*op. cit.*, 358–9) that Beaverbrook, who accompanied Van to Paris, intended to organize a joint Anglo-French press campaign in favour of the Hoare–Laval plan. If so, it sadly misfired. But the *Daily Express* stuck bravely to its proprietor's views, defending Van and Hoare and their policy until the end.

† Alexander George Montagu Cadogan (1884–1968): entered diplomatic service, 1908; served in Constantinople, Vienna, London; member of British delegation to League of Nations; British minister at Peking, 1933–36; Deputy Under Secretary of State, 1936–38; Permanent Under Secretary, 1938–46; Britain's permanent representative at United Nations, 1946–50.

say that he would leave the matter to Mr Eden's judgement and therefore concurs in this view. Mr Eden feels that this decision will meet with His Majesty's approval, not only on its merits, but because it will meet the risk, of which Mr Eden was acutely conscious, of permanent officials being implicated in the political decisions of their ministerial chiefs.[100]

Eden must also have been ultra sensitive to the gossip which eroded his professional relationship with Van: the contrast between an older, experienced, single-minded and powerful PUS, and a relatively inexperienced, and perhaps somewhat naïve and vain, minister. Rumour had it that Eden, because of his lack of experience, would be a popular appointment at the Foreign Office: 'It is said that he will speak his own mind, but it will be the mind of the Foreign Office officials'.[101] Eden shrank from being swamped by Van's stronger personality. 'He knew that when he spoke in cabinet twenty pairs of eyes turned on him with one thought: "His Master's Voice".'[102] It was natural enough that Eden should seek independence from his overmighty official.

In the long run these considerations counted far more than so-called differences over policy. Throughout the crisis, until the final agreement, Eden had not deviated seriously from the Foreign Office line, Van's line. He was privy to all the twists and turns of the negotiations. Perhaps his conscience stirred at the thought of a deal with Mussolini; but this did not deter him from arguing in favour of a 'frank exchange of territory'. Ultimately he shied at the last hurdle, claiming that the terms of the agreement were too onerous and, if accepted, would ruin the League and bring the government into disrepute.

It was this shilly-shallying that made certain the failure of British policy. This particular charge cannot be laid at Van's door. From the outset he had kept to his opinions with commendable consistency, in marked contrast to the vacillation of some of his ministers. Of course, there can be no guarantee that had Van's line been accepted a great victory would have ensued. But it is quite certain that failure to follow through a consistent policy invited catastrophe. In the event the League was ruined, Ethiopia sacrificed, Italy alienated, and Germany encouraged.

Van never recovered from the repercussions of the Hoare–Laval débâcle.* He had compromised himself, or so it was believed. His

* There can be no doubt that he was gravely embarrassed by the affair; and that the embarrassment remained, perhaps deepened, with the passage of time. This

reputation remained under a cloud. Although he was to continue in office for another two years, his great days were over. For the past six years he had flourished on a series of weak Foreign Secretaries. Now Eden had replaced them to remind him of the limitations of his position.*

NOTES

1. See G. Baer, *The Coming of the Ethiopian War* (Harvard University Press, 1967), ch. 1, which summarizes Italo-Ethiopian relations, 1889–1934.
2. See D. C. Watt, 'The Secret Laval-Mussolini Agreement of 1935 on Ethiopia' in *The Origins of the Second World War* (London, 1971), ed. E. M. Robertson.
3. Quoted by Rotunda, *op. cit.*, 183.
4. See Rotunda, *op. cit.*, 183–5; and Sir G. Thompson, *Front Line Diplomat* (London, 1959), 95.
5. Minutes of 19 February 1935, F.O. 371/19103, J. 608/1/1.
6. Minutes of 25 February 1935, F.O. 371/19105, J. 973/1/1.
7. See 'Memorandum on Questions for Discussion at Stresa', 4 April 1935, C.P. 79(35), CAB. 24/254.
8. For the text see Cmd. 4880, misc. no. 2 (1935).
9. See J. Gehl, *Austria, Germany and the Anschluss, 1931–38* (O.U.P., 1964), 114.
10. See *Lessons of My Life*, 46 and *M.P.*, 520.
11. Quoted in Baer, *op. cit.*, 128–9.
12. Van to Sir George Clerk, 18 November 1935, F.O. 371/19166, J. 8787/1/1.
13. See, for example, Baer, *op. cit.*, 127–8; and for a far more vigorous criticism, Rotunda, *op. cit.*, 215–45.
14. Quoted in Baer, *op. cit.*, 123.
15. See his correspondence with Drummond, *The Spectator*, 28 May, 4 and 18 June 1943; *Lessons of My Life*, 46; *M.P.*, 518–21.

---

is perfectly evident from the unusually reticent, sometimes misleading, account he later wrote of his role in the crisis. It was not so much what he included – though he placed undue emphasis on the fortuitous nature of his participation in the talks, and by implication diminishes his part in the negotiations which preceded them – as what he omitted. (See, *M.P.*, 537–43, and *Lessons of My Life*, 39–53; see also, below, p. 177.) This was a curious lapse; he was usually more forthright.

* The miserable Ethiopian affair dragged on until the summer of 1936. On 5 May the Italians entered Addis Ababa. On the 9th Ethiopia was formally incorporated into the new Italian empire. Sanctions were lifted a month later. There was one last, brief flare-up of controversy. From April to May the Foreign Office was split on the by now academic question of whether or not to close the canal to Italy. It was in any case hopelessly late to deter Mussolini; but the officials entered into the spirit of the debate with gusto. O'Malley, Peterson, and Strang strongly in favour; the heavier guns, Orme Sargent, Victor Wellesly, Lancelot Oliphant, Rex Leeper, Ashton-Gwatkin, and Ralph Wigram, against. Van remained true to form: 'the heart speaks for it and the head against it'. (See F.O. 371/20181, J. 5034/216/1. Sir Owen O'Malley also made available to me a copy of these papers.)

16. Rotunda, *op. cit.*, 223.
17. A private communication.
18. Thompson, *op. cit.*, 98; Baer, *op. cit.*, 128, n.27; and *M.P.*, 519.
19. Avon, *op. cit.*, 179; Thompson, *op. cit.*, 97; *M.P.*, 521; and *Lessons of My Life*, 40.
20. Baer, *op. cit.*, 122.
21. R. Churchill, *The Rise and Fall of Anthony Eden* (London, 1959), 85.
22. See *The Spectator*, 28 May 1943; *M.P.*, 520; Baer, *op. cit.*, 128; Rotunda, 219, *passim*.
23. Quoted by Rotunda, 29. For general opinions about Perth, see Rotunda, 12–13; and *M.P.*, 434.
24. *M.P.*, 549.
25. See Templewood, *op, cit.*, 100, 137.
26. *Ibid.*
27. Templewood, *op. cit.*, 138. See also Avon, *op. cit.*, 242.
28. A private communication.
29. *M.P.*, 522.
30. See F.O. 371/19112, J. 2334/1/1.
31. Minutes of 8 June 1935. F.O. 371/19112, J. 2389/1/1.
32. See F.O. 371/19113, J. 1459/1/1. Eden later claimed (*op. cit.*, 221) that he was 'not enthusiastic' about the proposals.
33. See cabinet conclusions in F.O. 371/19113, J. 2435/1/1. Eden was also saddled with the unhappy task of explaining the significance of the naval agreement to the French.
34. *Ibid.* For Eden's visit to Rome, see Mario Toscano, 'Eden's Mission to Rome on the Eve of the Italo-Ethiopian Conflict', in *Studies in Diplomatic History and Historiography in Honour of G. P. Gooch* (London, 1961), ed. A. O. Sarkissian.
35. Avon, *op. cit.*, 232.
36. See F.O. 371/19113. J. 2506/1/1; also Avon, 232.
37. *M.P.*, 530.
38. Minutes of 10 July 1935, F.O. 371/19916, J. 2816/1/1.
39. See Van to Hoare, 7 and 9 August 1935. F.O. 371/19123, J. 3614/1/1. For this general question, see Marder, 'The Royal Navy. . . ' *op. cit.*
40. *Ibid.*
41. The correspondence is in F.O. 371/19123, J. 3614/1/1. It includes two letters to Hoare, 7 and 9 August; one letter to Chatfield, 9 August, and one to Admiral Little (Deputy Chief of Naval Staff), 9 August. See also F. O. 800/295, Van to Hoare, 9 August 1935, with an enclosure of an equally dismal report by the Chiefs of Staff, C.O.S., 392.
42. Avon, *op. cit.*, 251, 349–53.
43. Thompson, *op. cit.*, 107.
44. Van to Hoare, 18 August 1935, tel., F.O. 371/19125, J. 3815/1/1.
45. See Van to Hoare, 7 and 9 August 1935, F.O. 800/294, or F.O. 371/19123, J. 3614/1/1.
46. See Hoare to Chamberlain, 18 August 1935, F.O. 800/295; printed in Templewood, *op. cit.*, 164–5.
47. See J. A. Cross, *Sir Samuel Hoare, a Political Biography* (London, 1977), 216.
48. Van to Hoare, 10 September 1935, tel., F.O. 800/195.
49. Templewood, *op. cit.*, 169–70.
50. Quoted in Avon, *op. cit.*, 262.

51. See F.O. 371/19140, J. 5556/1/1.
52. Van to Hoare, 7 October 1935, F.O. 371/19141, J. 5642/1/1; see also Van to Eden, 4 October 1935, tel., F.O. 371/19140, J. 5584/1/1.
53. Van to Eden, 4 October 1935, tel., *ibid*; see also James C. Robertson, 'The Hoare–Laval Plan', *Journal of Contemporary History* (July 1974), 435–6.
54. See minutes of 4–5 November 1935, F.O. 371/19158, J. 7317/1/1.
55. *Ibid.*
56. See for example, Peterson's note of 20 November 1935, F.O. 371/19163, J. 8363/1/1 and his tel. and accompanying notes, 25 November, F.O. 371/19163 J. 8384/1/1.
57. See a tel. from Sir Eric Drummond, F.O. 371/19150, J. 6333/1/1.
58. Minutes of 16 October 1935, F.O. 371/19150, J. 6333, 6372/1/1.
59. See Hoare to Sir George Clerk, 16 October 1935, *ibid.*
60. See his minutes of 12 November 1935, F.O. 371/19160. J. 7671/1/1.
61. See his minutes, 26 November 1935, F.O. 371/19164, J. 8423/1/1.
62. Notes of an interview between Van and Grandi, 4 December 1935, F.O. 371/19167, J. 8997/1/1; see also, Avon, *op. cit.*, 291–2.
63. See Record of a Conversation between Garibaldi and Van, 25 November 1935, C.P. 225(35), CAB. 24/257.
64. See F.O. 371/19164, J. 8419/1/1; see also the Van-Garibaldi conversations, *op. cit.*
65. Minutes of 26 November 1935, F.O. 371/19164, J. 8423/1/1.
66. Van to Hankey, 19 November 1935, F.O. 371/19166, J. 8767/1/1.
67. Van to Hoare and Eden, 24 November 1935, F.O. 371/19164, J. 8419/1/1.
68. Cabinet conclusions in CAB. 23/82. See also a note by Hoare and Eden with a Foreign Office memorandum on the question of oil sanctions and its implications on British foreign policy. C.P. 212(35), CAB. 24/271.
69. Templewood, *op. cit.*, 178.
70. *M.P.*, 539.
71. Avon, *op. cit.*, 298.
72. Hoare to Sir Clive Wigram, 2 December 1935, R.A., GV K2506/1.
73. See Templewood, *op. cit.*, 179.
74. See Record of the Conversations, C.P. 233(35), CAB. 24/257.
75. Templewood, *op. cit.*, 182.
76. The precise proposals are contained in C.P. 235(35), CAB. 24/257; or F.O. 371/19168, J. 8993/1/1.
77. Avon, 302–5.
78. The cabinet conclusions are in F.O. 371/19168, J. 9174/1/1; also CAB. 23/82.
79. These complicated negotiations may be followed in: F.O. 371/19168, J. 9083, 9108, 9145, 9175/1/1.
80. Avon. *op. cit.*, 309.
81. See cabinet conclusions, 19 December 1935, CAB. 23/82.
82. N. Nicolson, ed. *The Diaries and Letters of Harold Nicolson* (London, 1969), i, 226.
83. M. Peterson, *Both Sides of the Curtain* (London, 1950), 121.
84. This account is based mainly on interviews with Sir Clifford Norton (3 October 1972) and Lady Vansittart (18 August and 31 October 1972), some details of which first appeared in Colvin, *op. cit.*, 81–2.
85. *M.P.*, 541.

86. See *News Chronicle*, 17 December 1935.

87. *News Chronicle*, 23 December 1935.

88. See cabinet conclusions, CAB. 23/82, 17 December 1935; the discussion on Ethiopia on 18 December is to be found in CAB. 23/90B. Freddie Lonsdale, a socialite and playwright, knew that Van 'had kept back information about the camel corridor from cabinet' (K. Young, *op. cit.*, 335). The evidence does not bear out this charge. He did not, however, evade his share of responsibility for the crisis. Writing to Lord Runciman after the conclusion of the talks, he expressed his distress at having embarrassed the government, 'and of course particularly Sam'. (See J. A. Cross, *op. cit.*, 263.)

89. *M.P.*, 542.

90. *Ibid.*, 549. Chamberlain's advice was an unexpected blow. On 2 December, as Chancellor of Reading University, he had bestowed upon Van an Honorary doctorate. See *The Times*, 3 December 1935.

91. *Ibid.*, 542.

92. See Van to Phipps, 20 December 1935, Ph.P. 2/17.

93. Phipps to Hankey, 30 December 1935, H.P. 5/5.

94. Hankey to Phipps, 2 January 1936, H.P. 5/5.

95. Van to Beaverbrook, 20 December 1935, Beaverbrook Papers; see also Lady Vansittart to Beaverbrook, 19 December 1935, *ibid.* This letter was first published by A. J. P. Taylor, *Beaverbrook* (London, 1972), 360. Beaverbrook's letter to Van has not survived.

96. K. Young, *op. cit.*, 334.

97. See, for example, his minutes of 14 March 1940 (F.O. 371/24363) where he categorized Beaverbrook as a member of the 'Money-in-our-time Brigade'.

98. Avon, *op. cit.*, 242.

99. See Eden to King George V, 8 January 1936, R.A., GV K2506/8. In February 1936 Eden told Hugh Knatchbull-Hugesson that he was being sent to China to replace Cadogan who was being brought back to become PUS. See H. Knatchbull-Hugesson, *op. cit.*, 93.

100. Eden to King George V, 8 January 1936, R.A., GV. K2506/8.

101. A minute by A. J. Sylvester (Lloyd George's private secretary), 21 May 1935, Ll.G.P., G/22/10.

102. Private communications.

CHAPTER X

Eclipse

THE FOREIGN OFFICE made every attempt to learn from the experience of the Hoare–Laval affair, examining just where it had gone wrong. After the affair had exploded Van invited the heads of departments to an *ad hoc* meeting to consider the aftermath of the incident. O'Malley was immediately struck by Van's demeanour, he had never seen him looking so worried. Another participant commented: 'It was like a meeting of disgruntled shareholders listening to the head of the company describe what had and what had not happened.'[1] There was not, however, a great deal of criticism, at least not in the sense of putting forward an alternative policy. O'Malley registered his unhappiness with the policy, or perhaps with its failure. Collier alone took strong exception to Van's line, followed somewhat gingerly by George Rendel, who was not one of Van's most fervent admirers.[2] But on the whole the opposition was muted.

On one point at least all were agreed. Somehow it was necessary to bridge the gap between a largely ignorant public opinion, both at home and abroad, and the foreign policy decision-making process. Rex Leeper drafted a comprehensive plan of action which called for the mobilization of the mass media, the League of Nations Union, and possibly the churches, all functioning under the guidance of the News Department of the Foreign Office, Leeper's own department.[3] Judging by the alacrity with which Van accepted this programme, it is clear that he believed that the débâcle of the previous December stemmed not from the plan itself but from the manner of its presentation. Hence it was necessary to re-educate public opinion at home, together with the member states of the League. 'If we are to succeed, we must *all* be ready to the best of our ability not only in word but deed; and we must be ready to eventually go *in practice* as far as we are prepared to go *in theory*, otherwise we must fail.'[4] Leeper (acting yet again on Van's behalf?) visited Churchill the following April to conscript his support for this programme of mass re-education,[5] the aim of which was to weld into a coherent force the many diverse groups who were aware of the German menace but were unsure of how precisely to combat it. For Van, the fundamental issue remained constant: how to prevent Germany from extracting the maximum political capital from the Ethiopian imbroglio. Although the main thrust of his diplomacy had been directed towards Italy, his eye was still fixed upon Berlin.[6] Having completed this evaluation of the events of December 1935, an evaluation which did not shake any of his basic premises, Van returned to the idea of his long-delayed holiday. Whether or not he managed to snatch a few days' rest remains unclear. Certainly by mid-February he was back at his desk ready to resume his search for a German agreement.

The last stage in the negotiations with Germany had petered out in the summer of 1935. By late autumn the question of continuing the negotiations had been raised with a new sense of expectancy. This was mainly due to the authors of the initiative, Sargent and Wigram, two of the fiercest critics of Germany in the Office and both closely identified with Van. In a lengthy memorandum of 21 November 1935 they set out the case for coming to terms with Germany.[7] Recognizing the immense obstacles involved, they nevertheless concluded that an agreement was desirable, hinting that concessions in the Rhineland and in the colonial sphere could pave the way for an overall settlement. They reinforced their argument with a familiar theme:

> The British public will expect this policy to have been attempted, before we proceed to intensive rearmament, or to a further multiplication of defensive pacts which, in the circumstances now emerging in Europe, will soon differ little from what Germany before the war claimed to be the policy of 'encirclement'.

The Sargent–Wigram programme was daring, almost revolutionary, in concept but highly controversial in detail. Their proposals stimulated a loquacious debate among the officials. Collier rejected practically all the basic precepts in the Sargent–Wigram design, suggesting instead that it would be better to let sleeping dogs lie and not discourage those powers who were constructing barriers to Germany's ambitions by pacts and alliances. Ashton-Gwatkin pointed out the dangers of a 'lean Germany', hinting that substantial economic aid would reduce the German menace. Van set out his views in twelve pages of detailed minutes.[8] His attitude towards a German agreement has been too often simplified, particularly over colonial concessions,[9] so that it would be worthwhile to reconstruct the precise chain of events and circumstances which he felt were indispensible for the attainment of a lasting agreement.

Naturally Van entertained the gravest suspicions concerning German intentions. What German aims were 'logical, just, and reasonable'? he asked. 'Not', he answered, 'the absorption of the possessions of her neighbours, what she herself has never before possessed.' He called for precision in the definition of aims. What was meant, for example, by Germany ' "keeping within reasonable bounds" her Eastern and Central European policy? Does that mean that she might have Austria and Memel, but not Russia and Czechoslovakia?' He was not averse to an agreement, but he grasped immediately that to attain it Britain would have to pay a heavy price. The demilitarized zone of the Rhineland was one field where concessions were conceivable. Indeed, Van explained, this would be 'the strongest argument yet put forward for an early agreement'. There was little new in this. Since early 1935 the Foreign Office had been anticipating a German move to demilitarize the Rhineland.[10] Now clearly expecting a German *démarche* as inevitable, Van wished to capitalize on it to Britain's and Europe's advantage. Nor was he alone in this attitude.

The colonies were another field where compromise was possible. But Van did not contemplate any open-handed gesture. Concessions certainly, but to obtain them Germany would also have to make some sacrifice. Taking the German appetite for expansion as the *sine qua non* of German foreign policy, he wrote:

> I believe that Germany will expand somehow and sometime . . . If it can't be in Africa, it will be in Europe. And I would prefer it to be in Africa in regions with which we were always well able to dispense. I prefer in a word, that we should pay ourselves and honestly, rather than attempt or countenance any unworthy transaction at the expense of someone else. We cannot possibly be a good member of the League in Africa, and a shockingly bad one in Europe.

It was Van's hope to substitute German aggrandizement in Europe for colonial concessions in Africa. Should the Germans refuse to rise to his bait, then 'war is certain and unavoidable'. Van put his case succinctly to Bruce Lockhart:* 'he was quite prepared to give Germany colonies if this would bring peace. Is afraid however that concessions will do little good.'[11]

Put this way Van's argument was unanswerable. But there was a fatal flaw in it, for it was a policy born of weakness not of strength, and it contained little to make it attractive to Germany in her existing mood of confidence. In any case, Van was adamant that negotiations under the conditions then prevailing 'were worse than useless'. As he explained to Sir Clive Wigram, first it was necessary to re-equip the national defences, secondly to secure the cooperation of France, and only then would it be practicable to agree on the price to be paid to Germany.[12]

The question of a German agreement was again raised toward the end of January.[13] Van, in a twenty-page essay, summarized his own position and that of the Office.[14] It followed the general line of his previous minutes, with one addition. Van now thought it vital to test Germany's intentions in a limited agreement on a particular topic† before moving on to a more general settlement. He again emphasized

> that no lasting bargain can be made with present-day Germany without the payment of a high price – that is, provision for territorial expansion ... that such expansion can therefore only be provided at our own expense; that is, in Africa by the restitution of the former colonies of Germany. Unless we are prepared to face these facts, we should not delude ourselves with thinking that a real, as opposed to a paper, agreement is possible.

The immediate issue, therefore, was to decide on a specific question with which to launch the negotiations. There was a general consensus that the Rhineland would provide the most fruitful starting point. Van had long been in favour of grasping this nettle.[15] On 3 February, at a top-level meeting in the Foreign Office, Eden also pressed for using the demilitarized zone as a lever to ease Germany into a broader agreement. By 15 February a six-point programme

---

* Robert (Hamilton) Bruce Lockhart (1887–1970): diplomat, journalist, banker; entered consular service, 1911; achieved fame as head of Special Mission to Soviet Government in 1918; member of Political Intelligence Department of Foreign Office, 1939–40; deputy under Secretary of State at Foreign Office and Director-General of political Warfare Executive, 1941–45. Kn. 1943.

† He suggested four categories of the particular: (a) an air limitation convention; (b) an economic gambit; (c) revision of the Locarno agreements, i.e. the Rhineland question; or (d) revision of the League Covenant.

had been agreed upon which effectively covered all the elements of a general agreement;* these were brought before a cabinet committee two days later. After considering them without 'much enthusiasm', the committee finally acquiesced but substituted the air convention for the demilitarized zone as the starting-point.[16]

All these plans were frustrated by Hitler's sudden, though by no means unexpected, move into the Rhineland on the morning of 7 March. Some hours before German troops actually crossed the Rhine, Van received definite information from Christie about the Rhineland *Einmarsch*.[17] His information was extraordinarily detailed and, as it turned out, correct. It specified the number of German troops to be used, the timing of the action, the reason for it, and details about the forthcoming German diplomatic offensive.† Christie received the information in Paris, unquestionably from Ritter who was then attached to the German embassy, and immediately – about midnight – telephoned the news to Van at his home in Park Street.

Hitler's initiative threw the Foreign Office plans for a European settlement into disarray. The Germans had previously been notified that the British were preparing a comprehensive agreement.[18] Now Hitler had repeated his manœuvre of the previous year, taking what he knew was about to be offered. Suspicions as to his reliability

* The six points covered were: (a) revision of the Locarno agreements to include the termination of the demilitarized zone, mutual inspection of armaments, and the inclusion of Holland in the new agreement; (b) the limitation of air and ground armaments; (c) recognition by the Western powers of Germany's special interests in central and eastern Europe in return for a German promise not to exploit those interests in a manner contrary to the League Covenant; (d) economic concessions to Germany to include financial aid and tariff reductions; (e) postponement of Germany's return to the League until after the preliminary stages of the negotiations had been concluded; (f) to leave the colonial question for Germany to raise, but to ensure that Germany offered something concrete in return.

† Christie's figures corresponded closely with Jodl's testimony at Nürnberg, according to which only one division was employed in the occupation of the Rhineland while three battalions actually crossed the Rhine heading for Aachen, Trier, and Saarbrucken. Christie spoke of 'some battalions of infantry, some squadrons of airforce and some A.A. units'. In this connection see also, D. C. Watt, 'German Plans for the Occupation of the Rhineland', *Journal of Contemporary History* (1966, No. 4).) Less informed sources put the number of German troops much higher, at 'about 35,000' (see Churchill, v, 150). Christie listed the German diplomatic proposals as: 'Return to League. . . . ; Air Pact between England and Germany and France; Bilateral Pacts of Non Aggression with all neighbours of Germany; Guarantee of Integrity of Belgium and Holland for 25 years; and in consideration of this programme Germany will refrain at present from raising the colonial question.' These too were remarkably similar to the final German proposals. See *Germany No. 1*, Cmd. 5518 (H.M.S.O., 1936).

deepened. Was he capable of honouring any agreement? Further negotiations were not ruled out, but as Eden commented, 'we shall enter them at a disadvantage'.[19]

There was, of course, no question of forcing a German withdrawal, and all attempts to do so met with a stubborn refusal.[20] But it was decided to probe Germany's intentions further. A series of questions were formulated, mainly by Van and Wigram, and presented to the German government on 6 May. The original draft underwent considerable modification by the cabinet who flinched at its categoric tone and moderated its language to be 'as unsensational as possible'.[21] Naturally, all this prevarication greatly irritated Van. Even so, the document, in its final draft, was blunt enough, asking at one point whether Germany could signify whether 'she recognises and intends in future to respect the existing territorial and political status of Europe, except in so far as this might be subsequently modified by free negotiation and agreement'.[22]

By the end of May this particular initiative had run its full course. Hitler skilfully evaded replying to the questionnaire. According to Phipps, he believed that it had been sent 'to pillory him'. But there was a more decisive reason. The victories in France of the *Front Populaire* in the elections of April–May had dampened Hitler's enthusiasm for a general European settlement; his thoughts, again according to Phipps, were turning towards an Anglo-German agreement.[23] For Van this was final proof that Hitler was playing his own game, and had no intention of limiting his options in a general agreement:

> He has 'his usual outburst' about *Gleichberechtigung*. Ergo he is *not* yet, in his own view, in a position to conclude equal and enduring treaties. I wonder if anyone who knows his job really expected any other attitude than that. Hitler will not bind himself in a fluid Europe – fluid, that is, for an intending aggressor.[24]

Van was convinced that the chances of a genuine agreement based on mutual concessions were minimal. Nevertheless, he favoured continuing the talks, though without any illusion as to their outcome. His aim was to play Hitler in order to buy time to repair Britain's defence deficiencies. Without a credible defence capability, he posited, any meaningful negotiations with so perverse a power as Germany was outright self-deception, the worst of all possible sins.[25]

Thus the pattern of 1935 repeated itself in 1936; high hopes for an agreement early in the year, extreme disillusionment within a few weeks as a result of Hitler's unscrupulous behaviour. Throughout the summer and autumn of 1936 the Locarno powers were busy swapping memoranda, formulating possible substitutes for the agreements Hitler had destroyed in March.[26] These diplomatic feelers were exhausted by December. Van and his associates had managed 'to play' Hitler for little more than six months. Two major attempts to appease Germany, to integrate her peacefully into a European framework, had ended in failure. Small wonder that a sense of frustration began to take root in the Foreign Office. Hitler, in a very real sense, was a phenomenon beyond the comprehension of diplomatists trained according to nineteenth-century patterns of diplomatic behaviour and educated according to the ethics of Western liberal capitalism. Faced with such an enigma, the officials, and even more their political masters, were at a crippling disadvantage. They were quite simply unable to keep pace with this juggernaut which blithely ignored, or was perhaps unaware of, the accepted norms of the game.

One issue continued to remain at the core of any future agreement: the colonial issue. As we have seen, Van was not in favour of indiscriminately throwing sacrifices to the tiger, but of using colonial concessions to gain an advantage elsewhere in Europe, and for this too there were persuasive historical precedents. It would, however, be nearer the mark to claim that Van consistently exaggerated the importance the acquisition of colonies held in Germany's order of foreign policy priorities. In January 1935 he postulated that the colonial issue 'will probably replace the naval question of pre-war days',[27] a highly fanciful comparison by any reckoning. In fact, Germany's colonial campaign, despite its façade of official approval, was inaugurated and kept in motion mainly for its propaganda and prestige value. It was of secondary importance to the top Nazi leadership. Von Neurath confided as much to Sir Nevile Henderson,* while Göring revealed that 'the colonies were Dr Schacht's† hobby but were not regarded by Herr Hitler or himself as of the same immediate importance'.[28] Judging from the reports received by the Foreign Office, Schacht was indeed the main inspiration behind

* Nevile Meyrick Henderson (1882–1942): entered foreign service, 1905; served in St Petersburg, Tokyo, Rome, Paris; counsellor Constantinople, 1921–24; minister at Belgrade, 1929–35; Ambassador at Buenos Aires, 1935–37; at Berlin, 1937–39. Kn. 1932.

† Hjalmer Schacht (1877–1970): economist and banker; president of Reichsbank, 1924–30, 1933; Minister of Economics, 1934–37; German economic 'wizard'; tried at Nürnberg, but acquitted, 1946.

German colonial demands, spurred on, no doubt, by the vision of cheap and plentiful raw materials.[29]

In March 1936 the government set up the Plymouth Committee to examine this whole question. Its report was non-committal. The least objectionable course, it pointed out, would be for France to join Britain in the surrender of the whole or part of Togoland or the Cameroons, or both. In any case, it was apparent that the colonial issue would be a bad starting point for general negotiations, for it would entail yielding something concrete in return for vague declarations of good intent which could, and no doubt would, be violated at the first opportunity.[30]

Van shared this opinion, as did most of the officials.[31] But his attitude was by no means as hostile as Wigram's or Collier's. He was beset by a curious anxiety that failure to concede to German colonial pressure might lead to open hostilities.[32] In a mammoth paper circulated on 31 December 1936, Van marshalled his thoughts on this perennial topic:

> Is it coherent, he questioned, to maintain a refusal of even partial restitution without accelerating our progress towards security? Surely the trend of events points to one of the two definite courses. I do not of course recommend that we should contemplate restoring even the Cameroons except in return for at least the showing of full European appeasement in an adequate treaty observed over an adequate period. If it turned out to be worth nothing we could close down on any further conciliation ... a conditioned glimpse of an unpromised land would, if properly timed, attenuate what is still a plausible grievance, and remove a bone of contention that is barely worth a dog-fight or protracted snarls.[33]

Five months later, in May 1937, he slammed the colonial door shut. 'In her present state of exultation', Van wrote, 'Germany would [not] pay any substantial price for the mere return of the Cameroons, and therefore even if we were in a position to make the offer, the negotiations would probably be abortive.[34]

The main outlines of his colonial policy are clear. Attempts to label him as a colonial 'appeaser' bear little relation to the facts. His policy was no more than a tactical ploy designed to secure a strategic advantage. His mistake, if such it can be called, lay in his failure to assess accurately the importance the return of colonies held in Germany's scale of priorities. He persisted, in the face of a substantial amount of evidence to the contrary, in endowing German colonial demands with a significance not claimed by the German government itself. But it was not a failure of major proportions. From whatever position one evaluates it, the colonial issue remained a peripheral one.

Hitler's unfavourable response to the questionnaire coerced the government into reconsidering how far they wished to pursue the negotiations for an agreement. Van favoured the continuation of exploratory talks, provided they were conducted circumspectly and with due dignity. He hotly opposed running after the Germans. When the suggestion was first raised that perhaps a ministerial visit (Halifax's name was mentioned) to Berlin might brighten the prospects for an eventual settlement, he rejected the proposal as 'a futile humiliation'.[35] Yet within two months Van himself was in Berlin, on a semi-official visit, sounding out the Germans as to the prospects of an agreement. The Olympic Games of 1936 provided the occasion for his journey.

One sound reason for Van's *volte-face* was his desire to counterbalance the spate of private visits to Germany, usually culminating in interviews of dubious value with Hitler, by well-meaning but naïve public figures, which, in the eyes of the Foreign Office, seriously compromised British diplomacy. These innocent do-gooders, playing at diplomacy, were regarded with a mixture of scorn and alarm by the professionals. After Lothian's visit to Hitler in January 1935, Van had labelled him as 'an incurably superficial Johnny-Know-All',[36] a measured verdict which reflected his general attitude towards those who dared to trespass on the domain of the professional diplomatists. The Olympic Games would provide a fine backcloth for more meddlers in the Lothian mould, and Van was out to scotch their plans.*

He left London on 30 July and remained in Berlin until 13 August. Ostensibly his visit was a private one. Lady Phipps was indisposed, and her sister, Lady Vansittart, had agreed to act as hostess at the Berlin embassy for the duration of the Games. The fulfilment of this family obligation was but a thin disguise to mask an extremely hectic visit which inevitably assumed a quasi-official character.[37] During his fortnight in Berlin Van met most of the Nazi leaders, certainly

---

* He was not altogether successful. In September, barely a fortnight after he had left Berlin, Lloyd George arrived on a highly publicized visit. Even worse, Lothian reappeared in May 1937, amiably settling the affairs of Europe over a cup of tea with Hitler. This exercise in open diplomacy occasioned a blistering attack from the officials, with Van taking the lead. See F.O. 371/20735, C. 3621/270/18.

the most important of them: Göring, Goebbels, Hess, Frick, Ribbentrop, von Neurath, von Papen, General von Blomberg, to name but a few. On 8 August the Vansittarts hosted a grand reception at the embassy to which were invited over a thousand guests, including many of the Nazi chiefs. And on their last night in Berlin Hitler, apparently making a significant gesture of conciliation, gave a magnificent dinner in their honour in a resplendent new banqueting hall just completed according to his own design. They dined in style to the sound of Wagner, though Van noted that Hitler rationed himself to spinach and water.

Early on during the visit Van met Hitler face-to-face. The meeting had been arranged by Ribbentrop, by now ambassador-designate to London. He invited Van to lunch at the *Kaiserhof* hotel to prepare the ground for the Hitler interview. Their luncheon tête-à-tête did nothing if not clarify their differences. Ribbentrop's verdict was blunt and unambiguous: 'an Anglo-German understanding with Vansittart in office was out of the question'. But Van's verdict on Ribbentrop was equally crushing and far more pertinent: 'with that gentleman we shall have more trouble. I fear that he is shallow, self-seeking and not really friendly.' During one exchange, Ribbentrop displayed his true colours: ' "if England didn't give Germany the possibility to live" there would eventually be war between them, and one of them would be annihilated'.

This was hardly an encouraging prelude for the interview with Hitler. When they met on the morning of 5 August, he appeared to Van as

an amiably simple, rather shy, rotundly ascetic, *bourgeois*, with the fine hair and thin skin that accompany extreme sensitiveness, a man of almost obvious physical integrity, very much in earnest, not humorous, nor alarming, not magnetic, but convinced of a variable mission and able to impress himself so strongly that he impresses himself on those around him, perhaps I should say even on those constantly around him.

Although the interview was long and 'exceedingly friendly', it contained nothing of substance. Hitler showed a distinct preference for vague generalities. After the initial formalities, he launched into a long-winded justification of his past policies, particularly his domestic record. Van listened attentively, attempting to guide the discussion toward the projected five-power conference, but Hitler refused to be drawn. Instead, he veered off onto another favourite theme: the world-wide communist conspiracy and its latest manifestations, the Civil War in Spain* and Blum's† *Front Populaire* government in France.

The Spanish situation dominated the political side of his visit. Van met von Neurath on seven occasions 'and he spoke always of Spain'. From Van's point of view the war seriously prejudiced such chances as ever existed of obtaining a full European, as opposed to a strictly Western, settlement. And his talks in Berlin confirmed this impression. Clearly the Germans were reluctant to commit themselves. Von Neurath told Van that whatever the circumstances the five-power conference could not convene before mid-October; and he showed little disposition to be enticed into any detailed or preliminary discussion. Van emphatically rejected the notion of confining the settlement to Western Europe, preferring, as he expressed it, to broaden 'the area of appeasement'. Summing up his minimal conditions for a settlement, Van linked a multi-lateral Western agreement with bi-lateral pacts of arbitration, non-aggression and non-interference in Central Europe. The Soviet Union, in the existing climate of opinion in Germany, was excluded from this arrangement. This structure would stand or fall on two cardinal points on which there could be no compromise: no sacrifice of existing treaties (an obvious reference to the Franco-Soviet, Franco-Czech, agreements); and no disarmament for several years. Van did not rate the chances of a German agreement very high. On the other hand, if the Western alliance were sufficiently 'tactful and determined', as he hoped would be the case, an eventual settlement was not beyond the realms of possibility. In this sense at least he departed from Berlin 'with better hopes' than when he arrived.

Together with the serious side of his visit, Van was whisked around Berlin's social circuit. Parties and receptions pursued one another remorselessly. Goebbels, 'a limping, eloquent, slip of a Jacobin', succeeded in charming Van, despite, no doubt, the byzantine extravaganza he staged on the *Pfaueninsel* (known as the Peacock Island) for over 3,000 guests and which, according to the most subdued reports, terminated in an outburst of orgiastic revelry, much to Hitler's

* The Spanish Civil War began with a revolt of military commanders in Spanish Morocco on 18 July 1936. The fighting spread rapidly to the mainland, and it did not come to an end until March 1939. The extreme polarization of political forces inside Spain, together with the active intervention of Italy and Germany on behalf of the insurgents and the Soviet Union championing the forces of the left, turned the Spanish Civil War into the ideological *cause célèbre* of the 1930's.

† Leon Blum (1872–1950): French socialist politician of Jewish extraction; Prime Minister, June 1936–June 1937, March–April 1938, December 1946–January 1947; interned by the Germans, 1941–45.

chagrin. He was shown the sights of Berlin, including the quiescent Communist suburbs, by Göring, 'a Smith minor suddenly possessed of unlimited tick at the school stores', and Hess, about whom he maintained a meaningful silence.

This festive atmosphere was marred by one sombre incident. Wilfred Israel, a leader of the Jewish community of Berlin, was smuggled in by the back door of the embassy, 'plainly terrorized'. Israel called for more energetic intervention to alleviate the lot of German Jewry. On the advice of Phipps, Van replied that this would result in more harm than good, but, if an agreement were reached that autumn, it might perhaps deter the Germans from further persecution, or at least it would lend added weight to a moderating word from Britain. This was poor comfort indeed, as Van well appreciated: 'I did not relish this interview', he concluded.

One excellent reason for Van's visit was to dispel the notion that he was consumed by a blind and irrational hatred of Germany. Van exerted all of his great personal charm to this end, and in Phipps's judgment his efforts were 'more than sufficient to prick this dangerous bubble'. The ambassador's assessment was not entirely borne out on the German side. Reliable sources indicated that the German government, and Hitler in particular, rejected Van's tactical approach, and that if the West insisted on attaching an Eastern pendant to a Western Locarno there would 'be no conference'. Hitler, the sources claimed, would never sign an instrument which would freeze the *status quo* in Europe. And so it turned out.

On his way back to London Van stopped over in Paris to dine with Blum and Delbos, the French Foreign Minister, giving them a full account of his Berlin conversations. He then journeyed to Brittany, where he spent two weeks in the company of his friend, Alexis Léger. He was making a conspicuous effort to procure French support and to strengthen the *entente*. Neither the French nor the Belgians had been keen about Van's trip to Germany, suspecting perhaps a deal at their expense. Van set their minds at ease. He and Léger attained a community of purpose, though both dwelt on the difficulties of persuading the French left and the British opposition to accept the exclusion of the Soviet Union from the proposed agreement.

1936 ended badly for Van. His massive paper, 'The World Situation and British Rearmament',[38] reflected his own deep pessimism. It was a tale of unrelieved gloom. Circulated on New Year's Eve, it could hardly have added to his colleagues' seasonal gaieties. After seven years as head of the Office, all that he could offer his chiefs was an inordinately lengthy (31 pages) paper forecasting almost certain catastrophe. His enemies would certainly turn it against him as an admission of failure.

On New Year's Eve he heard of the sudden death of Ralph Wigram. Wigram was one of his closest associates. As head of the Central Department, he and Van had been in close accord over the German question and Wigram's minutes often triggered the inspiration for Van's own thoughts. Churchill's attacks on the government were based, in part, upon Wigram's periodical briefings; and they were made with Van's full knowledge and encouragement.[39] Van relied heavily upon Wigram's judgement and felt his loss deeply. He is reported as having told Wigram's wife: 'I don't think I have the strength to go on without him – alone'.[40]

His future was still under a cloud. Immediately on his return from Brittany in September, Eden renewed the offer of the Paris embassy. On 20 December Baldwin returned to the proposal and it was raised again in January.[41] It is clear that there was a general consensus among the politicians that he should go. Van declined the offer, for the third time in twelve months. He did so on both public and private grounds, pleading that the delicate health of Lady Vansittart would not permit such a change.[42] But more than anything he feared being removed from the centre of events and placing the Office in the hands of amateurs, however gifted, or even handing it over to professionals if their views differed from his. Supremely confident in the righteousness of his cause, he scorned the pomp and circumstance surrounding a modern ambassador's role. He was loath to accept a mere sinecure in exchange for his current position of real power. If left with no alternative, he would fight the system from the inside.* This was a classic case of self-deception. Van was already very much the fifth wheel of the coach. And there is no one quite as unpopular as the guest who deliberately overstays his welcome. He concluded his letter to Baldwin on an apologetic, pleading note:

> for nine years now I have done everything else that one man may do to serve and help another. This is a long slice of life, and I do not remember failing you. For some six of those nine years I've

---

* He later disclosed that he did not resign his position because, among other reasons, Churchill advised him 'to stick it out' (*Lessons of my Life, op. cit.*, 112). When Van wrote of personal grounds he may also have been referring to the well-known predilection of Phipps to take the Paris embassy. Had Van moved in first, exploiting his position of seniority, it would undoubtedly have strained their family relationship.

done the same for Anthony, and I think here also remembrance will mitigate any disappointment that he might also feel.

Eden's desire for change could not be postponed much longer. Nor in fact was there any logical reason why his wish should be denied. He was perfectly at liberty to promote the advisers of his choice. Early in the year he strengthened Cadogan's authority in the Office.[43] He was disarmingly frank about his lack of confidence in Van. He told his private secretary, Oliver Harvey,* that Van's judgement was suspect and that he was no longer in a fit state of health to hold down his job.[44] Something of Eden's doubts must have filtered through to two of the most influential figures in White-hall, Warren Fisher and Horace Wilson,† corroborating their own estimation of Van's inconsiderate and harmful behaviour. Consequently in May there occurred a bizarre incident which hinted at a backstairs cabal to oust Van from office. Both Fisher and Wilson were involved. They invited J. P. L. Thomas, Eden's Parliamentary Private Secretary, to tea, and told him that they

> were thoroughly dissatisfied with the Foreign Office and especially with Vansittart ... they told me that Vansittart was an alarmist, that he hampered all attempts of the Government to make friendly contact with the dictator states and that his influence over Anthony Eden was very great. For this reason they had strongly backed the idea that I, whom Horace Wilson knew well, should become P.P.S. at the Foreign Office because I would be in a position to help them build a bridge between 10 Downing Street and the Foreign Office, and to create a better understanding between the two Departments. This might lessen the damage done by the Foreign Office in general and Vansittart in particular.[45]

Thomas hastily turned down this suggestion. Van, of course, held Wilson in utter contempt, and this tea party may well have been the root of it. Fisher in particular seems to have been active against Van. Shortly after the above affair he told Lady Vansittart that Van must cease writing his memoranda as they were annoying his chiefs. She warned her husband to trust neither Fisher nor Wilson.[46]

* Oliver Charles Harvey (1893–1968): private secretary to Eden and Halifax, 1936–39, 1941–43; minister at British embassy in Paris, 1940; Assistant and Deputy Under Secretary of State at Foreign Office, 1943–47; Ambassador to France, 1948–54. Kn. 1946, Cr. Baron, 1954.
† Horace John Wilson (1882–1972): Permanent Under Secretary at Ministry of Labour, 1921–30; Chief Industrial Adviser to the Government, 1930–39; Permanent Under Secretary at the Treasury and Head of Civil Service, 1939–42; a close adviser to Chamberlain on all matters, including foreign affairs. Kn. 1924.

Whether Chamberlain, who had just succeeded to the premiership, was privy to these clumsy intrigues must remain a matter for
speculation. Certainly the opinions voiced by Fisher and Wilson
echoed those of their master. But this is really of secondary importance. The evidence is now irrefutable that by the early spring of
1937 there was a general movement in Whitehall to neutralize Van;
and this was common to his political chiefs, his civil service equals,
and even to some of his colleagues in the Foreign Office.[47] This
continuous tug-of-war must have had a damaging effect on the work
routine and morale of the Office. While not labouring the point,
Van's clinging to office in the teeth of such widespread opposition
created a kind of power vacuum at the top with others, Cadogan or
Wilson or Eden or Chamberlain, ready and anxious to fill the gap.

Nevertheless, Van continued to go through the motions as Eden's
principal adviser. In September he was photographed at Eden's side
at the celebrated Nyon conference.* The minutes flowed endlessly
from his pen, always hammering away at the same topics: greater
rearmament coupled with greater resistance to German bullying.
His attitude towards Italy was typically ambivalent. Throughout
1937 he took a more pronounced anti-Italian line: 'the Italians are
hostile to us . . . [and] the only thing that can change this attitude of
mind is not fair words but strength'.[48] He readily admitted the truth
of a Southern Department minute which explained that 'Italy is
always and forever to be mistrusted, and no foreign policy based on
a contrary assumption can ever be a sound foreign policy'. On the
other hand, he never lost sight of the 'more formidable menace of
Germany'.[49] And this led him back to his old policy of searching
for points of agreement with Italy. He favoured *de jure* recognition
of the Italian conquest of Ethiopia,[50] and supported the negotiations
which finally culminated in the Anglo-Italian agreement of April
1938. Not, he reasoned, in order to break the Rome–Berlin axis, but
to loosen it and 'to restore to Mussolini some latitude of manoeuvre
– if he so desires'.[51]

On 30 April 1937 Sir Nevile Henderson arrived in Berlin as the new
British ambassador to Germany. By any reckoning this was a dis-

---

* The conference (10–14 September 1937) had been convened to devise counter-
measures against Italian submarine pirate raiders in the western Mediterranean.
Since the outbreak of the Spanish War, there had been numerous attacks
against shipping in the area. The nine powers who participated decided to
initiate naval patrols in those areas most prone to attack, the main burden of
decision and action resting with Britain and France. In the event the patrols
proved an effective deterrent.

astrous appointment. Henderson's views on Germany were incredibly naïve and he held a grossly exaggerated belief in his own ability to effect a change in German policy. Eden bravely accepted responsibility for this lapse of judgement, but he hinted that, as he did not know Henderson personally, the appointment had been strongly urged upon him.[52] For this, Van must take full blame. Van knew Henderson very well. Indeed, judging from their early correspondence, they were on intimate terms.[53] When Henderson was in Yugoslavia, Van noted that he had 'a keenness which I naturally like'.[54] It has been suggested that Van's choice revealed a superficial judgement of character.[55] But there was no evidence until May 1937 to suggest that Henderson's appointment would prove as calamitous as it did. His career had been unspectacular but sound. In Foreign Office jargon he was 'a man and a good shot'.[56] Van's main consideration in recommending Henderson was to prevent a political appointment which would have been highly resented by the professionals and would have seriously impaired morale in the service.*

Henderson was soon at odds with his colleagues. The overall impression prevailed that he was too weak, too vain, too shallow; that his sources of information were inaccurate; and that he was too susceptible to Nazi pressure. All this, of course, was reflected in his despatches, some of which make quite remarkable reading. 'Sir N. Henderson evidently needs some stiffening up,' Van remarked, after reading one of Henderson's 'extraordinary' telegrams.[57]

> My apprehension is plainly that Sir Nevile Henderson will again mislead His Majesty's Government, and the more of this illusionist stuff that he imbibes and sends home the more he may possibly complicate your [Halifax's] task with some of the more naif of your colleagues. The Nazis are in fact convinced that they can make our Ambassador in Berlin believe anything they wish him to believe.[58]

Harold Nicolson was told that 'Henderson is a complete Nazi, and that the Foreign Office do not trust him to represent their real point of view'.[59] Van regarded Henderson's inept bungling in Berlin as a major factor in Britain's foreign policy failures of those years.

* Were there other alternatives to Henderson? Sir Percy Loraine and Sir Miles Lampson were both mentioned, but both occupied important posts in delicate areas, Loraine in Turkey and Lampson in Egypt, and no doubt it was thought unwise to shift either of them. There was another possibility. Had Van taken the Paris embassy there would have been no need to move Phipps, and Henderson would have stayed in a backwater where he belonged. But as we have seen, Van steadfastly refused this option.

Neville Chamberlain succeeded to his long-awaited premiership on 28 May 1937. Almost two months earlier he had submitted a paper to the Foreign Policy Committee of the cabinet setting out his views on Anglo-German relations and the possibility of a new approach to the dictator states.[60] His scheme contained no new revolutionary concepts. It was simply a rehash of the two major initiatives which had gone before and which had failed.* In general, the Foreign Office accepted this plan, but without any overt enthusiasm. Nor was this surprising. Having failed themselves on two separate occasions, they approached Chamberlain's fresh initiative in a spirit of extreme scepticism, particularly when orchestrated by one whom they considered to be naïve and inexperienced in foreign affairs.

It would be erroneous to assume that all the officials were of this opinion. Cadogan agreed, more than most, with Chamberlain's strategy, while other officials argued for 'an understanding with' or 'greater complacency towards' Germany.[61] The curious point here is that these views were usually expressed by those who held no direct responsibility for Anglo-German relations. O'Malley, head of the Southern Department, or ambassadors in far away places such as Lampson, were the chief exponents of a softer line towards Germany, believing that this would be the most expedient means of clipping Mussolini's wings and isolating Italy. For Van, and those who were directly concerned with Germany, the Central Department and Sargent, this was an absurd argument. Van expressed himself in his usual trenchant style:

> We all want a *good* agreement with Germany, if a good one can be got. But we should never be bluffed into any *bad* agreement with Germany through fear of Italy. If Germany has 'reasonable and legitimate' objectives no one but a fool would thwart them. The trouble is that most of her present objectives are unreasonable and illegitimate. But if there are any in the former variety in her bag she will have – indeed has already had – considerable opportunity of bringing them out.[62]

* Chamberlain proposed a four point programme: (a) the conclusion of a treaty or treaties of non aggression and guarantees for Western Europe to replace the Locarno agreements; (b) German assurances to the governments of Central and Eastern Europe, in treaty form or otherwise, to respect their territorial integrity with special reference to Czechoslovakia, and including some kind of indirect arrangement with the Soviet Union; (c) Germany's return to the League; (d) a disarmament convention. Colonial concessions were not excluded, but it was finally acknowledged that they could only take effect in West Africa and then largely at the expense of France.

It has been suggested that during Van's last months as PUS attempts were made to curtail his freedom of expression, and that on at least one occasion Eden suppressed an important paper of his.[63] Why Van minuted his memorandum on the state of German industry 'suppressed by Eden' must remain something of a mystery. Perhaps it was the result of some unrecorded quarrel with Eden, scribbled off in a fit of temper. In fact the memorandum was widely circulated, including its secret reports composed by members of the Association of Heavy Industries in the Rhineland (the *Langnamerein*), and a summary of his conversation with Gordeler.[64] Van had no cause for complaint that his views were not publicized in official circles, though whether they were listened to or not is another matter. If anything, as we have seen, the proliferation of his essays proved a factor in his downfall. Perhaps a measure of self-restraint would have paid more positive dividends.

At any rate, his last paper as PUS was more restrained in tone, and far shorter in length, than his previous publications.[65] Even his conclusions were more comforting. Germany, he now reasoned, was surrounded by untrustworthy associates and rent by grave internal divisions of 'policy, philosophy and creed'. There was little chance that she would embark on a large-scale action in the immediate future:

> We can therefore contemplate our own position with reasonable *sangfroid* and without the panic and precipitation that seem to animate some of our publicists.

This paper was based entirely on Van's secret sources of intelligence, chiefly from Christie.[66] They appear to be quite authentic.* Moreover, Van went out of his way to emphasize the unique role his private network played in gauging an accurate picture of internal German developments. Treat this information as 'exceptionally secret', he wrote, for any leakage would jeopardize the lives of his informants. Doubtless, this was a necessary caution. But from 1936 onwards his intelligence system grew steadily in importance and

---

* Van printed two appendices. The first contained extracts from secret monthly reports complied by Colonel (later General) George Thomas, head of the War Economy and Armaments Office, and which detailed the difficulties in obtaining sufficient quantities of strategic war materials, a factor which obviously limited Germany's capacity to wage a major war. The other contained a report by Dr Aschmann, head of the Press Department of the Foreign Ministry, which summarized the Hitler–Mussolini talks of September 1937. According to Aschmann the main point here was that in the event of a Nazi *putsch* against Austria, Mussolini promised not to intervene.

scale,[67] almost, one is tempted to conclude, in direct relation to the decline in his influence. Was he now deliberately flaunting his contacts to counterbalance his crumbling position? To demonstrate how indispensible he was, and how vital it was for him to remain at the centre of events? It would have been a logical reaction on Van's part.

In the autumn of 1937 Eden began to dwell yet again on Van's position, and his doubts were reinforced by those of Chamberlain, a far stronger and more decisive character than Baldwin.* Van was aware that 'the drive against him was as strong as ever'.[68] His opposition to the Halifax visit to Germany in November may well have proved the final straw in his relations with the Prime Minister. Most of the officials were uneasy about the visit, but accepted it for lack of a convincing alternative.[69] Their suspicions grew as the result of a telegram received from Henderson on the eve of the visit which summarized his preliminary talks with German leaders and expressed sympathy for the concept of autonomy for German minorities living outside Germany. This was tantamount to condoning German expansion in Central and Eastern Europe, and it provoked some sharp comments from Sargent and Van.[70] They rejected entirely the Henderson thesis as a starting point for Halifax's discussions.

On 13 November the *Evening Standard* scooped the story.[71] As a result, Chamberlain was compelled to make an official announcement in the House that the visit was on. This was to place the government in a ridiculous position, seemingly dragging its feet and having decisions forced upon it. Chamberlain may well have wondered how the *Evening Standard* had got hold of the story. One prominent journalist had a clear answer. Frederick Augustus Voigt† wrote to his editor that 'a high official in the F.O.' leaked the story 'so that

* Since his accession Chamberlain had expressed dissatisfaction with the negative attitude of the Foreign Office (see, for example, *Harvey Diaries*, 57–8). Van, as PUS, led the oppositionist camp, and his refusal to make way gracefully for Cadogan could not have endeared him to Chamberlain. Apart from differences in policy, there were of course vast differences in style and personality between the two men, and it would be foolish to ignore them. Apparently Chamberlain's suspicions were such that he authorized some surveillance on Van's social activities, thereby bringing to light, in fact confirming, Van's contacts with Churchill and Dalton and other opponents of his policy. (See I. Colvin, *The Chamberlain Cabinet* (London, 1971), 264.)

† Frederick Augustus Voigt (1892–1975): *Manchester Guardian* journalist; ed., *The Nineteenth Century and After*, 1938–46; edited own newsletter, *The Arrow*, 1939; described as 'the greatest British political journalist of the 1930's'. See also D. Ayerst, *Guardian. Biography of a Newspaper* (London, 1971), 501–4.

it would receive stunt publicity and be denied by the Germans', thereby destroying the forthcoming talks.[72] Was the high official none other than Van? If so, it would surely have sealed his fate as far as Chamberlain was concerned. Voigt was careful to mention no names, and indeed no evidence has yet emerged to confirm or deny the veracity of his story. As has been pointed out, it would have been 'a desperate step' for Van to have leaked the story.[73] But it is not inconceivable that one of his minions, Rex Leeper for example, would have done the job for him. Previous examples of such a combination are not lacking. Whatever the truth, Chamberlain would have held the Foreign Office, and ultimately Van, responsible.

By the beginning of December the essential decision regarding Van's removal had been taken. Chamberlain himself broke the news:

> Van has accepted my proposal. Indeed I did not give him any alternative. I think the change will make a great difference in the F.O. and when Anthony can work out his ideas with a sane, slow man, like Alick Cadogan, he will be much steadier. Van has had the effect of multiplying the extent of Anthony's natural vibrations and I am afraid his instincts were all against my policy.*

* Letter to Chamberlain, 12 December 1937, quoted by K. Middlemas, *op. cit.*, 78. Colvin adds a dramatic flourish to the interview (*op. cit.*, 171–2): 'I don't know whether I will accept or not', said Vansittart.
'What will you do then?'
'I may stand for Parliament.'
'What? You can't do that!' The Prime Minister leaned forward startled. 'You know too much.'
'I will think it over, Prime Minister, and let you have my answer.'
Colvin does not quote a source for this confrontation, but he might have relied on 'two long conversations with "Van" shortly before his death' (*op. cit.*, 16). The reference to Van standing for parliament has a strange ring at this stage in his career. Earlier in the year, in July, his name had cropped up in some political circles as a potential National Labour candidate for East Marylebone (see *The Dugdale Diaries*, entry for 13 July 1937, unpublished version at present in the possession of Mr Adam Fergusson). But it is quite clear that he was not consulted about the idea, and equally clear that he would have rejected it. In January 1938, in the immediate aftermath of the affair, he told Rex Leeper that he was thinking of 'resigning and going into politics' (K. Young, *op. cit.*, 385), a natural though non-committal reaction to his treatment at the hands of Eden and Chamberlain. Just over a year later, however, in January 1939, when the dust had settled, he was in fact approached by Lord Howard de Walderon to stand as Conservative candidate for Marylebone. He refused: 'matters had better remain as they are at present. The situation is so delicate that I feel that everybody will have to stand pat for the present until it clears.' (Correspondence, January 1939, in Vnst. 4/4.)

Van would be elevated to the high-sounding title of Chief Diplomatic Adviser to the government. He would be stripped of all executive power, but would be available for CID meetings, missions abroad, and international conferences. How would this affect Cadogan, his replacement as PUS? It was too early to draw any definite conclusions, for Van's new functions had been defined only in the most general terms and he may well have hoped to profit by the vagueness of his new status. He and Cadogan possessed deeply contrasting personalities, and a clash of style and policy would have resulted in disastrous consequences all round. This was a real danger. At any rate, it was necessary to avoid 'duality' at the top and to safeguard Cadogan's position, for as Harvey noted, 'Van was very active'.[74] Here was cause for much bickering in the future.

Realizing he had no option, Van accepted his new position without undue fuss. He rationalized that it was better not to resign, for resignation would have been regarded by the Germans as a triumph and by Britain's friends in Europe as a set-back.[75] He only insisted that the communiqué should make clear that he was not being '*dégommé*' (ousted), that no change in policy was contemplated, and that his status as senior to the PUS was assured.[76] All this was quite innocuous, in fact meaningless, but simply to have made these requests must have restored to him a measure of self-respect. His wishes were observed, though the final communiqué included one ominous phrase which underlined the true reality of Van's new post. The duties of the Chief Diplomatic Adviser, it stated, 'will include advising the Secretary of State upon all major questions of policy concerning foreign affairs remitted to him for that purpose'.[77] From this general collapse in his fortunes Van salvaged one minor success, wholly symbolic and devoid of any real significance. He retained the use of the PUS's room. It may have comforted him to maintain the façade of power. By then his detractors could afford to be generous, having so effectively dismantled the machinery of his authority.

The communiqué was issued to the press on 1 January 1938. It found the Vansittarts in Monte Carlo enjoying the Riviera weather. But while the Vansittarts were attracting the attention of the gossip columnists, Lady Vansittart for her elegant dresses and Van for his interest in *chemin de fer*,[78] in London instructions were being drafted defining in more precise detail the status of the Chief Diplomatic Adviser and the scope of his activities. On 22 January Eden released this document under his own signature, though it had been drafted by Gladwyn Jebb,* previously Van's private secretary but now Cadogan's.[79] The chain of responsibility in the Office was clearly set out. All papers were to be submitted to Cadogan who would then forward them directly to the Secretary of State. Should Eden desire Van's advice, the paper would be so marked before returning it to Cadogan. Outcoming papers from the Secretary of State were to be sent direct to Cadogan who would then pass them on to Van and other senior officials. The sting was in the following sentence: 'In the event of a paper requiring urgent action, it will be sent by Sir A. Cadogan direct to the Under Secretary concerned with a slip bearing the words "Sir R. Vansittart after action".' Interviews with ambassadors and other foreign dignitaries were also removed from his jurisdiction. There was an exception to these crippling limitations. Departmental minutes on CID papers were to be submitted direct to Van, who, in the absence of the Secretary of State, would represent the Office at its meetings and at those of its more important sub-committees.

One other crumb was thrown Van's way. Rex Leeper had proposed setting up a 'Coordinating Committee for Publicity in Foreign Countries', and Van had readily consented to act as its chairman considering it imperative that foreign directed propaganda should remain under the control of the Foreign Office.[80] Eden grasped at this flimsy straw to demonstrate to Chamberlain 'the kind of work the Chief Diplomatic Adviser can very usefully perform'. Although Van was depicted in the press as a mighty overlord of the British propaganda machine endowed with sweeping powers, the authorities regarded his new role with cool indifference. There is no evidence that Chamberlain took any special interest in the committee's activities despite Van's request that he should do so. By May 1938 Van was perturbed by 'the slowness of work and meagre financial support' offered to his committee. The Treasury was particularly hostile, regarding the committee as a kind of conspiracy to extract funds from its purse for a highly speculative project. 'The whole thing is very amateurish', proclaimed Fisher. Judging from his cutting remarks, and his past performance, Fisher no longer took Van seriously, and little remained of their old friendship. Regarding other Foreign Office officials his comments were even more scathing.

* Hubert Miles Gladwyn Jebb (1900–   ): entered diplomatic service, 1924; private secretary to PUS, 1937–40; served in Ministry of Economic Warfare, 1940; Head of Reconstruction Department, Foreign Office, 1942; representative to United Nations, 1950–54; Ambassador to France, 1954–60. Kn. 1949. Cr. Baron, 1960.

Rex Leeper, he noted caustically, was 'already overpaid, though I would be prepared to pay him more as a pension'. The committee was another convenient backwater where Van could discharge his energy without unduly disturbing those who were engaged in more serious business.

Naturally, the new appointment aroused a great deal of speculative comment. What was its deeper significance? Did it indicate a dual foreign policy? Did it presage a radical upheaval in British foreign policy aims? Or was it merely a tactical ploy? Or perhaps just time for a change? On the whole the British press accepted the communiqué at its face value, although it discerned the possibility of tension between Van and the Secretary of State on one side and the Foreign Office staff on the other.[81] Questions were raised in parliament, some provocative, but the true situation was evaded with exemplary skill. Lord Lothian, perhaps relying on his own experience, thought it dangerous that Van and Cadogan should work on parallel lines. 'Parallel lines never meet', rejoined Halifax to the sound of laughter, 'and therefore never clash.'[82]

Hankey was not so flippant. In a 'Most Secret and Personal' letter to Phipps he recounted the background to Van's dismissal.[83] Beginning with Baldwin, who 'was a weak man and shrank from anything drastic', Hankey insisted that the desire for change had never slackened:

> No one questions Van's patience, or ability and industry. But he is apt to get rather jumpy. He pays too much attention to the press of all countries, and to S. [ecret] S. [ervice] information – useful pointers in both cases, but bad guides. I think this is largely due to his taking too little leave, which usually warps people's judgement. Anyhow Van has got on a good many people's nerves, and there is an idea about that F.O. suspiciousness has prevented us from taking advantage of opportunities to get on better terms with Italy and perhaps with Germany.

Hankey was anxious to point out that 'Van is immensely popular with us all', and that he personally was 'immensely in his debt for help with the Defence programmes'. Although, unlike Fisher, he was not involved in any of the intrigues which surrounded Van, he was consulted and thought the present compromise a sensible and workable one. On the other hand, Churchill told Phipps that the appointment was 'very dangerous', and that 'it would be represented as a victory for the pro-Germans in England' and would 'arouse the suspicions of the French'.[84]

The Germans too were divided in their estimation of Van's new role. One opinion focused on Van's 'quite extraordinary ability', and could not 'envisage that Chamberlain would not want his co-operation'. German journalists stationed in London were also unable to unravel this mystery: six believed that Van had been sidetracked, six that he had been promoted, and the rest held opinions in between. As was to be expected, Ribbentrop, Hitler's British expert, was completely wide of the mark: 'Van our most important and toughest foe has been appointed by Chamberlain to a position where he can play a leading role in the diplomatic game against Germany.' Ernst Woermann, *chargé d'affaires* at the German embassy, came closer to the truth: Van, he remarked, did not fit in with Chamberlain's overall policy.[85]

In Italy, where Van had recently been paraded as *Il Padrone Segreto del 'Foreign Office'* (the Secret Master of the Foreign Office), Mussolini received the official explanation with equanimity, though he hastened to enquire 'whether Cagodan was not a Jewish name',[86] and expressed great admiration for Van's personality. American sources proved the most accurate:

> the communiqué from Downing Street [was] almost unprecedented ... [and] does not necessarily mean a change from a pro-French ... to a pro-German orientation of British foreign policy. The Cabinet, however, find Sir Robert too independent for a civil servant – too much inclined to take a line of his own and fight for it against the opinion of the political leaders of the government.[87]

Van did not abandon his old prerogatives without a struggle. He wished to insert a provision in the final instructions defining his status whereby papers of major importance should be sent through him to the Foreign Secretary. Cadogan vehemently objected, and 'Van collapsed'. 'I think', Cadogan concluded, 'Van is off his mental balance'.[88] When Eden resigned in February, Van attempted to exploit the change to enlarge his own role. He told Halifax that it had been agreed that he should have direct access to the Prime Minister. This particular scheme was quickly scotched, mainly at the insistence of Harvey who sprang to his new chief's defence.[89] Nor was Van above using the press in his periodical skirmishes with his superiors, both to inflate his own position and to criticize the policy of the government.[90] His lack of real authority was mirrored

by an exaggerated propensity to impress his views on every conceivable subject to as wide an audience as possible. From 1938 there
is an appreciable quickening in the tempo and range of his minutes.

None of this endeared him to his colleagues. Cadogan, the chief
butt of his actions, understandably resented his interference. 'I'm
all for Van having his boost but if it develops in any dangerous
direction, I'll blow it to bits.'[91] The situation was really quite absurd.
There was no constitutional precedent for a Chief Diplomatic
Adviser,* and the appointment was an anomalous one from the
outset. As far as Cadogan, Halifax and Chamberlain were concerned,
Van had turned into the Office pest.

> Van has been away all this week, but it doesn't make much dif-
> ference if he's here. He sends in minutes to the S of S snarling at
> some of Nevile H's telegrams which H[alifax] hands gloomily to
> me. I keep them for 2 or 3 days and then hand them back to H.
> and say, 'I'm very stupid: I can't remember what you told me to
> do about this.' He looks unutterably sad, and says, 'I think perhaps
> we might burn it now.'[92]

Even old comrades such as Tyrrell believed that Van had manœuvred himself into an unconstitutional position, and that he 'should
take a year's leave to recover his sanity'.[93] Oliphant expressed similar views.[94] Phipps had 'no idea' what the new appointment meant,
but something seemed to crack in his relations with Van. He suspected that Van, divested of all routine work, would 'spread himself
unduly and end by causing trouble'.[95] What really alarmed Phipps
was the manner in which the French press magnified the importance
of Van's new post. He assumed that Van was manipulating his extensive contacts in French society to deliberately inflate his own
position: 'that Van is now to all intents and purposes another Secretary of State, that he is the only true and enlightened friend of
France, etc. etc.' This quite obviously reflected badly on Phipps,
and he reacted vigorously to defend his position. He frustrated a
plan by Van to interview Chautemps† and Daladier‡ on the
grounds that 'such interviews would be given an altogether undue
importance, particularly as Van would be coming back here on

---

* Though there was a Chief Economic Adviser, Sir Frederick Leith-Ross, and a
Chief Industrial Adviser, Sir Horace Wilson.
† Camille Chautemps (1885–1963): French Prime Minister, June 1937–March
1938; member of Reynaud's cabinet and Pétain's cabinet, 1940.
‡ Edouard Daladier (1884–1970): French Minister of Foreign Affairs, 1934; of
War and Defence, 1936–38; Prime Minister, April 1938–March 1940.

Denham Place, the William and Mary home of Van and Sarita.
(Reproduced by kind permission of The Antique Collector)

The Drawing Room, Denham Place.
(Reproduced by kind permission of The Antique Collector)

purpose from England,* where he would be supposed to have been charged with a special and highly important mission by the Prime Minister'.[96]

There was an undeniable element of truth in Phipps's assertions. Van was certainly not averse to the praise showered on him by the French press, nor was he above pulling a few strings in his own favour. Whether he set out to deliberately undermine Phipps's position, or the policy of the government, is another matter. Phipps unquestionably believed this to be so, as his correspondence with Hankey indicates. Some months later he was again reporting on Van's subversive activities in Paris, this time to Sir Horace Wilson.[97] Phipps insisted that he was not telling these tales out of 'any feelings of petty jealousy'.[98] Yet this could only have been partially true. Phipps, whatever distinction he had attained, was a secondary figure when compared with Van. After having served as PUS for eight long years, Van could rise no further, as his present appointment indicated. Phipps could only rise in favour if he indicated beyond all doubt his loyalty to the government's policy, and yet here was Van seemingly sabotaging his efforts:

> These activities [Van's] are, I am well aware, only a sample of what has been going on throughout my time here as Ambassador – a time now rapidly drawing to a close. I can only hope that my successor will have an easier task here in this respect than I have had. Above all I earnestly hope that he will only be chosen after his loyalty to the Prime Minister's policy of appeasement has been proved 'beyond a peradventure'. Otherwise the danger to that policy, already none too easy of execution owing to intrigues on both sides of the channel, will be greater than it need be.[99]

One can discount the more extreme of Phipps's suspicions. Van was not motivated by such machiavellian thoughts. He simply had nothing better to do.

The passing of time saw no improvement in his situation; if anything it gradually deteriorated beyond repair. In April he was still fretting. When the Washington embassy became vacant owing to Lindsay's retirement, Van was pressed to take it as a graceful way of abandoning his ludicrous position. The Promotion Board and Halifax were strongly in favour, but apparently 'no one [has] the courage to tell him to go where he is told'.[100] Chamberlain, surely

---

* Van was forced to cut short his Riviera holiday and return to England because of the sudden death of his father on 10 January. He planned to return to France immediately after the funeral.

H

a measure of the absurdity of the situation, even toyed with the idea of appointing Van Director-General of the BBC in place of Lord Reith.[101]

The critical months before the outbreak of war saw Van more isolated and powerless than ever before. His role as an effective formulator of policy was strictly curtailed. His advice was scarcely sought. Confined to the fringes of diplomacy, he dissipated his energies in other directions: his secret service network; his contacts with Churchill and Dalton and other dissidents; and his relationship with the press. But this was no substitute for his previous position of authority. His stubbornness was commendable, but perhaps he would have been better off fighting the system from the outside. At any rate, he had no doubt where to place the ultimate responsibility for this deplorable state of affairs:

> Went to see Van. Still at same room in F.O. . . . quite catty about Eden. Been trying to edge him out for a long time . . . Eden had been jealous of him, thinking he had too much limelight. Had brought Cadogan back from China with intention of making him PUS. He wanted a tame and colourless Civil Servant with less character, less knowledge, and less persistence in arguing with politicians when he thought they were wrong . . .* Van said he thought of Eden as a man with whom he had often had to go out tiger shooting and who, in the end, had shot him in the back.[102]

NOTES

1. The precise date of this meeting remains unknown and no record of it has been discovered; and it is in fact extremely doubtful whether one was kept at all. All the surviving participants of the meeting whom the author interviewed were positive that it had occurred two or three weeks after Van's return from Paris. This account is based on a number of private communications.
2. K. Young, *op. cit.*, 356.
3. For his memo see F.O. 345/538, P. 224/46/150 and 325/541, P. 332/332/150.

---

* Van's remarks about Cadogan should not be taken at their face value. Only four months had elapsed since his 'elevation', and, no doubt egged on by Dalton's propensity for political gossip, he was still only too keen to vent his spleen on those whom he held responsible for his fall from grace. Cadogan was an obvious target. But he was in fact far from being the 'tame and colourless' civil servant Van portrayed in contrast to his own resolute and determined character. Any reading of the Cadogan Diaries makes this absolutely clear. In many respects, Cadogan's management of the Foreign Office was more efficient and businesslike than Van's; while his timid appearance masked strongly held opinions which enabled him to stand up to his political chiefs when the occasion demanded it.

4. *Ibid.*
5. See M. Gilbert, *Churchill*, v. 726.
6. See his minutes of 4 January 1936, F.O. 395/538, P. 224/46/150.
7. See F.O. 371/18851, C. 7522/55/18.
8. The papers may be seen in F.O. 371/18851, C. 7522/55/18. A copy of his minutes is in Vnst. 2/24, 1935.
9. See, for example, '*Chips*', *The Diaries of Sir Henry Channon*, ed. R. R. James (Penguin edn. 1970), 146; even Medlicott, *op. cit.*, 21, leaves this impression; see also N. Thompson, *The Anti-Appeasers. Conservative Opposition to Appeasement* (O.U.P., 1971), 44.
10. See, for example, Van's minutes of 28 February 1935, Vnst. 2/28. The theme of a German move into the Rhineland appears time and again in Van's minutes from his first 'old Adam' memo. until the actual event in March 1936.
11. K. Young, *op. cit.*, 361.
12. See Van to Sir Clive Wigram, 7 November 1935, Vnst. 2/27; also his minutes of 16 November 1935 on a despatch by Phipps on Germany's expansionsist aims, Vnst. 2/27.
13. See Medlicott, *op. cit.*, 20–21.
14. See, 'Britain, France and Germany', C.P. 42(36), CAB. 24/260 or F.O. 371/19935 C. 997/4/18. Sir Eric Phipps also participated in the formulation of this programme.
15. See C.P. 43(36), CAB. 24/260.
16. See Medlicott, *op. cit.*, 21–2.
17. Record of a telephone message about 12.45 am, 7 March 1936. Christie Papers, 1/17.
18. See E. M. Robertson, *Hitler's Pre-War Policy and Military Plans, 1933–39* (London, 1963), 72–3.
19. Medlicott, *op. cit.*, 24–5.
20. See F.P. (36)6, 13 July 1936. Copy in Vnst. 1/5.
21. See cabinet conclusions, 30 April 1936, 4 and 6 May 1936, CAB. 23/84, 89. Chamberlain took a prominent part in these discussions.
22. See 'Questions to be Addressed to the German Government', C.P. 127(36), CAB. 24/262.
23. See Phipps' despatch of 26 May 1936, Vnst. 2/26.
24. Van's minutes of 17 May and 1 June 1936, Vnst. 2/26, 38.
25. *Ibid.*
26. See C.P. 220(36), CAB. 24/263; C.P. 307(36), CAB. 24/265; also Medlicott, *op. cit.*, 29–30.
27. Minutes of 8 January 1935, F.O. 371/18891, C. 144/21/18.
28. See F.O. 371/20717, C. 3741/37/18; and Sargent's minutes, 8 June 1937, F.O. 371/20721, C. 4135/37/18.
29. See, for example, Record of Schacht's conversations with Blum, F.O. 371/20726, C. 635/48/18, 'The Colonial Question', F.O. 371/20735, C. 3260/48/19, and 'German Colonial Aspirations', March 1935, F.O. 371/18819, C. 1738/21/18. Schacht may well have been exploiting the colonial issue to protect and strengthen his own position within the power structure of the German government. By 1936–37, with Göring tightening his grip on the German economy, Schacht's position was considerably weakened, yet these very years witnessed a marked increase in his schemes to procure some kind of

colonial success. The German colonial question is discussed by K. Hilderbrand, *Vom Reich zum Weltreich. Hitler NSDAP und Koloniale Frage, 1919–1945* (Munich, 1969).

30. For the report and accompanying minutes, see F.O. 371/19927, C. 4275/97/18 and 19928, C. 5185, 5520/97/18. In this connection, see also Eden's statement in the House on 27 July that 'HMG hoped that with so many other international problems still unsolved but with new opportunity of advance towards their settlement having been afforded during the last few days, there will in no quarter be desired at this time to introduce further causes of serious differences between the nations.' (See P.D.C. v. 315, C. 1131–2.)

31. See F.O. 371/19906, C. 3746/4/18 and 19928, C. 5185/97/18.

32. See his minutes on Plymouth report, 24 June 1936, F.O. 371/19928, C. 5295/971/18; also in Vnst. 2/28. In this connection, see also Medlicott, *op. cit.*, 28.

33. 'The World Situation and British Rearmament', 31 December 1936, F.O. 371/19787, A. 9996/9996/1. Copies of this paper are to be found in the files of all departments in the Foreign Office.

34. Minutes of 7 May 1937, F.O. 371/20735, C. 3362/240/18.

35. Minutes of 1 June 1936, Vnst. 2/26; see also of 17 May 1936, Vnst. 2/28.

36. Quoted by Medlicott, *op, cit.*, 12n.

37. The following passage is based on 'A Busman's Holiday', September 1936, Vnst. 1/17 (a 14-page account of his visit); Sargent to Van, Van to Sargent, 6 August 1936, F.O. 371/19912, C. 5780, 5781/4/18; Phipps tels., 6, 13, and 14 August 1936, F.O. 371/19912, C. 5750, 5871, 5919/4/18; Eden to B. Newton, 11 September 1936, F.O. 3712/1992, C. 6431/4/18; minutes by Van, 17 September 1936, F.O. 371/19912, C. 6528/4/18; *G.D.*, C. v. nos. 508, 510; *The Ribbentrop Memoirs* (London, 1954), 65–7; P. Schmidt, *Hitler's Interpreter* (London, 1951), 50–51; *The Times*, August, 1936.

38. F.O. 371/19787, A. 9996/9996/1.

39. See M. Gilbert, *Churchill*, v. *op. cit.*, *passim*.

40. Quoted by Colvin, *op. cit.*, 120. See Van's tribute to him in *The Times*, 2 January 1937.

41. Van to Baldwin, 30 December 1936, Baldwin Papers, v. 171; interview with Lady Vansittart, 31 October 1972; *The Harvey Diaries*, *op. cit.*, 23; and *The Cadogan Diaries*, *op. cit.*, 13.

42. Hankey to Phipps, 11 January 1938, Ph.P. 3/3.

43. *The Cadogan Diaries*, 13.

44. *The Harvey Diaries*, 23.

45. Avon, 447–8.

46. Interview with Lady Vansittart, 9 March 1973.

47. Private communications.

48. Minutes of 12 October 1937, F.O. 371/21162, R. 6700/1/22. For further examples of his 'anti-Italianism' see F.O. 371/21159, R. 3656/1/22 and 21160, R. 4977/1/22, F.O. 371/21162, R. 7776/1/22.

49. Minutes of 25 October 1937, F.O. 371/21162, R. 6907/1/22.

50. Minutes of May 1937, F.O. 371/21158, R. 2879/1/22.

51. Minutes of 27 June 1937, Vnst. 2/39. See also, K. Young, *op. cit.*, 370.

52. Avon, *op. cit.*, 503–4.

53. See their correspondence, July–October 1923, F.O. 800/157.

54. Van to Sir Clive Wigram, 23 August 1934, R.A., GV. M. 2440/14.

55. A private communication.
56. See T. Jones, *op. cit.*, 314, 543.
57. Minutes of 28 February 1938, F.O. 371/21656, C. 1353/43/18.
58. Van to Halifax, 17 February 1939, F.O. 800/315; see also Van's comments on Henderson's last interview with Hitler, *B.D.*, 3, vii, 354–5. There are no end of quotations to exemplify this point. Van and Sargent were the most outspoken of Henderson's critics, but most of the officials joined in when given the opportunity.
59. *Nicolson Diaries*, i, 327. See also K. Young, *op. cit.*, 390.
60. See F.P. (36), 23, 2 April 1937, F.O. 371/20735, C. 2618/270/18.
61. *Cadogan Diaries*, 13–15; and minutes in F.O. 371/21159, R. 3795/1/22.
62. See Van's minutes, 3 June 1937, F.O. 371/21159, R. 3795/1/22 and 19 April 1937, Vnst. 2/34.
63. See Colvin, 151–2, followed by K. Middlemas, *Diplomacy of Illusion* (London, 1972), 77, who adds that Van's use of the word 'suppressed' might have been 'hyperbole'.
64. See F.O. 371/20733, C. 5933/165/18. This file includes Van's memorandum of 6 July 1937; appendices A–E include the above reports, and others, from Van's sources.
65. Undated but December 1937, Vnst. 1/21.
66. Compare with Christie Papers, 1/5, 1/21; see also T. P. Conwell-Evans, *None So Blind*, 73–102.
67. See Christie Papers, where there is a steady increase in intelligence reports from 1936, mounting to a veritable flood in 1939–40.
68. *Dalton Diaries*, 4 November 1937.
69. See *Harvey Diaries*, 57. Cadogan, Rex Leeper, Sargent, Strang, Cranborne and Harvey were of this opinion, as, finally, was Eden, who seemed to find it more difficult to make up his mind.
70. Minutes in F.O. 371/20737, C. 8293/270/18.
71. *Harvey Diaries*, 59; and F. R. Gannon, *The British Press and Germany, 1936–39* (O.U.P., 1971?, 129–31).
72. See Gannon, *op. cit.*, 130–31, quoting Voigt to Crozier, 17 November 1937.
73. Gannon, 131, n. 147.
74. *Harvey Diaries*, 63–4.
75. *Dalton Diaries*, 12 April 1938.
76. *Harvey Diaries*, 64.
77. For text of announcement, see F.O. 395/574.
78. See 'The Monte Carlo Merry-Go-Round', *The Sketch*, 5 January 1938.
79. See F.O. 370/539, L. 116/113/405.
80. See F.O. 395/596, P. 359, 476, 799/359/150, and PREM 1/272 for this paragraph.
81. For example, *The Times*, 1 January 1938.
82. See *P.D.*, Lords, v, 107, c. 784; also *The Times*, 18 February 1938.
83. Hankey to Phipps, 11 January 1938, Ph.P. 3/3. Hankey wrote two letters to Phipps that day, the first, 'Most Secret and Personal' (handwritten), the second 'Personal and Confidential' (typewritten).
84. Phipps to Hankey, 9 January 1938, Ph.P. 3/3.
85. See *G.D.*, D. i, nos. 93, 95, 101; and F.O. 371/22491, W. 127/27/50.
86. See F.O. 371/22402, R 290/23/22, 22491, W. 379/127/50.
87. F.O. 371/22491, W. 495/127/50.

88. *Cadogan Diaries*, 40–41.
89. *Harvey Diaries*, 107.
90. For example, *Harvey Diaries*, 66; *Cadogan Diaries*, 34, 91, 99. Also Phipps to Sir Horace Wilson, 13 December 1938, Ph.P. 3/5.
91. *Cadogan Diaries*, 34, 67.
92. *Cadogan Diaries*, 67.
93. *Harvey Diaries*, 168.
94. *Cadogan Diaries*, 71.
95. Phipps to Hankey, 9 January 1938, Ph.P. 3/3, two letters.
96. *Ibid.*, also Phipps to Vansittart, 9 January 1938. Ph.P. 3/3.
97. Phipps to Sir Horace Wilson, 13 December 1938. Ph.P. 3/3.
98. Phipps to Hankey, 9 January 1938, Ph.P. 3/3. This phrase was cut out of final draft.
99. Phipps to Sir Horace Wilson, 13 December 1938. Ph.P. 3/5.
100. *Harvey Diaries*, 148; also *Cadogan Diaries*, 78.
101. *Cadogan Diaries*, 82.
102. *Dalton Diaries*, 12 April 1938.

CHAPTER XI

Black Record

VAN STRUCK SOME OBSERVERS as being 'in the depths of glooms' in the early months of 1938.[1] But there were some consolations attached to his new dignity. In the New Year's Honours list he was created a Knight Grand Cross of the Bath (GCB); and although he feigned indifference to such honours, it must have satisfied his ego to have been included in this distinguished order. More to his liking, he found free time to devote to those leisurely pursuits he had been compelled to neglect in the recent past.

He returned to writing, and discovered a new outlet for his literary gifts. He collaborated with Miles Malleson, an old friend who had appeared in his play *Foolery* many years ago, on the film script of *Sixty Glorious Years*, an epic on Queen Victoria's reign starring Anna Neagle. According to the critics it was a huge success. The script was 'cultured, lucid, and well-stocked with memorable periods'.[2] Van was a great enthusiast of this medium. At the same time, he contracted with Sir Alexander Korda to write more scripts glorifying Britain's great imperial past: *Burmese Silver*, starring Sabu, 'the elephant boy', and *The Four Feathers*, a film extolling the British conquest of the Sudan, were perhaps the two best examples.

He was on firmer ground in the theatre. 'You shall now take seisin [possession] from me of this land', proclaimed Van, as he handed to George Bernard Shaw the title-deeds to the National Theatre at its prospective site in South Kensington. Shaw accepted the deeds, 'the earth and the twig' (feudal symbols of possession), modestly describing himself as 'the next best thing to Shakespeare'.[3]

Apart from jesting with Shaw, Van also wrote another play, *Dead Heat*, which was produced for the 11th Malvern Festival in August 1939. It was a light, romantic comedy, which, in Van's words, illustrated the dangers whereby man unwittingly hastens his own self-destruction. It might have been a parody on the last stage of his own career. *Dead Heat* was not well received. In content and dialogue it was nostalgically pre-war and scarcely distinguishable from his productions of those years.[4] He scored a far greater success when, together with Sir Seymour Hicks,* he staged the theatricals in honour of M. Lebrun, the French President, who arrived in London on a state visit in March 1939. A temporary theatre was planned by the well-known architect, Sir Edwin Lutyens, and erected in the glass-covered court of the India Office. The setting was magnificent, reviving ancient glories, and provided a splendid backcloth for a varied assortment of items ranging from *Romeo and Juliet* to an appearance by Cecily Courtneidge. Halifax thought it all 'amusingly original'.[5]

This was the lighter side of his work. The fact that Van held no administrative responsibility made his position at the Foreign Office largely humbug. It might have been possible to overcome this obstacle had his talents and experiences been exploited in another way. But this was not to be. He rarely attended the sessions of the Foreign Policy Committee of the cabinet† which, on the surface, would have been a perfect forum for him to ventilate his views. His feeling of impotence must have grown.

This can clearly be discerned in his role in the Austrian crisis which again became critical towards the middle of February.‡

* (Edward) Seymour (George) Hicks, (1871–1949): actor-manager and author; wrote *The Cherry Girl, The Gay Gordons, The Dashing Little Duke*; built Aldwych Theatre, 1905. Kn. 1935.

† This was of recent innovation, set up in April 1936 as a result of the Rhineland crisis. Van was first invited to attend on 3 February 1938 to hear a report by Sir Nevile Henderson, a precedent which he deplored. From then on his attendances were sporadic to an extreme, though Wilson and Cadogan participated more frequently. The sessions of the committee may be followed in CAB. 27/622, 623, 624.

‡ On 12 February 1938, Schuschnigg, the Austrian Chancellor, met Hitler at Berchtesgaden. He was treated to a furious lecture about the iniquities of Austrian policy and browbeaten into conceding far-reaching concessions to the Austrian Nazis. Schuschnigg tried to thwart Hitler's demands by insisting on a plebiscite on the question of Austrian independence. This forced Schuschnigg's resignation and his replacement by the Nazi, Seyss-Inquart, who, acting on Göring's telephone instructions, promptly 'invited' the German army to occupy Austria. This invasion began on 12 March. The same day Hitler entered Austria to a rapturous welcome. The following day he proclaimed the *Anschluss*. A month later, a Nazi-inspired plebiscite recorded a vote of 99·75 in favour of Hitler's action.

Although he was not officially excluded from the preliminary internal discussions on Austria there was a noticeable sigh of relief when he did not attend.[6] Obviously he was viewed as a disruptive and controversial influence. The independence of Austria had been a cardinal theme in Van's policy. What could the Western powers now do to avert Hitler's bid to extinguish it? Van favoured a joint *démarche* to warn the German government of the dangerous consequences of their adventurous policy. Believing that Germany 'may bluff herself' into a big adventure, he called for some 'plain speaking' at Berlin to avoid a general conflagration.[7]

Yet if Van considered that Germany 'may bluff herself', it must be admitted that there was a large element of bluff in Van's own proposal. Did Britain have the necessary muscle to stand up to Hitler? There may be some academic debate about this now, but it was the firm opinion of the Chiefs of Staff, the government's professional advisers, that the country was not yet in a position for a showdown with Germany.[8] The gap between political intent and military capability had never been so great.

A display of Western unity and resolution might have compelled the Germans to back down. At best, it remained a speculative proposition. In the final analysis, such action was dependent upon French cooperation. But at the time the French were exhausting their strength in futile political in-fighting, attempting to construct a new government. At no time was the moral and political disintegration of France more in evidence. And what if a vigorous warning provoked the Germans into a more daring adventure? That was the great imponderable to which no one could provide a convincing answer. Cadogan put it most bluntly:

Van, as far as I can make out, wants to talk big, but then – ? He's an idiot with an idée fixe – a very simple one. He's all façade and nothing else. Nothing constructive: with all his big *talk* he's got no idea at all. And *that* is what we are suffering from.[9]

For Cadogan, Van and Sargent represented 'the forces of evil'.[10] One may sympathize with Cadogan's impatience at Van's holier than thou minutes. But for all his carping, Cadogan had nothing better to offer, unless the absorption of Austria by Germany may be called a policy. Both the Chief Diplomatic Adviser and the PUS were caught in a cleft-stick not entirely of their own making.

Meanwhile, Van carefully nurtured his secret sources of information. The Foreign Office encouraged Van in this activity, for at least it added a new dimension to intelligence material even if the results were regarded with a pronounced degree of scepticism. Goerdeler was perhaps the classic example of this kind of contact. When they met in the summer of 1937 he appeared as an 'impressive person, wise and weighty, a man of great intelligence and courage, and a sincere patriot'.[11] Goerdeler was of course a member of the Nazi party, but as he explained to Van the party 'contains large numbers of decent, honest, idealistic, and now disillusioned people'. He was a genuine opponent of the Hitlerite régime and met a horrible fate in 1944. But he soon revealed himself to Van as an old-fashioned German nationalist hankering after a greater Germany. They met again in April 1938, after the *Anschluss*, when Goerdeler argued that the Sudeten-German territories should be ceded to Germany, an idea totally unacceptable to Van who would only consider a degree of local autonomy.[12] In December the same year he proposed a comprehensive scheme for the integration of Germany into the European community, a programme which led Van to portray him as 'a stalking horse for Germany's military expansion', and Cadogan to reject it as being 'too much like "Mein Kampf" '[13]. Van's true estimation of these fly-by-night visitors can be gauged from a letter he wrote after the war concerning Theo Kordt who had visited him in August 1939:

> I should say from my limited experience of the man that he was one of the Germans who did *not* want war with the West. On the other hand, I gradually discovered that what he really wanted was a German maximum without war with *us*. His real game was to get a free hand in expansion east, and expansion to the limit, including Russia. . . Kordt [read Goerdeler] was riddled with the notion of expansion. Otherwise he was a decent, humane man, and emphatically not a Nazi. Indeed I think he hated the Nazi Party for personal and public reasons. But of course he would have accepted, and rejoiced in, their conquests.[14]

A far more serious customer, at least in Van's estimation, was Konrad Henlein, leader of the *Sudetendeutsche Partei* (SDP). This did not spring from any intrinsic quality of virtue in Henlein's character, but rather from Van's implicit trust – often exaggerated – in Graham Christie's judgement. Christie acted as the main vehicle of communication between Henlein and Van. Since early 1935 he had been in close and continuous contact with Henlein. He firmly believed that Henlein represented the moderate faction within the SDP as opposed to the so-called radical elements, Kasper and

Haider. According to Christie, Henlein rejected a pan-German solution to the Sudeten problem. He demanded only that his people's legitimate rights, as guaranteed under the Czech constitution, be respected. This meant in effect greater local autonomy for the Sudeten German regions, a highly laudable aim which was being persistently sabotaged by the obstinacy and short-sightedness of the Czech government. The most vital problem, as Christie saw it, was to ensure that Henlein remained leader of the moderates and was not driven into the arms of the radicals who were demanding total absorption into the *Reich*.[15]

Van was deeply influenced by this analysis and in fact it represented a close approximation of Henlein's delicate position within his own party.[16] As late as July 1938 he wrote: 'Henlein has only been passing very reluctantly under German influence and has no love for his Nazi masters.'[17] Yet in a broader sense this was a lopsided view of Henlein's policy. Since January 1935 the German Foreign Ministry had been subsidizing the activities of the SDP, and Henlein was an acquiescent, if not enthusiastic, tool of German machinations.* But Henlein was the perfect figurehead for his Nazi masters. He certainly deceived Van, among many others, on his periodic visits to London.

He first arrived in London in December 1935. Christie made the necessary arrangements, encouraged by Van. He lectured at Chatham House, preaching his habitual message of goodwill and conciliation.[18] He returned in July 1936. Once again, Chatham House opened its doors to him. On this occasion he met Van who was 'very impressed with the uprightness of the young Sudeten leader'. So much so that when Van visited Berlin the following month he raised aspects of the Sudeten question.[19] Henlein must have left London encouraged by what he had heard. Van did not disguise his sympathy for his complaints, and promised to 'advise and help the Sudeten Germans'.[20]

When they next met in October 1937 Henlein still struck Van as being 'decent, honest and moderate, or anyhow relatively moderate'.[21] Henlein made the usual conciliatory gestures, asking for a measure of local autonomy and hinting that unless pressure were put on the Czechs to accede to his demands he might not be able to

---

* It has been questioned whether the acceptance of the subsidy signified Henlein's 'complete subservience' to Berlin (see K. Robbins, 'Konrad Henlein, the Sudeten Question and British Foreign Policy', *Historical Journal*, XII, 4(1969), 683). This is a matter on which it is impossible to decide conclusively one way or the other. 'Complete subservience' is in any case a relative term. But it is clear that Henlein did not act as a brake on German plans, and that ultimately he benefited from them.

restrain his wilder colleagues. But, he added prophetically, Beneš and company would never agree until after the *Anschluss*, for then they would have no option but to yield as Czechoslovakia would be 'ringed round on three sides'. Van listened patiently, neither quarrelling nor agreeing with him, only endeavouring to keep him 'as calm and moderate as possible and to dissuade him from any counsels of despair'.

Reporting on his visit to Berlin, Henlein painted Van's attitude in the most sympathetic colours. Van had assured him that the British government would work to secure 'the most far-reaching autonomy for the Sudeten Germans, but that Britain would be found at the side of France "if the Germans marched into Czechoslovakia" '.[22] It is highly unlikely that a skilled diplomat like Van would have committed himself in quite so unequivocal a manner; and certainly there is no evidence of this in the British record of the conversation. Perhaps Henlein deliberately inflated Van's attitude in order to secure his own position within the SDP and to prove to the Germans that, through his influential contacts in the West, he alone could extract the necessary concessions from the Czech government.

Nevertheless there was a grain of truth in his reports, just enough to endow them with a veneer of credibility. It was common cause for complaint in the West that the Czechs were too inflexible towards their German minority. Van was definitely of this opinion. He was bitingly critical of Beneš and the Czech government.[23] Van reportedly told Rutha, a close associate of Henlein's, that Beneš was an ' "old fox" who only dealt with "splinter parties" and "small people" ', and that it was Beneš's intransigence which endangered the peace of Europe.[24] This sounds suspiciously like Christie prompting Van; but it reflected fairly accurately opinion in the Office regarding Czech behaviour. Van was of course utterly opposed to a German *coup* against Czechoslovakia, particularly after the *Anschluss*. Equally he refused to submit to German threats designed to subvert the Czech state. But he did support the concept of local autonomy for the Sudeten Germans; and he certainly saw the British government playing the role of an honest broker to persuade the Czechs of the wisdom of such a policy. On the surface this would appear a painless and sensible way of removing a point of friction from the European map. There was therefore a meeting of minds between Van and Henlein's professed policy. With all the vast intelligence sources at his disposal, or perhaps because of them, Van failed to penetrate beneath the surface of Henlein's masquerading. Nor did he discern that Henlein's attempt to effect a balance between Prague and Berlin was foredoomed to failure. Henlein's more militant rivals within the SDP, some of whom were in contact with the more extreme elements within the SS in Germany, would ensure that he would never fulfil the role of the moderate which he seemingly aspired to play. It was a singular lapse in judgement, though not, as it turned out, a crucial one.

By May 1938, the occasion of their next meeting, the situation had altered dramatically. Austria had been absorbed and Czecho-slovakia, in Henlein's prophetic phrase, was now 'ringed round on three sides'. Hitler had decided to force the pace. Henlein was instructed to raise his demands to a degree unacceptable to the Czech government.* On 12 May, a day before he was due to meet Van, Henlein was in Berlin receiving further lessons on how best to dupe the English. On 15 May he returned to Germany to report to Hitler on the success of his mission.[25]

Van, Christie and Henlein met over dinner.[26] Van chastised Henlein: 'he had of late been no longer ostensibly the moderate Henlein that I had known and appreciated in previous years'. He attempted to wean Henlein away from the Karlsbad programme which 'exceeded the bounds of the possible'. The Western powers, Van assured him, were now acting in concert, and as a consequence 'serious offers' would be 'forthcoming' from the Czech government. Van stressed the necessity of isolating 'the perfectly legitimate question of the rectification of the internal grievances of the Sudeten Deutsch' from general questions of foreign policy. Only by so doing could war be avoided. This was perhaps the essence of Van's message.

Henlein took the point. He must have played his part to per-fection, the role of a basically moderate politician, concerned only to protect his people's rights but persistently harassed by rabid extrem-ists in Berlin and within his own party. Throughout their four hours of conversation, Van found him 'far more reasonable and amenable' than he had dared to hope for. They parted 'on as friendly terms as ever'.

Summing up the results of the discussion, Van proposed an even-handed policy: to persuade the Czech government to 'take its opportunity', while at the same time exerting pressure on Berlin 'not

---

* At Karlsbad, on 24 April, Henlein presented his eight-point-programme. It included: full equality of status for Germans and Czechs; delimitation of the German areas; full autonomy; removal of all injustices and reparation for damage suffered by the Germans since 1918; the right of the Germans to pro-claim their 'Germanism' and their adherence to the ideology of Germany; and the complete revision of Czech foreign policy.

to interfere with any acceptable solution'. On one point however he was categorical. Under no circumstances could British policy allow the 'dismemberment of Czechoslovakia with a view to facilitating Germany's eastward drive for which the complete domination of Europe is a prerequisite'. Such a catastrophe, which Britain had fought for centuries to avoid, would reduce her to the status of a second-class power. He concluded: 'I feel, however, that there is now some slight chance of avoiding this fatal consummation by means other than the alternative method of preventing it which would probably mean a European war.' He hardly exuded confidence. But it is clear that Henlein the moderate still played a large part in his calculations to avoid war; and he remained in contact with him through intermediaries such as Christie and Prince Hohenlohe, a Bohemian landowner, until mid-August, encouraging him to accept the British attempt at mediation through the Runciman mission.[27]

Three main points emerge from this discussion which are worthy of emphasis. Van had in effect committed himself to a measure of local autonomy for the Sudeten Germans, though he carefully refrained from entering into precise details of the internal settlement. He also made clear that the Western powers were prepared to exert pressure (he did not of course use such an indelicate turn of phrase) on the Czechs to adopt a more flexible attitude. But equally he was determined to prevent a repetition of the *Anschluss;* there could be no question of ceding Czech territories to Germany. The problem was fundamentally an internal one, to be settled by the parties in dispute in conjunction with the powers.

During the following months his attitude did not basically alter, but his sources continued to provide him with conclusive evidence that Hitler would not be satisfied merely with rectifying Sudeten Germans' grievances, but that he was bent on destroying Czechoslovakia by war.[28] On 18 August Ewald von Kleist-Schmewzin, another German visitor, revealed to him Hitler's timetable: 'After the 27th September it will be too late.'[29] Van was impressed, though not surprised. Von Kleist had only confirmed what he already knew. Other government figures did not take von Kleist's warning quite so seriously.[30]

Van, however, had no need of von Kleist's advice, or that of any other go-between to guide him. He had already decided on a policy of his own. Taking the July 1914 crisis as an example, he ventured to hope that disaster would not again emerge from silence.[31] It was necessary to drive home 'beyond peradventure' our attitude to Germany. As during the May crisis,* there was no other alternative but to adopt a tough line: 'If we leave Berlin under any illusion where we stand in a European war, there will be a European War.' In order to reinforce British policy, Van hinted that it might be necessary to mobilize the fleet and recall parliament.

But what if Germany should ignore the British warning, however pungently it was expressed? Just as at the time of the *Anschluss*, Van's proposals contained a large element of bluff. Moreover, as had been the case six months earlier, there was no question of a military showdown with Germany.[32] It could only be a political-diplomatic confrontation and the prize would go to the side who displayed the strongest nerves.

Van was extremely agitated at the way the government was handling the crisis. He was sleeping badly, at times only four hours a night, and was becoming increasingly dependent on drugs for his rest.[33] This could not have sharpened his judgement. In particular he was appalled at the influence Nevile Henderson seemed to exert on the Prime Minister.[34] He regarded Henderson's presence at the cabinet meeting on 30 August as 'a disastrous innovation'. The meeting was a crucial one.[35] It was decided not to give a public warning to Germany that if she invaded Czechoslovakia war would inevitably follow. The government would not go beyond Simon's Lanark speech.† Halifax pursued this theme in his usual non-com-

---

* On Henlein's return to Czechoslovakia from his visits to London and Berlin in May, disorders broke out in the Sudeten German regions. This situation, together with rumours of German troop movements and concentrations along the Czech border, led to a partial Czech mobilization. Great Britain and France took a firm stand, strongly warning Germany of the possible repercussions of her action. Germany retreated from this show of strength. The crisis blew over. It was generally interpreted as a humiliating setback for German policy. There has since developed a hot debate on the origins and motives of the crisis; whether Germany actually planned to launch an attack, or whether the Czechs provoked the crisis, or whether it was the result of jumpy nerves on both sides. What evidence there is seems to point to the latter conclusion. (See G. L. Weinberg, 'The May Crisis, 1938', *Journal of Modern History* (XXIX, 1957); W. V. Wallace, 'The Making of the May Crisis of 1938', *Slavonic and East European Review* (June, 1963); D. C. Watt, 'The May Crisis of 1938: A rejoinder to Mr. Wallace', and W. V. Wallace, 'A Reply to Mr. Watt', *Slavonic and East European Review* (July, 1966). See also D. C. Watt, 'Hitler's Visit to Rome and the May Weekend Crisis', *Journal of Contemporary History* (January, 1974).

† On 28 August Simon addressed a political demonstration at Lanark. His comments were made after consultation with Halifax. He said: 'This case of Czechoslovakia may be so critical for the future of Europe that it would be impossible to assume a limit to the disturbance that a conflict might involve, and everyone in

mittal manner, invoking Dominion hostility to intervention. Chamberlain was more decisive: 'no democratic state ought to make a threat of war unless it was both ready to carry it out and prepared to do so. This was a sound maxim.' Henderson's on-the spot evidence rounded off the 'anti-warning' attack.* Van's advice had been ignored.

For the next few days Van worked feverishly to get his view accepted. Halifax bore the main brunt of his campaign. This was an unfortunate, if inevitable, choice. Halifax's opinions ran hot and cold. Arguing with him was akin to pounding a pillow. At times he appeared to support Van, only to collapse at the critical moment before Chamberlain's authority. One senior official described him 'as a good listener and that was all. He exhausted his advisers.'[36] He most certainly must have exhausted Van. By 4 September he had succeeded in unsettling Halifax, and a note was drafted to the effect that Britain would intervene if France honoured her obligation to Czechoslovakia.[37] Van's success was short lived. Four days later Chamberlain announced to a closed circle – Halifax, Horace Wilson, Simon, and Cadogan – his intention to visit Hitler in person. Van was originally excluded from this confabulation, but was brought in, on Halifax's initiative, after Chamberlain had made his announcement. Alone among the participants, he fought the idea 'tooth and nail – "it was Henry IV going to Canossa again".'[38] But more than ever Van's was a voice in the wilderness. Estranged from Chamberlain, he had no faith in either Simon or Halifax and despised Wilson. 'It is a disaster', he told Dalton, 'that Horace Wilson had usurped my functions, and that with him is Nevile Henderson'.[39] Effectively excluded from the inner circle, Van had no one in authority to turn to. Halifax had proved to be a broken reed, and, as the crisis progressed, substantial differences emerged between himself and Cadogan.[40] To crown his misery, his old adversaries, his 'funk brigade', the Dawsons, Astors and Garvins, took courage and began to rear their heads even higher. He expressed contempt and disgust at *The Times* editorial of 7 September which suggested that the Czechs should cede the Sudeten territories outright.[41] He admitted to Dalton that his 'position had become very difficult and that he

every country who considers the consequences has to bear that in mind.' (Simon, *Retrospect*, 245.)

* It is now known that Chamberlain was already considering meeting Hitler in person to negotiate a solution. He had confided his plan to Horace Wilson and Henderson on either 29 or 30 August. Henderson thought 'it might save the situation'. (See I. Colvin, *The Chamberlain Cabinet*, 143, and *Cadogan Diaries*, 92.) If such was the case, it explains Chamberlain's opposition to an open warning. Halifax, on the other hand, was not informed until after the cabinet meeting.

could not go on indefinitely'. But he thought it was his duty to hold on for a time. If he resigned now it might seem that he was moved by personal resentment or ambition, which was not the case. His elimination from the scene would 'give great delight to the Germans and "Nevile Henderson would go through the roof with joy".'[42]

On 15 September Chamberlain flew to Germany to meet Hitler at Berchtesgaden. The last scenes of the drama were about to be enacted, but already parts of the scenario had been written. Towards the end of July Henderson had broached the idea of convening a four-power conference – Great Britain, France, Germany, and Italy – to settle the Czech problem. Van thought this a disastrous notion, and for two main reasons. First, the presence of Italy – 'She has really nothing to do with it' – would only stiffen the German attitude. Secondly, and of far greater importance, it 'would be the thin edge of the German wedge for excluding Russia from Europe'.[43] Van became increasingly preoccupied with the role the Soviet Union was destined to play in the present European crisis. He was no friend of the Soviet Union. On the contrary, he was resolutely opposed to its totalitarian system of government. But the German danger was paramount; and this demanded rallying to the democratic cause every potential ally. Two days before Chamberlain set out for Canossa, Van forecast in prophetic terms the consequences of his actions.

If the German spirit were fundamentally changed, there would be no objection to any form of conference or pact which tended to a solution of any specific question. But that spirit has *not* changed. In fact every hour that we live demonstrates more clearly that it is Germany, not Russia, that threatens the physical existence of every country and of its individual citizens. So long as this is the case it would surely be an unpardonable folly to assist Germany in driving off the map an associate whose weight we may need. It is precisely for this reason that Germany is trying to exclude Russia. If we lend ourselves to the beginning of this process, the future is fairly obvious – in two stages. In the first, Russia will be evicted and retire into sulky isolation. In the second she will be penetrated by Germany, and Bismarck's traditional policy of close Russo-German relations will follow. The consequences to Europe are too obvious to need enlargement here.[44]

Van was deliberately excluded from a Foreign Office conference the day Chamberlain left for Germany. On his return, Halifax hesitated whether or not to sanction his participation in the Anglo-French consultations, fearing that Van's oppositionist voice would mar the proceedings. Finally, it was agreed, after sounding out Chamberlain, to allow Van to attend, but only after Halifax had conveyed to him a 'severe warning'.[45] There is no record, however, of his having contributed to the discussion.[46] But there is a slight indication that he attempted to cook the proceedings in a more roundabout way. On 16 September Harvey, Halifax's private secretary, was informed that a message had arrived at Denham Place from Paris which hinted that if Daladier, the French premier, was being invited over for talks it was most important 'that his second man' (Bonnet?)* should not accompany him, and that any telegram to Paris on this subject should be delayed until Van arrived at the Foreign Office to clarify the situation in person.[47] This was most mysterious. Was it a ruse on the part of Van and Alexis Léger to stiffen the French delegation by excluding the defeatist Bonnet? Given the solitary nature of Van's position, this assumption is not as implausible as it first appears. Cadogan at least had cause to complain to Halifax of Van's intrigues with Léger.[48] Nevertheless, Bonnet accompanied Daladier, and his contributions to the discussions amply confirmed Van's estimation that the French 'were weak, especially Bonnet'.[49]

If Van failed to stiffen the French, he had not altogether abandoned hope of modifying the stand of his own government. Throughout this period he was in constant contact with the parliamentary opposition, both Labour and Conservative. He had known Churchill well for many years. In 1933 Van had been elected a member of the Other Club. Throughout the 1930's Churchill was a welcome visitor at Park Street; and he would often visit Van's room in the Foreign Office where he would 'test' his speeches before a critical but highly sympathetic audience of one. His meetings with Churchill, 'in cigar-smoke-filled rooms', were fairly common knowledge, though Van later was forced to concede that they 'cost me more than he knew'.[50] But Van also saw much of Dalton.[51] There was an air of conspiracy about these clandestine meetings. Of course the government was quite aware of his contacts with the dissidents of both parties. That they were not stopped was perhaps a reflection of his standing and reputation in the Office, though it has been pointed out that 'there was something in the atmosphere of the F.O. which

---

* Georges Bonnet (1889–1973): French politician; Minister of Finance, 1933; of Commerce, 1935: Ambassador to United States, 1937; Minister of Foreign Affairs, April 1938–September 1939. Considered by most observers as the archetypal appeaser of the 1930's.

allowed this ... [but it] would never have happened at the Home Office.'[52]

Dalton, an old colleague who held similar views, was an attentive listener to Van's angry tirades against his chiefs. When the Labour leaders met Chamberlain, Van hoped that Dalton 'would speak frankly'. He did, taking his guide from Van's briefings. The meeting itself was barren of any positive result, though Chamberlain was quite forthcoming: 'If we can avert war now, we are not certain that it will come later.' Dalton delighted Van by quoting Chamberlain: ' "I don't know whether any of you play poker", then looking at me direct, "perhaps Dalton does. Well what Henderson said to me was: If Hitler is bluffing, at any rate he has got a full house in his hand".'[53] Innocence in cards as in politics was a sure recipe for disaster.

Chamberlain's belief that he could 'avert war now' led him to Godesburg and later to Munich. The only course left open to Van was to continue to issue stern warnings.[54] But the most he achieved was to ensure that the fleet moved to Alexandria, a safety precaution as during the Ethiopian crisis, gaining Cadogan's and Chamberlain's consent after the event.[55] This was a mere gesture, symbolic of his real position, for he had been advocating the mobilization of the fleet since early August.[56] As the journeys to Canossa progressed uninterrupted, Foreign Office circles close to Van whispered among themselves a ditty describing Chamberlain's shuttle-diplomacy:

> 'If at first you can't concede,
> Fly, fly, fly, again.'[57]

As news of the Munich settlement* trickled through to London, Van's first thoughts were: 'The past is past. It is a terrible past but

---

* Following the first two Hitler–Chamberlain meetings at Berchtesgaden and Godesburg, a week of acute international tension followed, when it appeared as though the powers were tottering over the brink into war. Further Anglo-French consultations were held on 26 September. Chamberlain appealed for a conference so that the cession of the Sudeten German areas, already agreed upon in principle at Berchtesgaden, might be effected by discussion not force. On the 27th Roosevelt broached Hitler, as did Mussolini on the 28th after he himself was tackled by Chamberlain and Roosevelt. Hitler succumbed. On 29th September the four powers, Great Britain, France, Italy, and Germany, met at Munich to decide the fate of Czechoslovakia; the Russians and the Czechs were excluded. The agreement was signed soon after midnight. By it Germany would occupy the areas she claimed between 1–10 October under conditions supervised by an international commission which would also determine the plebiscite areas. As a result of the agreement, the Germans gained the vital Czech frontier fortress, important industrial–military installations, 10,000 square miles of Czech territory, and approximately 3·5 million extra population of whom about 700,000

we must forget about it. The next country that is going to be bumped
off is England. If we start recriminations we shall create splits. What
we have to do is to come together for the next danger.'[58] He urged
Harold Nicolson to shelve his differences with Chamberlain and
serve under him in a Government of Reconstruction. Nicolson
thought this plea 'very noble', but he hit out strongly at Chamberlain in a speech the following day for having ignored the warnings
of Van 'who had been consistently right', and for having listened
to Wilson, 'whose advice was never inconvenient'. Van accepted
Nicolson's praise philosophically: 'Nothing could make my position
worse than it is.' He forecast war within a year.[59]

The remaining months before the outbreak of war saw no improvement in his fortunes. Papers he sent to Chamberlain were returned
to him apparently unread.[60] He described the proceedings of the
international commission, defining the plebiscite areas in Czechoslovakia, as 'scandalous'.[61] Van had never ceased to believe that
Hitler's aim was to wipe Czechoslovakia off the map. During the
early weeks of 1939 his intelligence sources confirmed the persistent
rumours that Hitler finally intended to strike westwards.[62] By 20
February his voices told him that Hitler had resolved to liquidate
Czechoslovakia.[63] Once again, it was Christie who was supplying
the bulk of the information, though now ably assisted by T. P.
Conwell-Evans.* Conwell-Evans reported to Van in remarkably
prescient terms that

> Hitler had decided to devour the remains of Czechoslovakia in
> the very near future. The method which Hitler intends to adopt
> is to stir up a movement for independence among the Slovaks.
> Czech resistance to these claims will then give Hitler the oppor-
> tunity to intervene *manu militari*, or in other words to invade the
> remains of Czechoslovakia.[64]

---

were Czechs. The Western powers undertook to guarantee the new Czech
state. Polish and Hungarian claims were cashed on 2 and 9 October, the Poles
occupying Teschen, the Hungarians a strip of southern Slovakia and Ruthenia.
(For details of the settlement, see *B.D.*, 3, ii, no. 1227 and appendices.)

* Conwell-Evans had lectured at Konigsberg University from 1932–34. He was an
early admirer of Hitler and Nazi Germany and had a wide and influential
range of contacts in the German Foreign Ministry. As secretary of the Anglo-
German fellowship he had arranged Lord Lothian's trips to Germany, and had
keenly pursued the goal of Anglo-German friendship. At the height of the
Czech crisis, by now disillusioned with Nazi Germany, he became an active
'anti-appeaser'. His contacts with Van date from this period. From then
on they remained in close touch, Conwell-Evans being added to Van's list of
sources.

Cadogan tended to belittle the reliability of the sources.[65] And in truth the multiplicity of information forecasting where Hitler would strike next was confusing. But early in March the indications mounted that Czechoslovakia was now the main focus for German activity, with the week 12–19 March set as the most probable time for the occupation of Bohemia and Moravia.[66] The conquest was executed on 15 March, roughly in accordance with Conwell-Evans' predictions. The main weight of Van's wrath was turned against Henderson. He asked for the Ambassador's immediate return from Berlin. Henderson had failed in his most elementary duties. He had misled the government, 'leading us up the garden path again', by giving a hopelessly over-optimistic evaluation of the situation which made 'wellnigh incredible reading' after the latest German *coup*. His own warnings had been rejected. 'Nothing seems any good', he plaintively cried, 'it seems as if nobody will listen to or believe me. I shall never know why.'[67] But at least there was a generous acknowledgement from Cadogan, who had consistently fought Van since his appointment as PUS, sometimes in the most bitter terms: 'I must say it is turning out – at present – as Van predicted and as I never believed it would. If we want to stem the German expansion, I believe we must try to build a dam *now*.'[68]

The dam to which Cadogan referred was connected with the twin problems of Poland and the negotiations for a Soviet agreement. These questions stood at the centre of British diplomatic activity during the spring and summer of 1939. The final destruction of Czechoslovakia had led to a fresh burst of diplomatic initiative. On 17 March the Rumanian minister to London, M. Tilea, informed Orme Sargent and Van that his government had reason to believe that Germany intended to 'enslave' Hungary and to 'destroy' Rumania. What, he queried, did the British government propose to do in such an eventuality?[69] The response came swiftly enough, and in a quite unprecedented manner. A wave of British guarantees swept across eastern and south-eastern Europe: to Poland on 31 March; to Greece and Rumania on 13 April;* while on 12 May an Anglo-Turkish mutual assistance pact was concluded. Here was a definite British commitment which, if honoured, would deny to Hitler further easy pickings in Europe.

---

* The guarantees to Greece and Rumania followed immediately after the Italian invasion of Albania on 7 April. There was, however, a popular misconception at the time that the policies of the two Axis powers were coordinated, and the guarantees were intended as much to warn Germany as to limit further Italian expansion.

But the Anglo-French alliance system made little sense without the active cooperation of the Soviet Union. Only a cursory glance at the map of Europe sufficed to substantiate this elementary point. Certainly Van held no doubts on this score. Since, and even before the Munich settlement he had argued fervently in favour of including the Russians in any arrangement to check Germany. German threats towards Poland in the winter of 1938–39 only reinforced his convictions, for he was fully conversant with the minutest details of the German–Polish negotiations and the nature of the German demands.*

Not everyone shared Van's enthusiasm for a Soviet connection. In most official circles distrust of the Soviet Union ran deep. But the case for embarking on meaningful negotiations with the Russians was overwhelming. Parliamentary voices from the extreme left to oppositionist Conservatives called for the inclusion of the Soviet Union in an anti-German front, and their cries did not go unheeded by the public.[70] Moreover, it was known that the French were angling after a mutual assistance pact with the Russians, and the British were apprehensive about being dragged into a Russian alliance on the coat-tails of the French. It was a combination of these factors which induced the government to commence, albeit reluctantly, negotiations with the Soviet Union in April. The first British proposal required them to declare that, in the event of an act of aggression against any of her neighbours, Soviet assistance would be forthcoming 'if desired'.[71] This was tantamount to demanding a unilateral Soviet guarantee of Eastern Europe without reciprocal compensation for the Russians, for what if Soviet intervention was not 'desired', as was clearly the case with Poland and Rumania. The British had no unequivocal answer to this riddle.

---

* German pressure on Poland began to build up at the end of October 1938 when Ribbentrop presented to Joseph Lipski, the Polish Ambassador in Berlin, two main demands: the return of Danzig to the Reich; and the construction of a German extra-territorial road and railway link across the corridor to East Prussia. These demands were construed by the Poles as directly threatening their independence. The talks continued throughout the winter with Beck, the Polish Foreign Minister, stubbornly refusing to be browbeaten by the Germans. During March the pressure was increased. The occupation of Prague and the annexation of Memel (21 March) brought matters to a head. The British guarantee to Poland followed. On 28 April Hitler retaliated by abrogating the German–Polish agreement of 1934, and the Anglo-German naval agreement of 1935. The Polish question now became crucial; but the enigma of the Soviet Union hamstrung the Powers' response. See Van's minutes of 7 December 1938, Vnst. 2/39; of 17 February 1939, F.O. 371/22964, C. 1709/15/18; of 15 June 1939, Vnst. 2/43.

But the Russians did. Moscow responded by calling for a comprehensive political agreement between Great Britain, France, and the Soviet Union, to include a military convention which would cover acts of aggression against any one of the signatories or against any East European state situated between the Baltic and Black seas. The Foreign Office regarded this proposal with extreme unease, while Chamberlain's main preoccupation was how the offer 'might be most diplomatically rejected'.[72] It was not until mid-May that the cabinet finally accepted the idea of a triple pact. It now remained to work out the details.

Initially, Van tolerated the official line. But he quickly became disturbed at the delay in reaching an understanding with Russia. More than anything, he was apprehensive that Russia would relapse 'into isolation' from which she would emerge by establishing 'closer relations with Germany'.[73] For these reasons Van plumped for an early and successful conclusion of the talks.

It was the last factor which took precedence over all others. In Van's view a Soviet–German connection would be 'absolutely fatal'. There was nothing original in this analysis. The possibility of the revolutionary forces of Nazi Germany and Bolshevik Russia combining to overwhelm Western Europe had long been debated in the Foreign Office. Perhaps Van was more alive to this danger than most of his colleagues. By the middle of May, one of his intelligence contacts – this time 'an entirely reliable source' in the German General Staff – confirmed that German–Soviet negotiations had reached an advanced stage and the parties were on the verge of agreement.[74]

It was the ubiquitous Christie who was urging Van on.[75] Van lost no time in reporting to Halifax the gist of his information. According to this report, the Czech general, Jan Sirovny, was acting as the chief intermediary between Moscow and Berlin. The proposed deal was based on four points: the partition of Poland; Soviet annexation of Bessarabia; Soviet domination of the Dardanelles and the Bosphorus; and a German undertaking to aid a Russian invasion of India. Hitler, the report continued, was so confident of German military strength and national unity that he no longer feared collaboration with Russia, and even believed that it 'would be possible to Nazify Russia as a step towards world domination'. Much remains to be clarified about the exact state of German–Soviet relations at this stage;[76] but it is clear that the programme here outlined ran far in advance of anything yet decided upon, though it may well have reflected the basic aims of the protagonists of the alliance. What is certain is that the sudden spate and strength of these rumours forced the cabinet to take the Soviet negotiations far more seriously.

On the same day that Van informed Halifax of Christie's report, the Foreign Policy Committee of the cabinet authorized him to begin informal negotiations with Maisky to prepare the ground for joint Anglo-French-Soviet military talks, initially to guarantee Poland and Rumania but not excluding the possibility of extending the guarantee to other European countries.[77] There was little to distinguish between these proposals and the full-blown alliance the Soviets were demanding. By 24 May the cabinet too had reached this conclusion, and accepted in principle the idea of a Soviet alliance.[78] The decision had been taken tardily and grudgingly, and the oncoming negotiations, though raised as it were to a new level, were conducted with little conviction and even less enthusiasm.*

All this was noted by Van. He predicted war 'in or before September'. Only 'by sufficiently impressing the Germans' could the catastrophe be avoided. He suggested the immediate conclusion of an Anglo-Russian alliance. As for the Poles, who were being subjected to intolerable pressure, he even proposed doing 'something rather striking, such as giving [them] as a free gift a certain number of aeroplanes'. This would create a 'dramatic impression' of sufficient weight to deter the Germans.[79]

From mid-June the tone of his minutes became more jittery. Christie was bombarding him with reports, at least one a week, occasionally more. All related the same story with slight variations: intensive German preparations for a *coup* against Poland coupled with the danger of a German–Soviet alliance.[80] On 15 June he heard similar information about Hitler's plans but from a different source. That evening, at the Kensington home of Conwell-Evans he met the two German diplomatists, Erich and Theo Kordt. Hitler, Van was assured, had already taken concrete steps to secure the cooperation of the Soviet Union. This would safeguard his eastern flank and enable him to crush Poland without effective intervention from the West. Only an Anglo-Soviet alliance was likely to curb Hitler's ambitions. Here was direct confirmation from the *Wilhelmstrasse* of Van's own fears. He appeased the Kordts. The

---

* One factor which reinforced the government's hesitancy was the attitude of the Dominions. During the negotiations it had become clear that, with the exception of New Zealand, the Dominions were opposed to an alliance with Russia for fear of becoming involved in a war in Eastern Europe which, they argued, was of no concern to their vital interests. See R. Ovendale, *'Appeasement' and the English Speaking World* (Cardiff, 1975), 271.

British government, he confidently declared, was taking the Soviet negotiations very seriously; an agreement would be forthcoming.[81]

It has been asserted that Van lied to the Kordts, deliberately inflating the possibility of a Soviet agreement[82] and by so doing lulled the German conspirators into a false sense of security that there would be no war in 1939. But this is surely to misconstrue the situation. It is more logical to conclude that Van was not privy to the exact stage the negotiations had reached, and was simply expressing his own view of what should happen. If the fault lay anywhere, it lay in the Kordts' estimation of Van as a creditworthy vehicle of communication with those in authority. This was a wholly erroneous assumption, and Theo Kordt, resident in London, should have been aware of the fact. The Kordts' message contained nothing substantially new. In any case, every item of intelligence, however thin in content and however obscure the source, ultimately found its way to either Halifax or Chamberlain. The cloak-and-dagger style of the Kensington parley added little to Van's credibility as a reliable source. It is surely a measure of his loss of influence that he played, and was allowed to play, these subterranean games with such verve. For the sad truth was that there was little else for him to do. At this stage his admonitions had reached the point of diminishing returns.

On 22 August, the day news first reached London about the German–Soviet pact, Van was called in for the 'first time' for discussions at 10 Downing Street.[83] The situation was now clearly critical, though in Chamberlain's opinion the pact had not altered anything.[84] It is not too difficult to understand why Van was now brought into the inner circle. Events had developed pretty much as he had forecast, or rather in accordance with Christie's intelligence reports. As early as 27 June Christie had disclosed that war against Poland had been postponed until the beginning of September, the interval to be exploited to conduct a war of nerves against the West. Accompanying this political directive was a military one, by which the German armed forces would be placed on a full war basis (*Kriegsbereit*) from 27 August onwards.[85] By 17 August Christie, taking Ritter as his guide, was able to quote chapter and verse from the Italian-German talks held at Salzburg and the Berghof earlier in the month.[86] According to Ritter, the Italians were afraid that Hitler would unleash a European war for which they were unprepared. Hitler brushed aside the Italian anxieties: he would localize the Polish problem and the West would not intervene. All that he required from Italy was that she should adopt a position of benevolent neutrality when the crisis broke. Having thus demolished the Italian argument, or so he thought, Hitler set the date for the attack against Poland.* On the evening of the 18th, Van, in a state of high excitement, contacted Cadogan and Halifax and informed them that Hitler would strike between 25–28 August. Cadogan attempted to calm Van down, noting caustically: 'This is the beginning of the "War of Nerves". And I have seen the first casualty.'[87]

Van now wished to take the initiative in two ways. First, to warn Hitler in the most categorical terms that any action against Poland would spark off a European war. He was in favour of despatching a high-ranking, forceful personality to Berlin to warn Hitler in person, perhaps as a means of by-passing Henderson. General Ironside's[†] name was mentioned as a possible candidate. This never materialized. Henderson remained the official channel of communication with the German government. Secondly, Van wished to deepen the gap between Hitler and Mussolini, a time-worn theme of his. Earlier in the year he had opposed the Chamberlain–Halifax visit to Rome which ostensibly had the same purpose.[88] Now he drafted a telegram of 'pure appeasement to Rome'. It was never sent. The following day Sir Percy Loraine expressed confidence, rightly as it turned out, that Mussolini would not fight.[89]

On 26 August the ever resourceful Christie conveyed to Van precise details about Germany's operational plans against Poland. The German generals were confident of total success. Within three weeks a *Cannae* was predicted for the Polish armies 'somewhere around Warsaw'.[90] On 1 September, without any declaration of war, the German armies struck deep into Poland. Two days later Great

---

* Christie's information was remarkably accurate. Ciano, the Italian Foreign Minister, met Ribbentrop at Salzburg and Hitler at the Berghof between 11–13 August. The talks followed in general the lines related above. But Ciano was not deceived by the German assurances: 'I return to Rome completely disgusted with the Germans, with their leader, and with their way of doing things. They have betrayed us and lied to us. Now they are dragging us into a venture which we do not want...' By 21 August, a report had reached Henderson that Hitler had fixed the 25th as the date for the attack on Poland (Cmd 6115, para 24). It was not, however, until 23 August that Hitler finally set the date to attack Poland on the 26th. At Bechtesgaden he had merely spoken of solving the crisis at the end of August. See, A. Bullock, *Hitler. A Study in Tyranny* (London, 1969, Pelican ed.) 519–22, 529, and M. Muggeridge, ed., *Ciano's Diary, 1938–1943* (London, 1947), 124–25.

† William Edmund Ironside (1880–1959): governor and commander in chief, Gibraltar, 1938–39; Chief of Imperial General Staff, 1939–40; C.-in-C., Home Forces, 1940. Cr. Baron, 1941.

Britain and France were at war with Germany. By the end of the month the Polish campaign was over. That unhappy country had been crushed and partitioned by its two more powerful neighbours. The first battle of the European war Van had for so long prophesied was over.

Post mortems on the causes of the war were soon forthcoming. Sir Nevile Henderson set the pace. On 20 September he wrote a final account 'on the circumstance leading to the termination of his mission to Berlin'.[91] Covering more than twenty-six pages, it reads, as it was no doubt intended, as an apologia for the policy which Henderson represented and believed in. The tone and substance of Henderson's report roused Van to refute it, and in doing so he initiated a debate in the Foreign Office, remarkable for its unanimity of opinion, on the 'Origins of Germany's Fifth War'.[92]

Underlying Van's thesis was the basic fact that the present war was no accident, a notion suggested by Henderson.[93]

> Nothing could be further from the truth, [Van countered]. There was no brainstorm and no accident. From the advent of the Nazi régime . . . there was never the least chance that any course could or would be pursued other than that which was, in fact, pursued, step by step, with remorseless, systematic, calculated tenacity . . . it is on this view that I have from the first differed fundamentally from Sir N. Henderson and from all those here who have been of this persuasion. For the theory of accident is implicit in the doctrine of appeasement, which is necessarily motivated by the idea that, if only Germany could be satiated with instalments, she would become 'somehow good', and peace would be preserved.

If the war was not accidental, what then was its origin? It lay in Germany's recent history, for she 'has made five wars in seventy-five years', and 'Her percentage of responsibility has varied between 100 per cent and 80 per cent'. And why were these calculated wars sprung upon the world? 'Because three generations of Germans have desired to dominate the world. There was never any excuse for blinking this fact. Yet it *was* blinked, though Hitler was perfectly explicit in *Mein Kampf*.' There was a logical consequence to this lust for domination:

> No country can dominate the world without first destroying the British Empire. The Soviets too recognised that from the start; and, since both Nazism and Communism have always desired, and always must desire, to 'liquidate' us, there is nothing surprising in their latest alliance.

These successive wars were possible

> Because the Prussian military caste and system are always there on
> The Day, always ready spiritually, if ready materially, to lend
> themselves to the profession of Conquest for which they have been
> trained and hardened. So long as that system remains intact or
> unregenerate, the world can never be long at peace . . . we are
> fighting the German Army and the German people on whom the
> Army is based. We are fighting the *real*, and not the 'accidental',
> Germany. That the real Germany contains many good individual
> Germans is, of course, incontestable. The trouble is that they are
> never there corporatively on The Day, irrespective of the treat-
> ment Germany has received during the preceding years. History
> makes this incontestably plain.

All these facts led to one inescapable conclusion.

> Providence has twice been kind to us. We cannot count on a third
> indulgence to 'wishful' blindness. We must eradicate not only
> Hitlerism, but Prussianism, lest a Sixth War be that hitherto
> impossible thing, the Blitzkrieg in the West, which would take
> unaware democracy, ever unready for the recurrent 'Day' by
> its very nature and procedure.
>   These reluctant truths by the nature of things – for the nature
> of things political is peculiar – cannot have the same notoriety as
> the myth of accidentalism; but they should at least be known –
> lest once more 'the clouds return after the rain'. For one of the
> origins of Germany's Fifth War was the illusions that were cher-
> ished about her.

None of the officials – the German experts, Ivone Kirkpatrick*
and William Strang,† and Cadogan – who commented on Van's
paper seriously dissented from its contents. Indeed, they trod very
much in his path. Cadogan again graciously conceded that 'Nearly
everything that Sir R. Vansittart writes about the past is undeniably

---

* Ivone Augustine Kirkpatrick (1897–1964): entered diplomatic service, 1919;
  First secretary at British Embassy, Berlin, 1933–38; Assistant Under Secretary
  of State at Foreign Office, 1945; Permanent Under Secretary, 1953–57. Kn.
  1948.
† William Strang (1893–   ): entered Foreign Office, 1919; counsellor at
  British Embassy, Moscow, 1930; Head of Central Department, Foreign Office,
  1937–39; Assistant Under Secretary of State, 1939–43; Permanent Under Secretary, 1949–53. Kn. 1943. Cr. Baron, 1954.

right'. But he asked: 'How did Van propose to eradicate "Prussian-ism"?' Kirkpatrick was not so 'pessimistic as to believe that Germany must be wholly destroyed, and for ever, if we are to preserve peace in Europe' (not that Van suggested such a measure), while Strang thought that there would be no solution to the German problem 'until the evils of war are unmistakably brought home to the German people on German soil in a far greater degree than in 1918'.

As could be expected, Van did not shrink from committing himself where others hesitated. He gave a clearcut answer to Cadogan's query. Germany must be occupied and the ascendency of Prussia destroyed. In Van's phrase: 'Don't break up Germany: break up Prussia, and do it good and proper.' This would be realized by the creation of a German federation, a reversal to the pre-Bismarckian era, as a sure means of breaking for ever Prussia's hegemony over Germany.

These basic ideas about how to settle the German problem, ideas which Van scarcely deviated from during the course of the war, were influenced by a memorandum submitted by the 'South German group' and transmitted to him by Christie. It is difficult to identify the exact composition of this group, but it is certain that they were all Christie's men and that Christie maintained contact with them in Switzerland. Among them were: Prince Max Hohenlohe; Dr Joseph Wirth, the ex-Reichskanzler; Fritz Thyssen, the industrialist; Hermann Rauschning; and Hans Ritter. The main points of their programme may thus be summarized: the occupation of Germany, including Berlin; the complete demilitarization of Germany; the elimination of the Nazi party, root and branch; and the creation of a German federation. Van welcomed these general principles, though he was less happy with the group's territorial ambitions which included retention of the Sudetenland and the Polish corridor. He also did not entirely exclude the possibility of a French annexation of the left bank of the Rhine.[94]

The faintest suggestion of a compromise peace with the aggressor brought forth a strong reaction. Beaverbrook, who was flirting with such ideas in March 1940, was stigmatized as a member of 'the Fifth Column'.[95] Similarly, his answer to the Sumner Welles mission* was an indignant paper entitled, appropriately, 'The Nature of the

---

* Welles's mission was to obtain first-hand information of developments in Europe, to investigate the possibility of concluding a negotiated peace, and to ensure that Italy remained neutral. During February–March he visited London, Paris, Rome, and Berlin. On his return to Washington he reported to Cordell Hull and Roosevelt that there was no basis at that time for successful negotiations.

Beast'.[96] His views sharpened with each new German aggression. On the day the Germans invaded Norway and Denmark, he wrote to Halifax:

> I hope that what has happened today will be a final lesson to the innocents at home and abroad . . . who say that we must not aim at splitting up Germany, and that we should declare our anaemic intentions. We should on no account declare anything of the sort, and we should most certainly aim at splitting up Germany if we possibly can. If we can't small nations will continue to get their throats cut by this accursed German race.

His passions now thoroughly aroused, Van swept on to indulge in a turn of phrase which was later to cost him dear.

> This is not due to sin, but to a refusal to swallow the hard fact that eighty per cent of the German race are the political and moral scum of the earth. You cannot reform them by signatures and concessions. They have got to be hamstrung and broken up. So long as they remain coherent, the same 'skin game' will go on and on, and the world will continue to be the uninhabitable place that one race of bone-headed aggressors has made it for the last three generations.[97]

The dramatic events of April–June 1940 seemed to vindicate his almost blanket condemnation of 'the German race'. The German offensive in the West opened on 10 May. Within six weeks the German panzer divisions had cut through France and stood poised to strike across the English Channel. By mid-June the remnants of the Allied forces had been evacuated from Dunkirk. France had fallen; German armies lorded it over the entire Continent from the Atlantic to the Vistula. Great Britain stood alone against the might of the new German Empire.

For Van the fall of France was not only a political-military disaster of the first magnitude, it was also a personal tragedy. 'Chips' Channon had taunted him about France, 'his great love' and 'treacherous mistress'. Yes, Van acknowledged, 'they had had a lover's quarrel'.[98] Some days prior to this conversation Van had been involved in an attempt to patch up the quarrel. On 14 June he, together with Desmond Morton, Jean Monnet, and René Pleven, had drafted a declaration of union between Great Britain and France. It was presented to the French two days later. Although it called for an 'indissoluble union' between the two countries, it was in fact little more than a tactical stratagem to boost French morale and ensure her continued participation in the struggle against Germany. The proposal was received with varying degrees of stupefaction and annoyance on both sides of the Channel. By 23 June, only a week after the cabinet had approved the draft, Halifax assured a worried Hankey that the idea was 'completely dead'.[99] By the end of the month, when it became clear that the British would have to take action against the French fleet,* Van bade farewell to the *entente cordiale* in an emotional outburst which was published in *The Times* on 29 June.

Van also found little joy in the fact that his old confidant, Winston Churchill, was now Prime Minister.† Churchill did not put himself out to accommodate Van. It was said of him that he chose to surround himself with yes-men, preferring harmony to the controversy at the top. 'How do you fit a square peg into a round hole,' was one explanation for Churchill's neglect of Van.[100] Even with the change in government he remained an outsider. Dalton, who had admitted to being a 'Vanite',[101] was the one politician to whom he could turn for comfort. The Labour leader showed great patience and sympathy, but Van's never-ending tales of woe and personal misfortune led him to conclude that 'Van is a little egocentric in these days'.[102] Another friend and colleague believed that his prolonged period of 'non-employment' had resulted in 'a long phase of persecution mania'.[103] This seemed to be a generally accepted verdict of his frame of mind.

Eventually, he was found a job, of sorts. In addition to the Ministry of Economic Warfare, Churchill had asked Dalton to take charge of the Special Operations Executive (SOE).‡ He agreed to take Van on as his chief adviser, largely as a result of Rex Leeper's

* The French fleet, which lay at anchor at Portsmouth, Alexandria, Oran, and Mers-el-Kébir, was either seized or destroyed by British forces between 3–4 July. The heaviest French losses in men and ships occurred at Oran on 3 July.

† Churchill had been raised to the premiership on 10 May as a result of the debate in the House of Commons on the Norwegian fiasco. The government scraped through with a greatly reduced majority of eighty-one, a result widely interpreted as a vote of no confidence in Chamberlain's government.

‡ SOE was divided into two sections. SO1 (its name was later changed to Political Warfare Executive, PWE) was responsible for propaganda to enemy and enemy-occupied territories; Rex Leeper was put in charge, mainly at Van's instigation, and Richard Crossman worked under him. Gladwyn Jebb was in charge of the second section SO2, which coordinated all subversive and sabotage activity against the enemy overseas. Regarding Leeper's section, Dalton recalled: 'I often found the atmosphere highly charged with personal rivalries, and with apprehensive jealousy, often fully reciprocated, of other departments.' See *The Fateful Years*, 368.

persistent campaigning on his behalf, but also because of the unsuit-
ability of the alternative candidate, General Edward Spears.[104]*
It was not a happy appointment. Van was soon quarrelling with
two of Dalton's top subordinates, Gladwyn Jebb and Richard Crossman. Jebb, Van reflected, had 'got on so fast that he is bound to
have caused some jealousy.'[105]

His relations with Crossman were more complex. Crossman was
responsible for the propaganda campaign against Germany. He was
stationed at Woburn Abbey in the stables, and travelled to London
once a week to consult his superiors. As his work was also carried
out in conjunction with the Foreign Office, Van became a kind of
supervisor over Crossman's work. Their views clashed violently
over the character of the German-directed propaganda. Crossman,
a self-assertive intellectual with a mind of his own, explained that
although he recognized the fact that Nazism was supported by the
mass of the German people, he yet wished to exploit every opportunity to drive a wedge between Hitler and oppositionist elements
inside Germany which he was convinced did exist.[106] Van held no
such conviction. His faith in the ability of the German opposition to
act decisively against Hitler was nil. He believed it to be a virtually
non-existent and in any case totally ineffective entity. His debate with
Crossman often became acrimonious. Relations between them
soured, and this in turn affected his standing with Dalton – 'this
[quarrelling] is beginning to bore me'[107] – a good friend whom he
could ill afford to lose. There can be little doubt that by the end of
the year Van had succeeded in alienating almost all who came into
close contact with him.

In November–December 1940, on the authority of Duff Cooper,
Minister of Information, Van broadcast a series of seven talks on the
overseas service of the BBC to the English speaking peoples. Extracts
from the broadcasts appeared simultaneously in the *Sunday Times*.
Later, in January, the talks were published under the title: *Black
Record. Germans Past and Present. Black Record* aroused violent controversy from the outset. J. B. Priestley, who happened to be present
during a recording, stalked out of the studio in disgust at what he
had heard, slamming the door behind him.[108] The Dominion High
Commissioners were also upset by it; Cadogan thought it 'vulgar

* Edward Louis Spears (1886–1974): Brigadier-General, 1918; Conservative
M.P., 1931–45; Churchill's personal representative to French government,
May–June 1940; to General de Gaulle, 1940; Minister to Syria and Lebanon,
1942–44. Kn. 1942. Cr. Baronet, 1953.

and ridiculous'; while Halifax, who eventually sanctioned its publication, cautioned Van about its unrestrained language.[109]

Even today *Black Record* makes strong reading. To those conversant
with Van's thoughts and writings on this topic, the subject matter
of the pamphlet is all too familiar, and is almost identical in content
with his paper, the 'Origins of Germany's Fifth War'. Comparing
Germany with a butcher-bird 'which was steadily destroying all
its fellows',[110] he certified that Hitler was no accident. 'He is the
natural and continuous produce of a breed which from the dawn of
history has been predatory and bellicose.' And Van did indeed delve
into 'the dawn of history' to make his point. He cited Tacitus as an
authority: 'they [the Germanic tribes] think it weak to win with
sweat what can be won with blood'. He noted two further absolute
truths about the Germans: their unlimited urge for *Lebensraum*, and
the fact that 'they never kept a pledge or treaty'. What drove the
Germans to this barbaric behaviour? 'Envy, Self-Pity and Cruelty',
he answered confidently, these were the three characteristics which
typified the German psyche.

Van did not deny that there were good, individual Germans:

> Of course there have been, and are, Germans who may not have
> liked executing the programmes of their leaders; but with indivi-
> duals we are not concerned; the fact remains that the programmes
> of their leaders always *have* been executed . . . It is therefore danger-
> ous to persist in the hallucinations that there is in Germany an
> effective element of kindly and learned old gentlemen, and sweet
> pig-tailed maidens. That is unhappily a myth.

German liberals have always been 'a weak minority' and incapable
of impeding 'the iniquitous habits and causes of the majority'. Was,
then, Germany doomed for ever to remain a political pariah? Not
necessarily. But if she

> is ever to cease to be a curse to herself and to everyone else, she
> will have to undergo the most thorough spiritual cure in history;
> and part at least of that cure will have to be self-administered. It
> will have to comprise a complete change of heart, mind and
> soul; of taste and temperament and habit; a new set of morals
> and values, a new, a brand-new way of looking at life. Such an
> achievement is not inconceivable; it will at the very best be extre-
> mely difficult.

The main themes of *Black Record* are clear. It is first and foremost
an account of Germany's relations with her neighbours, an account
of how, by repeated bouts of planned aggression, the Germans

I

succeeded in imposing their hegemony over Europe. And secondly, by implication, it poses the perennial question: how can Germany, with such a turbulent history and tradition, be reconciled to a peaceful and settled Europe? The origin of the pamphlet as a series of broadcasts lent itself both to simplistic presentation and evaluations. It is undeniable that *Black Record* contains some embarrassing elements of instant history and psychology. But if Van was guilty of over-simplification, so too were his critics, perhaps to an even greater degree. To take the most obvious example, almost without exception they pounced upon his Tacitus quotations in order to 'disprove' his entire case. Most of them seem to have made a point of not having read his pamphlet thoroughly, or at best only superficially, in order to derive a vicarious satisfaction from knocking down their own intellectual aunt-sallies.[111] All the fancy theories attributed to Van were categorically rejected by him as 'devoid of meaning'. He aspired to no theories. His aim was to tell the truth about Germany to his fellow countrymen; and he did so as 'a working diplomat with his coat off'.[112]

Van did not advocate the destruction of Germany or of all Germans. Quite the contrary, he specifically held out hope of solving the German problem given certain minimal conditions. He did not lump together all Germans as evil beyond redemption, though he had an unfortunate habit of referring to 'the German race', but in fact held the opposite view and expressed it time after time. What he actually wrote was 'that the record is a black one, and that time and caution are essential' if it be rectified. Nothing that happened during the course of the war forced him to alter his opinion.

Black Record began a controversy which was not to end until the occupation and destruction of Nazi Germany.[113] Van placed himself proudly in the vanguard of this debate. A new political term was coined, 'Vansittartism', denoting an extreme and obsessive anti-Germanism. In the public's eye he became the champion, *par excellence*, of a tough, uncompromising settlement with a defeated Germany.

The broadcasts represent a summation of his views on Germany, though presented in a highly-simplified form for mass consumption. He made them, apparently, under severe nervous strain. His long period of inactivity had left him frustrated intellectually. But also, and perhaps as a result, his old physical complaints returned. He was again sleeping badly, on a nightly sedative, and suffering from stomach pains.[114] Did his mental and physical state so weaken his judgement as to make him more susceptible to extremist advice? Dalton certainly believed that his judgement at that time was 'very uncertain'.[115] It has been suggested that such was indeed the case, and that Van's 'evil genius' was no less a personage than Frederick Voigt.[116] Without question Voigt and Van held extraordinarily similar views regarding the twin dangers of Nazism and Communism. Voigt, as a prominent political journalist, would have had easy access to Van, though his chief, William Crozier, apparently conducted most of the interviews with him.[117] But this was not unusual as Van made himself accessible to most of the leading journalists of the day. In all probability, Voigt's chief source at the Foreign Office was Rex Leeper, who in turn often spoke in Van's voice. At any rate, no evidence has yet emerged which places Voigt among Van's inner circle. In this respect, he was most definitely not in the same class as Christie of whom it may truthfully be said that he was responsible for some of Van's wilder ideas. However, *Black Record* was Van's invention alone. He had no need of an *éminence grise* to formulate ideas he had been preaching incessantly for the past forty years.

The initial reactions to *Black Record* were mixed. The press was divided: the *Sunday Times* and *The Observer* waxed enthusiastic; other newspapers, the *Reynolds News*, the *News Chronicle* or the *Daily Herald* were openly critical. Dalton thought that on balance it would do good, 'though many highly educated and traditionally minded people will be shocked. Certainly, however, it may be criticised as being hysterical and venomous, even though true in substance'.[118] His old chief, Hoare, was less discriminating: 'They are, like everything you write, brilliant, personal and inspired by deep fervour.'[119] Opinion in the Foreign Office was equally divided. Among the juniors his ideas were well received, his general thesis regarded as 'correct' though his manner of presentation upset 'half, if not more, of those who heard it'.[120] At the top there was more opposition. Cadogan, who had just rejected as 'catastrophic' the idea of Van replacing Lord Lothian as Ambassador in Washington,[121] referred to 'the sterile policy of *Black Record*', while Eden, who confessed to not having read it, agreed with Cadogan's verdict.[122]

If Eden did not bother to read Van's polemic, there were tens, possibly hundreds of thousands of more ordinary people who did,* not only in Great Britain but also abroad. Two hundred and fifty copies were sent on request to Iceland alone,[123] and it is reasonable to assume that this was not an isolated incident. The reasons for its enormous popularity are not difficult to discern. Paradoxically, it

---

* It is difficult to calculate the exact number of copies sold, but one contemporary report put it at 'about a million copies', Koffler, *op. cit.*

was the same quality which Dalton thought would shock 'highly educated and traditionally minded people' which appealed to the less sophisticated. Van studiously avoided the tortuous style which so bewildered many of his colleagues; he kept his prose simple, un-complicated, and full of many lively passages–the mark of a successful controversialist. *Black Record* is in fact a highly readable philippic.

Secondly, Van's recital of Germany's black record obviously struck a deep and receptive chord in the minds of his fellow countrymen. Only his more intellectual critics, frantically searching for both sides of a question where perhaps only one existed, accused him of appealing to the baser instincts of the ordinary Englishman. Nor should it be assumed that he lacked support among intellectuals, or that aca-demics refused to climb down from their ivory tower. Some academic works were published, written of course in appropriately sober and less passionate language, which followed Van's general line.[124] In the context of the winter of 1940–41, when German bombers were nightly attacking London and other densely populated targets, the high-falutin' arguments of his critics appeared as nothing more than the irresolution of sanctimonious liberals who were out of touch with the real world. He could safely leave it to the political theologians to split hairs as to the precise degree of German guilt; for the mass of the population the answer to this particular question was crystal-clear.

But *Black Record* also affected Van's status as a senior government official. It would not be an exaggeration to say that he had become a notorious figure overnight. Hostile questions were first directed against him in the House on 17 December, and the probing continued until mid-April.[125] His broadcasts were assumed to have united the German people around Hitler, thereby strengthening his régime and lengthening the duration of the war. Van took the opposite view, declaring that 'the German people are already united behind Hitler'; and so, by implication, did the government.[126] His opponents remained unappeased. His resignation was called for.[127] Some ques-tions even imputed financial gain as a motive for the publication of *Black Record*.[128] But the truth was that Van donated his royalties to war-time charities such as the Spitfire fund.[129] It was his old adver-sary, Lord Londonderry, who raised the cardinal point, pointing out that an active civil servant should not

> come out into the open either by way of broadcasting or of pub-lishing his views on political matters which can come in certain circumstances, in the realm of controversy.[130]

The government was unable to give a convincing reply.

Shortly after the Lords debate, *The Times* followed suit. Van's actions had been 'an obvious breach in the whole tradition of the British Civil Service'. The precedent thus created was more important than the views expressed. Van, the leader implied, would have to choose, for it was inconceivable to be 'both a civil servant and a popular controversialist'.[131] Van, apparently, had already chosen. Some time after the publication of *Black Record*, he was asked by Clifford Norton why he didn't do anything constructive. Van replied: 'I've got a lot of nasty things to say about them yet'. Within a few weeks he had retired from public service.

NOTES

1. Nicolson Diaries, i, 315, 323.
2. See *Manchester Guardian*, 20 October 1938; also *The Observer*, 16 October 1938.
3. Reports in *The Yorkshire Post*, 23 April 1938; *The Times*, 23 April 1938.
4. See, for example, the review in *The Times*, 10 August 1939.
5. See *Fullness of Days*, 203, for his description. For the same occasion Van wrote two poems for 'France', which vividly expressed his emotional francophilia. See Vnst. 3/8, 1939.
6. *Cadogan Diaries*, 48.
7. See his minutes of 4 March 1938, Vnst. 2/39.
8. See *B.D.*, 3, i, no. 164. Record of Anglo-French conversations, 28–9 April 1938.
9. *Cadogan Diaries*, 47–8.
10. *Ibid.*, 62.
11. For report of their conversation, see F.O. 371/20733, C. 5933/165/18.
12. See G. Ritter, *The German Resistance, Carl Goerdeler's Struggle Against Tyranny* (London, 1958), 83–4.
13. *Cadogan Diaries*, 128–9.
14. Van to Cadogan, 5 October 1945, F.O. 371/48652, C. 6776/198/18.
15. This passage is based upon the correspondence in the Christie papers 1/11.
16. See R. M. Smelser, *The Sudeten Problem, 1933–38. Volkstumpolitik and the Formulation of Nazi Foreign Policy* (Folkestone, 1975).
17. See F.O. 371/21729, C. 7512/1941/18.
18. See Robbins, *op. cit.*, 675.
19. See 'A Busman's Holiday', Vnst. 1/17; also R. M. Smelser, *op. cit.*, 148.
20. See Henlein's account in *G.D.*, C, v, no. 465.
21. Record of their conversation, F.O. 371/2131, R. 6982/188/12.
22. *G.D.*, D, ii, nos. 13, 14, 31.
23. See Dalton Diaries, 5 September 1937.
24. Quoted by Robbins, *op. cit.*, 687–8.
25. *G.D.*, D, ii, nos. 149, 154.
26. The record is printed in *B.D.*, 3, i, appendix II. On the same visit Henlein met Churchill and Sir Archibald Sinclair (*ibid.*, 633–5), and a group of M.P.'s organized by Harold Nicolson on Van's initiative (see *Nicolson Diaries*, i, 333–4).
27. See F.O. 371/21729, C. 7591/1941/18 and 21721, C. 8118/1941/18.
28. Minutes of 10 August 1938, Vnst. 2/39; also minutes of 6 August, *ibid.* See

also his note to Halifax, July 1938, F.O. 371/21729, C. 7512/1941/18 and Van to Halifax, 31 August 1938, F.O. 800/314; and in particular F.O. 371/21736, C. 9591/1941/18. This last report, compiled on 2 August, included intelligence estimates from Van's anonymous sources in Germany; an account of Hohenlohe's talks with Henlein at the end of July; and information obtained from 'a prominent German officer', 'a very well-informed Sudeten Deutsch source', 'a highly placed German official', 'a leading German industrialist', and so on. Goerdeler was among the sources, referred to as usual as 'X'.

29. See *B.D.*, 3, ii, 683–6.
30. See Neville Chamberlain's comments to Halifax, 19 August 1938, *ibid.*
31. See his minutes of 9 August 1938, F.O. 371/21736, C. 9591/1941/18.
32. See Chiefs of Staff report, no. 755, CAB. 53/40.
33. *Dalton Diaries*, 5 September 1938.
34. Minutes of 23 April 1938, Vnst. 2/35, also of 9 August 1938, Vnst. 2/3. See also *Dalton Diaries*, 5 September 1938.
35. Minutes in CAB. 23/94; see also *Inskip Diaries*, 30 August 1938, Churchill College, Cambridge.
36. A private communication.
37. See *Inskip Diaries*, 8 September 1938.
38. *Ibid.* also *Cadogan Diaries*, 95.
39. *Dalton Diaries*, 24 September 1938.
40. *Cadogan Diaries*, 92 *passim*.
41. His minutes of 2 December 1937, F.O. 371/20737, C. 8411/270/18, and of 31 August and 7 September 1939, Vnst. 2/39.
42. *Dalton Diaries*, 19 September 1938.
43. Minutes of 25 July, F.O. 371/21729, C. 7375/1941/18. The proposal was contained in a telegram from Henderson, 21 July 1938. Halifax minuted Van's comments: 'There is much force in this.'
44. Minutes of 13 September 1938, Vnst. 2/39; see also those of 20 September, *ibid.*, and *Dalton Diaries*, 17 September 1938.
45. *Cadogan Diaries*, 98, 100.
46. See *B.D.*, 3, ii. no. 928.
47. *Harvey Diaries*, 182.
48. *Cadogan Diaries*, 100.
49. Van's remark to Dalton, *Dalton Diaries*, 17 September 1938.
50. See interview with Lady Vansittart, 31 October 1972; *M.P.*, 496–7; also M. Gilbert, *Churchill*, v, 566, 625, 978.1.
51. See *Dalton Diaries* for this period.
52. A private communication.
53. *Dalton Diaries*, 17 and 19 September 1938; also Dalton, *The Fateful Years* (London 1957), 176–83. Dalton very discreetly did not mention Van by name but referred to him as 'a poker-playing friend'.
54. See Vnst. 2/39.
55. *Cadogan Diaries*, 102.
56. See Van to Halifax, 30 June 1939, Vnst. 2/41, and minutes of 10 July 1939, Vnst. 2/43.
57. Quoted by B. Lockhart, *Comes The Reckoning* (London 1947), 9.
58. *Nicolson Diaries*, i, 366–7.
59. Lockhart, *op. cit.*, 18. Nicolson in fact never made the speech attributed to

him in the press. He had included in his original draft an attack on Wilson, Simon, and Hoare, but had then amended it fearing it would harm Van. Unfortunately, the National Labour Office had already sent a copy of the original draft to the press and in that form it was published. See *Nicolson Diaries*, i, 367.

60. See, for example, F.O. 371/22922, C. 358/281/17.
61. See his minutes of 11 October 1938, Vnst. 2/39.
62. See for example, 'An Estimation of German Intentions', January 1939, F.O. 371/22963, C. 1292/15/18; and Van to Halifax, 18 January 1939, *ibid.*
63. Van to Halifax, 20 February 1939, F.O. 371/22965, C. 2209/15/18.
64. *Ibid.*
65. Cadogan to Halifax, 26 February 1939, F.O. 800/294 (Cadogan Papers).
66. See Van to Halifax, undated but 11/12 March 1939, and Van to Halifax, 13 March 1939, F.O. 371/22966, C. 3234/15/18.
67. Minutes of 15 March 1939, Vnst. 2/43.
68. *Cadogan Diaires*, 163.
69. This strange affair, for long shrouded in mystery, is exhaustively discussed by S. Aster, *The Making of the Second World War* (London, 1973), 61–78. For another slant on this story, see N. A. Rose (ed.), *The Diaries of Blanche Dugdale* (London, 1973), 131–32.
70. See M. Cowling, *op. cit.*, 215, 244–5, 247, 252, 294, 342.
71. Halifax to Sir William Seeds, 14 April 1939, *B.D.*, 3, v, 205–6. The Anglo-Soviet negotiations may be followed in *B.D.*, 3, vols. iv (app. 3), v, vi, vii. See also R. Manne, 'The British Decision for an Alliance with Russia, May 1939'. *Journal of Contemporary History* (July 1974).
72. See R. Manne, *op. cit.*, 19.
73. His minutes of May 1939, Vnst. 2/43.
74. See Van's note to Halifax, 17 May 1939, F.O. 371/22972, C. 7253/15/18.
75. See Christie papers, 180/1/29. In particular a report by him dated 17 May 1939, which obviously served as the basis for Van's remarks to Halifax. Other reports had been arriving in London to the same effect. Ashton-Gwatkin had also received an indirect message from Goerdeler that the German generals had received 'a new and unexpected offer from the Soviet Union which may entirely change the situation', see F.O. 371/22972, C. 6794/15/18. See also the report sent by the British military attache in Berlin, Mason-MacFarlane, to London, *B.D.*, 3, v, no. 552.
76. See D. C. Watt, 'The Initiation of the Negotiations Leading to the Nazi-Soviet Pact: A Historical Problem', *Essays in Honour of E. H. Carr* (London, 1974), eds. C. Abramsky and B. Williams.
77. For Van's terms of reference see CAB. 27/625, 3876; also *B.D.*, 3, v, nos. 527, 581, 582, 621.
78. See CAB. 23/99, conclusion for 24 May 1939.
79. See his minutes of 4 May, 7, 15, 16 June 1939, Vnst. 2/43.
80. Christie Papers, 180/1/29, 30.
81. For E. Kordt's account see *Nicht Aus den Akten: Die Wilhelmstrasse in Frieden und Krieg* (Stuttgart, 1950), 313–19. Also, *B.D.*, 3, vi, appendix 1. L. Mosley, *On Borrowed Time. How World War Two Began* (London, 1969), 254–7, has a long and dramatic account of the meeting.
82. See Mosley, *op. cit.*, 257.
83. *Cadogan Diaries*, 199.

84. *Ibid.*
85. Christie to Van, 27 June 1939, Christie Papers, 180/1/29. See also *None So Blind*, 195–6.
86. Christie to Van, 17 August 1939, Christie Papers, 180/1/29.
87. *Cadogan Diaries*, 196, entry for 18 August 1939.
88. See Van to Halifax, 13 December 1938, Vnst. 2/38.
89. *Cadogan Diaries*, 199–200, entries for 22, 23 August 1939.
90. Christie to Van, 26 August 1939, Christie Papers, 180/1/129.
91. See Cmd. 6115 (HMSO, 1939), Germany no. 1.
92. The title of Van's memorandum, 28 November 1939, F.O. 371/22986, C. 19495/15/18.
93. See Cmd. 6115, para. 16.
94. For this passage see, his minutes of 20 January 1940. F.O. 371/22986, C. 19495/15/18; Christie's report of February 1940, F.O. 371/24389, C. 3439/6/18; and Christie's papers 180/1/33, 35. Sir David Kelly relates (*The Ruling Few*, 272–3) that, before he was due to leave for Switzerland in the summer of 1940, Van gave him the names of two Germans to whom he might listen if they approached him. Prince Hohenlohe was one of them.
95. Minutes of 14 March 1940, F.O. 371/24363, C. 4012/267/62. For Beaverbrook's motives, see A. J. P. Taylor, *Beaverbrook*, 403–6.
96. See F.O. 371/24389, C. 4229/6/18.
97. Van to Halifax, 9 April 1940, F.O. 371/24418, C. 5304/1285/18.
98. *Channon Diaries*, 264.
99. Halifax to Hankey, 23 June 1940, Hankey Papers, 4/32. See also, *Churchill*, ii, 180–84; and A. Shlaim, 'Prelude to Downfall: The British Offer of Union to France, June 1940', *Journal of Contemporary History* (July 1974).
100. A private communication.
101. *Dalton Diaries*, 5 June 1940.
102. *Ibid.*, 25 May 1940.
103. *Ibid.*, 7 July 1940.
104. *Ibid.*, 7 and 17 July 1940.
105. *Ibid.*, 17 November 1940. For the Van–Crossman and Jebb dispute, *ibid.*, 22 August 1940, and early part of 1941.
106. Interview with Crossman, 21 March 1973.
107. *Dalton Diaries*, 5 February 1941.
108. A private communication.
109. *Cadogan Diaries*, 337–8.
110. All the following quotations are from *Black Record* (London, 1941).
111. The amount of anti-Vansittart literature published during the war is enormous. I list here only the most prominent criticisms. H. Laski, *The Germans – Are They Human? A Reply to Sir Robert Vansittart* (London, 1941); Kingsley Martin, *Propaganda's Harvest* (London, 1941); and *Editorial* (London, 1968), 306–7; V. Gollancz, *Shall Our Children Live or Die? A Reply to Lord Vansittart* (London, 1942); Parliamentary Peace Aims Group, *Germany's Record: A Reply to Lord Vansittart* (London ?); N. H. Brailsford, *Germans and Nazis: A Reply to Lord Vansittart* (London Commonwealth Library, ?); H. Fraenkel, *Vansittart's Gift for Goebbels* (London, The Fabian Society, ?); F. Nielson, *Hate, The Enemy of Peace. A Reply to Lord Vansittart* (London, 1944). Some of these criticisms extend into the war-time debate on Vansittartism, and do not

relate specifically to the publication of *Black Record*, though of course they deal with the many questions raised in the pamphlet.

It should not be thought that Van was only the subject of criticism. He had many strong and vocal supporters both in and out of parliament. For a remarkable defence of his ideas, see D. Koffler, *Vansittartitus. A Polemic* (London, 1943). Koffler himself was a German refugee, a not unimportant fact in itself, as were many of his defenders. See, for example, the correspondence in *The Spectator*, 7, 21 and 28 February, 1941.

112. *Black Record*, preface.
113. For a full discussion on the nature of the controversy, see 'The War Years'.
114. *Dalton Diaries*, 16 November, and 17, 18 December 1940.
115. *Ibid.*, 18 December 1940.
116. A private communication.
117. See A. J. P. Taylor, *Off The Record, op. cit.*
118. *Dalton Diaries*, 2 February 1941.
119. Hoare to Van, 26 March 1941, Temp. Papers, XIII:18.
120. Private communication and Valentine Lawford's diary, 7 December 1940. See also W. Strang's minutes of 16 November 1941 (F.O. 371/30928, C. 647/118/18) where he refutes the arguments of Van's critics while accepting, though not *in toto*, Van's own ideas.
121. *Cadogan Diaries*, 339.
122. See F.O. 371/25532, C. 7782/154/18. Minutes of a Foreign Office meeting on British Propaganda to Germany, 10 July 1941.
123. See F.O. 371/29310, N. 2123/347/15.
124. See, for example, R. Butler, *The Roots of National Socialism* (London, 1942); L. B. Namier's articles on Germany in *The Spectator*, 28 February 1941, *Time and Tide*, 17 May 1941 and 5 July 1941, later reprinted in *Conflicts* (London, 1943), 78–93; A. J. P. Taylor, *The Course of German History* (London, 1945); also his preface to the 1961 edition; A. L. Rowse, *The End of an Epoch* (London, 1948); or 'German Political Ideas from Luther to Hitler' in G. P. Gooch, *Studies in German History* (London, 1948).
125. See *P.D.*, Commons, v. 367, c. 1101–02, 1238; v. 368, c. 1417–18, 923–24, 1516; v. 369, c. 383, 538, 1413; v. 370, c. 1410, 1525; also, *P.D.*, Lords, v. 118, c. 388–410.
126. See the debate in the Lords, *ibid*.
127. By R. R. Stokes on 8 April 1941, *P.D.*, Commons, v. 370, c. 1410.
128. Questions put by R. R. Stokes and R. Gibson, *P.D.*, Commons, v. 369, c. 538, 1413.
129. See F.O. 371/26658, C. 2583/2583/18. *Black Record* sold at 6d a copy; Van received ¼d royalties on each copy sold.
130. Debate in the Lords on Van's broadcasts, 18 February 1941, v. 118, c. 402.
131. *The Times*, 20 February 1941.

CHAPTER XII

The War Years

VAN'S RESIGNATION TOOK EFFECT from 25 June 1941, his sixtieth birthday. He was under no legal obligation to retire. Many precedents could be cited of diplomatists having continued in office well after the official retiring age, particularly at moments of national crisis. But he was under severe emotional strain. The *Black Record* broadcasts had catapulted him into the centre of a public controversy which was destined to grow in intensity as the war progressed. On that score alone his official position would have become untenable. But even more disturbing for his serenity of mind was his sense of isolation in his work. In 1938, when he reluctantly assumed the empty dignity of Chief Diplomatic Adviser, Halifax told him: 'Of course, you are the fifth wheel on the coach'.[1] Three years later, sadly disillusioned by his experience, he decided to put an end to a situation which had become anomalous and personally humiliating. Eden, who was mainly responsible for shunting Van off to the sidelines in 1938, returned to office as Foreign Secretary on 23 December 1940 to complete the job.* He made plain his feelings to Dalton early in January 1941.[2] Later the same month it was common gossip in the Office that Eden planned to retire a number of senior diplomatists, including Van, and was even negotiating with the Treasury about proportionate pensions.[3]

Van's relations with Churchill came to a head when the Prime Minister refused to sanction a series of broadcasts he was to make in

---

* There is an enigmatic entry in the *Channon Diaries* (for 19 February 1940, p. 286): 'I set the wheels in motion today to sack Vansittart, who I have decided to have made a Peer.' Channon, whatever his pretensions, was in no position to carry out his threat, but he may have been whispering in someone's ear in the wings, a form of pressure more suitable to his talents.

French on the overseas service of the BBC. Obviously anticipating a repetition of the *Black Record* episode, Churchill was understandably reluctant to grant his consent. Van drafted a long letter to the Prime Minister claiming that 'he is much the best-known and loved in France of all Englishmen', and that if 'he is not allowed to speak to them on the air, he will be completely discredited'.[4] His loss of face seemed complete. If he was not to be allowed to fulfil a minimal duty, the encouragement of French resistance, what use was there in his continuing in government service? Happily this incident resolved itself. After lunching with Churchill at Chequers the veto was removed. Churchill excused himself, claiming that he hadn't understood that the broadcasts were to be in French. In that case, he confided to Van, 'No member of the House of Lords will understand them'.[5] Apart from this concession, the meeting was unsatisfactory. Van made it clear that he was thinking of resigning as Chief Diplomatic Adviser. Isolated and neglected, he felt he had come to the end of his tether. In cabinet circles he was described as Dalton's *chef de cabinet*. But, as he reminded Dalton, he felt a little too old for a private secretary's job.[6]

Eden was absent from England during February on a tour of the eastern Mediterranean countries. His visit coincided with the Balkan crisis of the spring of 1941 and this delayed his return to London until 10 April. Van was not consulted about the trip and would in fact have advised against it. During this entire period Van was studiously ignored. His advice was not sought nor was he shown any papers.[7] This was the final straw. Immediately on Eden's return, Van wrote him 'a fiery letter' claiming that the promises made to him had been systematically broken but that he had never expected anything different.[8] On 18 April he met Eden and tendered his resignation. He rejected out of hand any notion of a political post in the government, or even of employment on the British Council. More than anything he wished to be free to write and speak and broadcast without fear of embarrassing either the government or his colleagues. He even thought it possible that Churchill or Eden would see fit to consult him from time to time. A month later *The Times* announced his impending resignation;[9] and in the birthday honours list he was raised to the Peerage as Baron Vansittart of Denham. On 16 July he took his oath in the House of Lords, sponsored by Lord Hankey and Lord Horder.[10] To complete his tarnished glory he was appointed a privy counsellor. Already he appeared a changed man. Dalton noted that 'he looks much better and happier' as he prepared to embark on a fresh career as 'a new, free man'.[11]

No sooner had he left the Foreign Office than he was involved in a lawsuit. On 2 June *Time* magazine published an article which held Van responsible for the 'hypocrisy, equivocation and confusion' of British foreign policy in the 1930's, and for having had a hand 'in all the steps which led to Britain's isolation'. Van was outraged at this slur upon his character and policies. He wrote immediately to Henry Luce, the owner-publisher of *Time* and an old friend of his, announcing that he intended to prosecute the magazine for libel.[12] His language was unrestrained. He failed to understand why 'you printed such slanderous muck', or why 'without the slightest cause, you have tried to stab in the back – with a dirty knife – a man who supposed himself to be your friend'. Luce replied in a friendly and soothing fashion. Offering as lucrative a peace offering as he could envisage, he hoped that when the time came his company would be allowed to publish Van's true record of the story.

Van was not placated by so transparent a gesture. Indeed, considering the full circumstances of his resignation and his past record, his anger is fully understandable. At the beginning of September the case was brought before the courts. Van was not interested in damages, only in clearing his name, and a tolerable compromise formula was agreed upon beforehand. Van had attained satisfaction. He wrote again to Luce expressing his pleasure that 'the legal action has been settled as between friends and gentlemen'.

Van made his maiden speech in the House of Lords on 18 March 1942, on a motion put by Viscount Elibank about the number of enemy aliens employed by the BBC in their German section. Elibank suggested that these aliens exploited their position to promote pan-German ideas, thereby diminishing the effectiveness of the British propaganda machine.[13] This was a topic tailor-made for Van. Throughout his career he had taken an interest in propaganda, and since 1938 he had been actively engaged in it. One of his favourite hobby-horses, dating from the First World War, was the manner by which German emigrés abused the hospitality of their country of refuge in order to advance their own subversive ideas. Moreover, Van had been personally traduced in one of these German broadcasts, or so he thought, having been described as 'an ordinary private citizen with whose views the Government were not in sympathy at all'.

His speech contained many of the motifs he was to develop as the war progressed. Referring only 'to the activities of a small portion of our visitors', he condemned their work as being incompatible 'with the interests of this country, or indeed of our Allies', for the perfectly simple reason 'that they have remained good Germans, and sometimes pan-Germans, and often strong nationalists'. Quite naturally he placed the German Right, 'that awful combination of militarism, Junkerdom and heavy industry', far beyond the pale, but he had no use also for the German Left: 'On that point experience has spoken, and we cannot be fooled twice.' These German propagandists, he claimed, wished to avoid unilateral disarmament and to preserve intact the German war machine. There was a simple explanation for this: 'German heavy industry is needed for a Greater Germany'. He cited Stalin, by now an impeccable source, in support of his views. 'Stalin says he does not identify the German people with Hitler. No more do I. I have never identified the hounds with the huntsmen, but I know, and all Europe knows only too well what hounds do when the huntsmen sound the horn that promises blood.'

Much of his speech was reserved for the kid-glove treatment meted out to the German army:

> Some of our propagandists appear not only to feel but to express admiration for it, and that is why, even in the Russian campaign, there has been practically, as far as I can make out, a ban on criticism of the military caste in whose hands Hitler has been a tool from the beginning.

For this overt currying to German militarism, Van could 'only blame Mr Crossman or his assistants or advisers'.*

The ensuing debate followed a pattern which was to become painfully repetitive as Van's parliamentary career progressed. He was accused of setting afoot a 'campaign of hate', of wishing to emulate the 'Haw Haw type' broadcasts, and, most insulting of all, of complicity in Chamberlain's appeasement policy Naturally he denounced these accusations as 'a complete travesty', even though they illustrated 'the technique I have become accustomed to in this controversy, that of putting words into my mouth which I have not said, and then to spend time demolishing them'. These were tricks of the trade which he had to learn the hard way.

Yet the unrestrained, often violent, nature of his language played into the hands of his enemies. The *Evening Standard* portrayed him as the man who 'makes more Nazis . . . [as] a kind of Nazi inside out'.[14] Undoubtedly his public exhortations provided a modicum

---

* Mr Crossman later claimed that this personal attack on a civil servant was quite unprecedented (interview, 21 March 1973), forgetting perhaps that Van had suffered far worse treatment.

of grist to the German propaganda mill.[15] Goebbels used Van's speeches in his 'Strength through Fear' campaign, maintaining German morale by invoking dark prophecies of what would happen if Germany lost the war and the Vansittarts got their way.[16] When Van published *Lessons of My Life* in April 1943, another highly polemical work, Goebbels rejoiced:

> This fellow Vansittart is worth his weight in gold to our propaganda. After the war a monument ought to be erected to him somewhere in Germany with the inscription: To the Englishman who rendered the greatest service to the German cause during the war.[17]

However, to describe Van as a vulgar racialist would be to divest that emotive word of its precise meaning. He did not deny the existence of anti-Nazi Germans. On the contrary, he was in contact with many of them and encouraged them in their activities. But he compared them with Euclid's definition of a point: they have position but not magnitude. He was convinced that 'the Nazi clique', to use his detractors' favourite phrase, was supported, tacitly or otherwise, by the overwhelming mass of the German people; and that the only way to destroy Nazism was to crush Germany completely, to occupy her, and to root out, if necessary by force, the last vestiges of militarism and Junkerdom. This was his message to the British people.[18]

His weakness lay in his incapacity to translate his highly-charged emotions into an easily acceptable political doctrine. His consistent overstating of his case deprived it of a sense of proportion. Quotations from Tacitus, or references to German barbarism during the Thirty Years War, were on a par with those highly elaborate and embellished memoranda which had so irritated his chiefs. Van supplied his enemies with an abundance of ammunition, and they in turn exploited it to label him as a dyed-in-the-wool racialist for whom the Germans, through some inherent blemish in their nature, had always been the scourge of the earth. The cruder aspects of Vansittartism were rejected as much by the author of the creed as by its most vocal opponents. Much of this discussion was beside the point. Van was primarily concerned with achieving the swiftest, the most efficient, and the most expedient way of defeating Nazi Germany. Even given the wisdom of hindsight, it would be difficult to deny the ultimate validity of his opinions.

Van's most formidable adversary in this interminable German debate was George Kennedy Allen Bell, Bishop of Chichester. Bell, a man of refined and cultured tastes, delighted in championing lost causes. But like Van, his moral fervour often succeeded in irritating his listeners as much as convincing them.[19]

He first clashed with Van in earnest in March 1943, when he moved a motion calling attention to Stalin's speech of 6 November 1942 which distinguished between Germany and the Hitlerite state and enquired whether the government made the same distinction.* Bell lauded the German opposition, singling out the Protestant church for particular praise. But the naïvety and over-simplification of his presentation defeated its own aim, and Van had little difficulty in rebutting the Bishop's sermon.[20]

Hardly a session passed without a confrontation between them. A typical squabble occurred in the debate on the massacre of forty-seven British officers at Stalag Luft III. Van raised the issue twice.[21] For him this premeditated butchery was decisive proof of German savagery and their preoccupation with, if not positive enjoyment of, cold-blooded murder. Where did the ultimate responsibility lie? Again Van was in no doubt. He advocated a form of collective punishment. Responsibility lay not only with those who actually perpetrated the crime, but also with those who inspired it, namely the German General Staff. If only the government would make it manifestly clear that it intended to punish to the maximum penalty of law all those responsible, it would have a deterrent effect, 'and a good many [Germans] in these last crucial, vital weeks and months will stay off the job and go underground'.

Bell questioned Van's doctrine, arguing that acceptance of it would merely exacerbate the plight of the prisoners for it would encourage the Gestapo to take over full responsibility for the camps. Van, he accused, was no friend of the allied prisoners-of-war. This touched on a raw spot, as Van was President of the Association of Relatives of Prisoners-of-War. He would not take this outrageous charge lying down.

> I was proposing today measures which would mitigate the risks to which the prisoners are going to be exposed. Out of the blue comes the right reverent Prelate and, with his one hundred per cent Germanphile views, takes exactly the opposite line, and pretends that there is nothing to be done. That is the worst possible way of protecting prisoners-of-war, and it is a very fair example of endeavouring to hit below the belt.

* Stalin had said: 'We have no such aim as to destroy Germany, for it is impossible to destroy Germany, just as it is impossible to destroy Russia; but the Hitlerite state can and should be destroyed, and our first task is in fact to destroy the Hitlerite state and its inspirers.'

Van's speeches in the Lords continued in this vein. At the end of 1943 he made a particularly impassioned contribution on the question of German war atrocities and the punishment of war criminals.[22] By now the stories of wholesale massacres of entire communities, particularly in Eastern Europe, were too well substantiated to be seriously questioned. Van entertained no doubt as to their authenticity, and demanded 'for reasons not only of justice and security but of bare humanity, to liquidate the entire Gestapo and all the Death's Head Guards at the concentration camps'.

His speeches, no matter how harsh their content, were always well-composed and delivered with an air of confidence and authority. He rarely spoke from written notes as the light in the House was too dim for his eyes,[23] but he never seemed at a loss for an epigram or quotation at the right moment. He hardly ever used slang and spoke in a rather literary manner. He swiftly established a reputation as a persuasive, knowledgeable and witty debater, successfully overcoming his natural nervousness and lack of experience at public speaking. Even his opponents were compelled to acknowledge his new-found virtuosity, for though he preached a 'doctrine of despair' he did so with his usual 'charm'.[24]

Van soon broadened his public campaign against Germany. Not content with enlightening their lordships a few times a year, he became involved in a form of fringe politics, associating with so-called extremist groups who were determined that Germany should not escape the consequences of her aggression. Fine-sounding organizations such as 'Never Again' or 'Fight for Freedom' were ready vehicles for his oratory and pamphleteering. Initially he was most closely linked with 'Never Again', an association whose declared aim was to whip up public opinion to such a degree that 'no outbreak of sentimentality shall rob the victims of German atrocities of justice and retribution'.[25] He first addressed them on 18 February 1942 at Grosvenor House, and laid down the guidelines of his German policy: a prolonged occupation by the allied forces; the complete destruction of the German army; drastic control of German heavy industry; the total disarmament of Germany; and the re-education of the German people. This was the essence of Vansittartism.

He learned the stock-in-trade tricks of every politician. He stumped the country expounding his cause, exposing himself both to hecklers and to enthusiastic supporters. Audiences of all persuasions listened to his case. He toured the provinces, addressed the rotary clubs of London, enlightened the 1922 committee, and lunched with the guilds of the City of London. At Cardiff, after a particularly rousing speech, he brought the audience to its feet singing 'For He's a Jolly Good Fellow'.[26] He sought public controversy and did not evade it. He became a favourite butt of the *New Statesman*, 'neither new nor statesmanlike',[27] and the *Daily Herald*, 'I shall forgive them for they do not know what they are doing'.[28] Left-wing intellectuals entered the fray, often exasperating Van beyond belief with their ill-defined cloudy theories. He debated regularly on the BBC, though the topic remained constant: 'What Shall We Do With Germany?'*

By 1943 Van had set up his own organization, the 'Win the Peace' movement, with himself installed as President.† The movement presented a twelve-point charter which detailed Van's ideas about the post-war German settlement. Briefly, it provided for the unconditional surrender of Germany; the occupation of Germany; the punishment of war criminals; complete disarmament; the decentralization and demilitarization of the police force; the abolition of military or semi-military training; the evacuation of all conquered territories; the restoration of, and compensation for, all war damage; effective control over German war potential; no financial aid for Germany without the joint approval of the Allies; school and university education to be under Allied guidance; and the mass media to be strictly controlled. Together with the charter, the movement published twelve day-to-day aims, the main point of which was to propagate and secure public support for the charter, considered to be the minimum requirement for a just peace.[29]

His organization, largely sustained, one suspects, by the generosity of the Vansittarts, developed into his main platform for storming the country and disseminating his views. It is, of course, almost impossible to estimate the exact numerical strength of his movement. But one source claimed that in Bristol alone the 'Win The Peace' association could muster 10,000 supporters.[30] Exaggerated though this figure may be, there can be little doubt that Van's campaign enjoyed a considerable measure of popular support throughout the country.

Vansittartism also took root in the United States. His book, *Lessons of My Life*, a devastating attack against Germany, was well received,

* See, for example, *The Listener*, 19 and 26 October and 7 December 1944. The other participants in this particular symposium were: Kingsley Martin, editor of *New Statesman*; Barbara Ward, assistant editor of *The Economist*; and A. J. P. Taylor, the historian, who also chaired the sessions. Van received support only from Taylor.

† The movement's headquarters were at 4 Dean's Yard, Westminster. Among its more prominent supporters were: Sir Samuel Turner, Clifford Bax, Lord Dunsany, Lewis Mumford, and Rom Landau.

and there were few who quarrelled with either his facts or his main conclusions.[31] One commentator tried to out-Vansittart Vansittart:

> This masterpiece of realistic anger and invective [he extolled] should be put into the hands of all our men in uniform and into the hands of all sentimental, pro-German custardbrains whose 'humanity' towards post-war Germany will put our children and grandchildren in uniform again to sail and march and fly against the perpetual enemy of the civilized world – Germany.

Towards the end of the war rumours were prevalent that Van intended travelling to the United States to establish a transatlantic version of his 'Win The Peace Campaign'.[32] The visit, which was to include promotional dinners and mass rallies, was to have been sponsored by a local organization, 'The League Against Aggression'. Nothing materialized from these fine schemes. For the first half of 1945 Van remained in England, campaigning on home territory.

Van's movement, whatever the rights and wrongs of the controversies it aroused, and that must still be a matter of dispute, was a serious and thoughtful attempt to solve 'the German problem'. The shock waves it produced forced upon the public an awareness of the gravity and complexity of the question which might otherwise have eluded them. This, perhaps, was its greatest contribution to the war effort. But the nature of Van's reputation attracted to his banner some unwelcome adherents. Cranks of assorted varieties saw in him a convenient tool to promote their own outlandish schemes. He declined to involve himself in any of their grotesque concoctions,[33] either the physical elimination of Germany or her partition among her neighbours. At home he enjoyed a wide measure of popular support simply because he entrenched himself in the mainstream of public thought about Germany. He ran no parliamentary candidate in his campaign. But judging from the attendance at his rallies, the reception given to his speeches, and an examination of the correspondence columns of the press, it may fairly be concluded that his views represented a genuine and widely held expression of the deep revulsion felt towards Germany throughout the country.

His group was by no means the most extreme among those campaigning against Germany. In fact he soon clashed with the *ultras* and was in turn violently denounced by them as a moderate. One of their most damning charges was that Van was collaborating with émigré Germans, in particular with Walter Loeb* whom one of the most fanatical of the *ultras*, a Mrs Eleanor Tennant, described as 'A German gangster'.[34]

There was much truth in this, though if anything, such benevolence should have been marked to his credit. Certainly one of the paradoxes of Van's career was the manner in which he befriended those whom he classified as good Germans. Wolfgang Putlitz was the outstanding example; it was common knowledge that Van provided him with food and shelter at Denham Place during the war. But he was not alone. Van also took up the cause of many other less prominent Germans. He brought their plight before the Foreign Office, or other government agencies, trying, mostly in vain, to alleviate their situation or to propagate their views.[35]

Loeb, however, was in a slightly different category. Van first met him as a result of his involvement in the nebulous world of émigré politics. Van was in continuous contact with the large number of Polish exiles in London. He had long known Count Raczynski, the Polish ambassador to London. They had met frequently, though not on a regular basis, and they were in close accord regarding the post-war German settlement.[36] Among the numerous émigré groups then operating in London was one composed of socialists from the occupied countries, mainly Poland, Czechoslovakia and Holland, named here for convenience, Ciolkocz's Committee.† Naturally enough, it had very clear-cut ideas about Germany's status in the post-war world, and they were almost identical with Van's charter. What particularly enraged Ciolkocz and his associates were the activities of anti-Nazi Germans and Austrians who had made considerable headway in convincing public opinion in Great Britain that a socialist revolution in Germany was the most practicable way of overthrowing the Nazi régime. This was in direct contradiction to the Ciolkocz Committee's views.

The Poles, who were apparently the chief inspirers of the Committee, attempted to win over the Labour party to their camp, and

* Walter Loeb (1895–1948): former president of state bank of Thuringen and member of Reichsrat; member of Social Democratic Party; resigned in protest after first Nazi controlled state government had been elected in Thuringen; left Germany in 1933; founder member of 'Fight for Freedom', and of its editorial board.

† Much of the information for this passage is based on an interview with Adam Ciolkocz (ex-member of the Polish parliament, the *Djem*; of Polish National Council, and of Central Executive Committee of Polish Socialist Party. He arrived in England in 1940), and on material, pamphlets and manifestos, supplied by him. Ciolkocz was a leading member of the above committee.

discovered a warm supporter in William Gillies, secretary of the International Department at Transport House. Gillies knew Loeb well, and together they would meet with members of Ciolkocz's group to discuss methods of broadening the scope of their activities, or blocking that of their rivals. Loeb was, in a sense, on the wrong side of the fence, for he could scarcely be called a socialist, and, although a German, he held no truck with those of his fellow countrymen who gambled all on an internal revolution to rid Germany of Hitler. From these meetings there developed the 'Fight for Freedom' society.*

By the very nature of their joint activities, Van's movement and Ciolkocz's Committee were bound to become partners of a kind. Loeb became the main point of contact between them. At the peak of their collaboration they met about once a week when Van would conduct a kind of seminar on international affairs, enlightening his pupils on the significance of current world events.

The reverse side to Van's cooperation with his good Germans was his relentless pursuit of those anti-Nazi Germans who, in his estimation, had abused British hospitality by publicizing pan-German opinions and denying the essential war guilt of the German people. He had always believed that anti-Nazism in itself was not a sufficient guarantee of their trustworthiness; that the old German nationalist ambitions were lying dormant, only waiting to be resuscitated by the misguided actions of these German patriots. Instead of advocating a social revolution doomed to failure, they should, in the interests of a free and democratic Germany, accept with good grace the unilateral disarmament, occupation and denazification of Germany.

No single subject fired Van's emotions more than this one.[37] In his eyes, no one person exemplified more this kind of German than a certain Friedrich Stampfer,† that 'full-blown pan-German type

---

* Many prominent personalities were associated with 'Fight for Freedom', including: Camille Huysmans, the Belgian socialist; Luis Arquistan, the Spanish diplomat; Curt Geyer, editor of *Neuer Vorwaerts*; Will Lawther, president of Mineworkers Federation of Great Britain; Rennie Smith, journalist and joint editor of *Central European Observer*; and Walter Loeb. The society published nineteen pamphlets in all with an overall circulation of about half a million. One of them contained an answer to Gollancz's attack on Van, *Black Record, Gollancz in German Wonderland*, by Curt Geyer and Walter Loeb.

† (1874–1975): Stampfer was Austrian born; became editor of the German Social Democratic party journal, *Vorwaerts* (Forward) in 1916; member of the party's executive committee; and member of Reichstag, 1920–33. During the Hitler period he was in exile in Great Britain and the United States.

masquerading as a Social-Democrat'.[38] Stampfer was now in the United States, but he had left behind in Britain enough disciples to carry on his work. Van attacked Stampfer on every conceivable opportunity. Eventually Stampfer retaliated in a violent article published in an American newspaper, *Alliance*, on 1 April 1944.[39] In it he scored the usual debating points:

> I agree entirely with Lord Vansittart that there are in Germany no underground fighters who are willing to risk their lives in order to realize the war aims of Lord Vansittart or other implacable enemies of the German people. There are no underground workers in Germany who want to see their country controlled for twenty years or more by Russians, British and Americans. There are none who want to see it mutilated or dismembered. These people are bitter enemies of the Nazis, but they are not – and cannot be expected to be – enemies of Germany or of the Germans.

But it was his final thrust which elicited a sharp rejoinder from Van. Stampfer recollected that in 1937, when in Prague organizing the German underground movement, he and his colleagues were instructed at the request of a foreign authority to cease their activities in order to avoid friction between Prague and Berlin. Stampfer had no doubt as to who was responsible for this untimely intervention, or its ultimate result. 'Thus the German underground movement fell as the first victim on the altar of appeasement. The foreign authority to which reference was made was the Foreign Office in London.' Van, as head of the Foreign Office at that time, was thus branded as the first appeaser. This was too much for Van. He contacted the Office and informed Strang of his intention 'to call him [Stampfer] a typical German liar in public', to issue 'in very rude terms, a denial of this characteristic refugee propaganda'.[40] This he did, revealing Stampfer as a militarist and a teller of fairy-tales whose German propaganda 'has led him into a rare jumble of fantasy'.[41] This war of words with Stampfer lasted well into the 1950's.

One subject which continued to attract Van's attention was the question of the reform of the Foreign Office. Early in his career he had profited greatly from the old system of patronage and personal favour, as he had equally profited from the gentle reforms enacted before the first war. Even so, he had always retained an open mind on the subject. Perfectly aware that the Foreign Office had to adapt itself to changing times, he accepted the necessity for change in its organizational structure and in its methods of recruitment. The Second World War, like the First, provided an impetus for reforms which were long overdue. By early 1943 proposals had been agreed upon and were placed before parliament.[42] They were debated in the Lords on 25 and 30 March.[43] Van was not present. He was on one of his provincial tours, speaking at Chester and Bradford. His intention was to join the debate on its second day. Unfortunately, he fell ill and for some days was confined to bed with a high temerature.[44]

His general feelings about the proposals were clear: he welcomed them. What distressed him was not the reforms *per se*, which in fact amounted to little more than a technical and administrative restructuring of the service, but the decline in the status of the professional diplomatists.[45] The service, he concluded, was over-staffed, while open conference diplomacy had been taken to an absurd extreme and left no scope for the skills of the professional. He deplored the relegation of diplomatists to the rank of messenger boys; he deprecated the modern tendency to appoint outsiders, politicians, to the great embassies; and, speaking from bitter personal experience, he emphatically disapproved of attacks on defenceless civil servants by the mass media. Should these tendencies continue to take root unchecked, they would ruin the service. To extract the utmost from new recruits it was essential 'neither to beat [them] in public nor cheat them of the higher appointments', but 'to treat them with complete trust and respect'. This was all rather nostalgic, yearning for the good old days from which he himself had been only too eager to escape. But as Viscount Cranborne* reminded him, when winding up for the government, the real problem was not just to criticize these developments, but to adapt them to contemporary conditions and by so doing ensure that they did not ruin the service.

The Eden reforms of 1943 passed off almost without a ripple of controversy, but they generated a far more contentious and acrimonious debate, and one that touched directly on Van's eight years as head of the Office. Some senior diplomatists, now retired, had expressed disquiet at the internal organization of the Foreign Office during the inter-war years, and had charged undue interference in matters of policy-making and senior appointments on the part of the head of the civil service, Sir Warren Fisher. The assumption

---

* R. A. J. Gascoyne-Cecil (1893–   ): Under Secretary of State for Foreign Affairs, 1935–38; Paymaster-General, 1940; Secretary of State for Dominions, 1940–42, 1943–45; for Colonies, 1942; Lord Privy Seal, 1942–43, 1951–52. Viscount Cranborne, 1903; Fifth Marquess of Salisbury, 1947.

was that Fisher had wielded too much power and in too arbitrary a manner, and that those unfortunates who dared to oppose his views soon discovered that they were losing in the promotion race. Sir Walford Selby led the attack in a letter to *The Times* on 28 August 1942; and although he failed to mention Fisher by name the inference was apparent to any informed reader. The same theme was developed by Lord Perth and Lord Salisbury in a stormy debate in the Lords in November 1942.[46] The reforms went some way to meet this criticism, though in the most technical fashion, by the separation of the Foreign Service from the Home Civil Service. But the historical implications in the Perth–Selby offensive stood unanswered.

For some years the discussion remained dormant. It was resurrected by the publication of Selby's book, *Diplomatic Twilight*, in the spring of 1953. Selby levelled the most specific and malicious charges against some of his former colleagues, and his book, if taken at its face value, was a grave indictment of the Foreign Office during Van's tenure of office.* Eventually the matter was raised in the Commons, and the government issued a strong and unequivocal denial of the charges.[47] Elibank returned to the attack two weeks later.[48] Replying for the government, the Marquess of Reading specifically refuted two of Selby's most damaging charges: that his despatches from Vienna were not properly considered, and that the most important of them were not brought to the notice of the cabinet.†

Van did not participate in these exchanges. But he finally came to his own defence in the correspondence columns of *The Times*, again as the result of Selby raking up past controversies. He had written (*Diplomatic Twilight*, p. 73) that Henlein, after his talks with Van in October 1937, had gained the impression that neither Great

---

* Selby's book was only one in a series of critical assessments of the role of the Foreign Office during this period. But whereas Selby emphasized the apparent shortcomings in diplomatic procedure, his fellow critics (F. Ashton-Gwatkin, *The British Foreign Service* (Syracuse, 1950); Lord Murray of Elibank, *Reflections on Some Aspects of British Foreign Policy between the Wars* (Edinburgh, 1946); and Sir V. Wellesley, *Diplomacy in Fetters* (London, 1945)), seized on the weakness of the economic aspects of foreign policy decision making. It should be noted that two of these critics, Ashton-Gwatkin and Wellesley, had been engaged in a running battle with the Treasury over the setting up of an economic section in the Office. For Van's part in this struggle, see pp. 99–100.

† Any examination of the records will bear out the inconsistencies in Selby's accusations. His despatches were seen and noted by the relevant Foreign Office and government bodies. Unfortunately, the advice he rendered was often quite impracticable and related only to the swollen image he entertained of his own importance. See below, pp. 64–65, 69, 88 n. 32.

Britain nor France 'would intervene to help Czechoslovakia, and that Sir Robert favoured a "military occupation" of Austria by Germany as a solution to the Austrian problem'. As has been argued, Selby's claim rests on the flimsiest of evidence, while any interpretation Henlein put on the talks must be taken with a large pinch of salt.*

In view of the personal and persistent character of Selby's campaign against him, and considering that it now spanned a full decade, Van was left with no alternative but to defend his own reputation. His response, however, revealed a degree of self-restraint not usually associated with his public utterances, and can only be explained by his reluctance to wash the Foreign Office's dirty linen in public. He declared his intention to make public the true facts, but then went on to ask: 'Why did not Selby verify all this with me?' Regarding the other points raised in Selby's book, Van was confident that he could refute them easily enough, but deemed them 'unworthy of reply'.[49] It was a lame answer, as Selby was quick to point out,[50] and Van would have done better to disprove the charges in detail, for however hard he denied them something of the mud stuck.

Van sat in the House of Lords as an independent. He had no stomach to identify himself with any of the political parties, jealously preserving his freedom of thought and expression from the encroachments of doctrinal party politics. As befitted a member of his class and social environment, he possessed strong Conservative views. While not averse to social or economic or political change, he would countenance it only if it did not radically alter the existing structure of society. Compared with many of his contemporaries he possessed

---

* The only evidence to support Selby's charge comes from the German side: either Henlein himself, a notoriously unreliable witness, or unnamed confidential sources. Thus the German chargé d'affaires in London, Woermann, a few days after the October talks: 'Vansittart gave Henlein to understand that Britain regarded the *Anschluss* as inevitable in the long run but pointed out the dangers if it were accomplished by a military *putsch* [von Neurath minuted: 'Henlein told me the same.'], and hence preferred military occupation to a *putsch*'. (See *G.D.*, D, ii, nos. 13, 41.) There can be no way of finally burying this rumour, except to note the implausible nature of the source and to emphasize that it ran counter to everything Van had espoused on the Austrian question since his appointment as PUS. In any case, Selby's book is extremely misleading, not to say inaccurate. He quotes from Van's meeting with Henlein in October 1937 yet gives as his British source the records of the May 1938 meeting. It is therefore impossible to know from his account what exactly was said and in what context and by whom. However, Selby's intention was obvious: to incriminate Van and his diplomacy. For an attempt to clear up this muddle, see below, *Black Record*, pp. 222–26.

an open mind, but it was open only up to a point. Nor did he frequently commit himself on social or economic topics. On the rare
occasions when he took the plunge he revealed himself as being well
satisfied, sometimes embarrassingly so, with the *status quo*.[51] Wisely,
perhaps, he aimed most of his public comments at questions of
foreign affairs.

He had of course been offered a safe Conservative seat in the Commons, but had unhesitatingly turned it down, commenting to his
wife: 'Party politics is a dirty business and you need "sewer-boots"
to wade through parliament.'[52] If outwardly he displayed a modicum
of restraint towards party politicians, in private he spoke in extreme
terms of contempt against those who willingly sacrificed their integrity on the altar of party politics. His ideal was to rise above the
squalor of party debate as an untainted defender of the national
interest. In attaining this aim he was fortified by the knowledge that
his consuming interest, foreign affairs, slipped neatly, if a little un-
easily, into this category. On more than one occasion Van suggested
substituting the term foreign affairs for national affairs.

He had long held the opinion that the true explanation for Great
Britain's shocking record of complacency in the 1930's was rooted
in the politicians' natural instinct to make political capital out of
every national issue. Neither major party could evade its share of the
responsibility. But he felt that the Conservatives, having in fact
governed the country since 1931, bore the major portion of the
blame. A classic example of the treatment he dispensed to politicians
occurred at the end of 1944. The Commons had debated the question
of the punishment of German war criminals.[53] But the discussion
soon roved into a dispute about the parties' responsibilities for the
events leading up to the outbreak of war. Van's name was soon
dragged into it. Eleanor Rathbone* accused him of wrecking 'a
splendid opportunity of creating in Germany a fifth column . . .
that would be fighting for us all the time'. This by now threadbare
argument was soon replaced by a somewhat insidious comparison:
the equation of the German Fifth Column's struggle against Hitler
from inside Germany with Van's decision to fight government policy
from within the Foreign Office and not outside it.[54] By any reckoning
this was a ludicrous analogy, and it invited an incisive response from
Van. He admitted that he had decided to remain in the machine

---

* Eleanor Rathbone (1873–1946): Independent M.P. for the Combined English
  Universities since 1929; member of executive of League of Nations Union;
  leader in struggle for equal rights for women; and for care of refugees from the
  dictator states during the 1930's.

rather than get out and hopelessly oppose both the Government and the opposition parties:

> If the decision was wrong, no party is qualified to criticize it . . . No position is more untenable than that of those who now aver that they were all for fighting in the Far East in 1931, in the Mediterranean in 1935, in Spain in 1937 – all in just causes – for standing up to Hitler (why not Germany?) from 1933 (why not before?), while at the same time depriving us – and the just causes – of the material means of doing so. Here also the field is unsuitable for party warfare.[55]

This was an emphatic challenge to the pre-war record of all parties, and the party *fonctionnaires* were not slow in rushing to the barricades. The assault came mainly from the Left, with Michael Foot* leading the charge.[56] Foot's case was simple, perhaps deceptively so. His party had cast its vote against rearmament because of its 'unalterable opposition to a fatal foreign policy'. Voting against the defence estimates was, apparently, a traditional way of protesting against government policy in general. Moreover, if Van himself was so unutterably opposed to the government's policy, why did he not resign his position and alert the country to the bankruptcy of that policy? Neither of these points were thoroughly convincing, the first being disingenuous, the second simplistic, and Van had little difficulty in scoring off them. Quoting from a sixteenth century source, Francis Russell, the second Earl of Bedford, he defended his own record and the reputation of every civil servant:

> 'Those that serve must be directed always, though oftentimes it be to their great grief to put in execution all that they be commanded.' The nation must still choose between that maxim and having no public service at all.

Foot spoiled his own case by the intemperate tone of his language – 'Writing at the top of his voice', in Van's phrase – and by needlessly dragging in Van's contemptuous attitude towards the so-called German opposition, a hardy perennial in the armoury of every professional anti-Vansittart, but a topic which he had ignored in his original letter. Benefiting from *The Times* liberal editorial policy towards him, Van managed to get in the last word:

* Michael Foot (1913–   ): Labour M.P. for Devonport, 1945–55; for Ebbw Vale since 1960; Secretary of State for Employment, 1974–76; Lord President of Council and Leader of the House of Commons, 1976–   ; assistant editor *Tribune* 1937–38, ed., 1948–52, 1955–60, managing director, 1945–74; acting editor *Evening Standard*, 1942.

It [the controversy] started because Mr Foot imported his brand of Germanophilia into a question of inter-war armament. I will not take Mr Foot's idols at their face value because I know their feet of clay. For that refusal I have long been a red rag to a pink calf.

He was a difficult opponent to pin down in public. 'As slippery as an eel', was how an exasperated Michael Foot finally saw him. This was the kind of controversy he thrived on, out in the open and not concealed behind the walls of the Foreign Office, and he made full use of his literary skills to demolish the arguments of his adversaries.

On 6 June the Allied armies landed on the beaches of Normandy. The liberation of France had begun. Van had never disguised his love for France;[57] and if there had been a Francophile school at the Foreign Office, he would surely have headed it. Admittedly, the French had on occasion gravely disappointed him. Their pre-war record was blemished no less, perhaps more, than that of the British government. Nevertheless, his grief at the castastrophic collapse of France in 1940 had been deep and genuine, symbolizing as it did the end of an era in French politics he had intimately known. He had no doubt that the occupation of France was but an interregnum in the long history of French *grandeur*. Now that the liberation had begun, France could again take her rightful place among the Great Powers.

This was not a viewpoint widely accepted at the time. In particular, the Americans shied at committing themselves. The immediate issue was the recognition of some form of provisional French government which would constitute an authoritative voice in Franco-Allied relations. In Van's opinion de Gaulle's National Committee was the logical choice, and the Americans' obstinate refusal to acknowledge it was bound in the long run to gravely prejudice Anglo-French relations. Van was not so much concerned with securing de Gaulle's political future, for he recognized him as an extremely awkward and contrary partner, but with putting France back on the political map.[58] This was the mainspring behind his lobbying, for he consistently advocated French participation in the occupation and administration of Germany once the war had come to an end.[59]

His long-term aim was to resurrect the *entente* with Great Britain as the dominant element to provide a counter-balance between the United States and the Soviet Union, thereby securing a measure of independence for British policy from the domination of either of the super powers. Happily for Van his advocacy was crowned with success, though not his long-term strategy, and the French eventually took their place on an equal basis among the occupying powers.

He received recognition for his labours on the afternoon of 28 June 1948. *L'Academie des Sciences Morales et Politiques* elected him as a foreign member in place, ironically, of the late President Roosevelt. At the ceremony he read a paper on Anglo-French relations, the past history of which he summarized with the words 'too little and too late'. But peering into the future he envisaged the revival of the *entente*, and considered it a 'categorical imperative' that Anglo-French relations remain close 'for the protection of their common heritage'.[60] Two world wars had not shaken his confidence in the *entente* as the cornerstone of British foreign policy.

As the war approached its finale, so too did the debate on the future of post-war Germany. Van contended that his views were being systematically misrepresented. He could not reiterate enough that he favoured a decentralized, not dismembered, Germany.[61] Only Prussia had no place in his new Germany. The re-education of Germany, the reformation of the German character, would fail in its purpose unless the Prussian stranglehold were broken.[62]

Van was always careful to point out that a drastic peace imposed on Germany need not be an inhuman one. But to achieve a satisfactory post-war settlement, territorial changes in Eastern Europe were inevitable and should be accepted. Did this contravene the letter and spirit of the Atlantic Charter, as his opponents claimed?[63] Van was certain that the Charter did not preclude the territorial diminution of Germany, and that its relevant clauses were only a self-denying ordinance on the part of the Allies.[64]* In any case, he rationalized, whenever there was a case of conflicting interests, 'the Allied interest' must always be paramount.[65] Not content with the decimation of old Prussia's authority, he warmly applauded the Soviet intention to sever East Prussia from Germany.[66] He did so on the simple and incontrovertible grounds that the victims of aggression have a greater right to justice, retribution, and compensation than

* A reading of the Charter bears out Van's 'self-denying' interpretation of it (see articles 1 and 2). How did this square with the Sovietization of Eastern Europe? Quite obviously, it did not; and Van hammered away at the Soviet Union for all he was worth and on every conceivable occasion (see above, pp. 279–82). But he would have argued that the movement westwards of Soviet frontiers at *Germany's expense alone* was quite a different matter.

the aggressors. Thus he argued that it was morally right for the Soviet Union to expand into East Prussia and for Poland to seize territories in the west at Germany's expense.

So the discussion about Germany rolled on. Both sides, the 'Vansittartes' and the 'Bellites', yielded not one inch to the other. If anything, Van's opinions grew increasingly militant, almost in direct relation to the approach of Germany's defeat. This was quite natural. He was afraid of a sell-out, of a repetition of Versailles, of a soft peace made possible by allied myopia and German deviousness. Blind magnanimity in the context of the horrors of Germany's fifth war would be not only misguided but also dangerous. Even Churchill was not above Van's suspicions as the war drew to its climax.[67] Of course, there were no absolute values in this discussion. Yet as the stark reality of the German New Order in Europe was exposed, it became incredibly difficult to sustain the 'good German' image with any conviction. No doubt Bell and his followers saw themselves as the carriers of great, universal humanist values; but in the wake of Belsen and Auschwitz and the mass exterminations in the east these values appeared to be totally unrelated to the harsh facts. Their dream of the German people rising up against their Nazi oppressors proved to be a pipe-dream. Good Germans existed, no one denied that, but as Van had so graphically described them they had only position, not magnitude. Van's doctrine, so easily prone to distortion, was closer to the truth; and it almost certainly represented the majority feeling in the country.

Nor could he have been profoundly disappointed at the way the German problem resolved itself, whatever his initial misgivings. Some essential points must have met with his approval. The prolonged allied occupation; the decentralization of German governmental authority; the eclipse of Prussian ascendancy; even the partition of Germany, however hard the Soviet incursion into Western Europe was to accept. It is true that he campaigned for an even tougher settlement, though without any illusions that all his demands would be met. Aspects of the German settlement displeased him: the slipshod process of denazification, for example; or the lax control system over German heavy industry. Yet the German problem, as Van had known it for the past fifty years, had in practice ceased to exist. Cold war rivalries, already in evidence before the end of the shooting war, would ensure that Germany remained quiescent. She had become the plaything of the Great Powers with no distinct international existence of her own. For the foreseeable future, Europe would no longer be plagued by the German question. And it is not too fanciful to detect a strong dose of Vansittartism in the post-1945 German solution.

Van's war terminated on a most bizarre note. Ribbentrop, now on trial for his life at Nürnberg, had made an application to call Van as a character witness on his behalf.* Ribbentrop wished Van to indicate to the military tribunal that he had worked consistently in favour of an Anglo-German alliance and was not therefore involved in the planning of an aggressive war. This was an extraordinary request. Van detested Ribbentrop. He rated him as 'over-weeningly ambitious, cold-blooded as a fish, cruel and pretentious – but stupid, detestable and tiresome, and an evil creature', a harsh verdict with which most of Ribbentrop's acquaintances would have agreed. In any case, Van possessed definite ideas about the fate which should await war criminals. From the outset of war he had advocated imposing the harshest penalty of the law. Unlike many, he harboured no doubts as to the moral and historical value of the Nürnberg trials.[68] Only by placing the leaders of Nazi Germany on public trial and exposing their foul record to the eyes of the world would it be possible to avoid another German war. Ribbentrop's request, so typical of his vanity, was an intolerable provocation, particularly as he had the impudence to include Van in the company of men who had opposed him, even intrigued against him, in the years before the outbreak of war. Van declined to testify. In any event, the evidence against him was too damning. On 16 October, he was hanged in Nürnberg prison.

NOTES

1. *Dalton Diaries*, 25 February 1941.
2. *Ibid.*, 1 January 1941.
3. *Ibid.*, 27 January 1941.
4. *Ibid.*, 25 February, 1941.
5. *Ibid.*, 2 March 1941.
6. *Ibid.*, 14 February and 2 March 1941.
7. *Ibid.*, 19 February 1941; *Cadogan Diaries*, 372–3.
8. *Ibid.*
9. *The Times*, 22 May 1941.

---

* Ribbentrop's list of potential witnesses was a distinguished one. It included: Lord Beaverbrook; Lord Kemsley; Lord Londonderry; Lord Dawson of Penn; and Geoffrey Dawson. Apparently he was unaware that Geoffrey Dawson and Dawson of Penn had since died. See F.O. 371/50995, U. 9119/16/73, and 51008, U. 10442/16/73; also reports in *The Times*, 21 and 29 November 1945.

10. *The Times*, 12 June, 12 and 17 July 1941.
11. *Dalton Diaries*, 27 May 1941.
12. The correspondence for this episode may be seen in Vnst. 4/6.
13. For the debate, see *P.D.*, Lords, v. 112, c. 301–43.
14. *Evening Standard*, 24 February 1942.
15. See L. P. Lochner, ed., *The Goebbels Diaries* (New York, 1949), 115, 166, 172.
16. See 'A report on the reactions of German propaganda to Vansittart's speech', 25 March 1942, F.O. 371/30928, C. 3210/11/18.
17. Lochner, *op. cit.*, 392–3.
18. See, for example, his speech in the debate on Germany and the Hitlerite state, 10 March 1943, *P.D.*, Lords, v, 126, c. 549–50.
19. See A. Calder *op. cit.*, 567–70, for a convincing sketch of Bell.
20. See *P.D.*, Lords, v. 126, c. 535–82.
21. *P.D.*, Lords, v. 131, c. 978–9. 25 May 1944, and v. 132, c. 915–22, 13 July 1944. See also his letter to *Daily Telegraph*, 2 June 1944.
22. *P.D.*, Lords, v. 130, c. 109–18, 7 December 1943; also his speech on 11 February 1943, v. 125, c. 1057–69.
23. Interview with Lady Vansittart, 9 March 1973.
24. *Channon Diaries*, 326.
25. See F.O. 371/30936, C. 5262/739/18.
26. Interview with Lady Vansittart, 18 August 1972.
27. *P.D.*, Lords, v. 122, c. 1075.
28. *Ibid.*, c. 1076.
29. The author is grateful to Mr Adam Ciolkocz for providing him with the original 'Charter' and 'Aims' of 'Win The Peace' movement.
30. B. Dean, *Theatre at War* (London, 1954); and *Bristol Evening Post*, 17 September 1943, and 19 November 1944, quoted by A. Calder, *op. cit.*, 564.
31. See F.O. 372/38597, AN. 116/116/45. This file contains an appraisal of the book's reception in the press. Only the *New Republic* challenged Van, and then in a most qualified manner: 'There is not much danger that Vansittartism in *its more truculent forms* will have many disciples in this country.' (Author's italics.) This report is also of interest because it shows that the Foreign Office was compelled to keep an eye on Van and his activities abroad.
32. See *New York Times*, 23 March 1945, and F.O. 371/44577, AN. 1576/38/45.
33. See F.O. 371/46866, C. 1072/267/18.
34. For a report on her speech and the activities of the 'Never Again' association, see F.O. 371/39158, C. 6962/6962/18.
35. See F.O. 371/46803, C. 4197/71/18; F.O. 371/46826, C. 4964/155/18; F.O. 371/46910, C. 9739/2069/1.
36. Interview with Count Raczynski, 5 March 1973.
37. See his many speeches in the House of Lords on this subject.
38. Van to William Strang, 20 April 1944, F.O. 371/39119, C. 5425/712/18.
39. See Vnst. 4/7.
40. Van to Strang, 20 April 1944, F.O. 371/39119, C. 5425/712/18. Basil Newton, who was British minister in Prague in 1937, referred to Stampfer's accusations as 'Pure, or rather malicious, invention as far as I am concerned.'
41. For full text see Vnst. 4/7.
42. See Cmd. 6420. The main proposals were: to amalgamate the diplomatic, consular, and commercial services, with the Foreign Office; the separation of the Foreign Service from the Home Civil Service; improvements in conditions of

service; 'democratization' of training and recruitment procedures; and changes in the administrative structure of the Office.

43. See *P.D.*, Lords, v. 126, c. 926–951, 961–1020. The Commons debated the paper on 18 March (*P.D.*, Commons, v. 387, c. 1357–1438), and approved it by a majority of 153 to 6.

44. *The Times*, 27 and 29 March 1943.

45. See his speeches on Foreign Office reform, 13 December 1944, *P.D.*, Lords, v. 134, c. 294–7; v. 143, c. 873–82, 30 October 1946; v. 194, c. 575–7, 16 November 1955; v. 196, c. 888–97, 14 March 1956. Also, his article, 'The Decline of Diplomacy', *Foreign Affairs* (January 1950).

46. *P.D.*, Lords, v. 125, c. 224–72, 25 November 1942, and c. 275–325, 26 November 1942.

47. *P.D.*, Commons, v. 516, c. 151–52, 24 June 1953.

48. *P.D.*, Lords, v. 183, c. 351–5.

49. *The Times*, 15 June 1953. Both Harold Nicolson and Wickham Steed came publicly to Van's defence. See, *The Times*, 5, 9 and 11 June; also *Nicolson Diaries*, i, 333–4.

50. *The Times*, 20 June 1953.

51. See, for example, his contribution in the debate on the reform of the laws governing homosexual behaviour, see below, pp. 73–74.

52. Interview with Lady Vansittart, 31 October 1972.

53. *P.D.*, Commons, v. 404, c. 1714–63.

54. *Ibid.*, c. 1729–30.

55. Letter to *The Times*, 14 November 1944.

56. The controversy may be followed in *The Times*, 14–24 November 1944. Van wrote four letters in all, on 14, 17, 20 and 24 November. Walter Elliot, M.P., opened for the Conservatives (16 November), defending the right of parliament to debate these issues, a fact which Van did not challenge. He was followed by Michael Foot (16 and 18 November) defending Labour's record. After him came Wilfred Roberts, M.P. (24 November), who took up the Liberal cause with slightly more success. Other participants in the discussion were: Lord Perth, Robert Bower, M.P., Beverley Baxter, M.P., 'Non-Partisan', Luis Arquistan, Austin Hopkinson, M.P., T. D. Galbraith, M.P., and Air Commodore P. F. M. Fellowes, all of whom took a similar line to Van's. In this respect, see also Van's letter to *Sunday Express*, 3 January 1944. Some of this correspondence is in Vnst. 4/7.

57. See his tribute to the liberation of France in *The Times*, 7 June 1944.

58. See his speech in the Lords, 25 May 1944, v. 131, c. 972–81. And his unpublished letter to *The Times*, 30 June 1944, Vnst. 4/7.

59. See, for example, his speech in the Lords on 26 September 1944, v. 133, c. 120–28.

60. Report in *The Times*, 29 June 1948.

61. See *The Times*, 2, 7 and 11 March 1944, where he warmly supported A. L. Rowse's 'wise advocacy of a decentralised Germany'.

62. Draft of a letter, 28 January 1944, Vnst. 4/7, and *The Times*, 19 January 1944.

63. See letter to *Manchester Guardian*, 20 May 1944. Among the signatories were: Karl Ausch; H. N. Brailsford; Julius Braunthal, Victor Gollancz; Wengel Jaksch; Harold Laski; Hector McNeil; A. Ramos Oliveira; P. Ollenhauer; G. P. Strauss; Hans Vogel; and L. Woolf.

64. Van's letter to Emrys Hughes, 26 May 1944, Vnst. 4/7; and his letter to

Manchester Guardian, 1 June 1944, on the same subject. Also; *P.D.*, Lords, v. 133, c. 120–28, debate on occupation of Germany, 26 September 1944, and v. 133, c. 409–34, 10 October 1944; v. 134, c. 913–44, 7 February 1945; v. 136, c. 75–82, 1 May 1945, on the same topic.

65. See his speech in May 1944, *P.D.*, Lords, v. 131, c. 975–6.
66. *Ibid.*
67. Interview with Lady Vansittart, 31 October 1972.
68. See, for example, his speeches in the Lords, v. 125, c. 1057–69, 11 February 1943; v. 130, c. 109–18, 7 December 1943; v. 132, c. 916–22, 13 July 1944. Also his letter to *The Times*, 6 April 1945.

Y

CHAPTER XIII

Retirement

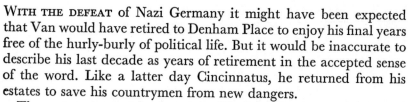

WITH THE DEFEAT of Nazi Germany it might have been expected that Van would have retired to Denham Place to enjoy his final years free of the hurly-burly of political life. But it would be inaccurate to describe his last decade as years of retirement in the accepted sense of the word. Like a latter day Cincinnatus, he returned from his estates to save his countrymen from new dangers.

There were two main themes to Van's post-1945 public career, and both were closely connected: his passionate belief in the political and economic integration of Western Europe; and his anti-Communist crusade. Through it all he emerged as an original, if enlightened, Cold War warrior. His suspicion of Russian ambitions was traditional and deep-rooted; and his acceptance of the Soviet Union as a wartime ally was an act of expediency, an extreme indication of his anti-Germanism. He first voiced in public his anti-Russian feelings in August 1944.[1] His excuse was the Russian refusal to assist the Warsaw uprising.* Protesting against Russian callousness, he invited the government to react sharply to 'this appalling and gratuitous tragedy'.[2] Here, for the first time, Van equated the similarity

---

* By the end of July the Russian armies had reached the outskirts of Warsaw. On 1 August, the commander of the Polish Home Army, general Tadeusz Bor-Komorowski, ordered his forces to liberate Warsaw from German rule and perhaps save her from Russian domination. The fighting lasted two months. Over 50,000 Poles were killed and 350,000 were deported to Germany. After the surrender, the Germans methodically destroyed what was left of the city. A great controversy followed. Could the Russians have saved the city and the Home Army? It now appears doubtful. The Russians had considerably overrun their supply and communication lines, and the Germans had reinforced their positions along the perimeter of the city. What is clear is that the Russians made no attempt to help the Poles, and obviously did not regret the annihilation of a force hostile to themselves.

of purpose and method between German and Soviet strategy. He later popularized the expression 'Communazis';[3] and it conformed perfectly to his estimation of the joint responsibility of the German and Russian generals for the Warsaw tragedy.

The first skirmishes of the Cold War were enacted on Polish territory. As the Russians advanced westwards they laid claim not only to the frontiers they had seized in September 1939, but also to the political and military domination of Poland through their creation, the Lublin Committee.* No amount of protestations from the West deflected the Soviet Union from its aim, or the Lublin Committee from its barrage of invective against its rivals in Poland and London. At first Van curbed himself, unwilling to exacerbate inter-allied relations while the main struggle against Germany was still undecided, and he took issue only with the 'intemperate' language of the Russian directed committee.[4] But after the Yalta decisions† and Churchill's statement that the freedom and sovereignty of Poland were more important than the actual line of frontiers, sentiments which Van generally endorsed,[5] he felt at liberty to ventilate his true feelings in public, for it was by now quite apparent that the Soviet Union was intent on bending Poland to her will. In a forthright letter to *The Times* he branded the Lublin Committee as a 'minority element' and stigmatized its activities as anti-democratic.[6]

Van's real target however was the Soviet Union. As the Russian armies swept through Eastern Europe, setting up Soviet-inspired governments on the way, his suspicions hardened. He noted with dismay the casual contempt displayed by the Soviet Union towards the minor powers and her repeated and successful attempts to trample underfoot their freedom of choice. Turning the Communists' political vocabulary upon its users, he traduced the Soviet Union as 'reactionary because it seeks to establish a new aristocracy of power'.[7] He pitched into the puppet régimes in Bulgaria, 'the bane

---

* The Polish Committee of National Liberation was established when the Red Army, together with Soviet-directed Polish forces, crossed the old Curzon line into Poland on 21 July 1944. In a manifesto published on the 25th the committee declared Lublin as the new capital of the new Poland. This body subsequently became known as the Lublin Committee.

† Regarding Poland, the conference (4–11 February 1945) agreed that the two rival Polish groups, the Lublin Committee and the Polish government-in-exile in London, should confer to concert some form of provisional régime. It was also proposed to hold 'free and unfettered elections . . . on the basis of universal suffrage and secret ballot', in which all democratic and anti-Nazi parties would have the right to participate. Although the question of Poland's frontiers was discussed, no final decision about them was reached.

of the Balkans', and Hungary, 'yet another police state'.[8] The troubles in Greece were attributed to 'A pertinacious attempt . . . to disrupt Greece, and to force her into the Communist bloc'.[9] He saddled the Communists with having 'violated every canon of fairness and humanity before our eyes, particularly in the field of justice'.[10] As an example he held up Czechoslovakia where 'terror was rampant' and 'innocent people [were] vanishing by the thousand'.[11] Time and again he inveighed against the violation of basic human rights behind the Iron Curtain, and exposed for public scrutiny the fate of political prisoners, including British citizens, who otherwise might have languished in Communist jails for years without a voice being raised on their behalf.[12]

Subversive activities by Communists in Great Britain was another topic which never failed to stir him. Allowing them virtually a free hand to spread their poison was, in his estimation, tantamount to cutting your own throat. Of course, he was influenced by his experience in the 1930's when he had constantly urged the suppression of Nazi–Fascist-like organizations, not, it must be admitted, with conspicuous success. In March 1950 he directed the attention of the House to the threat of Communist infiltration in the public services.[13] He did so at the height of the McCarthy witch-hunts in the United States, and although he immediately, and in the most unequivocal way, dissociated himself from the methods and aims of the junior senator from Wisconsin, 'the shy-making ballyhoo . . . the very way not to handle matters of this kind', the timing and contents of their respective campaigns left these two vastly contrasting characters as strange bed-fellows.

In a speech lasting one hour and ten minutes, Van surveyed the full extent of Communist subversion. No pillar of the establishment – the BBC, the Church, the educational system – escaped his probing. Names of Communist agents and tools flowed from his lips. Two per cent of the public service, he concluded, are Communist. And 'When I use the word "Communism",' he clarified, 'I simply mean "abominable cruelty".' This was a tough, uncompromising speech which moulded his image as a cold-war warrior. But his motion 'That continuous and resolute precautions are necessary for public security' was carried. A month later, however, a motion was put down by Viscount Stansgate* reprimanding Van that 'he

* William Wedgwood Benn (1877–1960): Liberal M.P., 1906–27; Labour M.P., 1927–31, 1937–42; Secretary of State for India, 1929–31; for Air, 1945–46. Cr. 1st Viscount Stansgate, 1941.

did not use due care in the exercise of the Privilege of Parliament'. Another full-scale debate ensued.[14] The House declined to rule in Stansgate's favour, despite Van's labelling him a 'fellow-passenger of fellow-travellers'. If Van wavered on the borderline of parliamentary privilege, he incontestably demonstrated his competence as a parliamentary tactician, forcefully presenting his case and skilfully evading any opposition or awkward questions. But his reputation also took a fresh leap forward. Some of his noble listeners shuddered at his 'Black Record Series, No. 2,' and sensed that they would soon be overwhelmed by series 'No. 3'. Certain newspapers – the *New Statesman* and *The Tribune* – abused him, a tradition they had begun during the first series. The *Reynolds News* dubbed him Lord Van Witchhunt; while the *Manchester Guardian* more elegantly referred to his personal crusade against Communism. But *Pravda* had the last word, and Van quoted it proudly, 'the senile yelpings of the half-drunken Lord Vansittart'.[15]

Van's fundamental political philosophy was motivated by a deep-rooted conviction that there could be no compromise whatever between liberal western democracy and any form of totalitarianism, whether it be Hitler's in the 1930's or Stalin's in the post-war era. 'You cannot do business with Totalitaria', he notified his lordships.[16] He asked: 'What is the difference between [Nazi] Germany and Russia?' And answered: 'It is colder in Russia.'[17] The struggle between these two diametrically opposed political systems could by no measure be bracketed with the political in-fighting basic to the party system. Van postulated that the international conflict had now moved into a new dimension. This was war, in fact 'the greatest war in history', and one either wins a war or loses it. Having seen Great Britain emerge only just victorious from the last war, he would do everything in his power to ensure that she did not lose this one by default. Van believed Stalin to be infinitely more dangerous than Hitler. For whereas Hitler had lost, Stalin had won. Half of Europe had fallen ransom to his whims. There was little the West could do now to reverse that situation; but she could and must remain constantly on the alert to prevent the other half from going the same way.[18] This now became Van's message to his countrymen.

The Communist *coup* in Czechoslovakia finally convinced him that there could never be any compromise with the Soviet *bloc*.*

---

* After the liberation, a National Front Government had been set up with the Communists playing a leading, but by no means dominant, role. On 17 February 1948, relations between the Communists and the non Communist parties grew extremely tense as a result of the Communist demand to implement far-reaching

The Czech tragedy was coupled with a human calamity, one which touched the Vansittarts personally. They were great friends of Jan Masaryk.* Shortly before returning to Prague, Masaryk had dined at Denham Place. Van warned him against returning to Czechoslovakia where he prophesied that a Communist takeover was imminent. Masaryk felt unable to heed his advice.[19] A few months after the Communist *coup* his dead body was discovered in the courtyard of the Czernis Palace, the Czech foreign ministry, at the foot of his apartment. Suicide or murder? The precise circumstances surrounding his death remain a mystery. But the ruthless display of Soviet ambition in Czechoslovakia convinced Van that Stalin would run the risk of a European war as recklessly as Hitler had done in the 1930's; and it was only the power of the United States, an unknown factor in 1938–39, which now restrained him.

But he was not wholly pessimistic as to the future. Peace could yet be attained subject to the following six basic conditions:[20] no undue reliance should be placed on treaties concluded with Russia, for she 'is possessed by the lust of world domination'; there should be no rapid disarmament, and no new ten-year rule; a long-term foreign policy must be formulated which should be 'uncompromisingly anti-totalitarian' and opposed to 'reactionary expansionism'; Western union should be encouraged; the closest possible relations should be maintained with the United States; and it was necessary, at all times, to repel 'all totalitarian myths and libels' directed against the West.

The key to his strategy lay in an integrated western policy which would be able to withstand, and even repulse, the Soviet steamroller.

---

and controversial nationalization plans, coupled with the decision of the Communist minister of the interior, Nosek, to flood the security forces with his own nominees and to purge them of non Communists. On 18 February the Communist Party issued a manifesto denouncing their government colleagues. Two days later the non Communists withdrew from the government. By the 25th, after mounting Communist pressure, Beneš, the Czech president, surrendered, and a new government was constructed which gave the Communists 12 out of 24 portfolios, Together with their Social Democrat hangers-on they commanded an overall majority. Thereafter the machinery of government was steadily communized and purged of all oppositionist elements. This was the Communist *coup* in Czechoslovakia. It was widely believed that Valentin Zorin, the Soviet Assistant Minister of Foreign Affairs who had arrived in Prague on 19 February ostensibly to supervise Soviet grain shipments, had orchestrated it.

* Jan Garrigue Masaryk (1886–1948): Czech minister to Great Britain, 1925–38; resigned in protest at Munich settlement; Czech foreign minister, 1940–48; Deputy Prime Minister, 1941–45; died 10 March 1948 in mysterious circumstances.

Once again, he was haunted by his memories of the 1930's. Hitler's bloodless victories of those years were made possible only because his victims had refused to combine and to act decisively against him. There must be no repetition of this fatal mistake. Van was an early advocate of Western unity. Since the end of the war he had on three occasions attempted to introduce a motion in the Lords calling for Western integration; three times the government had rebuffed him. Finally, in January 1946, he succeeded.[21] The Union he envisaged would bring immeasurable benefits: political cooperation; military strength; economic prosperity. At the outset, it would consist of the states of Western Europe and the Scandinavian countries. He was prepared to admit Italy (a relic from his pre-war fascination with that country), but there was no place in his scheme for Spain or Portugal, at least not until those régimes obtained a democratic form of government.

He saw no viable alternative to Western integration. In an era when world politics was destined to be dominated by the super powers, any other path would be 'tantamount to disappearing from the international scene and the ultimate loss of the last remnants of our independence'. Six months later he advocated an Anglo-French alliance as the first step towards, and cornerstone of, European unity.[22] By the end of the year the House of Lords, again as a result of his prompting, was debating the coordination of Western Europe.[23]

This last speech contained one significant innovation. It is a mark both of his realism and his appreciation of the Soviet threat that barely twenty months after the war had ended he began to toy with the idea of including West Germany in his programme of Western unity. He did so tentatively and with many qualifications. But it was only the forerunner of more explicit statements about the return of Germany to the European fold.

He viewed the prospect of German rearmament, however limited, with extreme disquiet,[24] reluctant as he was to accept the idea that German mentality had altered sufficiently to warrant such a step. But the magnitude of the crisis was such as to dictate extreme measures. There can be no mistaking the agonizing reappraisal he had to make: 'My lifelong antipathy to Germany is known, yet for once in all the blue moons of existence I acknowledge a German Government and tendency which might perhaps be turned to the account of Christian civilization.'[25] This was an astonishing *volte face* for Van to have made, and to justify it he needed to elaborate extreme political scenarios with the Russians on the brink of world, or at the very least European, conquest.[26] At the height of the Cold War it

was deceptively easy to point to many pertinent examples to substantiate the Communist urge to world domination. His anti-Communist crusade was a natural, inevitable continuation of his anti-
German campaign of yesteryear. Ideologically at least they both
stemmed from the same source.*

It would be a simple exercise to dismiss Van's immoderate anti-
Communist rhetoric; to regard him as an antiquated, pre-historic
survival of a bygone age out of touch in the post-1945 era. The
emotive, unyielding and persistent nature of his speeches and letters
– with their latent vein of violence – lend credence to this assessment.
No spirit of compromise crept into his *Weltanschauung*. By a curious
paradox he, like his Nazi or Communist adversaries, viewed international politics as an eternal struggle between the Children of Light
and the Children of Darkness. Peaceful coexistence or *detente*, those
fashionable catchphrases of contemporary times, would have been
regarded by Van at worst as a shabby confidence trick, or at best
as a goal to be approached with extreme care and to be abandoned
at the first sign of double-dealing. He adamantly refused to take
Communist protestations of peace at their face value. It is too early
to judge whether Van's fears were fully justified. The discussion is
still in full swing. But it is quite certain that recent Soviet policy
would not have eased his mind. The appearance of Soviet tanks in
Prague in August 1968 and the raising of a new dogma, the Brezhnev
doctrine, to say nothing of Russian meddling in the Middle East and
the Communist takeover in South East Asia, all would have suggested to him that the Communist appetite for world domination
had not been diminished by one iota.†

Apart from his official engagements, Van, during the last years of
his life, cut down his social activities to a minimum. He rarely tra-

* Some of his invective rubbed off onto China, another touchstone upon which
Van sharpened his cold war warrior image. He resolutely opposed the recognition of China, and emerged as a champion of Formosan independence. 'Shall
we build up hostile countries until they can fight us?' he asked. Neither would
he contemplate allowing China into the United Nations, at least not until she
called off her wars in Korea, Malaya, and Indo-China, for to do so would be the
appeasement of Communism, and 'Communism everywhere is our enemy'. See
his speeches in the Lords, v. 170, c. 299–300, 14 February 1951; v. 171, c. 618–31,
2 May 1951. And his letters to *The Times*, 23 January 1949, 17 and 14 January
1950, and 26 July 1950.
† Van died before the hitherto monolithic Communist world showed signs of
cracking. The Sino-Russian rift was still in its infancy; and it was still widely
believed that the anti-colonialist, revolutionary forces, wherever and whenever
they raised their heads, were firmly under the patronage of their Russian and

velled, and spent as much time as possible at Denham Place, meticulously answering his voluminous correspondence, writing his books, preparing his speeches, attending to the numerous demands of running his estate.[27] There is an absolute contrast here between the uninhibited socializing of his youth and the elderly, retired diplomatist avoiding the pleasures of high society. To a degree this process began after his second marriage, and was no doubt a natural reflection of his happy marital status. But it may also be interpreted as a deep-rooted, perhaps unconscious, desire to spurn the society which had rejected him. If there was little common language at the official level, why should he bother himself pandering to their social expectations? At any rate, Van retreated more and more into his shell, venturing out only occasionally to mix with his old cronies.

During his retirement Van devoted a great deal of time to writing, itself a solitary occupation. Pamphlets for his 'Win the Peace' campaign, or more substantial works such as *Lessons of My Life* or *Bones of Contention*, were produced in steady profusion. All of these publications were highly contentious, inspired only by memory and emotion. Even the most serious of them, *Lessons of My Life*, was written without reference to any official documents.[28] By the end of the war Van was contemplating recording a more authoritative account of his years in office. He filed an application to quote from his own official papers; but it was rejected, politely but firmly, on the grounds that no civil servant, whether serving or retired, 'may be permitted to publish privately memoranda written in his official capacity'.[29]

Van took exception to this ruling. A fundamental principle was involved. He could not possibly accept the suggestion

> that there should be one law for those who give their whole life to the Service of the State and another for politicians – [?]* failures at home – who take away from us professional diplomatists some of the few real rewards in our Service, and not infrequently make failures there also.[30]

Pointing to the example of Lloyd George, who was reported to have made £100,000 out of his memoirs, and anticipating an even greater

---

Chinese masters. This was the modern-day equivalent of the Axis conspiracy theory of the 1930's. Van would no doubt have wished to take tactical advantage of these differences to play off one criminal power against the other, as he had tried to play off Italy against Germany. But it is doubtful whether these ideological cum political disputes would have fundamentally altered his view of world politics as a clash between two rival systems. Totalitaria *versus* Democracy.

* The word in the original draft was 'often'. He then substituted it for another word which is illegible in the final draft.

sale for Churchill's books, he remonstrated against the manifest injustice of sanctioning vast profits for politicians while condemning the professional diplomatist to rusticate in silence and poverty. Convincing though this argument is to any reasonably sane person, it evinced scant response from the government.[31] When Van came to write his memoirs, he was most circumspect in his use of official papers, a fact which doubtless contributed to the abstruseness of *The Mist Procession*.

From the recollections of his employees, Van emerges as a somewhat idealized figure, benevolent and paternalistic, without any 'hang-up' about his *seigneurial* position, yet quite spontaneous in his day-to-day relations with his servants.[32] The Vansittarts took a benign interest in the welfare of the children of the estate, often inviting them to parties at their house or inviting themselves to festivities at their homes. Once a year they entertained at Denham Place a coach-load of working-class mothers and children sent on the initiative of his two sisters, Sibell and Marjorie, who were engaged in philanthropic work in the East End.

But by far the most vivid and intimate portrait of Van in domestic retirement emerges from a letter by a member of an old, sixteenth-century Denham family who knew the Vansittarts well. It is worth quoting extensively:[33]

My husband ... was born in a house, since converted, just outside the village entrance to Denham Place. We moved back into this house on the death of his mother in 1940, then having three small children. Immediately we found that Lord Vansittart and his wonderful wife took an interest in us and our children. They would stop and talk to them and to us and would remember them at Christmas and other festivities. My husband was a member of the Church Choir and as our sons grew up they joined the Choir too. Lord and Lady Vansittart always went to Evensong at 6.30 p.m., and the Lessons were always read by his Lordship. He had a preference for the Book of Ecclesiastes (I think he often read this in preference to the appointed lesson), and I have memories of his saying 'Vanity of vanities – all is vanity', and other phrases from that beautiful but rather cynical book.

After Church he would often stroll back down the village street with my husband and myself talking about all sorts of things. He took a lively and slightly mischievous interest in some items of village gossip. At other times he would ask our opinion of some item of public interest, but never with any condescension. We never at any time with him or Lady Vansittart had a feeling of the old feudal system, 'the rich man in his castle, the poor man at his gate'.

My daughter won a scholarship to the High School at High Wycombe, and he walked into my house one summer morning, it must have been in the summer of 1950, and gave her a lovely Parker Pen as a present. I remember he suffered from sciatica badly and walked with a stick at that time. Another son of mine was given the freedom of the grounds at Denham Place, and he gave him a 12 bore shotgun to shoot squirrels which were a pest at that time. He also kept pigs and my son used to help the pigman. He remembers the lively interest his Lordship took in the pigs, walking down every morning to look at them. This son of mine went into the Merchant Navy and Lord Vansittart would stop and ask how he was getting on. Sometimes I had a letter and he would read it with real interest. On one occasion my son mentioned the awful food and the fact that he was always hungry (this was at the training school). The next thing was that I had an excited letter from my son to say that an enormous hamper had arrived from Fortnum and Mason's from 'the Vansittarts'. There were many cases of kind little acts like this, and an interest was always taken in our doings. This may sound very much as if we were toadying for favour, but this was very far from the case. My husband and I being then very active members of the Labour Party, and we were rather social outcasts in the village because of this.

. . . [When we moved home] we missed the Village dreadfully, but the Vansittarts still kept in touch with us, always stopping to chat if we ever met. They gave each of our children a glowing reference when they left school and looked for jobs. When my eldest daughter married they gave her £100 as a wedding present . . .

. . . no-one ever meeting him as we did could imagine that this was the 'grey eminence' of the Foreign Office, the distinguished aristocratic diplomat, the entertainer, and guest of kings, etc. He was a kindly, courteous, elderly, good-looking man, with a twinkle in his grey-blue eyes and a lively interest in his fellowmen and a definite love of children.

One other incident springs to mind. In the middle of Denham Village is now a Green. This used to be a collection of dilapidated houses, which was condemned and pulled down. The land was bought by Lady Vansittart, but he often said that he wanted to

see a Village Green with the children playing and the men drink-
ing their beer on it. My children started playing on it as it was
outside our front door. This did not please the next-door lady.
One day we were told that this was the 'last day your children will
play on the Green as the Council are taking it over and it will be
railed round'. I felt that this was not what had been intended, and
went immediately to Denham Place and told them about this.
Great consternation and phonings for of course this was entirely
against his Lordship's wishes. So the Green was invested in the
Church Council and up to this day it is still a public green, given
by Lady Vansittart's brother in memory of their mother, but the
idea was Lord Vansittart's.*

During the winter of 1954–55 Van experienced another attack of
dermatitis.[34] The disease, psychosomatic in origin according to his
specialist, mainly affected his hands and arms. Van had a long
history of such attacks. He was advised to think about 'beautiful
things, roses, etc'. Eventually his meditation vanquished his afflic-
tion, and he slowly recovered his health. But soon after he suffered
a relapse.

In the autumn of 1956 Van was invited to Aberdeen to speak at
a public function. Whilst there he contracted a chill. He never fully
recovered from its effects. One night, after dining at Claridges, he
fainted. The fainting spells now began to occur with alarming regularity. A heart specialist was consulted but he found nothing or-
ganically wrong. However, Van as a young man had been an inveterate smoker, and his lungs, apparently, had been affected, for he
now had considerable difficulty in breathing normally. His health
and frame of mind, now generally uncertain, were also affected by
the international situation. On 26 July 1956 President Nasser of
Egypt nationalized the Suez canal, thus precipitating an international crisis of major proportions. The government, now presided
over by his old chief, Anthony Eden, distinguished itself only by its
lack of decision. Great Britain's international reputation plummeted
to a new low. Eden's inept handling of the crisis deeply depressed
Van.

Van held no brief for the new revolutionary régime in Egypt.†
Quite the contrary, he despised the colonels' dictatorship, to his
mind a squalid imitation of the more impressive European tyrannies.

* The commemoration plaque is still there.
† On 23 July 1952 King Farouk was overthrown in a military coup led by General
  Naguib. In April 1954 Nasser ousted Naguib, and two years later was elected
  President of the United Arab Republic.

Questions which had plagued Anglo-Egyptian relations since his days as Curzon's private secretary – the future of the Sudan and the Canal zone – came to the fore again as Egyptian nationalism soared to new heights of extremism. Egypt was now governed by a 'fundamentally unstable régime' which expressed 'dangerous xenophobic sentiments'. As for Nasser, he was nothing more than a 'crooked Anglophobe', 'a rabble-rouser', 'and a naked aggressor without even the loincloth of pretence. Give him a little more licence and he will set the whole East alight, beginning with Israel, just as surely as success was Hitler's fuel.'[35]

He knew that only a tough line would induce Nasser to back down. In a major speech in September 1956,[36] his last, he warned against placing too much reliance on the United Nations, while acknowledging that all diplomatic recourses must be exhausted before embarking on more drastic means to resolve the crisis. Re-living the past, he drew a parallel with Hitler and the events of the 1930's. His vision was truly apocalyptic. Nasser, like Hitler, wished first to destroy the Jews; then he would go on to unite all Arabia and Africa against the West. When Hitler had seized the Rhineland, it was argued that he could do as he pleased in his own country. Now, those same people were shouting the same defeatist slogans about Nasser. This was the last chance to avoid disaster in the East; but to do so it was essential to act, and to act decisively.

It was not only the lack of a firm and resolute government response which disturbed him. What he found most deplorable of all was the lack of national unity at a moment of supreme crisis. Instead, he found himself surrounded by pygmy-like politicians striving to extract the maximum political capital out of a national emergency. This was the surest recipe for national suicide. 'Before I die', he told the House, 'I should like to see again a day in which it is safe to be British.'[37] Unhappily, it was not to be. His last appearance in the House was spent in making enquiries about the fate of the unfortunate Lieutenant Moorhead.* But Eden's conduct, his fumbling and dithering, his inability to carry through a sustained course of action, had thoroughly disillusioned him. The last great international crisis through which he lived saw Great Britain humbled and humiliated as never before. It was a shameful finale to his country's role as a great power.

---

* On Christmas Day 1956 it was announced in London that the dead body of 2nd Lt Alan Moorhead had been recovered in Port Said. He had disappeared a few days earlier, presumably kidnapped by Egyptian irregulars. It was afterwards concluded that he had suffocated to death.

A week after his enquiries about Lt. Moorhead, he fell seriously ill. For the past month his health had been a matter for much concern. At the end of December, while watching an athletics competition on television, he complained to Lady Vansittart that he felt as though he himself had been running. His heart was like a 'fluttering bird'. The doctor diagnosed paraxysmal tachycardia, a very rapid, regular heart action, the rate ranging from 160 to 200 beats per minute. The condition is usually harmless unless it occurs as a complicating feature of some other form of heart disease, or in the elderly, or if it is prolonged. With Van all three factors were present. In addition to his heart condition he contracted a severe chill towards the beginning of February. He was confined to his bed, his condition gradually deteriorating. For two or three days he appeared to make a slight recovery. But he soon suffered a relapse and died in his sleep, peacefully and without pain, on the afternoon of 14 February 1957.*38 He was seventy-five years of age. His body was taken overnight to St Mary's church, Denham, from where it was removed to Woking, Surrey, for cremation according to his wishes. No national memorial exists for Van. But in the shadow of Denham church there lies a stone, now somewhat faded, to his memory.

NOTES

1. See his letter to the *Daily Mail*, 14 August 1944.
2. Van to Eden, 4 September 1944, F.O. 371/39496, C. 11943/1077/55.
3. *P.D.*, Lords, v. 154, c. 352–62, 3 March 1948.
4. See *P.D.*, Lords, v. 133, c. 280–82, 3 October 1944.
5. See his speech in the Lords, v. 135, c. 246–50.
6. See *The Times*, 13 March 1945.
7. *The Times*, 28 September 1945.
8. *The Times*, 21 August 1946, and 23 June 1947.
9. *The Times*, 29 July 1947 and 8 January 1948.
10. *The Times*, 1 September 1947; see also the issue for 27 November 1947.
11. *The Times*, 21 October 1949.
12. See for example, *P.D.*, Lords, v. 148, c. 529–42, 11 June 1947; v. 153, c. 600–608, 22 January 1948; v. 156, c. 78–86, 2 June 1948; v. 159, c. 693–706, 1 December 1948; v. 161, 177–78, 8 March 1948, c. 601–10, 23 March 1948; v. 163, c. 348–49, 28 June 1949. These examples are taken almost at random and could be duplicated many times over.

---

* The cause of death was certified as congestive cardinal failure accompanied by acute pulmonary oedema, a not uncommon combination. Pulmonary oedema may also result from changes in the permeability of the lung capillaries brought about by inhaling chemical mixtures, a condition which fits in well with Van's earlier smoking habits.

13. *P.D.*, Lords, v. 166, c. 607–31, 29 March 1950.
14. *P.D.*, Lords, v. 167, c. 3–53, 2 May 1950.
15. These quotations are taken from his speech in the Lords, v. 168, c. 837, on 27 July 1950.
16. *P.D.*, Lords, v. 158, c. 278–83.
17. *P.D.*, Lords, v. 154, c. 353.
18. These themes may be followed in, *P.D.*, Lords, v. 154, c. 352–62, 3 March 1948; v. 158, c. 278–83, 24 March 1948; v. 161, c. 87–89, 2 March 1949.
19. A private communication.
20. See his speech, *P.D.*, Lords, v. 154, c. 352–362, 3 March 1948.
21. *P.D.*, Lords, v. 138, c. 1089–1101, 24 January 1946.
22. *P.D.*, Lords, v. 142, c. 1053–1062, 29 July 1946.
23. *P.D.*, Lords, v. 144, c. 554–62, 3 December 1946. This theme was a characteristic of many of his speeches during this period. See in particular, Lords, v. 157, c. 1333–34; his letter to *The Times*, 24 March 1946; his speech to the Tool Makers Association, 19 May 1948, Vnst. 4/11.
24. See *P.D.*, Lords, v. 168, c. 837–45, 27 July 1950.
25. *The Times*, 31 May 1954.
26. See, for example, his letter to *The Times*, 28 September 1951.
27. Interview with Lady Vansittart; and a private communication from Mr Heffer, the Vansittarts' butler.
28. See Van to Sir Samuel Hoare, 18 June 1943, Templewood Papers XIII:19.
29. Sir Orme Sargent to Van, 30 October 1946, Vnst. 4/9.
30. Van to Sir Orme Sargent, 2 November 1946, Vnst. 4/9.
31. See Sir Orme Sargent to Van, 19 November 1946, Vnst. 4/9.
32. I am particularly indebted to the recollections of Mr Heffer for this passage.
33. I am deeply grateful to Mrs M. Delderfield for this communication, 1 March 1973. The letter has been edited only marginally.
34. The passages relating to Van's health are based on interviews with Lady Vansittart.
35. See *P.D.*, Lords, v. 199, c. 753–5, 13 September 1956. For Van's anti-Egyptian views, see also *P.D.*, Lords, v.181, c. 352–3; v. 184, c. 209–10; v. 185, c. 238–401, 1099–1100; v. 186, c. 880–81; v. 189, c. 1285–8; v. 194, c. 209; v. 196, c. 55–6, 388–97, 1099–1100; v. 199, c. 753–5. The dates of these comments range from March 1953–September 1956.
36. *P.D.*, Lords, v. 199, c. 753–5.
37. See *P.D.*, Lords, v. 201, c. 40–41, 23 January 1957.
38. See *The Times*, 9, 11, and 12 February 1957; and interviews with Lady Vansittart.

Epilogue

VAN CONCLUDED HIS MEMOIRS in a vein all too easily recognizable. 'Mine is a story of failure', he wrote, 'but it throws light on my time which failed too.'* This is a disarmingly generous, even-handed verdict on his life's work. One suspects, however, that he placed greater emphasis on the latter part of his summing-up than on the first. The times had failed him, not the other way round. In one sense this was certainly true. Few men of his generation perceived with greater clarity the predominant menace of the times through which he lived.

The German problem possessed him as violently as any *dyybuk;* and he was surely right on this most basic of issues. This is all the more surprising in that he was able to shake loose from his Edwardian inheritance, at least in part. Although he was brought up in the hey-day of British imperialism, he was almost wholly European-oriented in his approach to world politics. The Empire was important for him only in so far as it strengthened Britain's European position. Unlike many of his contemporaries, he instinctively understood that relatively minor changes in the European balance – even in far away places in central Europe – were in fact more vital to Britain's security and future than seemingly major changes on the periphery. He did not, however, entirely abandon the dream of a great, imperial role for Britain. This time, faithful to his Edwardian tradition, he was still deluded by visions of imperial *grandeur*, seduced by the nostalgia,

* *The Mist Procession* comes to a halt at the end of 1935. In a prefatory note, Lady Vansittart explained that Van wrote the Epilogue (*M.P.*, 550–52) in advance of completion of his book of reminiscences. 'During the writing he had a strong conviction that he might not be able to finish the book. The final pages were, therefore, written to conclude whatever chapter proved to be the last.'

the genuine opulence and the deceptive self-confidence of that era. The process of readjustment to the harsher realities of Britain's post-war position was as bewildering for him as for most of his countrymen. But his view was simply that a German hegemony in Europe signalled the end of the British Empire. Britain could not be a first-rate power in the Far East and a second-rate one in Europe. It was a classic exposition of the European balance of power doctrine in British foreign policy tradition.

No single explanation can account for his overriding concern with the European balance. Perhaps the key to his Europeanism lay in his gift for languages which in reality amounted to a gift for penetrating other cultures. At any rate, it is clear that his mastery of the major European languages gave him an insight into the political problems confronting Europe which many of his contemporaries lacked.

No doubt this 'cultural gap' was a serious hindrance to smooth relations between Van and his chiefs. Yet, as we have seen, his bitter complaint that he could recall 'no major issue' on which his advice was taken[1] rests on no foundation of fact. From 1930 to 1935 he stood in the front row of British foreign policy decision-makers and his influence, though lessened, remained formidable until the last months of 1937. The politicians listened to him, at least as much as they listened to any civil servant, though with a mounting degree of incredulity and alarm. It is perfectly true that he preached a message which his ministerial chiefs found increasingly difficult to accept, particularly during his last years as Permanent Under Secretary and as Chief Diplomatic Adviser. They were quite simply speaking on different wavelengths. Yet the complete explanation for his over-publicized 'failure' must also be sought in more personal terms. In the final analysis, he was reduced to helplessness as much by a combination of his own faults as by the mediocrity of the politicians he served.

His life-style, his intellectual vigour, his literary vanity, his flair for the dramatic, ensured that his relationships with his ministerial wards would be uncomfortable ones. He accepted the anonymous role of a civil servant with equanimity only when he sensed that, if the occasion demanded it, he could dominate the partnership between permanent official and minister. Nowhere is this more evident than in his relationship with Eden – by any reckoning a less formidable figure than he. Supremely confident in his own powers, he was an uneasy servant to lesser men.

It is pointless to speculate whether or not he should have gone after the Hoare–Laval affair. He did not do so for a variety of reasons, but ultimately because he convinced himself of his own indispensibility. Like countless others before him, he succumbed to the most deadly, and common, of human traits, that which the Greeks described as *hubris*. What is clear is that by staying on, his political masters came passionately to resent him, and that this feeling was communicated to some of his Whitehall associates. His ardent and mercurial temperament was out of keeping with the spirit of the times.

No public figure can or should remain immune from criticism. Van came in for his share, some of it legitimate, some of it wide of the mark. None of this detracts from his stature, and in a curious way, because of the issues involved, even adds to it. He remains a most attractive figure, warts and all. Miss Rebecca West, who knew him well, may have the last word: 'how very pleasant it was to know the last Renaissance man'.[2]

NOTES

1. *M.P.*, 550.
2. See her article in *The Sunday Times*, 4 May 1958.

A Bibliographical Note

GATHERING MATERIAL for this volume was not an easy matter. Unlike the subjects of some biographies, Van did not leave a vast, even if undigested, corpus of private papers. It is true that a Vansittart collection is deposited at Churchill College, Cambridge. But this collection is somewhat misleading. It is not a private archive in the accepted sense, but rather a selected edition of Van's official papers and minutes. This is not to decry its value, for it is undoubtedly convenient and time-saving to have access to this mass of raw material in one place and in an organized framework. But it has its drawbacks too. This is particularly evident concerning the anthologies of minutes he directed be made up during his last years in office. Valuable though they are, these minutes are unquestionably 'loaded'. They were intended to prove a case, Van's case, and they do so admirably. This is of course perfectly legitimate. It remains only to emphasize that the minutes must be treated with some caution. Often it has proved impossible to trace the context in which they were written, the original being buried somewhere beneath the mass of files in the PRO. But of more relevance, they reveal Van as being consistently right. From the confines of his archives he always pronounces, as it were, *ex cathedra*. As this is beyond the capacity of any earthly body, the Vansittart collection tends to give an unbalanced and far too undiscerning portrait of the man and his opinions.

The collection is also wholly dominated by its official correspondence; it is almost totally lacking in private papers. This is a serious handicap, and one that cannot be fully rectified either by interviews – in any case, an unreliable method of conducting historical research – or by consulting other collections of private papers. Nevertheless, many other private collections were consulted and many interviews conducted, and to a certain degree the gap has been bridged. Obviously there is an element of hit and miss involved. No method can be entirely watertight. For years the author lived in the hope that somewhere, somehow, a secret Vansittart diary would be unearthed which would reveal all – every researcher's fantasy! Perhaps someone either luckier or more thorough than he will be privileged to make this revelation. Until then, here are listed those archival and other sources consulted in the preparation of this work.

The vast majority of the material is in the PRO. Here are deposited all the CAB. and the F.O. series, the bulkiest of which are the political files (F.O. 371) of the Foreign Office. The F.O. 800 series contains the following collections of private papers consulted: Lord Bertie of Thame; Sir Alexander Cadogan; Lord Cecil; Sir Austen Chamberlain; Sir Eyre Crowe; Lord Curzon; Lord Halifax; Arthur Henderson; Sir Samuel Hoare; Sir John Simon; Sir Cecil Spring-Rice; and Ralph Wigram. It should be noted that these collections are almost always incomplete, the remainder, indeed often the most important part of the collection, being deposited elsewhere, as for example with the Curzon or Templewood papers. Other collections are misleading. The Wigram papers, to take an extreme example, consist solely of a series of his lectures on British foreign policy.

Other private collections consulted included those of: Group Captain M. G. Christie; Lord Hankey; Sir Eric Phipps; Sir Thomas Inskip; Sir Oliver Lyttleton. All these papers are at Churchill College, Cambridge. In addition: the Royal Archives, Windsor; the Templewood and Baldwin papers, University Library, Cambridge; the Beaverbrook and Lloyd George papers, Beaverbrook Library, London; the Lothian (Philip Kerr) papers, Scottish Record Office, Edinburgh; the Weizmann papers, Rehovoth; the Dalton diaries, LSE; the MacDonald papers, at the time of writing in the possession of Mr D. Marquand, M.P.; the Curzon papers, India Office, London. I have already noted elsewhere (see Acknowledgements) those individuals who kindly agreed to be interviewed in connection with this work. Their recollections proved to be invaluable when filling in gaps which otherwise would have remained embarrassingly empty.

I have also made extensive use of Hansard, Parliamentary Debates 5th series, Lords and Commons, and the Newspaper Library at Colindale, in particular for the period after 1941 when Van's career entered its public stage. In this connection, I must again place on record my thanks to Mr and Mrs D. Corfield who placed at my disposal a private collection of newspaper cuttings concerning Van's many activities.

Other Material

I make no attempt here to draw up a comprehensive bibliography or the life and times of Lord Vansittart. I note only those works which have been used directly in the writing of this book, or which have been found particularly useful when considering background material. The place of publication is London, unless stated otherwise.

Allen, R. C., *Great Britain and the United States* (1954)

Ashton-Gwatkin, F. T. A., *The British Foreign Service* (Syracuse, 1950)

Aster, S., *The Making of the Second World War* (1973)

Aster, S. (ed.), *The 'X' Documents* (1974)

Avon, Earl of, *Facing the Dictators* (1962)

Ayerst, D., *Guardian. Biography of a Newspaper* (1971)

Baer, G., *The Coming of the Ethiopian War* (Harvard University Press, 1967)

Barros, J., *Betrayed From Within* (Yale University Press, 1969)

Bialer, U., *Some Aspects of the Fear of Bombardment from the Air And the Making of British Defence and Foreign Policy, 1932–39* (unpublished Ph.D. thesis, University of London, 1974)

Bond, B. (ed.), *Chief of Staff. The Diaries of Lt. Gen. Sir Henry Pownell* (1972)

Brailsford, H., *Germans and Nazis: A Reply to Lord Vansittart* (n.d.)

Bullock, A., *Hitler. A Study in Tyranny* (1969)

Butler, R., *The Roots of National Socialism* (1942)

Calder, A., *The People's War* (1971)

Carlton, D., *MacDonald versus Henderson* (1970)

Cecil, R., *The Myth of the Master Race: Alfred Rosenberg and Nazi Ideology* (1972)

Churchill, R., *The Rise and Fall of Anthony Eden* (1959)

Collier, B., *The Defence of the United Kingdom* (1957)

Colvin, I., *Vansittart in Office* (1965); *The Chamberlain Cabinet* (1971)

Conwell-Evans, T., *None So Blind* (1947)

Cowling, M., *The Impact of Hitler: British Politics and British Policy, 1933–40* (Cambridge University Press, 1975)

Craig, G. A., and Gilbert, F., *The Diplomats, 1919–39* (New York, 1965)

D'Abernon, Lord, *An Ambassador of Peace* (1929)

Dalton, H., *Memoirs i: Call Back Yesterday* (1953)

Dalton, H., *Memoirs ii: The Fateful Years* (1957)

Dennis, P., *Decision by Default* (1972)

Dilks, D. (ed.), *The Diaries of Sir Alexander Cadogan, 1938–45* (1971)

Documents on British Foreign Policy, 1918–39 (1946–   )

Documents Diplomatiques Français, 1932–39 (Paris, 1962–   )

Documents on German Foreign Policy, 1918–45 (1948–   )

Fraenkel, Heinrich, *Vansittart's Gift for Goebbels* (n.d.)

Franckenstein, G., *Facts and Features of My Life* (1939)

Fry, G., *Statesmen in Disguise* (1969)

Gannon, F. R., *The British Press and Germany, 1936–39* (OUP, 1971)

Gehl, J., *Austria, Germany and the Anschluss* (OUP, 1964)

Gilbert, M., *Sir Horace Rumbold. Portrait of a Diplomat* (1973); *Churchill, vol. v* (1976)

Gollancz, V., *Shall Our Children Live or Die? A Reply to Lord Vansittart* (1942)

Gooch, G. P., *Studies in German History* (1948)

Gooch and Temperley, H., *British Documents on the Origins of the First World War, 1898–1914* (1929–38)

Gregory, J. D., *On the Edge of Diplomacy* (1928)

Grenville, J. A. S., *Lord Salisbury and Foreign Policy* (1964)

Halifax, Earl of, *Fulness of Days* (1957)

Hardinge, Lord, *Old Diplomacy* (1947)

Hildebrand, K., *Vom Reich zum Weltreich. Hitler, NSDAP und Koloniale Frage, 1919–1945* (Munich, 1969)

Howard, M., *The Continental Commitment* (1972)

Howard, Lord, *Theatre of Life* (1936)

James, R. R. (ed.), *'Chips'. The Diaries of Sir Henry Channon* (1970)

Jones, T., *A Diary with Letters, 1931–1950* (OUP, 1969)

Kelly, D., *The Ruling Few* (1952)

Knatchbull-Hugesson, H., *Diplomat in Peace and War* (1949)

Koffler, D., *Vansittartitus. A Polemic* (1943)

Kordt, E., *Nicht Aus den Akten. Die Wilhelmstrasse in Freiden und Krieg* (Stuttgart, 1950)

Lammers, D., 'The Engineers Trial (Moscow 1933) and Anglo-Soviet Relations', *The South Atlantic Quarterly* (Spring, 1963)

Larner, C., 'The Amalgamation of the Diplomatic Service with the Foreign Office', *Journal of Contemporary History* (1972), v. 7, nos. 1–2

Laski, H., *The Germans – Are They Human? A reply to Sir Robert Vansittart* (1941)

Lawford, V., *Bound For Diplomacy* (1963)

Lochner, L. (ed.), *The Goebbels Diaries* (New York, 1949)

Lockhart, B., *Memoirs of a British Agent* (1932); *Comes The Reckoning* (1947)

Londonderry, Lord, *Wings of Destiny* (1943)

Louis, W. R., *British Strategy in the Far East* (OUP, 1971)

Maisky, I., *Who Helped Hitler* (1965)

Manne, R., 'The British Decision for an Alliance with Russia, May 1939', *Journal of Contemporary History* (July 1974)

Marder, A., 'The Royal Navy and the Ethiopian Crisis of 1935–36', *American Historical Review* (June 1970)

Martin, K., *Propaganda's Harvest* (1941); *Editorial* (1968)

Medlicott, W. N., *Britain and Germany: The Search For An Agreement, 1930–37* (1969)

Middlemas, K. (ed.), *Whitehall Diaries* (1969)

Middlemas, K., *Diplomacy of Illusion* (1972)

Middlemas, K., and Barnes, J., *Baldwin* (1969)

Monger, G. W., *The End of Isolation* (1963)

Mosley, L., *On Borrowed Time. How World War Two Began* (1969)

Muggeridge, M. (ed.), *Ciano's Diary* (1947)

Murray, of Elibank, *Reflections on some Aspects of British policy between the Wars* (Edinburgh 1946)

Namier, L. B., *Avenues of History* (1950)

Nevakivi, J., *Britain, France and the Arab Middle East* (1969)

Nicolson, H., *Sir Arthur Nicolson Bart: First Lord Carnock: A Study in the Old Diplomacy* (1930); *Curzon: The Last Phase, 1919–1925* (1934); *Some People* (1939); *Peacemaking* (1969)

Nicolson, N. (ed.), *The Diaries and Letters of Harold Nicolson* (1969–71); *Portrait of a Marriage* (1973)

Nielson, F., *Hate. The Enemy of Peace. A Reply to Lord Vansittart* (1944)

Nightingale, R. T., *The Personnel of the British Foreign Office and Diplomatic Service* (1930)

O'Malley, O., *The Phantom Caravan* (1954)

Ovendale, R., *'Appeasement' and the English Speaking World* (Cardiff, 1975)

Overy, R. J., 'The German Pre-War Aircraft Production Plans: November 1936–April 1939', *English Historical Review* (October 1975)

Papers Relating to the Foreign Relations of the United States (Washington)

Parliamentary Peace Aims Group, *Germany's Record. A Reply to Lord Vansittart* (n.d.)

Peterson, M., *Both Sides of the Curtain* (1956)

Ribbentrop, J., *Memoirs* (1954)

Riddell, Lord, *Intimate Diaries of the Peace Conference and After* (1933)

Ritter, G., *The German Resistance. Carl Gordeler's Struggle Against Tyranny* (1958)

Robbins, K., 'Konrad Henlein, the Sudeten Question and British Foreign Policy' *The Historical Journal* (1969), XII, 4

Robertson, E. M., *Hitler's Pre-War Policy and Military Plans, 1933–39* (1963); Robertson, E. M. (ed.), *The Origins of the Second World War* (1971)

Robertson, J. C., 'The Hoare–Laval Plan', *Journal of Contemporary History* (July 1974)

Roskill, S., *Hankey. Man of Secrets*, 3 vols. (1970–74)

Rotunda, D., *The Rome Embassy of Sir Eric Drummond, 16th earl of Perth, 1933–39* (unpublished Ph.D. thesis, University of London, 1972)

Rowse, A. L., *The End of an Epoch* (1948)

Schmidt, P., *Hitler's Interpreter* (1951)

Selby, W., *Diplomatic Twilight, 1930-40* (1953)

Shlaim, A., 'Prelude to Downfall: The British Offer of Union to France, June 1940', *Journal of Contemporary History* (July 1974)

Simon, Viscount, *Retrospect* (1952)

Smelser, R. M., *The Sudeten Problem 1933–38. Volkstumpolitik and the Formulation of Nazi Foreign Policy* (Folkestone, 1975)

Steiner, Z., *The Foreign Office and Foreign Policy, 1898–1914* (Cambridge University Press, 1969)

Storrs, R., *Orientations* (1939)

Taylor, A. J. P., *The Course of German History* (1945); *Beaverbrook* (1972); Taylor, A. J. P. (ed.), *Off The Record. Political Interviews 1933–43* (1973)

Templewood, Viscount, *Nine Troubled Years* (1954)

Thompson, E., *The Augustan Poets* (1943)

Thompson, G., *Front Line Diplomat* (1959)

Thompson, N., *The Anti Appeasers. Conservative Opposition to Appeasement* (OUP, 1971)

Thorne, C., *The Limits of Foreign Policy. The West, the League and the Far Eastern Crisis of 1931–33* (1972)

Tilley, J., and Gasalee, S., *The Foreign Office* (1933)

Toscano, M., 'Eden's Mission to Rome on the Eve of the Italo-Ethiopian Conflict' in *Studies in Diplomatic History and Historiography in honour of G. P. Gooch* (1961), ed., A. O. Sarkissian

Trevor-Roper, H., *Hitler's Table Talk* (1953)

Vansittart, Lord, *Black Record. Germans Past and Present* (1941); *Lessons of My Life* (1943); *Green and Grey* (1944); 'The Decline of Diplomacy', *Foreign Affairs* (Jan. 1950); *The Mist Procession* (1958); *Bones of Contention* (n.d.); *Events and Shadows* (n.d.); *Even Now* (n.d.)

Waley, D., *British Public Opinion and the Abyssinian War, 1935–36* (1975)

Wallace, W. V., 'The Making of the May Crisis of 1938', *Slavonic and East European Review* (June 1963); 'A Reply to Mr Watt', *Slavonic and East European Review* (July 1966)

Warman, R. H., 'The Erosion of Foreign Office Influence in the Making of Foreign Policy, 1916–16', *The Historical Journal* (1972), XV, 1

Watt, D. C., 'The Anglo-German Naval Agreement of 1935. An Interim Judgement', *Journal of Modern History* (1956), v. xxviii, no. 2; *Personalities and Policies* (1965); 'The Secret Laval–Mussolini Agreement of 1935 on Ethiopia' in *The Origins of the Second World War* (1971), ed. E. M. Robertson; 'German Plans for the Occupation of the Rhineland', *Journal of Contemporary History* (1966), no. 4; 'The May Crisis of 1938: A Rejoinder to Mr. Wallace', *Slavonic and East European Review* (July 1966); 'Hitler's visit to Rome and the May Weekend Crisis', *Journal of Contemporary History* (January 1974); 'The Initiation of the Negotiations Leading to the Nazi–Soviet Pact: A Historical Problem' in *Essays in Honour of E. H. Carr* (1976), eds. C. Abramsky and B. Williams

Wellesley, V., *Diplomacy in Fetters* (1945)

Weinberg, G., 'The May Crisis of 1938', *Journal of Modern History* (1957), XXIX

Weizmann, C., *Trial and Error* (1950)

Index